LIMINAL MINORITIES

RELIGION AND CONFLICT

A series edited by Ron E. Hassner

A list of titles is available at cornellpress.cornell.edu

LIMINAL MINORITIES

RELIGIOUS DIFFERENCE AND MASS VIOLENCE IN MUSLIM SOCIETIES

GÜNEŞ MURAT TEZCÜR

CORNELL UNIVERSITY PRESS
Ithaca and London

Copyright © 2024 by Güneş Murat Tezcür

All rights reserved. Except for brief quotations in a review, this book, or parts thereof, must not be reproduced in any form without permission in writing from the publisher. For information, address Cornell University Press, Sage House, 512 East State Street, Ithaca, New York 14850. Visit our website at cornellpress.cornell.edu.

First published 2024 by Cornell University Press

Library of Congress Cataloging-in-Publication Data

Names: Tezcür, Güneş Murat, 1979– author.
Title: Liminal minorities : religious difference and mass violence in Muslim societies / Güneş Murat Tezcür.
Description: Ithaca [New York] : Cornell University Press, 2024. | Series: Religion and conflict | Includes bibliographical references and index.
Identifiers: LCCN 2023031796 (print) | LCCN 2023031797 (ebook) | ISBN 9781501774676 (hardcover) | ISBN 9781501774683 (paperback) | ISBN 9781501774706 (epub) | ISBN 9781501774690 (pdf)
Subjects: LCSH: Religious minorities—Violence against—Islamic countries. | Political violence—Religious aspects—Islam. | Muslims—Persecutions—Islamic countries. | Religious discrimination—Islamic countries. | Religious tolerance—Islam.
Classification: LCC HN768.Z9 V673 2024 (print) | LCC HN768.Z9 (ebook) | DDC 303.48/4091767—dc23/eng/20230925
LC record available at https://lccn.loc.gov/2023031796
LC ebook record available at https://lccn.loc.gov/2023031797

In memory of those we lost to the dark side of humanity in Maraş, Sivas, and Şingal

Contents

List of Figures and Tables ix

Acknowledgments xi

Prologue: Sinjar, August 2014   1

Introduction: Religious Liminality   9

1. A Theory of Religious Liminality and Violence   34

2. From Liminality to Genocidal Violence: Yezidis of Iraq   67

3. From Massacres to Denied Victimhood: Alevis of Turkey   110

4. Liminality in the Broader Muslim World: Baha'is and Ahmadis   153

5. Religious Liminality and Societal Discrimination in a Global Perspective   170

Conclusion: Transcending Liminality   191

Appendix for Chapter 2: Fieldwork among Yezidis   201

Appendix for Chapter 5: Statistical Results   207

References 209

Index 245

Figures and Tables

Figures

P.1.	Goya's plate 18 from *The Disasters of War*	7
I.1.	A causal schema of the main argument	12
1.1.	Jain temple, Murshidabad, India	57
2.1.	Lalish temple, Iraqi Kurdistan	77
2.2.	Yezidis celebrating the New Year's Eve	81
2.3.	Mount Sinjar and northwestern Iraq	85
2.4.	Photos of Yezidis of Kocho murdered on August 15, 2014	85
2.5.	Kocho in February 2014 and in October 2021	92
3.1.	Gazi Cemevi, Istanbul	117
3.2.	An Alevi ritual in Antalya	117
3.3.	Main locations of the Sivas massacre	134
3.4.	A commemoration of the twenty-fourth anniversary of the Sivas massacre, Ankara	148
4.1.	The Baha'i Gardens in Haifa, Israel	158
4.2.	An anti-Ahmadi protest in Lahore, Pakistan	166
5.1.	Liminal minorities across the globe	177
5.2.	Liminal and nonliminal minorities in Muslim and non-Muslim countries	181
5.3.	Societal discrimination, liminal minorities, and Muslim-majority countries	185
5.4.	The effects of religious demographics on societal discrimination against religious minorities	187

Tables

2.1	Explaining popular participation in mass violence against Yezidis	103
3.1	Anti-Alevi massacres in Turkey in the late twentieth century	119

FIGURES AND TABLES

3.2 Profiles of suspects in the Maraş massacre　124
3.3 Explaining popular participation in mass violence against Alevis　139
5.1 Liminal minorities and countries　177

Acknowledgments

Writing a book on mass violence is both a humbling and enlightening experience. It is humbling to meet with and read about people who suffer and demonstrate perseverance and resilience under extremely adverse conditions. It is equally enlightening to learn from their experiences as I strive to make sense of the conditions under which humans act extraordinarily, either in commendable or despicable ways. I realize that this journey has not only contributed to my scholarly growth but also expanded my personal horizons about the diversity of human condition itself and made me better appreciate the role of empathy to human relations. I remain grateful to all people I encounter in my journey.

My writing of this book has greatly benefited from inspiring conversations and exchanges with many colleagues. They include Majid Hassan Ali, Senem Aslan, Onur Bakıner, Banu Bargu, Christofer Berglund, Fırat Bozçalı, Paul Djupe, Tyler Fisher, Ekrem Karakoç, Bahadin Kerborani, Ohannes Kılıçdağı, Mark Moffett, Soli Özel, Hakan Özoğlu, Sadia Saeed, Kaya Şahin, Nükhet Sandal, Gülay Türkmen, Elisabeth Jean Wood, and Halil İbrahim Yenigün. I also had the opportunity to present different parts of this book in various academic avenues and developed my arguments in light of comments and questions I received. In particular, I thank participants in my presentations at the American Political Science Association meetings in Boston, Washington, D.C., and Seattle, the University of Indiana, Malmö University, and Religion in Public Forum.

Tutku Ayhan, who is currently a postdoctoral fellow at the Institut Barcelona Estudis Internacionals, was a doctoral student at the University of Central Florida (UCF) as I started to work on this project. She wrote a dissertation on the resilience and empowerment of Yezidi women in the wake of genocidal attacks under my supervision. Collaborating with Tutku as we both studied different aspects of the Yezidi genocide was a mutually rewarding experience. I am very much hoping to see her dissertation published as a book soon. Working with Josh Lambert, who also received his PhD from UCF, on the statistical analyses in chapter 5 has made the experience of writing less insulating and more enjoyable. Josh's sharp quantitative skills and visual acumen made that chapter a vital component of the book. Léa Faure, Doreen Horschig, and Sara Belligoni, my research assistants at UCF, provided much needed help as I worked on various iterations of this manuscript over the years. Serdar Yıldırım of Diyarbakır and Mardin provided meticulous transcriptions of many interviews used in this book. Mohammad al-Awwad, a UCF student, helped me explore various Arabic sources on religion and politics of Yezidis. My interactions with Myli Sangria, another UCF student who volunteered to teach English to Yezidis at the Sinjar Academy, were a source of optimism regarding the attention the plight of Yezidis attracted.

Watching Düzen Tekkal's visceral documentary, *Hawar: My Journey to Genocide*, in Orlando in February 2017 deepened my interest in the tragedy of Yezidis. The conversations I had with her and her family members including Şeyhmus Tekkal in Berlin later that year helped me develop a more acute understanding of the Yezidi experience. It was pleasure to exchange ideas and share intellectual companionship with Zeynep Kaya in Iraqi Kurdistan in spring 2018. Firat Esmer of Bremen, originally from Diyarbakır, was a joyful companion during our multiple visits to Iraqi Kurdistan. Jeen Maltayi of Duhok was a reliable, patient, and resilient translator and assistant during our fieldwork. The support of Bayar Dosky in that part of the world made our experience more hospitable. In Duhok, I greatly benefited from talking to Nesreen Berwari, Baba Chavoush, Khidir Domle, Dr. Nizar Ismet, Abdullah Sherem, and many other individuals, including survivors of atrocities, who should remain anonymous. Life-saving work of Dr. Gazi Zibari in Duhok and many other parts of the globe has been a source of great inspiration.

My interest in the Alevi question originated from my memories of the Sivas massacre as a teenager living in Turkey in the 1990s. As an avid reader of Aziz Nesin, the renowned Turkish writer whose visit to the city became a pretext for the attacks, watching him and his companions stranded in a burning hotel was a highly unsettling experience. This experience coupled with my family history of having roots in Sivas played a formative role in my quest to shed light on the dynamics of mass violence that took place in that city in 1993. It is my hope that what I discover in this book would facilitate a more self-reflexive collective approach among the residents of that central Anatolian city.

Ron Hassner, editor of Cornell University Press's nascent Religion and Conflict Series, has been a motivating force and an ardent supporter of this project from its inception. I am delighted to be in good company given other books in the series. When I initially approached the press with this project, Roger Malcolm Haydon astutely pushed me in the right direction and highlighted several core issues, especially the question of not talking to perpetrators, that need to be addressed. I remain grateful for his reflections. After his retirement, it has been my pleasure to work with Mahinder Kingra whose editorial guidance was crucial to my ability to bring this project to its conclusion. Critical remarks from three anonymous reviewers help me refine my argument and establish a greater coherence between the qualitative and quantitative empirical parts of the book. The dedicated work of India Miraglia, Kristen Gregg, and Karen Laun at the Press and Cheryl Hirsch at Westchester Publishing has made it a smooth experience to bring this book to publication.

I graciously acknowledge funding support from the Kurdish Political Science Program based at UCF and the Global Religion Research Initiative based at the University of Notre Dame. During my first six years at UCF, I was fortunate to have Kerstin Hamann as my chair and director. Her support was extremely valuable as I navigated various challenges of international travel in a part of the world not known for its political stability. At UCF, Sami Alpanda, Ulaş Bağcı, Jacopo Baggio, Scott Branting, Tom Dolan, Tiffany Early-Spadoni, Peter Jacques, Haidar Khezri, Kelsey Larsen, Julia Listengarten, Nikola Mirilovic, Jonathan Powell, Mustafa Kemal Topal, Paul Vasquez, Keri Watson, Bruce Wilson, Kenicia Wright, and Cyrus Zargar have created an intellectually stimulating environment that enriched my own scholarship.

As a nomadic couple, Nazlı and I aspire to instill a strong sense of empathy for the diversity of human experience among our sons, Babil and Metis, as they come of age. We are hoping that learning from the experiences of people who lost their homes and were forcefully displaced will make them more grounded and pursue more humane life choices.

LIMINAL MINORITIES

Prologue
Sinjar, August 2014

On a Saturday in late May 2018, we visited the Qadya Camp in Iraqi Kurdistan. The camp provided shelter to more than fifteen thousand displaced people living in three thousand container houses. Even though summer was yet to arrive, the heat already started to soar. Under the loud noise of a bulky and ineffective air conditioner, we listened to the story of Salim, a middle-aged Yezidi man. Salim and his family were captives of the self-styled Islamic State (IS) for nine months. After their escape, his wife and four children eventually made it to Germany as refugees. Salim was trying to join them. It came to me as a surprise when Salim mentioned that his ordeal at the hands of the IS was his second captivity. He had spent nine years as an Iraqi POW in Iranian prisons from 1981 to 1990. I thought only a Yezidi would have the experience of being imprisoned by both the IS and the Islamic Republic, archenemies of each other.

I was deeply touched by Salim's story. As we were about to leave, our host told me that there was an old man living in a nearby container. He was recovering from a major surgery. I decided to pay a visit to him out of courtesy. The old man looked very fragile and sorrowful. Immediately after exchanging pleasantries, he started to tell me the story of his village. By the time our conversation ended, I learned that he had lost around sixty members of his family, including his wife, three sons, his mother, and all his brothers. His story made me realize that I would have a sense of vindication if I could situate his experience within a universal understanding of human cruelty and resilience.

Towering over an arid and flat landscape, Mount Sinjar, located in the northwestern corner of Iraq, provided a semblance of safety to adherents of Yezidism, a monotheistic religion with its distinctive set of beliefs, for centuries. In the mid-1970s, the Ba'th regime forcefully dismantled Yezidi villages on the mountain and relocated their inhabitants to collective settlements on the plain. From the regime's perspective, these settlements would not only "civilize" the Yezidis but also make them easily controllable. As it would turn out, their relocation would make Yezidis vulnerable to an equally sinister force four decades later.

One of these new Yezidi settlements was Kocho, which is located around twenty kilometers south of Mount Sinjar. Like many other Yezidi settlements, Kocho was surrounded by Arab villages. On August 3, 2014, Kocho became a victim of its geography. By the time residents of Kocho became aware of the attacks, the IS blitzkrieg had already engulfed the entire area. While many Yezidis in villages farther north desperately sought refuge on Mount Sinjar, which remained beyond the reach of the IS, the people of Kocho found themselves surrounded by IS fighters.

At 9:00 a.m., a local IS commander known by his nom de guerre Abu Hamza visited Kocho and had a meeting with the village head, Ahmed Jasem. Abu Hamza, who was from a neighboring village and had known Jasem for years, assured him that the people of Kocho would be safe and demanded that they surrender their weapons. Jasem readily complied. In his next visit to Kocho, Abu Hamza became more intimidating. He told the people of Kocho to convert en masse to Islam within three days. He was accompanied by Dakhil, a former Yezidi singer. Dakhil's elder brother was killed after he had converted to Islam during the time of Saddam. The family then migrated to Ramadi, a Sunni Arab city in the south. To the surprise of Jasem, Dakhil now returned to Sinjar as a member of the ascendant Salafi-jihadist group. Jasem tried to buy time and frantically contacted Kurdish commanders and leaders of Sunni Arab tribes he had known for years.

Abu Hamza came back to Kocho three days later. "I have good news for you. Al Baghdadi [the IS leader] issued an amnesty for you. We will take you to Mount Sinjar soon." Meanwhile, IS advances created a sense of panic in Erbil, the capital of the Kurdistan Regional Government. Fearing the fall of the US consulate in Erbil, President Barack Obama ordered the conduct of airstrikes against IS targets around Erbil and Mount Sinjar on August 7. Two days later, the IS siege of Mount Sinjar was broken. Militants from PKK, a Kurdish armed organization established in 1978, and its Syrian affiliate YPG opened a corridor allowing Yezidis stranded on the barren top of Mount Sinjar to reach the safety of YPG-controlled lands in northeastern Syria. Nonetheless, many Yezidis, especially children and elderly, perished on the mountain due to lack of food and water and exposure to extreme heat. In the early hours of August 10, desperate residents of a smaller village seven kilometers north of Kocho fled to Mount Sinjar.

These developments changed how the IS decided to deal with the "Kocho question." On the morning of August 10, IS militants formed checkpoints around Kocho and started to enforce a curfew on the village. The people of Kocho were required to receive permissions to be able to tend their gardens. One of them tried to escape but was caught and executed. At the same time, a leader of Mitewtas, a local Sunni Arab tribe, attended his funeral, shared food with villagers, and tried to assure them that they would be fine. Another day, a Mitewta visited the health center in Kocho and had his blood pressure checked and received some medicine. He told the health clinic operator that the IS decided to take Kocho people to Mount Sinjar. Meanwhile, Ahmed Jasem fell ill. The IS took him temporarily to Ba'aj, a Sunni Arab town farther south, for treatment.

This eerie situation lasted until the morning of August 15 when a bulldozer appeared on the outskirts of the village. Half an hour later, another bulldozer arrived. An hour later, a large group of bearded IS militants wearing all black arrived in Kia pickup trucks mounting heavy weapons. Some villagers hoped that they would be taken to Mount Sinjar and released. Abu Hamza demanded all residents to assemble at the school. Women and children were sent to the upper floor. Abu Hamza addressed men who remained on the first floor: "We told you to convert to Islam. But you did not comply. Whoever is willing to convert can remain in Kocho." Nobody took his offer. Soon after, IS militants asked villagers to surrender their valuable possessions. Men were ushered out of the building in small groups and crowded into cargo beds of Kia pickups.

The first three pickups started to drive north, the direction of Mount Sinjar. Yezidi captives felt a sense of relief. Shortly after, however, the pickups turned southwest and stopped half a kilometer away from a vegetable garden and irrigation pool that belonged to Kocho. A group of six or seven IS militants were waiting there. After making Yezidi men lie down on the ground, they started to shoot at them from multiple directions. They aimed at their heads. Out of the group, only five survived the mass execution as bullets scraped their heads. As IS militants walked away, the survivors heard shots from a distance and realized that a new group of Kocho men were being murdered in the vegetable garden. The men crawled deep into the garden to hide themselves. They decided to move in the afternoon. One of them was badly wounded, so they left him behind. Another left the group to seek some help by himself.

The remaining survivors walked to a vegetable garden belonging to a Sunni Arab village. They were fortunate to meet with a villager who happened to be the godfather (*kiriv*) of the son of one man. The villager cried when he saw them. He gave them water and treated their wounds. When another Arab villager saw them, however, they had to leave. The survivors decided to take their chances and try to reach Mount Sinjar under the cover of darkness. After an arduous track, they made their way to a valley ascending toward the top of Mount Sinjar. With the guidance of a group of PKK militants, they eventually crossed the border to Syria. On August 18, the men reached Duhok where they were hospitalized.

The fate of women and children who were taken to the second floor of the school on August 15 varied. Women who were beyond their childbearing years were executed in the early hours of August 16. Their remains would be discovered in fields near the Solagh Technical Institute in the town of Sinjar in November 2015. Younger women and children, including boys who did not reach puberty, were taken away by IS militants. Many boys were incorporated into the military arm of the IS and some of them were sent on suicide missions. Women and girls were enslaved by IS militants and collaborators in Iraq and Syria. Out of a village population of 1,161 at the eve of the attack, 533 were reported dead or missing. More than 90 percent of men above the age of twenty did not survive; most boys and girls under the age of ten survived. Younger women, many of whom were eventually ransomed, had a higher likelihood of survival than older women (Cetorelli and Ashraph 2019, 15–20). Overall, around 3,000 Yezidis lost their lives and the IS kidnapped around 6,800 of them in Sinjar in early August 2014 (Cetorelli et al. 2017).

Some residents of Kocho tried to flee during those twelve fateful days in August 2014. Many of them, including Salim, his wife, and their four small children, were captured before reaching the relative safety of Mount Sinjar. Salim was initially separated from his family. On August 6, he and around one hundred Yezidi men were quizzed by IS judges. "How come your Muslim neighbors did not ask you to convert?" The Yezidis responded, "Our relations with them were informed by tribal norms. We coexisted." Then the judges asked them to convert to Islam on the spot. Thirty-six Yezidis refused to do so. They were bound, blindfolded, and taken away. Nothing was ever heard of them again.

The remaining men, who pretended to convert, were taken to Tal Afar. Salim rejoined his family. Most IS militants who were guarding them were locals. They accused Yezidis of being polytheists and not having a "book." Salim and his family, like many other Yezidi families, were given the task of tending a flock of sheep on the outskirts of Tal Afar. Kurdish Peshmerga occasionally sent guides to help Yezidis escape. With the help of a guide, Salim and his family were among the last Yezidis who managed to reach the Kurdish-controlled territory. On the evening of April 26, the remaining Yezidis were assembled and divided into three groups. As in Kocho, bound and blindfolded men were put into vehicles that took them to an unknown location. Women were distributed among IS militants. Boys were taken to IS training camps.

The Act of Killing: Close-Up

The Third of May 1808 of Francisco Goya (1746–1828), now part of the collection of the Museo Nacional del Prado in Madrid, was a watershed in the history of painting as it "portrays human suffering" in war "in all its sordidness" (Chu 2010, 156). In his iconic painting, Goya depicts the execution of a group of captured Spanish rebels at the hands of a French firing squad. The victims act in unison in their despair; the killers appear as faceless automatons. The appearance and behavior of the latter, forces of "merciless conformity," exemplifies an "inhuman repetition" (Clark 1959, 126–27). The contrast between the courageous humanity of victims with their visceral reactions and the faceless and emotionless firing squad naturally evokes sympathy for the former. The physical proximity between the executed and the executioners makes the intimacy of space deeply unsettling. The influence of Goya is apparent in Édouard Manet's *Execution of Emperor Maximilian (1868–69)* regarding the portrayal of the act of killing. Whereas the emperor displays a noble composure in the face of imminent death, members of the firing squad act as if they are practicing a routine business. There is no indicator that they act out of hatred, revenge, or resentment. In Pablo Picasso's *Massacre in Korea*, painted during the US intervention in the Korean Peninsula and part of the collection of Musée Picasso in Paris, the bifurcated composition between the act of dying and the act of killing gains a gendered dimension. A tight group of males wearing armor point their guns at a helpless group of naked pregnant women, girls, and boys. In all three paintings, the brutality of war is expressed via the humanity of victims and inhumanity of killers. The humanity of the condemned makes the executioners, a relentless force acting in cold blood, horrifying.

This bifurcated image of the act of killing has a huge influence on how we make sense of political atrocities in modern times. What makes the killers so effective and remorseless has little to do with their beliefs and emotions. An organized force (i.e., the state) provides the means that make such large-scale violence feasible and the justifications to make it meaningful. This portrayal of mass violence that seeks to flesh out an underlying political logic is an effective antidote to simplistic and popular perceptions of communal violence as a reflection of deep-seated and intractable ethnoreligious hostilities. It exposes the role of political elites behind seemingly irrational violence, demonstrates its predictable nature, and identifies policies that could reduce its destructiveness and frequency. It also makes violence appear as an outcome of alienation rather than a reflection of deeply ingrained human beliefs and emotions.

Goya's *The Disasters of War* (*Los desastres de la guerra*), a series of eighty-two etchings that depict the French invasion of Spain from 1808 to 1814 and its aftermath, provides a dramatically different perspective about violence (figure P.1 shows plate 18 from the series). In contrast to *The Third of May 1808*, which was officially commissioned by the government and had a populist appeal, these etchings represent Goya's artistic consciousness and his personal mission to document the dark side of humanity and demonstrate the naked reality of violence (Todorov 2019, 143–45). They would not be publicly available for thirty-five years after the painter's death. They leave no room for any melodrama, glory, or heroism in warfare. As Tzvetan Todorov incisively argues, horror is the only emotion triggered by these works of art. The painful suffering of the body is the most poignant truth of violence. Ideologies matter only as rhetoric that aim to justify horrendous violence. They are all vulnerable to descent into madness. Victims of today could be easily tormentors of tomorrow. Violence brutalizes all involved and corrupts all moral precepts and ideological postures. Ordinary people have an extraordinary capacity to commit crimes of unspeakable nature.

Jahangir Razmi's serial photos visualizing the moment of an execution of a group of Kurdish rebels in Iran in August 1979 are stark testimony to the intimate forms of killing (Prager 2006). The firing squad, composed of a ragtag group of revolutionaries, lacks the aura of anonymity and merciless repetition. These photographs follow the lineage of *The Disasters of War* with their macabre yet mundane portrayal of violence leaving no room for any moral consolation. The medium of portrayal changes, but the effect remains the same.

In making sense of murderous violence by ordinary people, Goya of *The Disasters of War* rather than *The Third of May 1808* becomes an intellectual lode-

Figure P.1. Francisco Goya, plate 18 from *The Disasters of War (Los desastres de la guerra): Bury Them and Keep Quiet (Enterrar y callar)* (Credit: Metropolitan Museum of Art)

star guiding this book. The artist's legacy is to make us alert to the potential of humans to engage in acts of barbarism across ideologies, partisanship, and cultures. The task of a scholar is to recognize this potential while trying to come to terms with the question of why some groups become the victims of such acts at the hands of some other groups. It is a search for a meaning in motives even if the very act of violence is deprived of any moral meaning.

The old Yezidi man's recounting of his survival of a firing squad evoked a violence that is eerie and intimate. In Kocho, the killers were not anonymous and nameless strangers. To the contrary, they were neighbors who attended Yezidi weddings, served as godfathers to Yezidi boys, and traded with the Yezidis. An extremist organization guided the atrocities, but the locals were the ones who killed their neighbors before enslaving their women and children and looting their properties.

Why do certain faith groups become targets of mass violence at the hands of ordinary people who often include their neighbors? I call these groups, such as Yezidis, *liminal minorities* who lack theological recognition and social acceptance from a dominant religious group. They are subject to multiple layers of stigmatization originating from religious differences and persisting across generations. These forms of stigmatization make the situation of a liminal minority particularly precarious during turbulent political periods fomenting resentment among members of a majority group. This combination of religious stigmatization and political resentment becomes the spark resulting in episodes of popular violence targeting liminal minorities in contemporary times. Consequently, the politics of recognition transforming liminal minorities into legitimate faith groups is indispensable for sustainable intercommunal coexistence and peace.

Introduction
Religious Liminality

The IS campaign against Yezidis, a Kurdish-speaking minority with distinctive monotheistic religious beliefs, in northern Iraq involves two puzzles. First, although the IS left a trail of death and destruction in the areas it occupied, its treatment of Yezidis qua Yezidis was uniquely vicious and ferocious. The militant group systematically executed, kidnapped, enslaved, and forcefully converted only Yezidis in large numbers. What explains the exceptionally brutal nature of the IS's anti-Yezidi violence? Next, a significant number of local people, many of whom were neighbors of Yezidis, actively took part in the atrocities. Attackers were no strangers to victims and continued to interact daily with them until the day of reckoning. Not only did they participate in lootings and shootings but also enslaved Yezidi women and children for months and years. What factors brought the total collapse of interreligious coexistence? What made ordinary people prey on their Yezidi neighbors and transformed them into looters, enslavers, and murderers?

The tragic experience of Yezidis reflects a global pattern of discrimination and violence against minorities in contemporary times. In many different parts of the world, minorities become targets of bloody attacks, often led by inflamed mobs. The "fear of small numbers" is aggravated by globalization exacerbating new uncertainties and status anxieties. Under these circumstances, numerical majorities often displace their anger and engage in predatory violence against minorities (Appadurai 2006). But why do some minorities more than others provoke the ire of majorities? In particular, why do religious minorities lacking any significant power and presenting no significant threat become the objects of popular fear and rage?

Intercommunal violence among believers in the Abrahamic religions of Christianity, Islam, and Judaism as well as violence involving these religions and major non-Abrahamic religions such as Buddhism and Hinduism have been subject of intense scholarly interest. Yet our understanding of the dynamics of violence targeting smaller faith groups is lacking. I aim to fill this knowledge gap and develop a theory of mass violence that aims to explain why certain religious minorities have been subjects of mass atrocities committed by ordinary people. I argue that popular perceptions of certain religious groups harboring illegitimate beliefs and conducting immoral practices have historically made them subjects of widespread stigmatization that assigns discrediting attributes to all members of these groups because of their religious faith, fosters discrimination, and reduces their life opportunities (Goffman 1963). Building on Arpad Szakolczai (2015) who argues that liminality should be a core term in social inquiry, I call these faith groups *liminal minorities* who are historically subject to holier-than-thou hostility and whose belief systems lack proper theological recognition and social acceptance in the eyes of a dominant religion. Religious justifications of violence have a formidable mobilization power and are likely to go unchallenged when they are directed against liminal minorities. For sure, historical configurations of a religious group as a liminal minority do not predetermine acts of mass violence against the group. A fragile religious coexistence could be maintained as long as the liminal group remains subordinate and does not actively challenge the status quo. When a dominant religious group experiences a status loss during a period of political change, however, it is very likely to displace its grievances onto a liminal minority perceived as being allied with rival and ascending groups. Under these conditions, hatred informed by religious stigmas (i.e., antagonism against a group by virtue of its purported core beliefs and innate characteristics) and political resentfulness become a combustible combination generating mass violence.

Guided by this theoretical framework, the book offers the first comparative-historical study of mass atrocities targeting liminal minorities in Muslim societies. Forms of liminality are not unique to Islam and emerge in social contexts dominated by other monotheistic religions such as Christianity. As my conceptual framework and empirical analyses will make it clear, the notion of religious liminality is applicable to marginalized groups in non-Muslim settings (e.g., Jehovah's Witnesses) where religious differences exhibit similar patterns of illegibility and potential for violent conflict. At the same time, the continuing centrality of Islam to sociopolitical affairs in many contemporary Muslim societies make the study of religious liminality a more urgent and relevant task than anywhere else. Given this motivation, I present empirically rich case studies of violence targeting two of such groups, Alevis in contemporary Turkey and Yezidis in contemporary Iraq. I also offer brief discussions of Baha'is in Iran and Ahmadis in Indonesia and Pakistan as two other liminal minorities.

To make it clear from the beginning, I aim to understand *bottom-up violence* by nonstate actors as different from *top-down violence* by state actors. Although these two forms of violence often happen simultaneously, state-led violence has dynamics that are qualitatively different from acts of violence initiated by private individuals. The latter form violence is often deceptively spontaneous. It typically requires organizations providing guidance, legitimacy, and benefits to participation (Luft 2019, 10). At the same time, an exclusive focus on elites and organizations often come at the expense of the agency of ordinary people who perpetuate the attacks. My approach highlights the agency of ordinary people in initiating and committing mass atrocities, a process also emphasized by Omar McDoom (2021) in his recent study of the Rwandan genocide. As case studies in this book demonstrate, my main goal is to make sense of the motives of these people.

Argument

Liminal minorities have been targets of both state and nonstate violence since the early modern times. Liminality emerges during a historical critical juncture when religious authorities allied with state elites start denying recognition to certain groups whose beliefs they deemed illegitimate. To adopt the terminology of James Scott (1998), these groups are *illegible* in the sense that their core beliefs and practices were confusing and nebulous for representatives of religious orthodoxy. In the Ottoman Empire, this illegibility and lack of recognition put "heretical" groups, as different from the People of the Book, outside of the prevalent politico-legal order and informed templates justifying armed expeditions on religious grounds. Alevis and Yezidi liminality originated in the early sixteenth century with the rise of Sunni orthodoxy in the Ottoman Empire and Baha'i and Ahmadi liminality in Iran and India, respectively, in the late nineteenth century when leading clerical figures condemned these messianic movements as direct threats to their authority. They were perceived to be allied with hostile foreign powers or inhabit strategically important areas beyond the imperial reach. Religious liminality aggravates such threat perceptions. Political loyalties of liminal minorities remain suspicious primarily because of its beliefs contradicting the prevailing religious orthodoxy. Members of these groups suffer a wide set of discriminatory practices and are vulnerable to campaigns of persecution at the hands of state authorities.

The advent of secular modernity and nationalism transforms how the states deal with liminal minorities. Although modern states pursue assimilatory practices toward these groups, they are less likely to sponsor violent campaigns against these groups justified on religious grounds. Meanwhile, religious discourses stigmatizing liminal minorities are rarely challenged and continue to generate animosity against members of these groups at the popular levels. This stigmatization, originally based on religious differences, often involves multiple layers and feeds into popular conceptions of a liminal minority as a treacherous political group. Bottom-up violence fueled by religious-inspired hatred is likely to happen when a dominant religious group (usually but not always a majority) experiences a loss of political status in an environment of weak or fragmented state capacity. The important point to emphasize is that such a status loss makes the group resentful not only against the now-dominant group but also against the liminal minority that is perceived to be a beneficiary of the new status quo, even when perception is disassociated from social reality. In contrast, if state authorities happen to be responsive to popular animosities and sponsor policies that persecute liminal minorities, outbreaks of bottom-up violence are less likely to happen and less fierce when they happen. In a sense, the codification of religious differences into the positive law and state practices make such violence redundant. Figure I.1 offers a schematic visual-

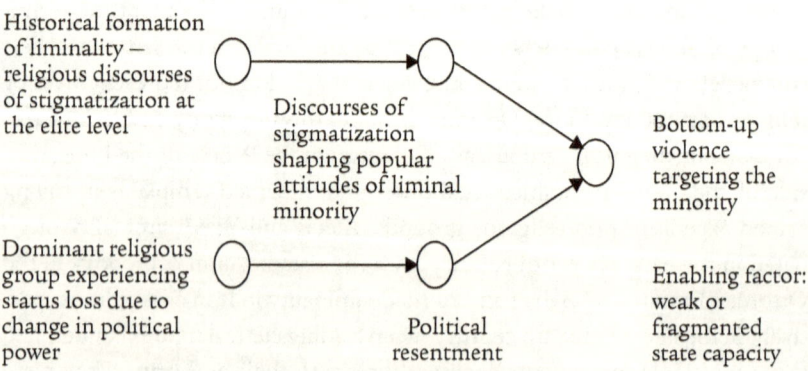

FIGURE I.1. A causal schema of the main argument

ization of this theoretical argument that combines predispositional (i.e., religious stigmatization) and situationist (i.e., political resentment) perspectives in explaining mass atrocities targeting a religious minority.

As I discuss in greater detail in chapter 2, this theoretical framework provides a more satisfactory understanding of the patterns of violence characterizing the IS attack against Yezidis compared to alternative explanations. Many IS militants who killed and enslaved the community were locals who used to interact with Yezidis on a regular basis. Although Yezidis' economic status somehow improved in the post-2003 period, they remained one of the most deprived communities in Iraq. Hence, greed and envy could not be central to the motives of the attackers. Moreover, Yezidis, a marginalized community during both the Ottoman times and under the Iraqi state, lacked political and military power. They were completely reliant on Kurdish forces, who controlled the Sinjar region, for their security after 2003. They did not even have their militia force. Once these forces fled unexpectedly, they were at the mercy of their attackers. Consequently, an explanation based on threat does not explain the political logic of anti-Yezidi atrocities either. In contrast, resentment was central to local Sunni animosity toward Yezidis. The post-2003 period saw the rise of Kurdish power that made systematic efforts to co-opt Yezidis. Yezidis, a historically stigmatized group, achieved minor gains in terms of greater public visibility and political representation. Increasing political visibility of Yezidis thanks to Kurdish patronage, albeit limited and symbolic, fueled resentment among local Sunnis, mostly Arabs but also Turkomans, who experienced a dramatic status loss in the new political order and lacked access to state resources.

Resentment becomes a particularly destructive force when a liminal minority becomes its object. Yezidis were the only group who were raped and sexually enslaved in large numbers by IS militants and collaborators in Iraq and Syria. Such brutal practices were permissible and justifiable only because the IS capitalized on centuries-old orthodox Islamic teachings and norms depicting Yezidis as "devil worshippers." This anti-Yezidi orthodoxy had a popular resonance and was actively circulated among local people by Salafi preachers since the early 1990s. These views provided a template of popular mobilization and predisposition for exterminationist violence. Such templates were less readily available for other groups targeted by the IS including Christians, Shiite Turkomans, and Sunni Kurds and Arabs affiliated with rival organizations. Although these groups also suffered, the Yezidis bore the brunt of violence. The ferocity and frequency of attacks targeting Yezidis reached unprecedented levels.

As covered in chapter 3, similar dynamics were also present during the anti-Alevi pogroms in central Anatolian towns in the late twentieth century, the worst massacres perpetrated by nonstate actors in modern Turkish history. Alevis achieved some social mobility thanks to processes of secularization and socioeconomic development that made religious differences less salient in the second half of the twentieth century. Nonetheless, they continued to remain at the margins of political power and sought alliances with stronger forces. Alevis disproportionately joined leftist movements starting in the 1970s and sided with the secularist forces in the face of rising Islamist activism in the 1990s. This dynamic would fuel Sunni Turkish resentment with Alevis especially in conservative Anatolian towns that became political backwater. Hence, it is not a coincidence that the bloodiest massacres targeting Alevis in Turkey and Yezidis in Iraq took place during periods when these groups felt excluded from power. Moreover, in both contexts, religious stigmas directly aggravated resentment felt by a previously dominant group, Sunni Turks in central Anatolia and Sunni Arabs in northern Iraq, against a relatively weak liminal minority. As I will demonstrate in latter chapters, justifications based on religious differences directly shaped what Francisco Gutiérrez-Sanín and Elisabeth Jean Wood (2017, 23) call the repertoire of violence, "the forms of violence including homicide, rape, sexual enslavement, enforced disappearances, forceful displacement," against both Yezidis and Alevis.

The difference in the scale of violence in both contexts could be explained by different political contexts. The IS violence against Yezidis was genocidal as it *intended to* destroy the very existence of this religious community. Genocidal campaigns, which are contingent rather than predetermined events, tend to take place during wars (Midlarsky 2005). The Holocaust "would not—and could not—have happened" had World War II not taken place (Bergen 2016, 1). More broadly, Martin Shaw (2003) observes that genocide could be conceptualized as an extension of degenerate war where a largely unarmed civilian population becomes the target of violence. Large-scale armed conflicts characterized by aggravated threat perceptions, uncertainty, and widespread sanctioning of lethal violence generate an enabling context for the realization of murderous projects targeting entire communities (Weitz 2003; Mann 2005; Straus 2006). Such was the situation in post-Saddam Iraq ravaged by an ongoing sectarian civil war and mayhem. In comparison, the anti-Alevi violence in twentieth-century Turkey were massacres that aimed to intimidate and subdue the community rather than eliminate the targeted minority. Even though the Turkish state authority lost its monopoly over violence for a brief period, it was able to impose order and bring an end to mass violence. This crucial difference in the political context, rather than the nature of intercommunal animosities, explains why the scope of violence was much broader in Iraq in 2014 than in Turkey in the late twentieth century.

Mass violence targeting liminal minorities is often condoned and rarely punished by authorities. When the perpetrators suffer few if any negative consequences for their heinous actions, they are emboldened to act in similar manners in future occasions. This pattern is what Manus Midlarsky (2005, 62) calls validation, a pattern that could be only broken by dismantling prevalent cultures of impunity. Relatedly, policies and initiatives aiming to transform exclusionary beliefs and norms about liminal minorities at both theological and popular levels are essential for the sustainability of religious pluralism. Such a transformation inevitably entails not only legal but also popular recognition of these groups with beliefs and practices deserving respect and dignity.

This argument differs from the constructivist approach in the study of mass violence in a crucial regard. In her posthumously published book, Lee Ann Fujii (2021) conceptualizes violence as "a *process* of group making rather than a product of groups" (6; original emphasis) that radically rewrites "what it means to belong to a given category" (8). From her perspective, group boundaries are malleable and context dependent than typically assumed. The very act of enacting mass violence constitutes collective identities and aims to fix categories of identity. It has a transformative impact as individuals who participate in public displays of violence develop a new sense of belonging and construct a new social order. I suggest that differences informed by religious liminality are less malleable. Such differences foment social distance and harbor animosities across generations that make violence against certain types of minorities more justifiable and thinkable than others. Although it is true that acts of violence harden group boundaries and set groups apart, they would not happen in the absence of historically formed religious differences. Consequently, the past has a long shadow that informs intergroup relations. The ways in which societies deal with the past either enable them to outgrow this past or remain encapsulated by its gloom.

Religious Minorities and Mass Atrocities

Many other religious minorities have been subject to waves of mass atrocities in similar periods and geographies. The Young Turks pursued a campaign of extermination against the Ottoman Armenians during World War I (Üngör 2012; Suny 2015). A vicious riot, instigated by the government and involving large crowds, brought the decimation of the Greek community in Istanbul and several other cities in September 1955 (Kuyucu 2005; Güven 2006). Assyrians became the victims of a massacre in northern Iraq in 1933 (Zubaida 2000). Post-Saddam Iraq saw the near extinction of Christian communities, who inhabited Mesopotamia since ancient times, due to widespread terror attacks. What distinguishes these historical episodes of violence against liminal and nonliminal minorities?

From a comparative perspective, violence against liminal minorities has two distinctive characteristics. First, it exhibits a more *continuous* historical pattern informed by religious stigmatization. Compared to liminal minorities such as Alevis and Yezidis, officially recognized minorities such as Armenians, Greeks, and Jews had enjoyed relatively higher levels of tolerance and safety under the Ottoman rule until the nineteenth century (Barkey 2008; M. Greene 2020). The Armenians whose millennial presence in Anatolia would come to a tragic end in the early twentieth century were not targeted in major violent campaigns until the second half of the nineteenth century. For sure, the Ottoman-Safavid wars in the sixteenth and seventeenth centuries brought devastation to Armenian communities inhabiting the borderlands between these two empires. Shah Abbas deported a large number of Armenians into Persia (Kouymjian 1997, 14–21). Yet neither the Ottomans nor the Safavids engaged in deliberate ethnic cleansing of the Armenians during this period. Even if the last Armenian kingdom ceased to exist by the fourteenth century, a large Armenian community in Cilicia and eastern Anatolia survived until the early twentieth century. The Armenian Church was incorporated into the Ottoman millet system and preserved the cultural distinctiveness of the community. Eastern Armenia, which remained under Iranian influence until the early nineteenth century, continued to host centers of vibrant commercial and cultural activity (Bournoutian 1997).

Given this history, we can make better sense of the Armenian genocide by studying sociopolitical developments since the last decades of the nineteenth century rather than seeking its origins in perennial religious differences (Suny 2015). An unintended consequence of the Ottoman modernization involving the promise of equal citizenship was the growing resentfulness among Sunni Muslim populations of the empire (Lewis 1968, 127–28, 355–56). They were fearful of losing their position at the top of the imperial ethnoreligious hierarchy. The idea of political equality transcending religious differences, the main promise of Ottomanism, had limited resonance among Sunni Muslims who historically occupied a superior political status over non-Muslims. In comparison, the Armenians, like the Greeks and the Jews, capitalized on their foreign connections and took advantage of increasing educational and commercial opportunities (Kurt 2021). They were better positioned than their Muslim neighbors to take advantage of the reforms that aimed to replace the hierarchical imperial system based on well-defined religious differences. They also aspired to improve their status thanks to their linkages with the Christian foreign powers and the leverage of these states over a diminished Ottoman Empire.

International context characterized by fierce geopolitical rivalries also aggravated Muslim animosity toward the Armenians. The Ottomans experienced territorial losses to the stronger imperial powers such as Russia and Austria-Hungary and new Christian states such as Greece and Bulgaria. In this context, Armenians who experienced a period of renaissance and cultivated foreign linkages increasingly became threatening (Melson 1982). In particular, the widespread perception of Armenian economic and social progress became the driving source of Muslim enmity at the local level. In many different occasions during the last decades of the empire, this enmity fueled outbursts of open hostilities given political weakness of the Armenians and the prevailing impunity (Kılıçdağı 2014, 172–80). These observations suggest that anti-Armenian violence during the late-Ottoman times was a modern phenomenon, a pattern consistent with the broader observation about the aggravating effects of colonization on ethnic polarization (Lange 2017; Mamdani 2020). There was nothing inevitable and predetermined about the genocidal violence. The communal tensions summarized above did not automatically escalate into the genocidal campaign of 1915. The outbreak of World War I became the ultimate enabling factor wiping out the constraints and empowering political actors intent on resolving the conflict via extreme means (Turkyilmaz 2011, 332–33).

In contrast, liminal minorities had a more precarious position in the Ottoman politico-legal order well before the advent of modernization and foreign encroachments. As summarized in more detail in chapters 3 and 4, respectively, both Yezidis and Alevis were the targets of various massacres during the sixteenth and seventeenth centuries, the classical age of the empire. Although the expeditions leading to massacres had a security dimension (i.e., Alevis presumed to be loyal to the Safavid shahs and Yezidis perceived to threaten Ottoman lines of communication and transportation), they were justified primarily on grounds that these communities fell beyond the pale of tolerated faiths. Both groups were demonized as holding beliefs in defiance of Sunni Islam and engaging in immoral practices. A common discursive practice was false rumors that their collective rituals involved sexual orgies.

The official justification for the deportation and killing of the Armenians were their alleged disloyalty and linkages with the Russians even if religious justifications, such as the depiction of Armenians as infidels, were present at the popular levels (Aktar and Kırmızı 2013, 307). The Simele massacre against the Assyrians in northern Iraq in 1933 took place following Iraq's nominal independence from the United Kingdom. The widespread perception that the

Assyrians were aligned with the British was a decisive factor triggering mass atrocities. The Istanbul riots of 1955 took place during the Turkish and Greek struggle over Cyprus. Turkish nationalism rather than an Islamist worldview that perceived non-Muslims as unassimilable was the main ideological drive of the attacks. In comparison, religious justifications of violence have played a decisive role in the acts of violence targeting a liminal minority. Religious symbols and discourses were central to anti-Alevi violence in central Anatolian towns of Maraş in 1978 and Sivas in 1993. The IS violence against Yezidis in Sinjar in 2014 was justified entirely on religious grounds.

Another important distinction between liminal and nonliminal religious minorities concerns the level of threat they presented to the dominant groups and their linkages with external actors. In contemporary India, anti-Christian violence is often a reaction to Western secular modernity. Local Christian groups become "a more convenient, available, and vulnerable scapegoat" for popular Hindu resentment with the global encroachments of Western sociopolitical order (Bauman 2020, 60). A similar pattern was present during the twilight years of the Ottoman Empire when Christians subjects of the sultan accumulated significant economic power (Hanioğlu 2008, 26; Kurt 2021). Moreover, starting with the Greek revolt in the 1820s, they also established independent states often thanks to the selective interventions of European powers that were framed as "humanitarian" missions protecting fellow Christians from the barbarity of the "uncivilized" Ottomans (Rodogno 2012, 11–12). Although the Armenian communities never became a significant military force that could have contested the Ottoman control in eastern Anatolia, the Berlin Treaty of 1878 paved the way for the direct involvement of European powers in the region. Consequently, Armenian linkages with Christian powers, especially with Russia, became a major concern for the Ottoman rulers and Muslim populace during this period (Morris and Ze'evi 2019, 39–43). The formation of the Hamidiye Cavalry composed of Kurdish tribal forces in 1890, which significantly contributed to lawlessness and violence in the region, was the sultan's attempt to contain the "Armenian threat" in the region (Klein 2011, 2–3). In contrast, foreign linkages and patronage were either nonexistent or much weaker in the case of Alevis and Yezidis. Even though both groups were also subjects of various missionary activism, they lacked strong external patrons who could exert sustained pressure on the Ottoman authorities on their behalf. This pattern did not change significantly after the demise of the empire and the advent of the modern state system in the Middle East. For instance, during the mandate period in Iraq, the British patronage to Yezidis remained negligent (Fuccaro 1999). In summary, arguments highlighting the role of international context and external forces in exacerbating interreligious tensions are of limited use in making sense of mass violence against liminal minorities.

Religion and Political Violence Debate

The relationship between religion and political violence has been the subject of intense public and scholarly debate since the early 1990s. Whereas some scholars argue that religion features prominently in violent political struggles in the post–Cold War era (Toft, Philpott, and Shah 2011), others express skepticism whether religion plays a role in the occurrence and intensity of civil wars (Maoz and Henderson 2020). From a secular perspective, religious wars that are motivated by absolute faith and promises of otherworldly salvation cause horrifying suffering (Dawkins 2016, 316, 341–48). In early modern Western Europe, state elites aimed to bolster the allegiance of the masses by discriminating against popularly stigmatized minorities and letting them become subjects of mass violence. In this sense, religious exclusion was central to the formation of nationalism (Marx 2003). In both historical and contemporary times, sacred spaces, locations profoundly valued by believers for offering "the possibility of communicating with the divine, receiving divine favors, and achieving insight into the deeper meanings of their faith," are prone to conflict (Hassner 2009, 2). When rival branches of a religion or two religions make competing claims over such a space, which is indivisible by its very nature, the potential for political violence is intensified.

An opposing perspective remains skeptical about the notion of "religious violence" and suggests that there is nothing unique about religion that promotes violence. Instigators of and participants in conflicts labeled as "religious warfare" have mundane motives—the pursuit of political power, economic profit, or social status (Cavanaugh 2009). This perspective reflects a general scholarly tendency to identify self-interest as the ultimate driver of human behavior and downplay the importance of emotional factors. As elegantly argued by Albert Hirschman (1997), illustrious figures both during the formative periods of capitalism and throughout the twentieth century justified capitalist practices on grounds that it would generate a system where interest-motivated behavior would prevail over destructive proclivities such as the passion for conquest and domination. For Hirschman, this remains an intended but unrealized effect of capitalism given the preponderance of resentment and alienation it continues to generate.

From a historical perspective, there is a close affiliation between the rise of nationalism and mass violence in modern times. Eric Weitz (2003), Michael

Mann (2005), and Cathie Carmicheal (2009) identify the rise of nationalism and the demise of multiethnic empires as the main factors that planted the seeds of genocidal violence by states in many different parts of the world by the early twentieth century. Racism that divides humans into exclusive and fixed categories and fosters eliminationist violence is a modern phenomenon that reached its zenith in the late nineteenth and early twentieth centuries (Weitz 2003, 32–42). Correspondingly, the rise of colonial practices informed by racist ideas that reify and politicize ethnic differences (Mamdani 2001; Lange 2017) and the struggle over the control of the state among ethnic groups (Wimmer 2013) contributed to spikes in political violence since the late nineteenth century. In other cases, the struggle over territory was a dynamic central to the logic of ethnic cleansing and mass violence (Hayden 1996; Toft 2003; Mann 2005).

Friedrich Nietzsche suggests that states historically instrumentalized religion to keep the population content and divert attention from their own shortcomings. Political elites relied on the religious establishment to legitimize their rule. However, the advent of democratic politics is inevitably associated with the secularization of political rule whereby religion becomes a privatized affair. This secularization fosters enmity among religious people against the new political order. This enmity in turn makes irreligious groups, including elites, embrace the state as a sacred entity and substitute religion with a total devotion to the state (Nietzsche 1910, 337–40).[1] We can think of this devotion as being synonymous with nationalism. Accordingly, the nation, which is "the highest-level social group of real significance for the vast majority of people around the world" (Mearsheimer 2018, 200), has been the main object of political sacrifice in modern times. The idea of nationhood has made "it possible, over the past two centuries, for so many millions of people, not so much to kill, as willingly to die for such limited imaginings" (Anderson 1991, 7). Since the French Revolution, levy en masse has been a defining aspect of how nation-states mobilize their citizens for war-making purposes (Berman 2020, 65). Likewise, self-determination movements in many different parts of the world successfully recruit a large number of individuals who risk their lives for a collective purpose (Tezcür 2016).

In her study of challenges facing liberal-democratic governance in Muslim countries, Jocelyn Cesari (2014, 2021) offers a similar perspective. She argues

---

1. Nietzsche also predicted the gradual disappearance of the state. As it loses its religious aura, people approach it purely from an instrumental perspective. Nietzsche's prediction has not been fulfilled as the state continues to command the absolute loyalty of people in many different parts of the world.

that the rise of nation-states in the Muslim world brought the formation of new forms of intolerance and restrictions on freedom of expression and belief. As the state privileged a certain religious faith at the expense of others, Islam gained a hegemonic characteristic. Even the ostensibly secular regimes in Muslim countries such as Tunisia and Turkey promoted majoritarian religion while restricting freedom of belief. Muslim-majority countries where Islam enjoys a hegemonic institutional status are more likely to experience higher levels of political violence compared to Muslim-majority countries where Islam is less institutionalized (Cesari 2014, 16–17). Consequently, both political illiberalism and violence are by-products of how Islam was institutionally privileged by the modern nation-states rather than reflections of Islamic traditions and culture.

In summary, nationalism has dwarfed religion when it comes to directing and instigating political violence in modern times. This scholarly recognition is an effective antidote against perspectives that portray armed conflict between religious groups as the exploitation of centuries-old lingering animosities and grievances (e.g., Chua 2018, 97). At the same time, dismissing the role of religious beliefs in motivating human action out of hand lacks a compelling basis. As discussed in the next chapter, there is a plethora of experimental and interdisciplinary evidence that demonstrates how monotheistic beliefs can be a very strong motivator of both prosocial behaviors and aggression toward outsiders. People do engage in acts of sacrifice not only in the name of the nation but also in the name of the religious community they seek to protect from "infidels." The appeal of Salafi jihadism that glorifies acts of sacrifice including suicide attacks in the last two decades is the most recent testimony to this very violent pattern (Moghadam 2009). Exclusivist religious beliefs often lie at the heart of genocidal ideologies in modern times, from the Spanish conquest of South America in the sixteenth century to al-Qaeda's indiscriminate attacks in the late twentieth century (Kiernan 2007).

I contribute to this debate by offering a nuanced and refined understanding of how certain religious differences become a source of political violence. I develop a historically grounded middle-range theory that fleshes out the mechanisms through which religious beliefs are associated with mass atrocities. This theoretical framework aims to bridge a predispositional perspective about collective hatred toward a religious minority and a situational perspective about resentfulness caused by political changes, similar to McDoom's study of the Rwandan genocide (2021). Mechanisms are central to causal claims in this framework (Hedström and Ylikoski 2010). As elaborated by Charles Tilly (2001), a theoretical understanding based on mechanisms differs sharply from covering law accounts that claim to identify a universal relationship between religion and violence. Although religious differences formed across centuries do not predetermine the contours of political struggles, they do remain relevant to understanding the outbreaks of violence targeting minorities. The scholarly task is to identify the historical and political dynamics under which religious markers become a life-and-death matter. Accordingly, I differ from most scholarly research on the subject that deals with more conventional forms of differences such as Islam-Christianity, Christianity-Judaism, Islam-Hinduism that have been the focus of most scholarly research. This conceptual move allows me to identify a distinct pattern, which is not covered by the extant literature, featuring violence against religious minorities.

My approach stands in contrast to both classical Marxist perspectives that tend to reduce politics to class conflict, and rational choice approaches prioritizing self-interest maximization in human motives. The former remains inadequate when individuals behave in ways that defy their material or class interests. The latter does not provide any insights about political behavior that tend to sacrifice personal well-being for collective goals. In certain historical periods, groups who are perceived to challenge the prevailing religious doctrine find themselves at the receiving end of mass violence. In other periods, apocalyptic beliefs foster acts of aggression targeting a variety of groups. I argue that motives of perpetrators of both types of violence could not be captured only by concerns about security, pursuit of pecuniary gains or social status, revenge, or desire for power. Following Anthony Marx (2003), I suggest that the desire to please God remains a powerful motivator of political action at popular levels and is what makes large-scale violence possible in such situations.

I also differ from scholars who suggest that "religious identities are no more inherently prone to violence than any other identities" (Bauman 2020, 25). I argue that we should take the *substance* of religious differences seriously. As Ron Hassner (2016) aptly argues, religion could act as "a force multiplier"—sacred leaders, symbols, rituals, and time could restrain or exacerbate warmaking practices in contemporary times. At the one end of the spectrum, religious differences have a long and institutionalized history of interfaith dialogue and mutual respect. Religious leaders could employ their expertise to actively engage in resolution of armed conflicts, as in Northern Ireland (Sandal 2017). They also have considerable power to reconfigure popular meanings attached to sacred spaces contested by multiple faith groups and play constructive roles in the resolution of violent conflicts (Hassner 2009, 157–59). At the opposite end of the spectrum, religious differences informed by centuries-long exclusivist teachings and norms could facilitate aggression against certain out-groups. More specifically, the ambivalence and internal pluralism of the great Abrahamic religions (Appleby 2000), fails to provide protection for liminal minorities who lack recognition and are prone to stigmatization by the virtue of their beliefs. The very existence of these minorities presents a direct challenge to the predominant religious doctrine and the moral order it underlines. It is also a source of existential insecurity and collective anxiety for members of the predominant group. When this group becomes resentful due to power loss, these insecurity and anxiety pave the way for acts of mass violence against members of a liminal minority.

I agree with the oft-made point that cultural factors including religious differences by themselves cannot explain the outbursts of communal violence (Semelin 2001). Mass violence is typically a rare event that follows long periods of religious coexistence and erupts with the collapse of norms regulating intergroup affairs. As long as these norms, which usually sustain a highly hierarchical sociopolitical order, remain intact, popular stigmatization of liminal minorities, who occupy a subordinate position in this order, is unlikely to be translated into acts of mass violence. During periods of political change characterized by status reversals, however, differences based on sacred beliefs and rituals are easily activated to make religious minorities the object of mass violence and reveal the historical curse of liminality. Consequently, violence against liminal minorities is directly shaped by the historical formation and perpetuation of religious differences.

Finally, my conceptualization of religion as a distinct source of group identity goes against the conventional approach in political science. Scholars studying ethnic conflict often treat religion as one of many identity markers that could become the basis of violent mobilization. Subsumed under the category of ethnic identity, religion is not substantively different from language, tribe, geographical origin, caste, clan, or race (Horowitz 2000; Chandra 2006). The substance of these markers is less important than the ways in which they shape group boundaries (Wimmer 2008). While Roger Brubaker (2015) identifies six mechanisms through which religion can foster violence, he also argues that none of those mechanisms are intrinsic to religion itself. In contrast, this book is based on the premise that the belief in an omnipotent God ruling over human affairs could motivate distinctive types of political behavior, both prosocial and destructive. Consequently, I identify the desire to please or be in favor of God as a major factor in explaining political violence directed against a religious minority.

Research Design and Methodological Approach

The theoretical framework in this book explicitly recognizes the role of normative ideas, cognitive ideas, and collective emotions in shaping violent political behavior. Methodological challenges of inferring political behavior from ideas and emotions are well documented. Ideational mechanisms often correlate with a set of plausible and material mechanisms and could be difficult to measure (Jacobs 2015). Moreover, inferring motives of perpetrators is a highly arduous task in the absence of "smoking gun" evidence such as internal correspondence among perpetrators during the attacks. Even public discourses used by the perpetrators to describe and justify their actions could be misleading when such discourses aim to cover ulterior motives. Hence, a theoretical framework that argues for the causal role of ideas in shaping behavior faces the challenge of indeterminacy.

I aim to address this challenge by employing process tracing, a method that measures and tests causal mechanisms at the meso level (Bennett and Checkel 2015). Process tracing utilizing a rich array of original sources helps me develop a deductive theory-testing approach and examine the observable implications of both religious and nonreligious explanations of participation in political violence against members of a liminal minority. More specifically, I conduct a series of "hoop tests" to falsify competing hypotheses about the motives for violence by consulting the available empirical evidence. If a hypothesis fails a hoop test, it is eliminated. Yet passing a hoop test does not confirm a hypothesis. Hence, passing a hoop test is necessary but not sufficient for confirming a hypothesis (Collier 2011).

My main unit of analyses are groups who share the same religious identity (i.e., Yezidis and Sunni Muslims in northern Iraq, Alevis and Sunni Muslim Turks in central Anatolia). I focus on general tendencies characterizing political behavior of these groups. I am fully aware that analyzing behavior at the group level is a simplification that could not account for important intragroup differences. Many members of a dominant group acted brutally toward their members of a liminal minority; some others showed altruism toward the outgroup. As in other violent contexts, some people, typically a minority, were better able to integrate an ethical perspective into their worldview than others (Monroe 2008). As already shown in the prologue, personal friendships and previous experiences of cooperation could also induce some individuals to actively help members of an out-group even at personal risk. Explaining this variation requires granular data at the individual level that have been unavailable. I am hoping that future studies will be better positioned to address the question of intragroup variation during communal atrocities.

Case Studies: Yezidis and Alevis

The main empirical focus of this book is liminal minorities in the broader Muslim world. Since the times of Muhammad, certain non-Muslim groups were offered protection and legal existence in return for payment of a special tax, a status called *dhimma* (Lapidus 2002, 36). Known as People of the Book (*Ahl al-Kitāb*), such groups included Christians and Jews (and to a more limited extent Zoroastrians) (Berkey 2003, 100–101). They were clearly distinguished from polytheists whose existence was much less tolerated (Cronin 2004, 371). Historically speaking, religious groups such as Ahmadis, Alawites, Alevis, Baha'is, Druzes, and Yezidis perceived to split from Islam (hence defying the core Islamic belief that Muhammad is the last prophet) lacked the dhimma status. Religious stigmatization of these groups could be expected to be more pervasive and readily actable than any other religious minority in the broader Muslim world. From a historical perspective, I consider these communities as liminal minorities par excellence. Accordingly, my primary empirical focus is on two paradigmatic cases, Yezidis and Alevis, that exemplifies general characteristics of such groups (Flyvbjerg 2006, 232–33). I also offer succinct overviews of Baha'is and Ahmadis. These empirical observations together provide significant variation in terms of intercommunal relations, ranging from accommodation to mass violence across both time and space.

The Yezidis are a predominantly Kurdish-speaking community historically based in northern Iraq and southeastern Turkey (Ali 2021). A significant number of them migrated to the Caucasus ruled by tsarist Russia in the aftermath of the Russo-Ottoman wars during the nineteenth and early twentieth centuries. In the late twentieth century, they migrated to Western European countries such as Germany, France, and the Netherlands. The Yezidi faith, which has its own distinctive characteristics, evolved in interaction with Islam, Christianity, and Zoroastrianism. It is widely accepted that Sheikh Adi (b. in Lebanon in 1075), who played a pivotal role in the emergence of Yezidism as a separate faith, was a well-known Muslim mystic and Sufi. He settled in the mountainous border zone between contemporary Turkey and Iraq by 1111. His tomb in the Lalish valley, which is located in contemporary Iraqi Kurdistan, gradually became the holiest place of Yezidism (Kreyenbroek 1995). According to one interpretation, Yezidism became a distinct religion through Kurdish syncretism of Islamic and Christian beliefs during the thirteenth and fourteenth centuries. An alternative historical reading, which is favored by most Yezidis, suggests that Yezidism has ancient roots preceding both Islam and Christianity but adopted some of their traditions for survival purposes in the face of hostility from ruling entities and neighboring communities (Guest 1993, 29).

The lack of a written body of teachings hindered the development of an official, monolithic Yezidi theology, which in turn contributed to Muslim perceptions of Yezidis as a "deviant sect" with ill-defined and ambivalent beliefs. According to Islamic orthodoxy, which goes back to the sixteenth century (Dehqan 2008; Kerborani 2021), the Yezidis lack the status "People of the Book." In fact, they have been labeled as devil worshippers by both Muslims and Christians who often confuse the holiest angel in the Yezidi faith, Tawus-i Melek, with Satan (*iblīs/şeytan*), the adversary of God in the Abrahamic religions. As late as the 1970s, many Iraqis believed that Yezidis indulged in sexual orgies and practiced a form of droit du seigneur, offering their brides to their holy men, during their communal gathering (al-Jabiri 1981, 3). Many Muslims continue to view Yezidis as impure and refuse to eat food they prepare. In turn, Yezidi oral traditions cultivate a culture of victimhood (Gökçen 2015). To paraphrase the Polish poet Czesław Miłosz, Yezidi collective identity is primarily a memory of wounds.

Alevism emerged from religious diversity and political fragmentation characterizing late-medieval Anatolia. It became a distinctive faith during the Ottoman-Safavid geopolitical struggle that started in the early sixteenth century (Karakaya-Stump 2020). Similar to the experience of Yezidis, the rise of the Sunni Ottoman Empire that projected its power into eastern Anatolia and Mesopotamia by the sixteenth century was a critical juncture in the formation of Alevi liminality. As the Ottomans viewed Alevi communities, which include both Turkic- and Kurdish-speaking groups, as being loyal to the Safavid shah, they pursued violent campaigns to eradicate and subdue them. The Sunni religious authorities declared Alevis as heretics beyond the pale of Islam deserving no protection. Also similar to Yezidis, what fundamentally distinguished Alevis from their neighbors was not what they believed in but what they did not practice. They had no mosques, no Friday prayers, no fasting during Ramadan, and no pilgrimage to Mecca. In the face of the Ottoman persecution, Alevi communities dispersed across Anatolia developed systematized religious rituals and practices that facilitated the formation of a more salient collective identity. Different from Yezidis, who have a supreme religious authority in the name of Baba Sheikh, Alevis have not developed a hierarchical structure under the authority of a single religious cleric. Nor do they have a focal pilgrimage site, comparable to Lalish in Yezidism. Nonetheless, they managed to maintain their differences from the surrounding Sunni communities until the Ottoman modernization and state-building efforts in the late nineteenth century.

A core aspect of Alevi liminality is about the very definition of the community. In contemporary times, many Alevis and non-Alevis participate in public debates about whether Alevism represents a distinct religious faith, a way of life, or a cultural heritage. An influential view is to label Alevism as a "folk Islam" that syncretize pre-Islamic beliefs and practices of Turkic groups. This view often finds acceptance among some contemporary Alevis as it helps them minimize their differences with the Sunni Turkish majority on grounds that their faith is inherently Turkish. Such an option is less available not only to Kurdish-speaking Yezidis but also Kurdish Alevis. At the same time, the articulation of Alevism as syncretic belief system indicates the clear subordination of Alevism to Sunni Islam in a hierarchy of faiths. The Turkish Republic has continued the state policies aiming to assimilate Alevis into Sunni Islam, including the construction of mosques in Alevi villages and compulsory religious courses that promote Sunni Islam in public education (Lord 2018). The state offers no official recognition to Alevis as a distinctive faith community and views them as "Muslims." This practice finds its most vocal expression in the oft-repeated phrase that claims that Turkey is "99 percent Muslim."

Two other groups covered in this book are the Baha'is in Iran and the Ahmadis in Indonesia and Pakistan. Compared to Yezidis and Alevis, these faith groups have a shorter history going back to the late nineteenth century. They were also subject to intense religious stigmatization as their core beliefs presented a direct theological challenge to Islamic orthodoxy. Although both groups became targets of popular hostilities since their emergence, the rise of Islamic influences over state policies in Iran, Pakistan, and Indonesia made their situation more precarious since the late twentieth century. Paradoxically, the intensity of state-led discrimination and persecution of these communities made it less urgent for popular actors to engage in acts of mass violence targeting Baha'is and Ahmadis.

A Note on Data Collection

The book is based on a rich variety of empirical sources. My discussion of the Yezidis draws on 103 semi-structured in-depth interviews with 95 individuals or groups of individuals and original documents in primary sources, primarily Kurdish and Turkish. Detailed information about the fieldwork as well as a listing of the interviewees, locations, and dates is provided in the printed and online appendixes (see table AO.1 at https://hdl.handle.net/1813/113348). For research purposes, I traveled to Duhok, Iraqi Kurdistan in September 2017 and May–June 2018 and Berlin, Germany in June 2017. Many of the interviews took place in camps for displaced Yezidis. Additionally, I rely on dozens of interviews conducted by Tutku Ayhan, who was a doctoral candidate at the University of Central Florida, primarily in Iraqi Kurdistan in April and

May 2019.[2] In terms of printed and online sources, I consult (a) declarations by Yezidi leaders, (b) statements by Kurdish, Iraqi, and Turkish authorities, and (c) books and newspaper and magazine articles written by Muslims and Westerners about Yezidis, and (d) official statements in both Ottoman and contemporary times.

In the aftermath of the IS attacks in August 2014, the media discourse has cultivated a gendered image of Yezidi victimhood obscuring the intragroup diversity and minimizing the agency of survivors (Buffon and Allison 2016). To avoid simplistic representations of the community, we adopted an intersectional approach (Crenshaw 1991) in our fieldwork and aimed to remain alert to power dynamics characterizing our relations with our interviewees and relations among them. Talking to both female and male survivors was valuable especially for learning about the scope of local Sunni involvement in the atrocities. At the same time, cognizant of dubious ethical practices characterizing journalistic interviews of women survivors (Foster and Minwalla 2018), we refrained from asking any direct questions about their experience of sexual violence during their captivity (Ayhan 2021). Some survivors may prefer to speak up about their tragic experiences to gain a sense of agency. For others, forgetting such experiences could be the only way to reestablish their lives (Erdener 2017).

My discussion about the episodes of mass violence targeting Alevis in Turkey in the late twentieth century is informed by a wealth of primary sources including court documents, memoirs, victim testimonies, newspapers and magazines, and parliamentary and governmental reports. Consulting all these different sources enables me to paint a detailed picture about the widespread local involvement in atrocities that took place in the Anatolian cities of Maraş in December 1978 and Sivas in July 1993. Most relevant for the purposes of this book, court documents provide rich information about the characteristics of perpetrators of violence in both episodes. Finally, in chapter 5, in collaboration with Joshua Lambert, we aim to identify broader patterns about how liminality is associated with discrimination against religious minorities across the globe employing large-N data sets and statistical models.

A potential methodological limitation is the absence of any interviews with perpetrators in the Yezidi case study. Talking to perpetrators of violence could be very insightful about their motivations. In some cases, it has been possible for scholars to interview people who were active participants in mass

---

2. The fieldwork is based on the protocol approved by the institutional review board of the University of Central Florida (# IRB00001138).

violence. A primary example is Fujii (2009), which aims to flesh out dynamics of local participation in the Rwandan genocide. Legacies of violence shape the availability of perpetuators as human subjects in research. Transitional mechanisms such as truth and reconciliation commissions facilitate reckoning with the past via testimonies by victims and bystanders, confessions by perpetrators asking for forgiveness to seek acquittal, and detailed reports by independent entities. They typically emerge in the aftermath of democratization or defeat of the regime/organization responsible for the atrocities. At the other end of the spectrum lie settings where violence undersigns a new political order characterized by a culture of impunity. Joshua Oppenheimer's documentary *The Act of Killing* (2012) is a visceral example of how mass killings in Indonesia in 1965–66 vindicated its perpetrators who brag about their active participation in atrocities and believe in their righteousness after many decades.

Neither of these conditions is present in the Yezidi case. Although many IS fighters and supporters were captured and imprisoned in both Iraq and Syria, not a single individual was put on trial and punished specifically for sexual violence targeting Yezidi women and children. Moreover, prospects for intercommunal reconciliation remain dim. Perpetrators have no incentive to come clean and accept responsibility. The Sinjar district, where massacres took place in August 2014, remains a highly contested and insecure zone making research in the area infeasible. Some local people who previously supported the IS have now been incorporated into the Iraqi forces, aggravating Yezidi anxieties. Consequently, talking to the perpetrators remains an elusive task under the prevailing circumstances.

Under these circumstances, I do rely on interviews with a wide range of individuals and not just survivors. The in-depth interviewees provide different interpretations about the motives of attackers while suggesting a widespread consensus on the widespread participation of locals in the violence. Moreover, I compile a variety of documents including reports based on field research and testimonies in journalistic sources about the local patterns of violence. Utilizing these diverse sources, I employ triangulation to assess the relative merits of these competing interpretations, whether attackers were primarily motivated by greed, fear, guilt, resentment, or hatred. To minimize confirmation bias that would privilege material that seems to support my hypothesis, I cross-check the information I obtained from interviews with each other and from other sources. It is ultimately up to the readers to decide if my interpretation of the motives of perpetrators is compelling on the basis of the presented evidence.

An Overview of the Book

Chapter 1 presents an original theoretical framework about the role of religious beliefs (i.e., defending a sacred doctrine against outsider groups) in mass violence. This argument is distinct from *instrumentalist* perspectives that suggest that elites exploit religious beliefs and passions at the popular level for their own parochial agendas. A limitation of these perspectives is that an exclusive focus on elite stratagems does not tell us much about the reasons why ordinary people take religion seriously to engage in acts of violence, often at personal cost. I build on both historical—for example, the study of the French Wars of Religion—and experimental studies to suggest that the belief in the supernatural could be a powerful motivator of aggression toward out-groups as well as altruism toward members of an in-group. I then argue that eschatological beliefs, categorization of certain groups as "heretical," and desire to remake the sociopolitical order in the image of God generate a disposition toward violence.

Building on these insights, I propose that certain faith groups, liminal minorities, are more vulnerable to religiously motivated violence than others. The very existence of these groups presents an affront to the constructed sacred order and foments insecurity and anxiety among believers of a dominant faith. The age of secularity as conceptualized by Charles Taylor (2007) does not ameliorate these insecurities and anxieties. To the contrary, it often generates a siege mentality among believers who feel their sacred values are under threat with the rise of widespread secular practices. Under these circumstances, liminal minorities, given their political and numerical weakness, make a convenient target of scapegoating at the hands of a resentful religious majority when the state capacity remains too weak or fragmented. This chapter discusses the mechanisms of religious hatred, resentment, fear, greed, and guilt in motivating participation in mass atrocities.

Chapters 2 and 3 provide case studies of violence targeting Yezidis and Alevis, respectively. After providing historical summaries of the experience of both groups, the narrative focuses on specific episodes of mass violence against Yezidis in post-2003 Iraq and Alevis in late twentieth-century Turkey. In both cases, my primary focus is on the agency and motives of ordinary people who actively took part in atrocities. I argue that the historically constructed and popularly available templates of religious stigmatization of Yezidis and Alevis played a central role in enabling mass participation in the atrocities at the hands of resentful religious majorities. I conclude both chapters discussing the prospects of the politics of recognition that offer a stark alternative to the politics of liminality.

Historical patterns characterizing the relations between Yezidis and their mostly Sunni Muslim neighbors exhibit complexity and countervailing tendencies that could not be accurately captured by a prism of victimhood. At the same time, religious stigmatization of Alevis and Yezidis exhibits a consistent and predominant historical pattern. The absence of any notable Islamic discourse that explicitly challenged and refuted widespread pejorative views of the Yezidis left the community particularly vulnerable to campaigns inspired by religious hatred. The US invasion in 2003 paved the way for the rise of Salafi jihadist movements capitalizing on Sunni Muslim resentment and aggravated the precariousness of the Yezidis in Iraq. At the societal level, anti-Yezidi norms and beliefs made extreme levels of violence permissible and facilitated widespread local participation in the atrocities. Without such norms and beliefs, IS violence would have remained more constrained in terms of targeting, repertoire, and frequency. More specifically, the IS would not have targeted Yezidis with such intensity and engaged in sexual slavery of the community in the absence of religious stigmatization. I end the chapter on a more positive note and suggest that a long-term and paradoxical implication may be the eventual liberation of Yezidis from their liminal status.

Alevis remain the largest non–Sunni Muslim group in contemporary Turkey. Since the early sixteenth century, they remained out of the Ottoman Sunni politico-legal order and were subject to periodic campaigns of persecution. Although the formation of the secular republic in the 1920s provided breathing space for and ended the insulation of Alevi communities, the rise of religious nationalism in Turkey in the second half of the twentieth century resulted in a series of massacres. The most lethal events took place in two central Anatolian towns, Maraş in 1978 and Sivas in 1993. In both episodes, thousands of local people, mostly men, took part in acts of violence resulting in the deaths of dozens of people. These intimate killings were the bloodiest acts of nonstate violence in the history of the Turkish Republic. I argue that macrolevel political and socioeconomic perspectives, which are prevalent in the limited scholarship on the attacks, are insufficient to understand the dynamics characterizing mass violence in these cases. I propose that Sunni Muslim communities perceived ruling governments as being hostile to their values and became resentful of Alevis who achieved greater political visibility. Their participation in the massacres was facilitated by widespread religious templates of Alevis as an immoral group. In the aftermath of the atrocities, the Alevi demands for recognition have achieved tangible gains but also met with opposition and deflection from the broader society and the ruling government. The hegemonic discourse espoused by the government identified "both sides" as victims of conspiracies aiming to undermine public order and poison sectarian relations. Consequently, the Alevi politics of remembrance continues to occupy a liminal public space and is tolerated only when it *unremembers* that victims were targeted because of their Alevi identities.

In chapter 4, I adopt a comparative approach and offer discussions of the evolution of Baha'i and Ahmadiyya faiths. The Baha'i faith emerged as an offshoot of Twelver Shiism in nineteenth-century Iran before evolving into a distinct religious faith. Followers of the Baha'i faith faced campaigns of discrimination and persecution often instigated by the Shiite clerical establishment. An anti-Baha'i riot that was instigated by the clergy with the complicity of state officials took place in 1955 during the ostentatiously secular Pahlavi regime. Their situation took a significantly worse turn after the foundation of the Islamic Republic in 1979. The Baha'i community was declared outcasts and subject to intense forms of persecution at the hands of state authorities. Like the Baha'i faith, the Ahmadiyya faith emerged as a messianic movement and was established by a person claiming to be *mahdī* in the late nineteenth century. It also attracted the ire of Muslim clerics who perceived Ahmadis as a "deviant sect." Originated in British India, the group has established sizable communities in Indonesia and Pakistan. A violent riot targeting the community in 1953 and enactment of discriminatory laws and policies since the 1970s demonstrate the depth of anti-Ahmadi animosities in Pakistan. Moreover, the community has been subject to various acts of violence and discrimination in Indonesia since the establishment of electoral democracy. I argue that the rise of religious nationalism, which makes citizenship rights conditional on membership in the dominant faith group, aggravates the precariousness of both Baha'is and Ahmadis.

Chapter 5, coauthored with Joshua Lambert, takes a broader empirical perspective and investigates the relationship between religious liminality and discrimination across the globe. Utilizing information from the Religion and State Project Minorities Module, Round 3, it identifies eleven distinct liminal minorities that exist in fifty-one different countries. Cross-regional analyses demonstrate that the notion of liminality advances our understanding of discrimination against religious minorities beyond the Muslim world. Liminal minorities are more likely to be targets of societal discrimination in non-Muslim countries than nonliminal groups. Societal discrimination intensifies against all religious minorities in Muslim-majority countries. A combination of various factors, including collective threat perceptions aggravated by the perceived ascendancy of Western secularism as well as geopolitical struggles, generate hostility toward religious minorities, including Jews, Christians, and Hindus, in Muslim-majority countries. The findings also suggest that the size of a religious minority has no effect on the likelihood that it would be discriminated against. That finding is consistent with the experience of liminal minorities whose share of the national population remains typically very small. They are subject to discrimination not because of their large demographics, mobilization capacity, or threatening nature but because of deeply rooted patterns of religious stigmatization.

In the conclusion, I reflect on the normative implications of the notion of religious liminality. After offering a discussion about how the pursuit of recognition could stand up to the challenge of religious nationalism and present a more promising future for liminal minorities, I conclude with a brief discussion about the contribution of this book to the study of religious differences and violence.

Chapter 1

A Theory of Religious Liminality and Violence

This chapter presents a novel theoretical framework to explain certain forms of religious violence. It focuses on the role of beliefs in the supernatural in intimate forms of violence—for example, neighbors attacking neighbors who happen to belong to a different faith group. Motives, reasons why individuals engage in violence, are central to this definition of religious violence. Violence is classified as religious only when there is plausible empirical support for the contention that perpetrators have been, at least partially, motivated by a desire to please or be in favor of a supernatural entity—that is, God. Building on both historical and experimental studies, I propose that religious belief may have distinctive characteristics motivating violent political action. More specifically, religious stigmatization plays an enabling role in violent attacks against certain faith groups.

While other sets of ideas, such as secular nationalism or utopian ideologies, are equally powerful enough to motivate aggression against members of an out-group, violence against certain groups of people is thinkable and executable only when it is articulated in reference to religious values. I call these groups *liminal minorities*, whose core beliefs are subject to fabrications, misapprehensions, and slurs. These historically constituted characteristics make them particularly vulnerable to outbreaks of religious violence. Liminality is in the eye of the beholder. Powerful groups magnify the stereotypical ideas they wield. For members of a dominant religious group, the very existence of a liminal minority is a source of anxiety and threat. Although I primarily focus on groups that originated in Muslim societies, this conceptualization is applicable to religious minorities in other parts of the world.

The advent of modernity has been a mixed blessing for liminal minorities. On the one hand, such groups are less likely to be targets of large-scale violent campaigns by secular states even if they continue to be subject to various forms of discrimination. On the other hand, during times of religious revivalism, they become a lightning rod and attract popular ire. As ostensibly secular states aim to appease religious majorities, they often remain complicit during moments of popular rage targeting liminal minorities. In such contexts, political resentment becomes the main dynamic translating religious stigmatization into collective acts of violence.

To consider normative implications of the notion of religious violence, I engage with Walter Benjamin's typologies of violence and Jacques Derrida's deconstruction of these typologies. Religious violence is inherently based on natural law; it is justified primarily on the justness of its ends. At the same time, it could also be coded into the positive law. That is the practice in political systems where discrimination against a religious group is institutionalized. Contemporary examples include the experience of Baha'is in the Islamic Republic of Iran and Ahmadis in Pakistan. Regardless of whether it is perpetuated by private groups operating outside the legal system or by the state enforcing the full force of the law, religious violence is a form of what Benjamin calls mythic violence, which is capricious, ambiguous, and arbitrary. I then drew on Derrida to argue that religious violence has an inherent contradiction. Seeking its origins in a revolutionary moment—that is, revelation—religious violence seeks to be the violence of foundation and claims superiority over "human-made laws." However, by the same logic, it remains vulnerable to any future claims of revelation. Established religions tend to smear new and competing claims of revelation as being heretical and to condemn carriers of such claims to social or physical death. Hence, how religious violence operates is subject to Derrida's "paradox of iterability," whereas the distinction between foundational and law preserving violence collapses. The foundational nature of religious violence is unsustainable unless it expresses itself in acts of law preservation and punishes the "heretics" who deviate from its core precepts.

How Is Violence Religious?

One of the earliest known forms of violence justified on religious grounds and enforced by the legality and power of the state took place in ancient Athens, the cradle of democracy. Socrates was put on trial for "impiety" in 399 BC. He was accused of "introducing new gods in place of those recognized by the city" and sentenced to death (Filonik 2013, 53). More than two millennia later, in the summer of 1988, Ayatollah Khomeini, the revolutionary Shiite cleric who founded the Islamic Republic of Iran, would order the mass execution of political prisoners using a similar religious justification. The regime used an explicit religious test to decide whom to execute. After hastily organized interrogations about the prisoners' upbringings and willingness to denounce their comrades, thousands of them were accused with the crime of fighting against God (*moharebeh*) or being apostates (*mortad*) based on a religious order (fatwa) issued by Khomeini. They were then swiftly executed in secrecy (Talebi 2011). The scale of the killings has been unprecedented in the modern history of Iran.

A stifling atmosphere of political anxiety was prevailing in both situations otherwise characterized by vast differences. Athens was a highly fragile democracy after its defeat in the Peloponnesian Wars that ended in 404 BC; Iran was a highly authoritarian regime that just ended its war with Saddam's Iraq after eight years of bloodbath. The trial of Socrates took place during a time of communal tensions. Following the Spartan victory in the Peloponnesian Wars, a group of oligarchs imposed a brief reign of terror. Although democratic rule was restored in 403, popular feelings of betrayal and resentment and demands for retribution were rampant. As Socrates and his friends were perceived to be complicit in the oligarchic takeover of Athens, his punishment and execution was politically motivated (Filonik 2013, 54–57, 80). Khomeini was tormented about Iran's inability to prevail over Saddam's Iraq. Although he eventually accepted the United Nations Security Council Resolution of 588 in July 1988 that called for a cease-fire between the two sides, he also lamented that the decision was "more deadly than taking poison" (Pear 1988). As his health was ailing, he was concerned about the question of succession. He would die less than a year later. The mass executions were his attempt to forge unity among his closest comrades to ensure the long-term viability of the regime. His designated successor protested the executions and was immediately sidelined. The remaining cadres who were baptized in a bloodbath, however, would be steadfast to his legacy (Abrahamian 1999, 218–20).

There was an *instrumentalist* logic both to the Athenian citizens' condemnation of Socrates to death and Khomeini's sending of thousands of prisoners to the gallows. Although the charges were religiously framed and justified, they served particular *political* goals. In this sense, these episodes are consistent with Niccolò Machiavelli's discussion of the role of religion in politics. For Machiavelli, religion has a strong political utility that could make people obey authority and stay united. Hence, rulers should appear religious even if they need to be free from religious principles (Tarcov 2014).

Can we then downplay the substantive role of religion in these two episodes of violence on grounds that religious discourse was a cover hiding ulterior political motives: retribution against political opponents in the Athenian democracy and stratagem of elite cohesion in the Islamic Republic? That would be too dismissive. Even though political considerations may have informed the legalistic decisions, Socrates and Iranian prisoners were charged with religious crimes. In both cases, life and death decisions were made based on religious differences, either in believing in different gods or unbelieving. It is important not to marginalize *politics* of religious difference; it is equally crucial not to ignore the religious basis of political decisions. Certain violent patterns "cannot exist without the doctrinal templates and rhetorical justifications of religion" (Grzymała-Busse 2016, 347).

Before presenting my own theory of religious violence, it is apt to survey a venerable intellectual tradition that is dismissive of religion as a cause of mass-scale violence. In his study of peasant rebellions in Germany in the sixteenth century, Friedrich Engels ([1850] 1926, 27) writes, "Those wars were class wars just as were the later collisions in England and France. . . . If the interests, requirements and demands of the various classes hid themselves behind a religious screen, it little changes the actual situation." If so, religious rhetoric and discourse are fig leaves hiding economic interests and power politics (Midlarsky 2020; for an opposing perspective, see Selengut 2003, 17–23). William Cavanaugh (2009, 177) similarly suggests that it is analytically impossible to separate religious motives from social, economic, and political causes of violent conflict in his review of "the so-called religious wars" of early modern Europe. He refutes the argument that religion "is necessarily more inclined toward violence than are ideologies and institutions that are identified as secular" (5). John Mueller (2000) raises a similar criticism and opposes the categorization of the wars in former Yugoslavia and Rwanda as "ethnic war" informed by religious differences (e.g., Muslims vs. Orthodox Christians). He suggests that underlying motives and dynamics of violence in such conflicts do not differ substantially from those in nonethnic wars. Arguing against perspectives that explain violence as the eruption of long-suppressed "ancient hatreds" at the mass level, he suggests that both types of wars are often fought by a small group of opportunistic and nonideological people—that is, armed thugs—who intimidate and control the broader populations. In his important study of ethnic riots in rural India, Paul Brass (1997) also argues against perspectives that suggest that ordinary people are primarily motivated by faith and sentiments. He instead focuses on the critical role of elites who instrumentalize mundane disputes for partisan and ideological purposes. Behind the appearance of spontaneous outbreak of religious passions lies highly organized riot specialists who instigate violence in competitive struggles for power. Similarly, Steven Wilkinson (2004) identifies electoral calculations as the primary reason why some Indian politicians are more likely to foment and let riots happen than others. Consequently, what is deemed as religious violence, which often involves self-sacrifice on behalf of its perpetrators, is a strategic tool in the hands of shrewd politicians who mobilize its world-denying potential for utterly mundane goals.

Purist versions of the instrumentalist approach assume that religious beliefs are peripheral to the motives of ordinary people who follow their own self-interest as much as their leaders. Even if they are mobilized by religious discourses, they do not necessarily believe in the substance of these messages and have their own mundane reasons to engage in violence. In some cases, they are primarily motivated by greed and seek material gains. In other cases, they are motivated by resentment of another's group relative achievements and seek to restore intergroup hierarchies. In all these cases, both elites and their followers use religious mobilization strategically to hide and divert attention from their underlying motives. Religion becomes just a political tool serving *both* group and elite interests.

This instrumentalist approach has an obvious shortcoming given its assumption that violent political action is exclusively motivated by self-interest maximization in pursuit of this-worldly benefits (Varshney 2003). Yet nonreligious motives are not mutually exclusive of religious ones. A man may be envious of his wealthy neighbor and may seek an opportunity to rob him and possess his properties. Yet this feeling of envy could be actable and socially legitimate only when the neighbor belongs to a despised religious group. To put it succinctly, greed would not have any political relevance in the absence of religious stigmas.

Other scholars suggest that while the elite and entrepreneurs are interest-oriented actors, their followers happen to be "true believers" whose passions could be inflamed with the right messages (Tambiah 1997, 24; Maoz and Henderson 2020, 46). This perspective still prioritizes elite calculations and strategies in fostering mass violence (Semelin 2001). For instance, the Ottoman rulers who initiated and organized the mass killings of Armenians were motivated by imperialistic designs. Their pursuit of religious homogenization aimed to sustain Ottoman rule in Anatolia. In contrast, for many ordinary people, including Ottoman soldiers and Kurdish villagers who actively took part in the massacres, killing and looting Armenians, demonized as infidels, was a religious duty (Balakian 2009, 95, 100, 144, 146; Çelik and Dinç 2015, 298).

According to this alternative approach, religious beliefs and passions, which have significant mobilizing power at the popular levels, are *instrumentalized* in the service of worldly goals pursued by the elites.

A prominent contribution in this regard is Anthony Marx's (2003) historical study of the emergence of nationalism in England, France, and to a much-limited extent, Spain in the sixteenth and seventeenth centuries. Challenging theories that associate civic nationalism with Western liberalism, Marx emphatically argues that intolerance and exclusion of religious minorities (i.e., Catholics in England and Huguenots in France) was central to the formation of nationalism, defined as a "collective sentiment . . . binding together those individuals who share a sense of large-scale political solidarity aimed at creating, legitimating, or challenging states . . . mass sentiment for or against state power" (6–7). Despite operating in very different context, the ruling elites in both England and France successfully harnessed the masses' passionate intolerance of religious minorities for the dual purposes of state and nation building. This is because "religious passions and intolerance remained more salient among the populace than more secular attachments" (164). As the states engaged in widespread discriminatory and often violent practices against religious minorities, they established stronger allegiance among the masses, who enthusiastically supported such practices. In turn, these bonds helped the rulers build stronger states involving taxation, conscription, and centralization. Consequently, nationalism gained a popular character thanks to the politicization of religious faith that enabled political mobilization from below.

By and large, however, the question of why and how religious mobilization has a decisively strong appeal among the masses remains unaddressed. After all, elites would be inclined to use religious appeals and justifications only when they have good reasons to believe that such discourses would find a receptive audience. For instance, Turkish political leader Recep Tayyip Erdoğan played the "Islam card" to consolidate his support base on many occasions. Erdoğan's pursuit of the so-called Islamist advantage is the subject of a broader scholarly debate that explores how ideational commitments or social services contribute to the ability of Islamist parties and social movements in mobilizing public support (Masoud 2014; Brooke 2017). Most notoriously, he falsely accused protesters of "drinking beer" in a mosque, an act violating a sacred space, during the popular Gezi uprising in June 2013. During campaigning for the 2019 local elections, he had shown footage from a video taken by an attacker who massacred dozens in a mosque in New Zealand in March of the same year and paired it with statements of the main opposition leader (*New York Times* 2019). Although his strategy had some success by driving a wedge between the protesters and conservative segments of society in 2013, his attempts to frame the opposition as "anti-Islamic" failed in 2019.

In conclusion, the reason why some people take religion so seriously to act violently needs to be explained rather than just simply assumed. It is too facile to argue that elites are the only ones who can see the utility of religious beliefs and norms, while believers lack perception to see through their partisan agendas. How does religion have an intrinsic appeal that could incite people to political violence?

Wars of Religion in France: Heretics and Eschatology

The historiography of the Wars of Religion between the Catholics and Huguenots (Protestants) in early modern France (1562–98) provides some unique insights about the role of religious beliefs in instigating bottom-up violence (Clarke 2019). In fact, the word *massacre* gained its contemporary meaning during this period and became the Protestant term for popular sectarian hatreds generating violence (Greengrass 1999). In her paradigmatic study, Natalie Zemon Davis (1973) offers an incisive criticism of perspectives that reduce popular violence into socioeconomic issues, a form of class conflict. For her, the Catholic participation in the Saint Bartholomew massacre in Paris in 1572, the bloodiest event during the wars, could not be understood without popular cultural frameworks and moral values.

For the Catholic crowd, the widespread killings of Huguenots were an act of defense of true doctrine from heresy and of collective purification; the Huguenots were perceived as symbols of pollution. Ominously, the Catholics accused the Huguenots of engaging in illicit sexual intercourses including incest after their nocturnal rituals (Roberts 2012). Similar accusations of immorality were repeated against liminal minorities, we would see later, in very different historical contexts. The Huguenots, independent of their actual numbers and strength, were perceived as an infection eroding the moral fabric of the society (Diefendorf 1985). When the political authorities failed to fulfill their duties and sought compromises with these "heretics," the crowd acted to expunge the infection from the body social (Davis 1973, 70). In this sense, the ritualistic nature of the killings was central to their cruelty involving mutilation of bodies. Such uncompromising positions were not unique to the Catholics. John Calvin rejected Thomas Aquinas's moderate interpretation of Exodus 32:26–28 and built on Saint Augustine's interpretation that called for the persecution of heretics by magistrates. For Calvin, religious persecution was not an exclusive prerogative of magistrates, and ordinary believers could act as the instruments of divine will (Walzer 1968).

Denis Crouzet (1990) identifies a different dimension of the sacred in the acts of violence during early modern France. For him, eschatological beliefs were the primary mechanism of popular violence during this period. Distinctive from Davis's discussion of the desire to purify the world from heretics, such beliefs shaped collective psychology on the eve of the Wars of Religion and convinced Catholic believers about the immanence of God and the coming end of the world, the apocalyptic moment. This "eschatological anguish" established a close connection between the end of time and the Catholic violence against Huguenots (Holt 1993). In this sectarian apocalyptic view, the very existence of Huguenots stood for the denial of God's immanence. Such beliefs about the imminent end of the world would also play roles in religious violence by a significant number of groups in the late twentieth century (Juergensmeyer 2000).

These two ideational patterns, the defense of doctrinal truth and apocalypticism, had been part and parcel of European political and religious scenes well before the Wars of Religion. In fact, the general idea that humans wage war on behalf of God (wars originated by God, *deo auctore bella*) was pervasive and nourished collective imaginations since the late medieval ages (Housley 2008).[1] This does not mean that religiously inspired ideas made warfare inevitable. But they provided a well-established repertoire of "strategies of actions" (Swidler 1986) readily available for political entrepreneurs to justify and mobilize broad support for violence against religious others.

The sharp contrast between "bloody France" and "peaceful Netherlands" suggests that religious coexistence and tolerance was still possible in the late sixteenth century. In the latter context, Catholic clergymen acted with restraint and encouraged believers to focus on their personal shortcomings rather than to take violent action against heretics. For Dutch clerics, heresy was "a moral rather than a doctrinal problem, as God's punishment for collective sin" (Pollmann 2006, 118). Besides, the practice of "clandestine churches" (*schuilkerk*) in the Netherlands sustained a cultural fiction of public and private distinction and neutralized the threat of religious dissent to the official church. As long as the religious minority observed this fictional separation, kept its rituals to well-defined and designated spaces, and did not openly challenge its second-class legal status, public order was sustained. The sustainability of

---

1. Housley (2008, 190–93) identifies two additional patterns central to the justifications of war on religious grounds: national messianism of "chosen people" vested with a divine mission and crusading (e.g., Reconquista in the Iberian Peninsula). These patterns continue to be relevant in the contemporary world. For instance, national-religious Zionism espouses a messianistic endeavor and perceives the expansion of the State of Israel into the West Bank as a fulfillment of this endeavor (Brenner 2018, 274–75). These patterns are less pertinent when studying violence against liminal minorities.

religious toleration in the Dutch Republic depended on this hierarchical order (B. Kaplan 2002). Consequently, religious coexistence was achieved "not by eliminating confessional boundaries, but by clarifying and reinforcing them" (Holt 2012, 61).

Building on these insights derived from the literature on the Wars of Religion, I suggest that the motive to defend the religious truth and doctrine from heretics is a core aspect of political violence against liminal minorities. As such, it needs to be theorized as an independent motive of human action that is irreducible to nonreligious motives including pursuit of security, material gain, social status, or revenge. What is required is a detailed empirical strategy to disentangle religious motives from nonreligious motives given the complexity of human action. I now elaborate on my definition of religious violence.

"The Virtue of the Absurd": Religious Faith, Sacrifice, and Altruistic Punishment

In *Fear and Trembling*, Søren Kierkegaard ([1843] 2021) addresses the question of religious faith and devotion as a source of human action. He offers an incisive interpretation of the well-known biblical story of Abraham's attempted sacrifice of his son, Isaac. Abraham finds himself in a limbo as true faith (i.e., following God's orders) and worldly ethics (i.e., the absolute wrongness of killing one's own son) collide. According to Kierkegaard, the only way for Abraham to ease this tension is to put his faith in God's notion of evil and good and to suspend his ethics. Human reason is incapable to decide whether Abraham's decision to murder his son is a testament to him following God's order or being self-delusional. Consequently, true faith believes by "the virtue of the absurd." Abraham relies on his faith that God will not make him actually kill his son.

For Kierkegaard, what makes religious faith exceptionally strong in motivating human action is its ability to suspend morality in the name of belief in God. Faith could make a person engage in an act of ultimate self-sacrifice. Friedrich Nietzsche's critique of Martin Luther's reformation follows a similar premise. According to Nietzsche (1977, 184), Luther's permission for the clergy to abandon sexual abstinence and to marry ultimately destroyed the Catholic ideal of religious man. If a man is capable of sexual abstinence, a superhuman sacrificing the worldly pleasure for his faith, he is exceptional also in other regards. Once this source of awe was taken away, the Church's authority among the people was fundamentally weakened, Nietzsche argues.

If religious faith motivates world-denying sacrificial acts, it could provide an even stronger motive for acts that do not involve a trade-off between self-preservation and worldly attainments. Contributions in social psychology, neurology, and behavioral economics in the last two decades employing experimental designs suggest that monotheistic religious beliefs can provide exceptionally strong justifications for prosocial behaviors as well as bias and aggression against groups perceived to fall outside one's moral order. Groups whose identity revolves around belief in supernatural omnipotent beings tend to exhibit higher levels of prosocial behavior that give them an evolutionary advantage over rival groups (Haidt 2012, 298–306; Norenzayan 2013, 143). Members of these groups believe that their actions are monitored by a supernatural being who can dispense otherworldly benefits. Although such beliefs foster intragroup cooperation and solidarity, they also foster high levels of distrust of out-groups who are perceived not to engage in an exchange relationship with the same supernatural being.

There is a plethora of influential experimental studies testing how religious beliefs and framings may affect human behavior. Subjects primed by concepts about God act less selfishly and allocate more money to anonymous strangers, suggesting that humans exhibit greater prosocial behavior when they believe that they are being watched by a supernatural being (Shariff and Norenzayan 2007). At the same time, priming subjects with religious words makes them develop pejorative views of out-groups perceived to violate subjects' religious values (Johnson, Rowatt, and LaBouff 2012). Similarly, individuals subjected to similar forms of priming and previously donated to a religious organization exhibit higher levels of costly punishment (McKay et al. 2011). Moreover, individuals situated in a religious context, a churchyard, express more negative views of individuals who are not members of that religious group (LaBouff et al. 2012). Most relevant for the purposes of this book, individuals exposed to scriptural justifications of violence exhibit higher levels of aggressive behavior than individuals exposed to nonreligious ones. This effect is also more pronounced among believers (Bushman et al. 2007). Similarly, subjects exhibit greater aggression toward members of religious out-groups perceived to hold alternative beliefs challenging the validity of their own. This effect is more pronounced when subjects are reminded of death and feel existential insecurity (Pyszczynski et al. 2006).

Overall, religious beliefs are conducive to parochial altruism—that is, believers engaging in hostile and personally costly action against nonbelievers in defense of their group (Fehr and Gächter 2002; Choi and Bowles 2007; Bowles 2008; Sapolsky 2017, 621–26). Such beliefs enable humans to overcome strong emotional inhibitions against premeditated violence (Grossman 1995; J. Greene 2013, 36–37, 225–53). Believers are more likely to risk their personal well-being and fight when they perceive their sacred values are under threat

(Gómez et al. 2017). Observational studies also suggest that religious beliefs with their promise of otherworldly salvation motivate individuals to target groups of "unbelievers" at a significant personal cost (Toft 2007; M. Horowitz 2009) and forgo compromise in pursuit of a higher good (Juergensmeyer 2009).

In summary, historical studies and randomized control trials present strong reasons to expect that religious beliefs could play a direct role in fostering violence against members of an out-group. Consequently, I define religious violence as *physical harm committed against members of a certain group and motivated primarily by antagonism toward that group's purported deviance from a particular way of believing in the supernatural (i.e., God)*. The notion of supernatural in this definition builds on Robert Bellah's notion of "sacred" and Charles Taylor's notion of "transcendence." Bellah (2011, 1) defines religion as "a system of beliefs and practices relative to the sacred that unite those who adhere to them in a moral community." For Taylor (2007, 20; my emphasis), a crucial feature of religion is the belief in "some agency or power *transcending* the immanent order." Although this definition is about physical harm, other forms of harm including the lack of recognition, socioeconomic discrimination, and denial of remembrance could be also analyzed using this conceptual framework.

This definition has two characteristics worth emphasizing. First, religion obviously has multiple dimensions involving belief, behavior, and belonging. These dimensions may reflect distinct motives (e.g., searching for purpose, maintaining tradition, etc.) and have different impacts on political attitudes and behavior at the individual level (Ben-Nun Bloom, Arikan, and Vishkin 2021). The definition proposed here is primarily about how the belief dimension of religiosity that is motivated by a concern to satisfy God affects propensity to participate in political violence. More precisely, it focuses on how humans act in certain ways and refrain from other types of actions to avoid supernatural punishments (Johnson and Krüger 2004) and to obtain otherworldly rewards (Stark and Finke 2000, 91–99) that only come from Gods, "*conscious supernatural beings*" (Stark 2001, 10; original emphasis). Monotheistic religions, including the Abrahamic faiths, have an advantage over both nongodly and polytheistic religions, as they encourage believers to engage in a long-term and exclusive commitment to achieve such rewards, realized only after death (Stark 2001, 18–19; Norenzayan 2013). Next, the definition focuses on the *motives* to commit violence rather than whether parties to the conflict belong to different faith groups or issues at stake are religious in nature, approaches common in quantitative studies. As discussed above, the underlying conflict could be primarily about socioeconomic and political factors completely unrelated to religious belief systems. Moreover, just because participants in a violent conflict make opposing religious claims does not mean that the conflict is caused by religious differences. The conceptualization of religious violence in terms of *motives* directly addresses the widespread skepticism that religious differences and claims are peripheral to what violence is primarily about, whether material interests, social status, or political power. It also sets a high empirical bar to identify any incidence of violence as "religious."

Benjamin's Critique of Violence and Derrida's Paradox of Iterability

Before I switch my attention to liminal minorities, I would like to make a brief normative detour and to take a stance against the morality of religious violence. In his celebrated article titled "Critique of Violence" (Zur Kritik der Gewalt) originally published in 1921, Walter Benjamin (2003) presents a series of binary distinctions starting with violence justified by natural law versus positive law.[2] Whereas the former justifies violence by the justness of its ends, positive law guarantees "the justness of the ends through the justification of the means" (237). For Benjamin, positive law—that is, modern European juridico-legal systems—is terrified of violence committed by private individuals and justified by natural law. Such violence directly collides with the legal system and presents a direct challenge to the state's claim to be the guardian of public order. The occurrence of violence outside of the legal sphere undermines the very preservation of the law (238–39).

Utilizing Benjamin's distinction, religious violence, by its very nature, is justified by natural law—that is, revelation—a presumed eternal message. When individuals claim to exercise violence in the name of God, they also expose the fragility of a political order based on positive law and present a direct challenge to its legitimacy claims. The raison d'être of the state is the preservation of its monopoly over violence. It aims to divest people of violence even if such violence claims to serve ends favored by the state. The state is by its very nature anxious of religious violence that claims to derive its legitimacy from a transcending source in defiance of the modern concept of sovereignty.

A rigid distinction between religious violence and positive law, however, is problematic for obvious reasons. There are many situations when religious differences are coded into positive law. Violence against a faith group, both in terms of physical punishments and discriminatory practices, often follow legalistic procedures. The trial of Socrates and the mass executions in the Islamic

---

2. The German word *Gewalt* is conventionally translated as "violence" but could also mean "power" and "force" in broader senses.

Republic exemplify forms of religious violence embodied in positive law. In contemporary affairs, secularism remains an incomplete affair and religious markers continue to be highly relevant to how states and their citizens interact with each other (Fox 2020). As discussed in chapter 4, religious discrimination against Baha'is in Iran and Ahmadis in Pakistan are explicitly incorporated into the constitutional order.

Whether outside of or in fusion with positive law, normative nature of religious violence could be assessed by another conceptual distinction made by Benjamin, that of between "mythic" and "divine" violence. According to Walter Benjamin, divine violence, based on the principle of justice, has an emancipatory characteristic. In contrast, power is "the principle of all mythic lawmaking" that is "intimately bound to violence" (248). It demands sacrifice and involves "bloody power over all life for the sake of living" (250). Both mythic violence and the law-preserving violence that serves it are violent. Positive law that has the legal backing of a state could also exhibit the characteristics of mythic violence when it embodies unpredictability, ambiguity, and arbitrariness. Benjamin's notion of mythic violence is applicable not only to irrational religious violence stemming from fanatical beliefs but also rational and secular violence representing modernity. States pursuing modernist ideologies, including the French revolutionary regimes and the nascent Turkish Republic, used the threat of fanatical and uncivilized religious violence to justify their own mythical forms of violence (for the relevance of this point in contemporary Turkey, see Yonucu 2018).

I argue that religious violence is an expression of mythic violence despite its claims to have a law-founding characteristic. In making this proposition, I rely on Jacques Derrida's deconstruction of Benjamin's three binaries: (1) founding violence that institutes law and preserving violence that maintains it, (2) mythic violence that makes law and divine violence that annihilates it, and (3) power as the underlying principle of mythic violence and justice as the principle of justice underlying divine violence (Derrida 2002, 264–65). For Derrida, these binaries are unsustainable. He suggests that the glorification of divine violence undergird by justice could easily erode into mythic violence undergird by power. Hence, Benjamin's espousal of divine violence as an emancipatory force has the potential to lapse into worst forms of terror—that is, the Holocaust (298). Not surprisingly, this interpretation that identifies an affinity between Benjamin's divine violence and anti-liberal democratic glorifications of violence remains the subject of intense controversy (Sinnerbrink 2006).

What is most relevant for my purposes is Derrida's (2002, 272) insight that there could be no "rigorous opposition" between the violence of foundation and that of preservation as they contaminate each other. This deconstructive perspective is crucial for seeing the contradiction inherent to religious violence. By its very nature, religious violence claims to derive its legitimacy from a revolutionary moment, that of revelation, and aspires to establish law *superior* to any existing human-made frameworks or previous instances of revelation. Correspondingly, the fact that it is ulterior to any preexisting legal system makes it immune to criticisms articulated within these systems. Since it does not need their justification, it cannot be summoned to appear before any court or judge representing them. In this sense, it is visionary.

At the same time, this visionary orientation embodies an inevitable vulnerability. Any new claim of revelation could marshal the same arguments to claim immunity from preexisting law, whether secular or religious in origin. In those moments of competing revelations, sheer coercion is the only tool that could decide the winner. To return to Benjamin's binary, power rather than justice would decide what law would remain supreme and what law would be subdued. The side that employs coercion more deftly than the other would prevail. Hence, founding violence would be meaningless without preserving violence. In the absence of the latter, the former is a sandcastle that would survive only during ebb tide. Religious violence, beyond its founding revolutionary movement when it annihilates the pre-revelationary order, inevitably leads to future sanctioning of groups and individuals perceived to challenge, defy, or ignore God's word. While it claims to be a form of divine violence, to use Benjamin's parlance, it could exist only as a form of mythic violence. This perspective helps us understand why the transformation of a persecuted religious minority into a ruling group would not make it more tolerant and self-confident. To give a historical example, the establishment of a Christian empire after Constantine's conversion to Christianity did not ease the insecurities and anxieties of some believers who perceived the very existence of heretics and pagans as an affront to God's will (Gaddis 2015, 6–7).

Consequently, I suggest that religious violence is subject to what Derrida (2002, 278–79) calls "the paradox of iterability" that makes the distinction between law-making and law-preserving violence unsustainable. There could be no sustainable founding of law without an entity, such as police, dedicated to its conservation. Foundation is meaningless unless it projects into the future, which remains undecidable. As Derrida writes, "Iterability precludes the possibility of pure and great founders, initiators, lawmakers" (278). Only through repetition (i.e., acts of enforcement) could religion preserve itself. Religious violence that posits revelation as the foundation of law necessitates acts of sanctioning against the ones who reinterpret, challenge, or deny God's word. In the absence of sanctions, the sacred becomes unintelligible and replaceable. The act of revelation loses its founding aura.

Who Stands at the Receiving End of Religious Violence?

This normative detour posits that the act of preservation is central to the logic of religious violence. This does not imply that violence is central to the essence of religious teachings and experience. In fact, many religious traditions, out of genuine commitment or resignation, have come into terms with what Hannah Arendt (1958, 202) calls "the essential human condition of plurality, the acting and speaking together, which is the condition of all forms of political organization." To give a prominent historical example, a monumental change took place during the Second Vatican Council (1962–65) when the Catholic Church transformed its position regarding many critical issues. Paul VI's *Dignitatis Humanae* endorsed the principle of religious freedom in 1965 (Philpott 2004; Wilde 2007). Moreover, for some Muslim scholars, the notion of religious pluralism is enshrined in the canonical texts of Islam (An-Na'im 2008).

There is also a potent sense of ambivalence in all major religious traditions regarding the treatment of other religions. The Christian views of Judaism are instructive in this regard. David Nirenberg (2013) lucidly demonstrates how thinking about Judaism has been central to the Christian self-understandings throughout the centuries. The fear of Judaism did not abate with the rise of Christendom by the fourth century. On the contrary, the very presence of Jews was portrayed as a challenge to Christ's sovereignty. Ambrose, bishop of Milan, argued that the supremacy of the heavenly law in the Christian empire could only be established with the expulsion or exclusion of the Jews (119). In comparison, Augustine of Hippo, a contemporary of Ambrose, pointed to the continued but residual existence of the Jews as a guarantee of the intelligibility of scripture (131–33). By rejecting Christianity, Jews were condemned to live as social outcasts. What Nirenberg calls the "Augustinian paradox" of simultaneous punishment and exile would have a long legacy over how the Christian leaders and thinkers would deal with the Jews in Europe.

Religious differences continue to inform and shape state policies in many different parts of the world and foster various forms of discrimination against groups marked as religious outsiders or deemed to behave in ways religiously inappropriate. One of the main focuses of the contemporary scholarship on politics of religion has been the nature of the institutional and ideological relationship between the majority religion and the state (Philpott 2007; Kuru 2009; Cesari 2014; Lord 2018; Fox 2020). The practices ranging from assigning certain citizenship benefits on the basis of religious affiliation and punishing members of a group for practicing their religious beliefs and rituals remain prevalent in different parts of the world. At the extreme level, when religious belief is enforced by power of the state, heresy becomes synonymous with treason (Stark 2001, 120). Secularism, which may actually aggravate religious differences in practice, is not necessarily a savior of persecuted religious groups (Mahmood 2015). To return to Benjamin, positive law often encodes and enforces what natural law (i.e., revelation) demands. The tension arises, as mentioned earlier, when natural law is claimed by a group of individuals in defiance of positive law.

My contribution to the literature on religion and politics is that some faith groups more than any others present an ontological challenge to the prevailing religious order, sanctified by either natural law alone or both natural and positive laws. The very existence of such groups, however small their numbers are, presents an existential insecurity and anxiety for many members of a dominant religion. This insecurity and anxiety generate a historically constructed pejorative *disposition* toward these groups and make them more likely to be the targets of religious violence. This predisposition is most conspicuous when majorities animated by natural law directly defy the state authorities to target such groups. In contrast to Benjamin's expectations, the state often remains complicit or impotent in the face of collectivities who express their rage via performative acts of violence. In such situations, positive law remains hostage to mythic violence.

This explicit focus on the identity of victimized groups addresses the skepticism often expressed about the unique nature of religious violence. For some scholars, religion with its tendency to sacralize human existence and transcendental goals beyond utilitarian calculations and worldly political goals has an extraordinary power in inciting violence in the name of God (Selengut 2003). For other scholars, however, the disappearance of religion would not make violence disappear, simply because religion would be replaced by other forms of collective identity such as nationalism, communism, or tribalism that would crystallize group boundaries and incite aggression against others (e.g., Meral 2018, 179). Charles Taylor (2007) offers a more eloquent elaboration of the point that religion and violence do not have a uniquely intrinsic relationship. He identifies two mechanisms through which religion begets violence: (1) scapegoating that targets groups perceived to transgress the sacred boundaries and (2) crusading where believers engage in war to conquer the ones outside of their religious-moral order (686–88).

In an enchanted world, the belief in God is default and the boundaries between the physical and spiritual worlds are porous—that is, supernatural entities are perceived to interfere in nature and human affairs. In that world, conformism and intolerance prevail. Heretics are persecuted as the well-being of the community is perceived to depend on collective belief (Taylor 2007, 43–44). In Taylor's view, a distinctive characteristic of the secular age is the rise of self-sufficient humanism where "the eclipse of all goals beyond human flourishing becomes conceivable; or better, it falls within the range of an imaginable life for masses of people" (19–20). Secular age also brings disenchantment, "a move from society where belief in God is unchallenged and indeed, unproblematic, to one in which it is understood to be one option among others" (3). Yet its rise does not necessarily bring the decline of what we call as sacred violence. This is because secularity, as vividly demonstrated by terror during the French Revolution, brings its own moralizing tendencies that continue to justify collective forms of violence. In fact, biblical narratives about exclusive identities born via acts of violence have been central to the emergence of myths of secular nationalism in modern times (Schwartz 1997). Scapegoating and crusading have lost their religious auras but continue to mark collective enemies and channel popular passions to fight them. Consequently, secular age is not immune from sacred violence (Taylor 2007, 686–88).

This is a well-founded argument especially given the tremendous capacity of secular ideologies to mobilize large groups of people to fight collective goals often at the expense of their well-being. Religion is not the only force that could sacralize human affairs and motive violence to defend this sacred understanding. As Benedict Anderson (1991, 7) acutely observes, millions of people not only kill but also willingly die for the imagined idea of nation. Yet religion is the only force that forms collective identities based on the belief in the supernatural and excludes certain groups from these collectivities for purported deficiencies and absences in their faith. As such, religion, more than any other identity marker, has an extraordinary capacity to instigate violence against these groups, what I label *liminal minorities*.

Religious Liminality and Its Historical Configurations

The notion of liminality comes from the Latin word *limen*, which means threshold and stands for in-between and transitory situations. It also has a long pedigree in the social sciences going back to Arnold van Gennep's *Rites de passage*, published in 1909, which discusses how ritualistic ceremonies, such as marriage, funerals, and conversions, are formative experiences through which social status of individuals are being transformed. The liminal phase is when an individual eschews the attributes of her old status yet to gain the attributes of her new status. This phase is characterized by ambiguity and uncertainty. Victor Turner (1969, 368) has revitalized van Gennep's concept by suggesting that liminal situations and roles defy ordered boundaries and are often perceived as "dangerous, inauspicious, or polluting" and a threat to the established structure and norms. In both van Gennep's and Turner's conceptualizations, liminality embodies unsettledness, uncertainty and ambivalence that generate a sense of collective anxiety as well as potential for change. In the last decade, the term has attracted increasing attention among social scientists given its promise to transcend ubiquitous but simplistic binary oppositions such as rational versus emotional, war versus peace, and West versus East. Scholars have used the term skillfully to make sense of the perpetuation of conflict during the war on terror in the post-9/11 period (Mälksoo 2012) as well as the complexities of the Turkish–European Union relations (Rumelili 2012). Following Thomassen's (2015) call that liminality should be treated as a master concept in social inquiry, I suggest that the notion of liminality neatly captures the experience of certain religious groups and their unique and lasting vulnerabilities and fragilities.

I define liminal minorities as *groups whose core religious beliefs and practices remain ambivalent, ill-defined, and stigmatized in the eyes of elite and ordinary members of a dominant group*. Differences based on liminality differ from racialized differences, which are perceived to be immutable and fixed. In most cases, liminal groups could be assimilated, often forcefully, into the dominant religious group. In that regard, liminal differences do not typically preclude conversions and could have more porous boundaries than racial differences perceived to be fixed and natural and underlie white supremacist orders (King and Smith 2005; Fredrickson 2015).[3] Even though liminal minorities share many characteristics in common, there is not a single characteristic all of them share. I identify two core characteristics of liminal minorities. A religious group can be defined as a liminal minority as long as it shares both of the characteristics (Goertz 2006, 29).

First, liminal minorities tend to lack official and theological recognition from a dominant religious group who find the very existence of these groups as subversive and unsettling and transgressing of well-established boundaries and norms. Their belief systems are perceived to be illegible and beyond the pale of theological legitimacy and social acceptance. The Abrahamic religions, despite their occasionally hostile relations with each other throughout history, exhibit mutual theological recognition. For instance, the Ottoman millet system based on the Islamic understanding of Christians and Jews as People of the Book is a historical legacy of this recognition (Barkey 2005). While

---

3. At the same time, even certain racial categories could have more fluid boundaries. In the United States, one example of such liminality is Black-white multiracial bodies that challenge preconceived notions of race and generate ambivalence and uncertainties (Brunsma, Delgado, and Rockquemore 2013; Reed 2022).

anti-Judaism has been a central theme in the evolution of both Christian and Islamic traditions (Nirenberg 2013), Jews are not a liminal group from the perspective of the latter. Antisemitism originated from religious differences (i.e., configurations of Jews as enemies of Christ; Moore 2007, 32–36) and drew on traditional prejudices (Bergen 2016). It also evolved significantly and had a distinctively modern and racist orientation by the late nineteenth century (Weitz 2003, 46; Hayes 2017, 7–20). In particular, the stab-in-the-back myth that identifies "Jewish betrayal" as the main reason for the German defeat in World War I became a core aspect of the Nazi propaganda.

Next, stigmatization, which reflects historically formed social, political, or economic power asymmetries, is central to the experience of liminal groups. In his classical study, Erving Goffman (1963, 3–4) conceptualizes stigma as a bodily mark, individual characteristic, or collective attribute that is devalued in a certain context. Individuals or group of individuals who are perceived to carry a stigma are subjects of discrimination and suffer reduced life chances unless they could pass as "normal" or mobilize resources to resist stigmatization that associate human differences with negative attributes. Dominant groups use stigmatization to keep "other people down" by controlling, exploiting, or excluding others and reinforce existing racial, ethnic, class, and gender hierarchies (Link and Phelan 2014). This ability to stigmatize collectives depends on the possession of symbolic power—that is, the ability "to make something exist in the objectified, public, formal state which only previously existed in an implicit state" (Bourdieu 1987, 14). The accumulation of symbolic power has been a central aspect of the modern state formation, which entails the ability to naturalize certain practices and discourses so that they resonate with broader society (Loveman 2005). At the same time, the exercise of symbolic power via stigmatization is more likely to be successful when stigmas "reflect the fault lines in a society at any point" (Pescosolido and Martin 2015, 91). Stigmatized individuals and groups are shunned and often perceived as dangerous and potentially violence (97). Attempts to remove stigmas via public awareness and education campaigns (e.g., ending the stigma associated with mental health) often overlook structural inequalities and processes that produce patterns of discriminations associated with such stigmas (Tyler and Slater 2018).

Liminal minorities have historically been objects of a litany of stigmas including charges of sexual promiscuity and impurity. They are identified as a threat to moral order and feared as a source of symbolic pollution (Douglas 1966). A common pattern is that liminal minorities are often alleged to have lax sexual morals threatening the gendered moral order (Davis 1973, 57–58). This conflation of religious and sexual deviancy has pernicious implications especially when morality is defined in terms of piety, patriarchy, and sexual conformism. Stigmatization begets various forms of discrimination, both at the personal and structural levels, against members of a liminal minority (Link and Phelan 2001). Moreover, given these patterns of historical stigmatization, any perceived negative behavior by a member of a liminal minority is attributed to the innate and undesirable characteristics of the group (Pettigrew 1979). What makes a religious group liminal is how elite and ordinary members of a dominant majority perceive its belief and rituals, rather than any particular characteristics intrinsic to that group. Liminality is in the eyes of the beholder, that of dominant religious groups (cf. Moore 2007). One cannot learn much about liminal groups by studying their stereotypical portrayals but learn a great deal about prejudices, anxieties, and fears of a community that harbor these stereotypes. Members of a liminal minority typically are aware of their stereotypical representation in the collective imaginary of members of a dominant group, and their public behaviors could be directly affected by such representations (Major and O'Brien 2005). Although they could also harbor stereotypical perceptions of other groups, they generally lack the power and status to impose their beliefs and pursue discriminatory practices.

Given these two characteristics, liminality has a propensity to culminate in religiously motivated violence. To paraphrase Henry Adams, politics of liminal minorities is often the systematic organization of hatred informed by religious stigmas. Following Roger Petersen (2002, 63), I define hatred as a historically formed "schema" that fosters antagonism against a group by virtue of its purported core beliefs and innate characteristics. When religious hatred is a relevant factor motivating violence, the group is attacked with "similar justifications over a lengthy time period" (62). Liminal minorities remain vulnerable to religiously sanctioned extreme forms of violence and certain repertoires of violence including sexual attacks. Religious beliefs demeaning members of these groups contribute to their dehumanization, an intergroup process that is often a necessary factor in mass atrocities (D. L. Smith 2011). Attacks against them, some of which could be unusually vicious, are more likely to feature more explicit justifications supported on scriptural grounds and demonizing their belief systems.

Scholarly treatments of politics of religion often exhibit blindness when it comes to liminal minorities. To give a prominent example, Alfred Stepan (2000) develops the notion of twin tolerations, as an alternative to secularism, as being central to the role of religion in a polity. He defines this notion as "the minimal boundaries of freedom of action that must somehow be crafted for political institutions vis-à-vis religious authorities, and for religious individuals and groups vis-à-vis political institutions" (37). Although Stepan aims to ensure equal and fair treatment of all religious groups, his focus on "religious authorities" makes his definition biased against liminal minorities whose beliefs often exhibit an amorphous character with no clearly designated hierarchies. In fact, the very act of constructing authority figures who could represent liminal figures in official capacity is a political process often directly controlled by ruling governments via the exercise of symbolic power.

Relatedly, focusing on historical experiences of liminal minorities help us develop a more nuanced understanding of the notion of religious pluralism that is conventionally measured in terms of the number/ratio of people who subscribe to one of the main religious traditions—namely, Christianity, Islam, Hinduism, Buddhism, and Judaism (Hackett and McClendon 2017). Although it is also customary to recognize main sectarian distinctions within these traditions (e.g., Catholics, Orthodox Christians, Protestants, Sunnis, Shiites), such classifications present an ahistorical depiction of religious collectivities as being internally coherent and homogenous. To provide a striking example, *CIA World Factbook* describes religious affiliations of people in Turkey as 99.8 percent Muslim ("mostly Sunni") and 0.2 percent other ("mostly Christians and Jews") (CIA 2021). This classification pushes Alevis, the largest religious minority in Turkey, to invisibility. Alevis, often "accused" of lacking a sacred book and proper places of worship, struggle to get even mentioned as a distinctive group in the religious landscape in contemporary Turkey. This lack of recognition, which has its roots in the Ottoman policies, is a form of silencing essential for sustaining the hegemonic image of Turkey as a religiously homogeneous country that is "99.8 percent Muslim." When the response to liminality is not physical violence or expulsion, it is often assimilation. And the absence of recognition greatly facilitates the latter.

Religious liminality is a historically formed process rather than reflecting essentialized differences. It is true that shared identity markers have been central to how anonymous human societies have been organized and expanded since hunter-gatherer bands (Moffett 2019). Individuals perceived not to share these markers become outcasts and are deprived from access to collective benefits. Given the high stakes involved, however, identities are often fiercely contested. From this historical perspective, the formation, persistence, and erosion of liminal identities reflect intergroup relations characterized by power asymmetries. The inception and dissemination of religious liminality are contingent and happen in certain historical periods and locations more than others. For instance, a liminal group that is heavily persecuted in one country may be tolerated in a neighboring country. The contrasting experience of the Nuqtavi Sufi order in Safavid Iran (persecuted) and Mogul India (tolerated) in the sixteenth century exemplifies this pattern (Saeed 2021a).

In certain historical contexts, communities that converted from one Abrahamic religion to another might also have a liminal existence. The experience of the followers of the rabbi Shabbatai Tzevi (the Dönme) in Salonica in the late seventeenth-century Ottoman Empire is an example of such a community. Although the Dönme converted to Islam and followed its basic tenets including fasting and praying in mosques, they continued to believe that Shabbatai Tzevi was a messiah, practiced endogamy and secret rituals, and remained a distinct community. The foundation of the Turkish Republic did not necessarily facilitate the assimilation of the Dönme under the banner of secular nationalism. They remained subject to discriminatory practices (Baer 2004). Throughout the twentieth and early twenty-first centuries, they were targets of various antisemitic conspiracy theories alleging their involvement in malicious plots (Baer 2013).

Liminality is also a matter of degree. Some liminal groups may gradually gain mainstream acceptance and recognition. Mormons in the United States (D. T. Smith 2015; Saeed 2021b) and Huguenots in France are prototypical examples of such a transition. In contrast, other groups could be relegated to a further liminal existence in times of religious revivalism. The experience of Baha'is after the Iranian revolution exemplifies this dynamic (Amanat 2017, 853–58). Similarly, a religious group that may have a liminal status in one religious context may be recognized as a legitimate entity in another one (e.g., Alevi organizations legally recognized as religious communities in Germany). Finally, liminality is primarily about how *mainstream* religious tradition, and not just niche and extremist interpretations, constructs a "deviant" group. Consequently, the antidote against violence targeting these groups is "less about pacifying 'deviants' and more about changing the central values" of a religious community (Davis 1973, 91).

Although liminality and heresy have overlaps, they are not synonymous. Both concepts are relational and reflect historically evolving power asymmetries. Beliefs and views of a religious majority typically form the core of the orthodoxy that defines what counts as the legitimate belief, demands conformism with this definition, and aims to back up this demand by force (Berlinerblau 2001). Both liminal and heretical groups are typically erstwhile insiders who deviate from the orthodoxy by virtue of their dissident beliefs and practices and become targets of persecution (Kurtz 2015, 293–94). At the same time, liminality has certain distinctive characteristics. First, the notions of heresy or heterodoxy are inadequate to make sense of the trajectory of a number of religious groups that evolved into separate faiths. From the perspective of Islamic orthodoxy, groups such as Ahmadis, Alevis, Baha'is, and Yezidis originated from heretical beliefs and practices (Langer and Simon 2008). Yet Baha'is and Yezidis are now separate religions that have little in common with Islam. Although some Alevis describe themselves as Muslims, many others define Alevism as a separate religion, a way of life, or a philosophy. In contrast, Ahmadis self-identify as Muslim despite their unacceptance by the broader Muslim community in countries like Pakistan and Indonesia. Labeling all these faith groups as heterodox or heretical is both empirically misleading and normatively egregious. Next, from a historical perspective, heresy did not necessarily translate into intolerance and persecution. In Islamic history, a variety of terms (e.g., *zindīq*, *mulhid*) were used to label beliefs and practices that deviate from the path. Whereas the punishment for the "deviants" exhibited great historical variation, in general, Muslims who "testify to the unity of God and the apostolate of Mohammed" received acceptance (Lewis 1953, 60). Consequently, liminality captures the degree of uncertainty, ambivalence, and exclusion characterizing interreligious relations much better than both heresy and heterodoxy.

I propose that certain religious traditions are more likely to be tolerant of "false beliefs." For instance, in contrast to Islam and Catholicism, Hinduism lacks a well-defined distinction between believers and unbelievers and is often characterized by polytheism at the popular level (Cook 2016, 60, 195, 415). Different from the Abrahamic religions, doctrine plays a less central role in Hinduism, which has no single founder and attaches less importance to temple worship (Verghese 2020). Consequently, compared to both Islam and Catholicism, Hindu heritage is less likely to historically generate categories of liminal minorities. The observable implication is that Hindu nationalism, which exhibits strong hostility and aggression against Muslims in India (Jaffrelot 2007), is less likely to target faith groups on grounds that they espouse stigmatized practices and ambivalent beliefs.

Jainism, a religious faith that originated in the Ganges basin around 2,500 years ago, captures this pattern (see figure 1.1). Jainism shares a common sociocultural and linguistic background with both Hinduism and Buddhism. It has twenty-four Tīrthaṅkaras, historical or mythical figures perceived as saviors who lead the way to salvation via a stream of rebirths. Vardhamāna Mahāvīra is the latest of Tīrthaṅkaras and believed to live in the sixth century BC. He is also known as the historic founder of Jainism (Zimmer 1951, 182). The notion of ahiṁsā (noninjury) is central to the Jain faith, which condemns injuring or killing of a living being as a worst offense (250). Jains, who tend to be more educated and wealthier than the rest of the society overall, make a tiny minority in contemporary India; there are around 3.3 million of them in a country with more than 1.4 billion people. Popular knowledge of Jains remains limited in India. Only 19 percent of Hindus think that they have "a lot

FIGURE 1.1. Adinath Digamber Jain Temple in Murshidabad, India, January 2023 (Credit: Author)

in common" with Jains, and only 18 percent of them claim that they know "a great deal" or "some" about Jains. In contrast, two-thirds of Jains argue that they have a lot in common with Hindus (Pew Research Center 2021, 72–74).

In contemporary India, the very question of Jainism as a religious faith separate from Hinduism remains highly contested and is entangled with the politics of caste and secular modernity, with significant judicial and legal applications (Sethi 2021). Article 25 of the Constitution of 1950 explicitly subsumes Jainism, Buddhism, and Sikhism under the broader category of Hinduism. At the same time, the Jain community's demands to be recognized as a "minority religion" at the national level gave fruit when the government of India granted that recognition in 2014 (Teater and Jenkins 2020). Furthermore, a large plurality of Jains argue that it is very important to be a Hindu to be truly Indian and a strong majority of Jains identify the BJP (Bharatiya Janata Party), the Hindu nationalist party, as the party they feel closest to (Pew Research Center 2021, 130, 133). To my best knowledge, there are no records of large-scale violence targeting members of the Jain religion in contemporary times. Accordingly, the experience of Jains in a Hindu-majority society exhibits qualitative differences than the experience of liminal minorities such as Baha'is and Yezidis in Muslim-majority societies.

The advent of political modernity does not diminish the potential of antiliminal violence for a variety of reasons. On the one hand, the rise of secular ideologies aiming to reduce the influence of religion in sociopolitical affairs make it less likely that liminal minorities would be targeted because of their religious beliefs. Yezidis had a higher degree of security under the tyrannical but secularly oriented government of Saddam Hussein than during more pluralistic but highly polarized post-2003 Iraq. Moreover, the formation of associations with the rise of modern civil society transcending religious differences and attracting members from diverse faith groups who work under common goals and interests would dampen the potential for violence (Varshney 2001).

On the other hand, there are equally if not stronger reasons to expect that modernity contributes to the precarity of liminal minorities. First, political modernity involves significant increase in the scope of political mobilization making popular appeals. It is characterized by a much deeper and extensive ideological penetration at a sociological level (Malešević 2017, 53). Accordingly, theological ideas and norms that were previously restricted to a narrow group of religious and political elites are now more likely to be disseminated among larger publics, especially in contexts characterized by the rise of religious revivalist movements. Ordinary people exposed to such ideas and norms are more likely to act on them. Paradoxically, popular religious hatred toward a liminal minority is more relevant for understanding mass violence in modern times than in the past. Next, the conventional distinction between secular and religious regimes (Philpott 2019) does not capture the variation in the way liminal minorities are treated. Political secularity is not necessarily a savior of liminal minorities. Under the guise of religious neutrality, it could unexpectedly aggravate and hierarchize religious differences and institutionalize privileges for the religious majority at the expense of minorities (Mahmood 2015). Overall, religious freedom remains a precarious value in many different parts of the world. Even in nominally secular countries, new faiths are often perceived as direct threats to the established religions and authorities often persecute individuals who become adherents of these faiths (Emont 2017).

Finally, globalization produces new forms of uncertainties, hierarchies, and insecurities that could easily aggravate the anxieties of a majority whose members "can always be mobilized to think that they are in danger of becoming minor (culturally and numerically) and to fear that minorities, conversely, can become major" (Appadurai 2006, 83). As majorities become concerned that they no longer have control over their policies in an increasingly globalized world, they become predatory and displace their rage onto small and vulnerable groups. Liminal minorities are particularly vulnerable to such violence given their insider-outsider status threatening the completeness and wholeness of the majority identity. The ambivalent nature of their identities blurs their separation from the majority and facilitates their labeling as "the enemy among us" during a time of conflict (Tambiah 1997, 276).

This conceptual discussion suggests that members of a liminal minority are targets of stigmas fostering hatred by virtue of their religious beliefs and practices. But then, how can we make sense of the timing of the outbursts of mass violence against them? How could we understand the difference between periods of religious coexistence and periods of communal violence? To answer these questions, we need to develop a more situationist perspective and focus on the notion of political resentment.

Resentment

Didier Fassin (2013) suggests that the experience of historically marginalized groups could be captured by the Nietzschean term, *ressentiment*. He defines ressentiment as an anthropological condition characterized by pervasive historical injustices and domination. He provides the South African apartheid as a historical example. Ressentiment condones neither forgetfulness nor forgiveness. It demands recognition without demanding revenge. In contrast, resentment does not necessarily have an objective factual basis and is often experienced by frustrated and discontented groups who displace their negative emotions onto others who have nothing to do with the causes of these frustrations and discontent. It is a sense of "an ideological alienation: the reality is blurred, leading to frequently misdirected rancor" (261). Fassin provides French police who patrol housing projects or their counterparts in the United States who patrol Black neighborhoods as examples of resentful groups. The police are discontent with the state of affairs but displaces their anger to civilian populations they despise and exercise control over. A progressive view would justify ressentiment but not resentment. Fassin's distinction between ressentiment and resentment is normatively valuable: groups who have been deprived of their human dignity have legitimate grounds to make demands for betterment of their conditions. The emotional state of indignation captures the collective mindset of these groups (e.g., the Black experience in the United States, the Kurdish experience in Turkey) whose anger is caused by unfair treatments. At the same time, it does not help us understand how ressentiment, a potentially progressive position, could degrade into resentment, a reactionary and divisive position. Previously marginalized and dominated groups could develop an absolutist mindset of victimhood and oppress others (and not only their former oppressors) once they capture power (Mamdani 2001). Transitional justice mechanisms including truth commission, spaces of memorialization, apologies, trials of former rulers, and reparations may address the root causes of resentment in certain contexts but not others (Ure 2015).

Max Scheler ([1915] 1994), also building on Nietzsche, offers a less sanguine view of the notion of ressentiment. He defines ressentiment as "a self-poisoning of the mind" (29) and a constant and negative emotive state fueled by intergroup comparisons and feelings of impotence and envy. It emerges when a group feels injured but lacks the capacity to improve their status and means to pursue vengeance against another group they envy. It is most intense in societies characterized by a significant "*discrepancy* between the political, constitutional, or traditional status of a group and its *factual* power" (33; original emphasis). Accordingly, it is strongest in democratic systems that institutionalize formal political and social equality but also has "wide factual differences in power, property, and education" (33). In particular, groups who develop a nostalgic view of the past where they enjoyed higher status than the present are amenable to developing ressentiment (49). The politics of nostalgia entails the rejection of the current state of affairs that purportedly deliver greater public recognition, status, and power to previously subdued groups. The feeling of existential envy, "which is directed against the other person's very *nature*, is the strongest source of *ressentiment*" (35; original emphases). This powerful and irreconcilable feeling of envy is directed against the very essence and being of a group regardless of its political actions (55).

For conceptual simplicity, throughout this book, I use resentment interchangeably with Scheler's conceptualization of ressentiment (as different from Fassin's) and primarily focus on how changes in access to political power, as distinct from access to economic wealth and social status, foments this collective mindset. Resentment is a collective state of mind based on intergroup status comparisons. It comes into existence and fuels revenge when a group perceives that another group occupies a relatively higher but undeserved status in the political hierarchy. It involves schadenfreude, pleasure one derives from the misfortune of another, but cannot be satisfied without a relative betterment in the status of one's group. Resentment is a potentially destructive force that could result in popular rage and further injustices.

Susan Fiske's two-dimensional conceptualization of intergroup relations, based on competence and warmth, offers an insightful understanding of the role of resentment, as conceptualized above, in episodes of mass violence (Fiske et al. 2002). Competence concerns the perceived abilities and merits of a group; warmth is about the perceived distance between the two groups. Groups perceived to have low competence and warmth (e.g., welfare recipients and poor Blacks in the United States) generate contempt and disgust among members of the dominant group; groups perceived to have high competence but low warmth (e.g., Jews in Eastern Europe and Chinese in Indonesia) generate envy, which is the basis of resentment. The latter dynamic suggests significant potential for instability and violence when a majority perceives a despised minority achieving a higher political status (Petersen 2002). The fact that a small number of Jews achieved positions of influence and power as financiers and administrators fueled popular antisemitism and led to a major pogrom in Barcelona in 1391 (Wolff 1971). In a very different context, after the Nazi invasion in 1941, local pogroms were more frequent in parts of eastern Poland where Jews were politically more assertive and demanding, a pattern consistent with the expectations of group threat theory (Kopstein and Wittenberg 2018).

Echoing Fassin, resentment does not need to have any objective basis. In fact, as an experimental study shows, a group who feels inferior in certain respects shows schadenfreude toward another group even if that latter group neither presents a threat to the former group nor is the reason for its inferiority (Leach and Spears 2008). Accordingly, even a slightly increased public presence of a minority group could aggravate a majority who would displace its broader grievances onto this group. In particular, a minority that is no longer content to occupy an invisible and subdued societal role could easily attract the ire of a majority (cf. Holt 2012). The lynching of thousands of Black people in the American South from the late nineteenth to early twentieth centuries were acts of popular terror that aimed to preserve the segregated racial order after the abolishment of slavery. These acts of terror often involved the participation of entire communities as perpetrators and spectators and took place after fabricated charges of sexual assault of a white woman by a Black man

(Tolnay and Beck 1995, 48). In some instances, such as the mass killings in Wilmington, North Carolina in 1898, the primary motive was to reverse political gains made by the Blacks during Reconstruction and reimpose the white political order (Dray 2003, 122–27).

Overall, resentment provides a dynamic account of how historical stigmatization of liminal minorities leads to actual outbreaks of violence. It provides a powerful conceptual tool to make sense of the breakdown of fragile religious coexistence leading to bottom-up violence. Liminal minorities, historically low-warmth groups, are convenient targets of popular resentment when they are perceived to make relative symbolic gains. As discussed in chapter 2, the IS opportunistically capitalized on deep discontentment of Sunni Arabs with the post-Saddam political order. Although Yezidis continued to be a marginalized group, they made some relative political gains under the new order while Sunni Arabs experienced a huge power loss. Alongside with religious hatred, resentment played a powerful motive in Sunni Arab targeting of Yezidis. Especially in the Sinjar area where Sunni Arabs and Yezidis cohabited, Sunni Arab resentment of Yezidis was a function of "last-place aversion" (Kuziemko et al. 2014). Sunni Arabs were anxious that Yezidis, a despised group historically placed at the bottom of the societal hierarchy, were making gains thanks to the increasing Kurdish patronage and power after 2003. Similarly, as discussed in chapter 3, the growing political activism and public presence of Alevis in the late twentieth century in Turkey became a major source of resentment among conservative Sunni Turkish populations of central Anatolia discontent with the secular republic and the rise of leftist parties. Coupled with deeply rooted anti-Alevi beliefs, this resentment fueled major episodes of mass violence against local Alevi communities in the late 1970s and early 1990s. Recalling Benjamin's typology, in these occasions, the crowds claimed the mantle of natural law in defiance of positive law and perpetuated lethal violence against a scapegoated minority.

This discussion suggests that a liminal minority is likely to be a target of violence during times of a broader conflict between stronger sides. In Iraq, the main nemesis of the Sunni Arabs were the Shiite Arabs and the Sunni Kurds. In Turkey, the main political cleavages were between the leftists and rightists in the 1970s and the secularist and Islamist forces in the 1990s. These patterns are similar to outbursts of antisemitism violence as a "collateral damage" during times of religious conflict among Christian sects or between Christians and Muslims in medieval and early modern Europe (Stark 2001, 122–24). Alevis in Turkey, Yezidis in Iraq, and Jews in medieval and early modern times were easy prey for larger groups suffering losses in broader struggles for power.

Fear, Greed, and Guilt

Drawing on the rich literature on mass violence, I discuss three additional microlevel mechanisms that motivate ordinary people to attack and kill their neighbors who happen to be members of another religious group: greed, fear, and guilt. These mechanisms, which are not mutually exclusive, represent distinct reasons why ordinary people participate in acts of mass violence such as riots and pogroms. I engage in process tracing utilizing hoop tests to flesh out which one of these mechanisms, if any, are pertinent in massacres targeting Yezidis and Alevis in chapters 2 and 3, respectively.

Fear

Fear involves perceptions of collective threat. This mechanism is the basis of security dilemma arguments that offer a rationalist model to explain how mutual insecurity leads to interethnic violence in the wake of state collapse (Posen 1993). Attempts by each group to augment its defense generates an atmosphere of mistrust and uncertainty and gives incentives to each group to strike preemptively. To give a historical example, Armenian attempts to arm themselves in self-defense aggravated Muslim suspicions of Armenian goals of seeking an independent state during the Adana massacres of 1909 (Der Matossian 2022). Other scholars pay more attention to emotional processes and develop nonrationalist versions of this argument. In the Rwandan genocide, wartime uncertainty and widespread perception of existential threats aggravated fears conducive to violent aggression (Straus 2006). Collective fear contributes to intergroup polarization, while material and structural opportunities translate fear into violence (McDoom 2012). States that already experienced territorial or population losses are particularly amenable to develop an existential threat perception justifying excessive violence against a group perceived to be threatening (Midlarsky 2005). It should be noted that a despised out-group, such as a liminal minority, could be perceived as threatening independent of its actions and capabilities. To make a historical analogy, the Jews of Germany did not present a threat to the Nazi regime while the Tutsi rebels did present a threat to the Hutu-dominated regime in Rwanda. The fact that the Nazis perceived an existential threat was purely reflective of their extreme ideology in the absence of any Jewish collective action against German national interests. The fear mechanism discussed in this book applies to situations when an out-group engages in observable military preparations and operations and has some capacity to inflict significant damage on an in-group.

Greed

Greed suggests that the pursuit of material benefits is the main reason why members of a group attack members of another group. It has been a motivator of violent behavior in many different conflicts especially when the targeted group is perceived to be a source of economic envy. People can participate in violence for opportunistic reasons such as looting. Greed is more likely to be a strong motivator when costs of engaging in violence are low—that is, perpetuators act with impunity against defenseless victims, and tangible benefits are substantial (Collier and Hoeffler 1998; Mueller 2000). During the Holocaust, non-Jewish populations of Eastern Europe seized properties of Jews who were killed or deported by the occupying German authorities (Gross and Gross 2016; Charnysh and Finkel 2017). Local participation in the killing of Jews and the seizing of their properties generated a social class benefiting from the German rule (Snyder 2015, 185). After the Soviet defeat of the Nazis, this massive robbery of property was not challenged and became a point of contact between the communist system and local populations (285). Many locals who participated in the Armenian massacres in the Ottoman city of Adana in 1909 were motivated by the prospect of plunder (Der Matossian 2022). Several years later, during the Armenian genocide, local notables in Antep who actively organized the deportations of the Armenians became the main beneficiaries of the expropriation and plunder of their properties (Kurt 2021).

Guilt

Guilt is a less-studied mechanism that is particularly relevant in political settings characterized by fundamental and swift transformations in power relations. According to this mechanism, members of a group attack members of another group so that they could dissociate themselves from their past allegiances and instead make the latter responsible for crimes of the ancien régime. Timothy Snyder (2015) offers a compelling account of the dynamics of local participation in mass violence against the Jews after the German invasion of the Soviet-occupied part of Poland and the Soviet Union in the summer of 1941. The Nazis propagated the myth of Judeo-Bolshevism, which identified Jews as the core of power in the Soviet Union. According to this myth, the extermination of Jews would be the end of communism. Local people had no such illusions about the nature of Soviet rule. In fact, only a small number of Jews actually became part of the communist system. Yet locals conveniently utilized the myth to detach themselves from the crumbling Soviet order with which they collaborated and vindicate themselves in the eyes of the Nazis, which became the new supreme power. Blaming Jews for the communist rule allowed local populations to associate themselves with the Nazi power.

I conceptualize religious violence in terms of perpetrator motivations. Eschatological beliefs about the coming end of the world, animosity toward "heretical" groups perceived to violate the sacred order, and exhortations to remake the worldly affair in the image of God generate a propensity toward violence in human affairs. I also argue that certain groups, liminal minorities, are more likely to be subjects of such violence. This is because their very existence has been a historical source of anxiety and uneasiness for dominant faith groups. Although the advent of political modernity has occasionally generated greater opportunities for members of these groups, their increasing visibility and participation in the polity become a direct affront to majoritarian religious sensibilities and a source of popular resentment.

This framework helps us better understand why liminal minorities, such as Ahmadis, Alevis, Baha'is, and Yezidis, are likely to be targets of religious violence in both historical and contemporary times. Dominant groups harbor historically formed stereotypical perceptions of these groups that facilitate their stigmatization which becomes lethal when combined with resentfulness that occurs during times of political change when a dominant group experiences a loss in power. A liminal minority becomes a scapegoat of majoritarian anger especially when it seeks greater political rights and public visibility. Religious justifications of violence have a stronger mobilization power and appeal and typically go unchallenged when they are directed against these minorities. A direct implication of this argument is that policies and initiatives aiming to transform exclusionary beliefs and norms about liminal minorities at both theological and popular levels are essential for the sustainability of religious pluralism. As we cannot make sense of lynchings in the American South without discussing the centrality of racism to popular values and norms, any analysis of violence targeting liminal minorities is lacking without recognizing the role of preexisting religious stigmas against such groups. While religious traditions have many ambivalent characteristics, there has been little disagreement when it comes to liminal minorities, which are deprived of respect, recognition, and equal treatment.

It is worth reemphasizing that this discussion does not mean that religiously motivated antiliminal violence is inevitable. Episodes of bottom-up violence are rare; periods of coexistence are common. Liminal minorities are usually tolerated, or at least not directly targeted, as long as they keep to themselves, resign to their subordination, and remain politically docile. Moreover, state authorities, authoritarian or democratic, do not necessarily condone acts of bottom-up violence against liminal groups. After all, as Walter Benjamin observes, violence seeking to claim the mantle of natural law presents a direct challenge to positive law and the state's claims to monopoly over means of legitimate coercion. Yet this tension between religiously inspired natural law and positive law is itself a constant source of precarity for liminal minorities. As we will see in chapter 4 about Baha'is and Ahmadis, the state authorities may remain complicit and impotent in the face of defiant mobs engaging in performative acts of mass violence. Such eruptions of violence tragically reveal how an ostensibly secular state could not live up to its own image of treating all faith groups equally.

Chapter 2

From Liminality to Genocidal Violence
Yezidis of Iraq

> There are no oil wells where we were living,
>   in Shingal,
> but I assure you, we are rich in mass graves.
>
> —Saad Shivan, "The Clock Shows 1 A.M."[1]

On August 14, 2007, four suicide bombers driving a fuel tanker and several vans targeted two impoverished rural towns in northwestern Iraq. These towns were Til Ezer and Siba Sheikh Khidir located around twenty-five kilometers south of Mount Sinjar. The coordinated attacks involving tons of explosives flattened entire neighborhoods and killed several hundreds of people. The incident was the most lethal single terror attack in post-2003 Iraq. Most of the victims were Yezidis who were forcefully located to these towns by the Saddam regime in the second half of the 1970s. In the aftermath of the attacks, security forces of the Kurdistan Regional Government (KRG) expanded their control into the area, sandwiched between the Syrian border and Tal Afar and Mosul, two cities with a heavy presence of Salafi jihadists. The relations between local Yezidis and Arabs, neighbors of each other across generations, further deteriorated.

The worst was yet to come for the Yezidis. After the outbreak of a protracted civil war in Syria and the rise of cross-border Salafi jihadist networks, the situation in Sinjar became increasingly perilous. The fall of Mosul, which hosted thousands of Iraqi security forces, to a small group of militants pledging allegiance to the IS in June 2014 cut Sinjar from the rest of Iraq. It was just

---

1. Saad Shivan's poem, cited in the epigraph, is translated by Mairéad Smith and David Shookran, "Bar Codes and Mass Graves: A Reading by Seven Emerging Êzîdî Poets," Poetry Foundation, 2018.

a matter of time before the IS moved into Sinjar, which remained the only "unconquered territory" on the main road linking Mosul and Raqqa, the two most important cities of the IS's self-declared caliphate. The IS's Sinjar campaign, which started on the early morning of August 3, was swift and ruthless. As Kurdish Peshmerga fled in disarray, the Yezidis became easy prey. At least 1,500 Yezidis, mostly adult males, were executed; around 1,500 others, many of them children and the elderly, died on Mount Sinjar from dehydration or starvation. IS militants kidnapped and enslaved around 6,800 Yezidis, mostly women and children (Cetorelli et al. 2017). Around three thousand abductees remained missing seven years after the attacks (Araf and Khaleel 2021). Most of them were presumed dead. The entire Yezidi community of Sinjar, several hundred thousand people, lost their homes and were displaced. In a matter of a few days, the IS killed or captured about 4 percent of around 250,000 Yezidis living in Sinjar (UNHABITAT 2015, 8). Assuming a global Yezidi population of half a million, the ferocity of the IS attack resulted in the deaths or captivity of one in every fifty Yezidis in the world. If not for the US military intervention that started on August 7, the IS genocidal campaign would have been more complete.

I argue that the IS genocidal campaign against the Yezidis was an extreme form of religious violence. The IS explicitly called for the forced conversion, enslavement, or murder of Yezidis on the grounds that they were "devil worshippers" whose very existence was an anathema to Islam. The IS treatment of Yezidis was vicious even by its own brutal standards. At the same time, a conceptualization of the IS as a monolithic and centralized organization overlooks even more macabre patterns. The campaign against Yezidis was successful because of the active and widespread participation of local Sunni Muslims. In fact, a striking feature of survival testimonies is the surprise and anguish experienced by Yezidis when they realized that most of their tormentors were their neighbors with whom they interacted almost daily. While the role of foreign fighters in the IS has been subject of considerable scholarly and public debate, the IS's embeddedness in the local communities stranding the Syria-Iraq border was the primary reason for its resilience and initial successes, including its occupation of Sinjar. Then why did the local people, primarily Sunni Arabs and Turkomans, become willing executioners, enslavers, and looters of their Yezidi neighbors? This chapter demonstrates that perpetrators of violence were motivated by hatred based on centuries-old religious stigmatization as well as political resentment caused by power changes in the post-2003 order.

In some postconflict settings, transitional justice mechanisms provide a relatively transparent and accurate understanding of the motives of the perpetrators. The truth commissions include testimonies from perpetrators and declassified official documents. In this case, however, no such sources are available given the ongoing conflict situation involving multiple layers of rivalries. Many of the perpetrators remain at large, and the trials of suspected IS militants in Iraq lack transparency and due process. What I lack in access to perpetrators, however, I make up for in access to survivors, bystanders, and informed observers. In particular, I rely on a plethora of testimonies by survivors—the ones who fled the IS assault on that fateful August day and the ones who remained in IS captivity before being released or liberated. At the same time, I approach these testimonies with a critical perspective and engage in triangulation by marshaling a wide variety of additional sources including in-depth interviews with non-Yezidis, IS documents, extensive field reports by international and local organizations, and historical documents. Overall, these sources provide unique insights into the nature and dynamics of the anti-Yezidi attacks and local participation.

Historical Formations of Yezidi Liminality

The Yezidis are a predominantly Kurdish (Kurmanji dialect)-speaking ethnic-religious group with a distinct monotheistic religion. Although some Yezidis embrace Kurdishness as an integral part of their identity, others perceive their religion as the basis of a distinct ethnic identity. Peacock Angel (Malak Ṭā'ūs), the highest of the seven angels ruling the world, is God's enabler in the world according to the Yezidi faith. Yezidis have historically inhabited the terrain that spans the contemporary border between Turkey and Iraq. The number of Yezidis in Turkey dwindled due to both discriminatory state and societal practices in the late twentieth century. Many of them started to migrate to Germany by the late 1960s and early 1970s (Interviewee #1, June 28, 2017; Interviewee #95, October 12, 2019). After the 1980 coup, which promoted Islamization as an antidote to leftist activism, state authorities started to explicitly deny Yezidism as a religion and put an X mark in the religious box of their national identification cards (Öztürk 1996, 60). Although most Yezidis continue to live in Iraq, there has been a sizable Yezidi community in Transcaucasia, especially in Armenia, since the nineteenth century and in Europe, especially in Germany, since the late twentieth century. After 2003 and 2014, many Yezidis left Iraq as refugees and formed diaspora communities in several countries including Australia, Canada, and the United States.

The very origins of Yezidis, very much like Alevis, has been the subject of intense controversy and ambiguity. Since the nineteenth century, many travelers, scholars, and intellectuals, both Muslim and Western, made various attempts to identify the origins of the group they often characterized as exotic and arcane (Allison 2008; Gökçen 2012). The widespread classification of Yezidis as a "syncretic religion" influenced and shaped by multiple other religious traditions, as in the case of Alevis, implies its perceived lack of authenticity and authoritativeness. Some scholars suggest that Yezidism was deeply influenced by Zoroastrianism, the predominant religion in Iran before the advent of Islam, and other pre-Islamic Iranian beliefs (Kreyenbroek 1995). From the mainstream Islamic perspective, however, Yezidis had been followers of the second Umayyad caliph Yazid ibn Mu'awiya (d. 683). They chose a "deviant path" after the death of Sheikh Adi ibn Musafir (b. 1162), a prominent Sufi sheikh (Okçu 1993; Teymûr 2008, 64). Accordingly, they were labeled as a "heretical group" that abandoned Islam (al-Jabiri 1981, 87). These divergent positions notwithstanding, there is widespread consensus that Sheikh Adi reorganized Yezidism and established a clerical order, parallel to monolithic religions. Over time, Yezidis developed a caste system with the three main categories being sheikhs, pirs, and ordinary people (murids) (Açıkyıldız 2010). In practice, one's membership in these social categories has been inherited from one's parents. Marriage has been endogenous and only permitted among members of one's own socioreligious group.

The controversy also extends to the question of whether Yezidis have sacred books of their own (Kreyenbroek 1995, 10–16). Although contemporary Yezidis acknowledge the existence of two such books attributed to Sheikh Adi, they play no important role in the community's religious practices (Açıkyıldız 2010, 88–91). Moreover, Yezidis have gone to great lengths to hide their purported books from outsiders. That contrasts with Mandaeans, another ethnoreligious group with deep historical roots in Iraq, who claimed to have sacred books of their own to escape persecution in the hands of powerful Muslim rulers (Khenchelaoui and Burrell 1999, 23–25). Such disagreements about the origins of the faith and its basic tenets were not only prevalent among outside observers but also among the Yezidis themselves.

A main challenge facing the attempts to identify historical origins and evolution of the community is that Yezidism, as a set of beliefs and practices, has historically relied on oral transmission across generations. Accordingly, oral traditions have been central to the actual experience of Yezidis (Kreyenbroek 1995). This historical pattern has precluded the formation of a dogmatic and official form of faith based on authoritative and canonical texts. Meanwhile, the insulated and endogenous nature of the group and the lack of an official dogma made the group illegible for outsiders who often relied on highly distorted and stigmatized views of the group. For instance, writing in the early fifteenth century, a prominent Arab historian, Al-Maqrīzī, mentioned Yezidis as a group who engaged in anthropomorphism (i.e., assigning human traits to God) and practiced adultery (Turan 1989, 62–63). The latter smear has persisted among the populace well into contemporary times (Öz 2007, 56).

The most blatant and pejorative example of stigmatization targeting Yezidis is the epithet that describes the community as "devil worshippers." This epithet derives from the conflation of Peacock Angel, which has a sacred status in the Yezidi faith, with Iblīs, a figure who fell from God's grace for refusing to bow to Adam according to the Islamic belief. Ibn Taymiyyah, the prominent Muslim theologian and scholar of the late thirteenth and early fourteenth centuries, wrote a treatise critical of the followers of Sheikh Adi. Although he condemned the sheikh's followers for corrupting his teachings, he did not refer to them as "devil worshippers" (Teymûr 2008, 58, 62–63). However, the epithet apparently gained widespread usage among Muslim ulema by the sixteenth century (Dehqan 2008). The Ottoman ulema, including both the leading mufti of the empire and local religious authorities, issued various fatwas demonizing Yezidis as devil worshippers who let their women have sex with their religious leaders. They also justified the plundering of their properties, the killing of their men, and the enslavement of their women and children (Hodgson 1974, 111; al-Jabiri 1981, 166; Murad 1993, 59–60; Kerborani 2021). It did not help that Yezidis were often conflated with supporters of Yazid ibn Mu'awiya, the Umayyad caliph, who was vilified for ordering the massacre of Hussein, grandson of Prophet Muhammad, in Karbala in 680 (Erginbaş 2020, 457–58). In this critical historical juncture, the formation of an imperial order imposing a Hanefi-Sunni orthodoxy facilitated the otherization of the Yezidis, as much as Alevis. Since Yezidis were not considered People of the Book, they lacked the relative recognition and protection offered to Christians and Jewish communities in the Ottoman Empire.

Stigmatized views of Yezidis were also embraced by westerners starting with the nineteenth century and continued to be widespread in modern times. For instance, a *New York Times* article from 1935 described Yezidis as "devil worshippers" (*New York Times* 1935). Similarly, an article published in *Le Monde* in 1972 read, "the picturesque Yezidis, who worship the devil" (*Le Monde* 1972). At the local level, Christians in northern Kurdistan were also reported to use the epithet of devil worshippers when talking about Yezidis as recently as the late twentieth century (Allison 2001, 37).

Given this historical stigmatization, a strong sense of victimhood has been central to Yezidi self-identification. Until the 2007 and 2014 attacks, the Yezidis tended to describe their history in terms of seventy-two military campaigns (*firmans*) by Muslim rulers (Murad 1993, 63). This number has a symbolic importance, rather than being a historically accurate count. In the Yezidi version of the myth of the Creation, while seventy-two races emerged from Adam and Eve, Yezidis had distinctive parents (Murad 1993, 281; Gökçen 2015, 46). Al-Jabiri (1981, 166) counts fifty-three anti-Yezidis massacres; Murad (1993, 62–63) identifies twenty-five Ottoman military campaigns targeting Yezidis from 1246 to 1918. Similarly, Cindî Reşo (2014) writes that a plurality of firmans were Ottoman expeditions against the Yezidis of Sinjar.

In this cyclical view of history, these religiously motivated campaigns had genocidal intentions and precipitated the decline of Yezidis into a tiny minority by the twentieth century (Ali 2019b). As I will demonstrate, hatred stemming from religious stigmatization was a salient factor in making sense of anti-Yezidi violence in post-2003 Iraq. Nonetheless, it is too simplistic to reduce the history of Yezidis into a history of unbroken religious persecution. Not all military campaigns had primarily religious motivations. Nor were Yezidi relations with Muslim rulers and neighbors all conflictual (Ayhan and Tezcür 2021). Several Yezidi leaders were even appointed to positions of provincial power by the Ottoman sultans in the sixteenth and seventeenth centuries. For instance, a Yezidi tribal leader joined the Baghdad expedition of Sultan Murad IV and was appointed as governor of Mosul for a year (Murad 1993, 61–62; Guest 1993, 49). In the early nineteenth century, a local Yezidi leader ruled over Yezidi, Muslim, and Christian communities until the Ottoman centralization drive in 1837 (Fuccaro 1999, 63).

There were also long periods when Sunni Kurds and Yezidis belonged to the same tribe or tribal confederation. At times, they formed alliances; other times, they fought each other. For instance, an Ottoman pasha organized an expedition against the Yezidis of Sinjar in 1655 because they were allied with a rebellious Kurdish chieftain (Guest 1993, 50). Evliya Çelebi (2013, 50), the illustrious Ottoman traveler who participated in the campaign, described the Yezidis of Sinjar as "wild savages, rebellious, ghoul faced, hairy infidels" who worshipped a black dog in his *Seyahatname*. According to Evliya Çelebi's account, the campaign resulted in the looting of Yezidi properties and animals and the enslavement of girls and boys (Kerborani 2021). A local Kurdish ruler, Mohammad Kor of Soran, viciously attacked Yezidis allied with a rival Kurdish emirate in 1832 (Layard 1850, 276–77; Longrigg 1925, 28; Guest 1993, 67–69; Eppel 2016, 51–6; Ali 2019b). His indiscriminate and sexual violence left a lasting impact on Yezidi collective memory (Allison 2001, 215–58). In the words of a Yezidi religious leader, "They took away a thousand of our girls [in 1832]. A thousand was plenty. Our population was much smaller by that time.... You now see lots of Kurds around. Their fourth- or fifth-generation ancestors were Yezidis" (Interviewee #3, September 27, 2017). In fact, many Yezidis including younger and more educated ones believe that most Kurds originally adhered to the Yezidi faith before being forcefully converted to Islam (Interviewee #73, May 8, 2019).

A primary reason why the Ottoman rulers staged expeditions against the Yezidis was related to strategic concerns. Mount Sinjar (*Çiyayê Shingal* in Kurdish), reaching an elevation of close to 1,500 meters and inhabited by several prominent Yezidi tribes, had a commanding position over the caravan routes linking the cities of Aleppo, Diyerbekir, and Mardin on the northwest and Baghdad and Mosul on the southeast. To borrow from James Scott (2009, 13), Mount Sinjar was a stateless zone with a long history of indigenous resistance to the state. Accordingly, a major Ottoman concern was to ensure the security of these routes. Sharaf Khan, the celebrated author of *Sharafnama* chronicling Kurdish dynasties (1596–99) (Alsancakli 2017), described Yezidis as "pundits who live off from agriculture and robbery" (Allison 2001, 33). Local Ottoman rulers conducted a series of punitive expeditions against Mount Sinjar to prevent Yezidi banditry and raids during the eighteenth century (Longrigg 1925, 126; Olson 1973, 332–33; Guest 1993, 60). Interestingly, these Ottoman expeditions left little trace in the Yezidi collective memory and oral traditions (Kreyenbroek 1995, 36).

At the same time, the Yezidis of Mount Sinjar presented more than a threat of banditry for the Ottomans. Karen Barkey (2005, 10) contends that religious or sectarian differences were not a major reason why non-Muslim groups were persecuted by the Ottomans. These persecutions had a political logic and were responses to perceived threats. Barkey's contention captures the experience of some religious groups, such as the Armenians, under Ottoman rule but does not explain how the Ottoman-Yezidi relations evolved. The very identity of Yezidis as a liminal minority outside of the Ottoman moral order was a source of security concern for the imperial and local rulers. Although this concern did not predetermine Ottoman actions, it fostered the perception that Yezidis were inherently rebellious and disloyal by virtue of their religion. In fact, the Sinjar expeditions were often justified in Islamic terms and involved indiscriminate violence. For instance, the official justification of an expedition in 1795 described Yezidis as infidels and heretics whose women and children could be enslaved according to Islamic law (Gölbaşı 2013, 3–4). Similarly, an Ottoman governor of Baghdad in the early nineteenth century declared Yezidis as apostates (*murtad*) to justify his military expedition on Mount Sinjar (Abca 2006, 179–80).

In summary, the Yezidis remained an illegible community in the eyes of Ottoman rulers who ruled over territories inhabited by the group for four hundred years, from the early sixteenth to the early twentieth century. They were never incorporated into the millet system as an officially recognized religious group. At the same time, Yezidi leaders, far from being defenseless and helpless subjects, were actively involved in regional politics with significant capacity for coalition building, negotiation, and resistance.

Encounters with Political Modernity

With the advent of the nineteenth century, increasing Western encroachments and Ottoman centralization efforts led to an unprecedented degree of encounters between Yezidis and outsiders. Western travelers, missionaries, and scholars who encountered Yezidis showed great interest about their "ancient faith," while readily adopting the prevailing Muslim stereotypical views of the group (e.g., Forbes 1839, 424–25). Meanwhile, Yezidis with their "deviant" beliefs remained a problem for the Ottoman rulers who increasingly perceived political loyalty in terms of identification with Sunni Islam, contrary to the argument that the Ottomans targeted Yezidis only when the group threatened public order (Gülsoy 2002, 134–35). The attempts to assimilate the Yezidis via co-optation, coercion, or indoctrination into the dominant Sunni Muslim order reached their zenith under Sultan Abdülhamid II (r. 1876–1909) who pursued a policy of "correction of beliefs" (*tashih-i akaid*).

The characterization of Yezidis as a group of devil-worshipping infidels with no sacred book would persist among Muslim religious authorities and population throughout the twentieth century. In modern Turkey, Yezidis were not only called devil worshippers but also infidels, enemies of Ali, the son-in-law of Prophet Muhammad, the ones with eight mustaches, and unbelievers (Çakar 2007, 7). A 1926 article by Mehmed Şerafeddin, who would become the highest ranking cleric in the Turkish Republic in 1942, described Yezidis as devil-worshipping infidels with no sacred book (Bulut 2017).[2] Similarly, a series of articles that appeared in a prominent Islamist magazine in Turkey in the mid-twentieth century routinely described Yezidis as "backward" and "savage" people worshipping devil they called Peacock Angel. The influential Islamist magazine *Sebîlürreşad* was published from 1908 to 1966, except for a hiatus between 1925 and 1948 (Arabacı 2004). The articles in this magazine also denied that Sheikh Adi, portrayed as an illustrious Islamic scholar, was the founder of the community and argued that the "religious order" emerged several centuries before his death (*Sebîlürreşad* 1954, 1962, 1965). An article published in another Islamist magazine in 1965 claimed that Yezidi murids "were proud to have their wives to be impregnated by their sheikhs." According to

---

2. I thank Bahadin Kerborani for bringing this article to my attention.

the author, Yezidis practiced what was forbidden for Muslims and did not practice what was legitimate for Muslims (*Tohum* 1965).

Several decades later, many Muslim activists and authorities condemned IS violence against Yezidis as being un-Islamic. Yet such condemnations did not amount to a recognition of Yezidism as a legitimate belief system. For instance, a Muslim theologian in Turkey condemned IS enslavement of Yezidis, a group that "deviated from Islamic faith" and "honor the devil," on the grounds that they were civilians and did not fight the IS (Öğmüş 2014). To give another example, a well-known Islamist journalist wrote in November 2014, several months after the IS attacks: "There is a common perception among people that Yezidis worship the devil. Yezidis oppose this claim and argue that they do not worship the devil. However, the reality is not what Yezidis tell. . . . Peacock Angel is the devil. Yezidis believe that Peacock Angel, rather than God, should be worshipped and Peacock Angel, rather than God, is the source of good and evil" (Özköse 2014, 22).[3]

The Ottoman *Mission Civilisatrice*

The Ottoman modernization (the Tanzimat era, 1839–76) brought some important changes in how the Ottomans perceived and dealt with Yezidis. It involved policies that aimed to pacify and incorporate "primitive" and "uncivilized" groups such as Yezidis into the imperial order via "civilizing campaigns." The large-scale kidnappings and enslavements of Yezidis as well as other non-Muslim groups declined (Erdem 1996, 46, 59–60). Moreover, the Ottoman portrayal of Yezidis changed from "apostates," who are subject to killings and enslavement, to "heretics," who should be converted back to the true faith by various methods including indoctrination and violence (Gölbaşı 2013, 4–5). The Ottoman state also became a fixture in the lands inhabited by the group. After a series of expeditions, the Ottomans managed to establish permanent garrisons on the slopes of Mount Sinjar by the late 1840s (Forbes 1839, 409–11; Layard 1850, 314, Guest 1993, 74–75; Fuccaro 1999, 4). Yet the Ottomans had little success in conscripting Yezidi men to their standing army (Gölbaşı 2009). A Yezidi delegation visiting Istanbul secured the intervention of a powerful British diplomat to obtain an exemption from conscription in 1849 (Guest 1993, 104–8; Gölbaşı 2009, 95). Even if the Ottoman authorities did not recognize Yezidis as part of the millet system, they let Yezidis make a payment instead of serving in the imperial army. In the face of new Ottoman attempts to recruit them as soldiers, a group of Yezidi leaders

---

3. The same author used the same words to describe Yezidis also five years ago (Özköse 2009).

petitioned the government in 1872. The group argued that Yezidi men should be exempted from military service on religious grounds. This petition, written in Turkish, Arabic, and French, was the first known document of how Yezidis portrayed their faith to outsiders. It enabled the community to avoid conscription for almost two decades.

The Ottoman policy toward Yezidis gained new impetus with the ascendancy of Abdülhamid II to the throne. By 1890, the sultan consolidated his power and vigorously pursued his ideological vision, which increasingly associated political loyalty with being Sunni Islam. Consistent with this vision, the conversion of peripheral groups such as Yezidis, Druzes, and Alevis into the dominant Sunni faith gained a new urgency in the face of increasing missionary activity and circulation of nationalist ideas. As the sultan developed an aggravated threat perception and feared the dissolution of his empire, he expected that the conscription of these liminal groups would facilitate their conversion to Sunni Islam and ensure their loyalty. The Russo-Turkish war of 1876–77, which resulted in a bitter Ottoman defeat and paved the way for increasing foreign influence over eastern Anatolia and upper Mesopotamia, also resulted in thousands of Yezidis fleeing to the Russian side (Nicolaus and Yuce 2019). In 1885, the Ottoman government concluded that Yezidis, just like Muslims, had to be recruited into the army.

After initial efforts in obtaining the community's cooperation failed, an Ottoman official, Omar Wehbi Pasha, was dispatched to Mosul to deal with the "Yezidi question" in 1892. To break the Yezidi resistance to conscription and taxation, he unleashed a campaign of terror involving the killing of hundreds of Yezidis, the kidnapping of women and their forced marriage to Ottoman soldiers, the forced conversion of Lalish, the main Yezidi temple and tomb of Sheikh Adi (see figure 2.1), into a madrassa, the confiscation of the Yezidi sacred objects, the construction of villages in Yezidi villages, and the forced conversion of Yezidi leaders (Parry 1895, 253–54, 257–58; Guest 1993, 134–40; Gölbaşı 2009, 117–26, 129–31). His violent campaign left a deep scar among the Yezidis and became the subject of a well-known elegy, *Feriq Pasha* (Gökçen 2015, 34). His brutal methods eventually backfired, as they exposed the insecurity of the imperial order in a time of intense geopolitical rivalry. The pasha was recalled. It would take some years before Lalish and some of the sacred objects would be returned to the community (Deringil 1999, 71–75).

The remaining years of the empire did not see any other large-scale anti-Yezidi violence except for several expeditions against Sinjar during World War I when groups of Armenians fleeing from genocidal Ottoman attacks took refuge in Mount Sinjar (Ternon 2014). The war ultimately brought an end to the centuries-old Ottoman rule over Yezidis. By 1918, a leading Yezidi was already

FIGURE 2.1. Lalish Temple, Iraqi Kurdistan, September 2017 (Credit: Author)

in communication with the British army, which captured Baghdad in March 1917 (Guest 1993, 178–80). The formation of the Turkish-Iraqi border in the 1920s would result in further fragmentation of the Yezidi community.

On the Margins of the Iraqi State

With the end of the Ottoman rule and the start of the British occupation over Mosul province, Yezidis would be subject to a non-Muslim authority for the first time since the time of Sheikh Adi. During the contestation over the

Iraqi-Turkish border, most Yezidi leaders preferred Iraq under a European mandate over either Turkish or Arabic rule (League of Nations 1925). Ultimately, most Yezidis became citizens of the new Iraqi state formed under British tutelage. Although religiously inspired violence against the community declined, Yezidis continued to be a marginalized group in the new political order (Fuccaro 1999). In a telling anecdote, opponents of Faisal, who would be appointed king of Iraq by the British in 1921, branded him as a "Yezidi" (i.e., an apostate) to undermine his claim to the throne (Bet-Shlimon 2019, 46). As in Ottoman times, conscription continued to be a primary source of contention between Yezidis and the state authorities in Baghdad. Meanwhile, Sinjar gained a new strategic importance as a border zone between Syria and Iraq (Fuccaro 1997). Yezidis engaged in small-scale rebellions and tried to evade conscription by taking advantage of the porous borders with French-dominated Syria. They also asked for British intervention in conflicts with their Arab neighbors, the Shammar tribe, over land (Gökçen 2012, 431–34, 438). Their demands to have a Christian district governor was unsuccessful and the district continued to have a Muslim governor (482).

The 1940s witnessed the rise of modern forms of political participation, including party and union activism, among different ethnic groups in Iraq (Tripp 2007). The bloody 1958 coup that replaced the Hashemite monarchy with a republican regime not only accelerated mass political participation but also contributed to political instability and violence in the absence of resilient institutions (Huntington 1968, 202). In particular, the Communist Party of Iraq found a receptive audience among Christians, Kurds, and Shiite Arabs. However, Yezidi representation in the party and other mass organizations remained very limited (Batatu 1978, 1190). As most of the community remained poor and rural with little or no schooling, its involvement in modern forms of mass politics remained low.

The 1958 coup also enabled Moustafa Barzani, the Kurdish leader who was in exile in the Soviet Union since 1947, to return to Iraq (Schmidt 1964). Barzani soon found himself at loggerheads with the rulers in Baghdad and raised the banner of rebellion in 1961. These developments made Nineveh province, where Sinjar and Sheikhan/Lalish are located, and the city of Mosul a conflict zone. The increasing influence of Kurdish nationalism among Yezidis would be a concern for Baghdad. The Iraqi regime and the Barzani movement, both of which espoused secular ideologies, downplayed religious differences in favor of encompassing ethnic platforms to increase their influence in Nineveh, a region home to multiple religious faiths (Ali 2019a). The former propagated that Yezidis were the descendants of the Umayyads, a dynasty that ruled over the Islamic empire from 661 to 750, via the lineage of Sheikh Adi

(Guest 1993, 15; Fuccaro 1999, 174). The Yezidi reverence of Yazid ibn Mu'awiya, the second Umayyad caliph, became a core aspect of the regime's attempts to reconfigure the Yezidi identity in ways compatible with Sunni Arab nationalism. The Ba'th party (r. 1968–2003) co-opted prominent Yezidis to its Umayyad office and officially recognized Yezidi holidays in 1972 (*al-Thawrah* 1972, 5; Ali 2021). This association of Yezidis with Yazid, the most hated figure in Shiite historiography for his execution of Hussein, grandson of Prophet Muhammad, in Karbala in 680, did not do them any favors in the eyes of Shiite clerics who referred to them as "unbelievers" and "infidels."[4] In comparison, the Kurdish movement espoused the idea that Yezidism had its roots in Zoroastrianism, which was reconfigured as the original religion of Kurds. The secular Kurdish perspective, to the chagrin of Kurdish Islamists, implied that Yezidis were the carriers of pre-Islamic Kurdish heritage and set the Kurds apart from their Muslim neighbors. This ideological contestation over the origins and nature of the Yezidi identity generated rifts among the community at both the popular and elite levels. Whereas some Yezidis joined the Peshmerga, others were recruited into the Iraqi army.

The shah of Iran, who had been the main supporter of the Barzani rebellion, made a deal with the Ba'th regime in 1975. This brought the collapse of the Kurdish insurgency. In the wake of this victory, the regime initiated a systematic campaign of Arabization and resettlement in Kurdish and Yezidi lands. Yezidis were forced to leave their centuries-old villages on Mount Sinjar. They were relocated to eleven collective settlements on the plain, which were surrounded by Arabs receiving preferential treatment, especially regarding land access, from the regime (Savelsberg, Hajo, and Dulz 2010). This forced resettlement policy enabled the regime to increase its physical and ideological control over the Yezidis who continued to experience high levels of poverty, unemployment, and illiteracy (Maisel 2008). Meanwhile, the regime brought Arab families to south Sinjar and distributed them land.

In the 1980s, a significant number of Yezidi men were conscripted to the Iraqi army, a practice that generated resentment among Yezidis (Interviewee #18, May 22, 2018). Many of them were killed or became POWs in the war with the Islamic Republic of Iran. A middle-aged Yezidi man had spent nine years, from 1981 to 1990, in Iran as a POW. Incidentally, he and his family would be captives of the IS for nine months in 2014–15 (Interviewee #30, May 26, 2018). Older Yezidis who embraced the Kurdish identity viewed the Saddam years in a negative light (Interviewee #33, May 26, 2018). In contrast, Yezidis

---

4. For instance, see an anti-Yezidi sermon by a Shiite cleric from 2011 at https://youtu.be/6xGe-b8dXD4 (accessed March 26, 2023).

who kept a distance from the Kurdish nationalist movement talked positively about relative safety offered by the authoritarian Saddam rule. In the words of a displaced Yezidi woman who lost her uncle during the Iran-Iraq War, "Nobody dared to do anything against Yezidis during Saddam. He controlled everything" (Interviewee #79, May 11, 2019).

In summary, the territorial conflict between the Kurdish movement and Iraqi government had ambivalent effects for the Yezidis in the second half of the twentieth century. On the one hand, the attempts by both sides to co-opt Yezidis resulted in some symbolic recognition of their religion after centuries of stigmatization. In this sense, this competition between two opposing nationalist worldviews ameliorated Yezidi liminality. On the other hand, Yezidis found themselves amid a power struggle between Arab and Kurdish nationalisms over which they had no influence. The catastrophic events of August 2014 would be the culmination of this relentless struggle.

Under Kurdish Rule

Following Saddam's crushing of the Kurdish rebellion, the United Nations Security Council Resolution 688 in 1991 imposed a no-fly zone over northern Iraq (Karadaghi 1993). This decision led to the formation of de facto Kurdish autonomy. Whereas some Yezidi communities, including northern parts of the Sheikhan district and Lalish, fell under the Kurdish rule, Sinjar, located in the northwestern edge of Nineveh province, remained under Iraqi control until 2003. While postinvasion Iraq was mired in violence and chaos, the Kurdish region became the main beneficiary of the invasion and emerged as a relative oasis of stability. The growing Kurdish power and economic opportunities in Kurdistan, on the one hand, and sectarian violence ripping apart Iraqi society, on the other hand, led to the incorporation of Sinjar and other Yezidi lands into the Kurdish orbit. Especially after the August 2007 suicide attacks targeting Yezidi settlements in Sinjar and killing hundreds of people, the KDP (Partiya Demokrat a Kurdistanê), the most powerful Kurdish party in Iraq, took over de facto control over the Sinjar district (Dinç 2017, 81–82). The KDP provided patronage to prominent Yezidi leaders, Mir Tahsin Beg and Baba Sheikh, who aligned themselves with the secular Kurdish nationalist cause.

In this political context, the question of whether Yezidis formed a separate ethnic group or were Kurds with a distinctive set of beliefs remained a highly contested issue (figure 2.2 shows a Yezidi religious ceremony). For the major Kurdish parties, including the KDP, Yezidis are Kurds who just happen to have a different religious faith. On the first anniversary of the IS attacks, Nechirvan Barzani said, "Kurdish Yezidis are our pride. Kurdish Yezidis preserved the

FIGURE 2.2. Yezidis celebrating the New Year's Eve in Lalish, Kurdistan, Iraq, April 2017 (Editorial credit: Lena Ha/Shutterstock.com)

Kurdish national identity. They preserved Kurdish language and culture" (Rudaw 2015). Accordingly, the KRG parliament reserves seats for Assyrians, Armenians, Chaldeans, and Turkomans but none for Yezidis, who are treated as ethnic Kurds. Moreover, Article 7 of the constitution that was approved by the KRG parliament in 2009 identifies Islamic law as a source of legislation while indicating that the rights and freedoms of Christians and Yezidis are to be protected. It also describes Sinjar as part of Kurdistan (Kelly 2010). The Yezidis of Sinjar, however, could not vote in the KRG parliamentary elections.

In postinvasion Iraq, Yezidi support became essential to Kurdish claims over the disputed territories in Nineveh province, one of the most contested areas in the entire country.[5] A decisive moment came during the 2005 referendum on the new Iraqi constitution. Had two-thirds of voters in three out of Iraq's eighteen provinces said no, the constitution would have been rejected. Whereas heavy majorities in Sunni Arab–dominated provinces of Anbar and Salahuddin voted no, the percentage of no votes remained around 55 percent in Nineveh, which includes Sinjar (BBC News 2005). Essentially, Kurdish mobilization of the Yezidi vote prevented the defeat of the new constitution and

---

5. Article 140 of the Iraqi constitution of 2005 calls for a referendum in Kirkuk and other disputed territories, stretching from Diyala on the border with Iran to Sinjar on the border with Syria, by the end of 2007. Such a referendum was never held.

made many Sunni Arabs furious. After 2005, the Kurdish parties increased their support among Yezidis at the expense of autonomous Yezidi parties. The Kurdish alliance increased its vote share from 60 percent in the December 2005 parliamentary elections to 78 percent in the January 2009 provincial elections in the Sinjar district and Qahtaniya subdistrict populated by Yezidis. In comparison, the vote share of independent Yezidi parties declined from 22 percent to 6 percent between these two elections amid allegations of widespread fraud (UNAMI 2009; USIP 2011). A significant number of Yezidis were worried that their community became a pawn in the Kurdish-Arab territorial struggle and complained about "Kurdification" of Sinjar (UNAMI 2009; HRW 2009).[6] These developments would be a source of Sunni Arab and Turkoman resentment against Yezidis perceived as a lackey in the Kurdish quest for control over Nineveh (Interviewee #38, May 28, 2018).

The post-2003 era generated some advancement opportunities and economic benefits for the Yezidis in Sinjar (Spät 2018). A Yezidi man became the governor of the district for the first time. Many Yezidis found employment opportunities in the Kurdish region during the boom years of 2007–14. Others joined the Peshmerga as foot soldiers and worked as translators for the US occupation forces. Educational attainment among Yezidis increased. Many Yezidi interviewees from Sinjar noted that they built better houses and purchased cars. They also indicated that Kurdish authorities made infrastructural investments by building roads, schools, and water tanks and improving phone and internet access (Interviewee #50, May 31, 2018; Interviewee #80, May 12, 2019; Interviewee #91, May 18, 2019). At the same time, Yezidis continued to lack land tenure in the collective villages they were forcibly resettled by the Ba'th regime (UNHABITAT 2015). Whereas Yezidis who were integrated into the KDP patronage networks derived political and economic benefits, many others remained outside of these networks, were critical of corrupt practices, and became disenchanted with Kurdish rule (Interviewee #47, May 30, 2018).

Sinjar remained as one of the most underdeveloped regions of Iraq. A Yezidi member of a Kurdish party drew a parallel between Sinjar and the Darfur region of Sudan, a deprived area that experienced genocidal violence in 2003–4 (Interviewee #34, May 27, 2018). A United Nations Development Programme survey in 2006 categorized the overall deprivation in Sinjar as "very extreme" with very limited water sources and basic infrastructure and high levels of poverty and illiteracy (cited in UNAMI 2009). This underdevelopment had deleterious effects on gender relations among Yezidis of Sinjar (Interviewee #87, May 16, 2019). A young Yezidi woman from Sinjar argued that living in

---

6. I thank Peter Bartu for sharing the UNAMI report with me.

close proximity to Muslims contributed to their lack of mobility as Yezidis were fearful that Muslim men would take over their women (Interviewee #94, May 20, 2019).

In post-2003 Iraq, religious differences became politically more salient than ever. As Shiite and Sunni extremist groups engaged in tit-for-tat sectarian violence, Iraq became an extremely dangerous place for all religious minorities including various Christian groups, Mandaeans, Kākā'is, and Shabaks. Mosul, Ba'aj, and Tal Afar became the hotbeds of Sunni insurgency and extremism. As early as 2004, Yezidis were victims of targeted assassinations because of their religious identity (UNHCR 2005). Yezidi civilians traveling to Mosul for business, education, or health reasons became particularly vulnerable to killings and kidnappings. Al-Qaeda distributed pamphlets describing Yezidis as infidels and calling for their murder. The Islamic State of Iraq (ISI) imposed a blockade over the delivery of food, fuel, and construction materials to the Yezidis of Sinjar in 2006 (UNAMI 2009). A university-educated Yezidi woman managing a local nongovernmental organization (NGO) observed that many Yezidi students had to abandon their university education in Mosul because of death threats during this period (Interviewee #40, May 28, 2018).

After a Yezidi girl was stoned to death by her relatives for allegedly having an affair with a Sunni man in April 2007, a group of militants hijacked a bus carrying a group of workers, checked passengers' ID cards listing religious affiliation, let others go, and executed twenty-three Yezidi men (HRW 2009). The devastating suicide bombings in two Yezidi collective towns, mentioned in the beginning of this chapter, happened four months later.[7] Many Yezidi interviewees noted that their relations with their Sunni Arab neighbors became more constrained and distanced after the bombings. They were suspicious that local Arabs were actively involved in the planning and execution of the attacks. Consequently, Yezidis became heavily dependent on their Kurdish connections and military presence in Sinjar for their very survival.

To summarize, the fall of the decades-old Ba'th regime (*sukut*) was a mixed blessing for Yezidis. Although the new political order generated greater employment and educational opportunities and access to some resources, it exacerbated the precariousness of the community for two reasons. First, religious differences were enmeshed with partisan politics in an environment of intense sectarianization. In this environment, Yezidis, as a liminal minority, were

---

7. Some Islamist groups explicitly condemned these attacks without offering recognition to the Yezidi faith. A column in a Turkish Islamist magazine, critical of Salafi jihadist violence, reads, "Regardless of who was responsible, this attack targeting the Yezidi community was inhumane and against Islam. The fact that Yezidis are *infidels* does not justify their massacre, including of their children. Muslim's fight is with oppressors, not with infidels" (*Haksöz* 2007; my emphasis).

especially prone to discourses of hate informed by centuries-old religious stigmas. Second, the Kurdish-Arab struggle over Nineveh and the rise of Salafi jihadism left Yezidis with no option but to side with the Kurdish forces to survive. That would fuel local Sunni Arab and Turkoman scapegoating of Yezidis.

The Catastrophe (the Last Firman)

The outbreak of a vicious civil war in Syria and the discriminatory sectarian policies pursued by the Nouri al-Maliki government generated an ideal environment for the revival of extremist Salafi jihadism in Iraq by 2013 (Gerges 2016). The plains of Nineveh and the city of Mosul became the operational bases of the IS that was already well entrenched in the region since the initial days of the US occupation. The IS pursued a campaign of intimidation involving suicide attacks, ambushes, and assassinations. In early June 2014, the second division of the Iraqi army in charge of security in Nineveh collapsed in the face of an IS onslaught (Aarseth 2021). As Iraqi soldiers retreated in disarray, the IS came into possession of a vast array of advanced weapons, vehicles, and supplies. Large numbers of people, including Shiite Muslims, displaced from Mosul and Tal Afar took refuge in Sinjar (Kamal 2017, 45). The only force blocking IS advance into the Sinjar area was the presence of thousands of Peshmerga forces. Given the recent history of Salafi jihadist violence targeting Yezidis qua Yezidis, there was no doubt about the fierce IS animosity toward the group, which was cultivated by historical identification of Yezidis as unbelievers. Nonetheless, what happened in the early hours of August 3 came as a complete shock to most Yezidis.

The IS launched a coordinated attack that initially targeted Yezidi settlements south and southwest of Mount Sinjar. Sibah Sheikh Khidir and Til Ezer, directly exposed to Sunni Arab villages, were hit hard (see figure 2.3). The attacks continued throughout the morning with assaults on the villages in the north and the east of Sinjar. Some fighters were from Syria; others were Sunni Turkomans from Tal Afar. A common pattern in Yezidi testimonials is that members of neighboring Sunni tribes such as Tayy, Khawatina, and Mitewta actively took part in the assault (Interviewee #18, May 22, 2018; Interviewee #38, May 5, 2019; Interviewee #51, May 13, 2018). According to a female survivor from Kocho, the scene of mass executions and kidnappings on August 15 (see figure 2.4), Sunni Arabs from the surrounding villages were among the perpetrators (Domle 2015, 16–17; Interviewee #2, June 30, 2017). A male survivor from Kocho noted that most of the attackers were Sunni Muslims from

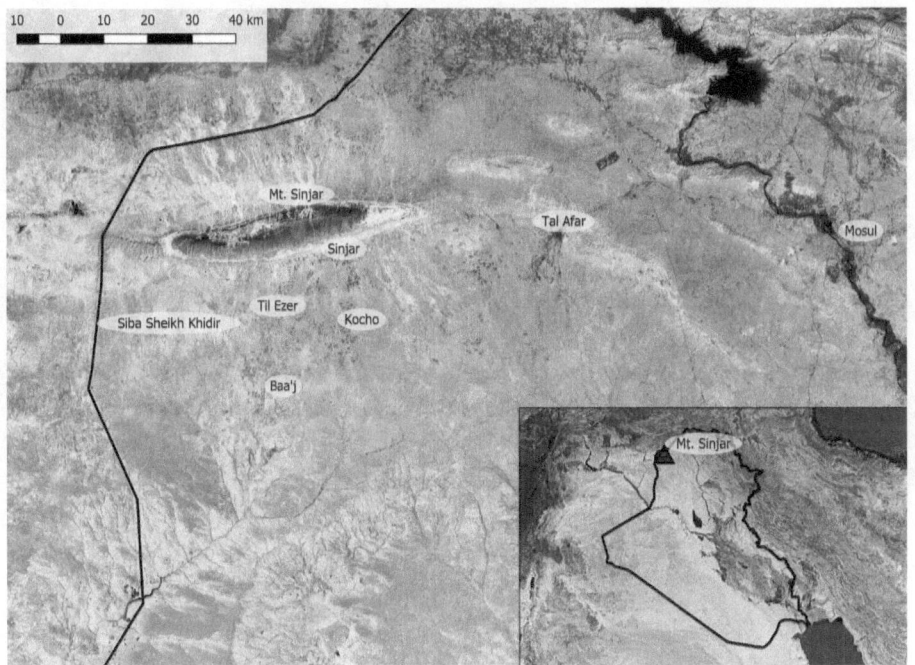

FIGURE 2.3. Mount Sinjar and northwestern Iraq (Credit: Joshua Lambert)

FIGURE 2.4. Photos of Yezidis of Kocho murdered on August 15, 2014 (Credit: Author)

neighboring villages whom the people of Kocho used to invite to their weddings (Interviewee #31, May 26, 2018). Yet another male survivor who remained in IS captivity for nine months, said that IS forces included many local Arabs he personally knew (Interviewee #30, May 26, 2018).

Some of the attackers were *kirivs*, godfathers of Yezidi boys (Domle 2015, 89–90). Yezidis practiced this custom to establish rapport with their Sunni neighbors, both Kurdish and Arab. As a kiriv held the boy on his lap during the circumcision, the latter's blood spoiled his white robe. The boy's family then washed the robes and returned it to the man—establishing a blood-based relationship between two families and precluding any attempt by the Sunni family to seek girls from the Yezidi family as wives. The custom came to an abrupt end with the attacks (Interviewee #59, April 29, 2019).

Although several Peshmerga contingents including Yezidi fighters resisted, they were soon overwhelmed in the absence of any aid. The bulk of the Peshmerga fled in panic leaving the local population to its fate. Kurdish leaders argued that Peshmerga forces were too overstretched to put up any meaningful resistance against the onslaught targeting Sinjar as the IS was also threatening Erbil, the KRG capital. For many Yezidis, however, the inability and unwillingness of the Kurdish forces to defend Sinjar would become a lingering source of disillusionment, bitterness, and betrayal. Tens of thousands of Yezidis, in cars or on foot, fled to Mount Sinjar. The ones who could not make it to the mountain were killed or enslaved (OHCHR 2016). At least 1,500 Yezidis were executed; around 6,800 Yezidis, mostly women and children, were captured by the IS. Almost 1,500 Yezidis died on Mount Sinjar from dehydration and starvation until a humanitarian corridor linking the northern side of the mountain to the PYD (Partiya Yekîtiya Demokrat)–controlled territory in northwestern Syria was established (Cetorelli et al. 2017). Hundreds of thousands of Yezidis were eventually settled in camps in Iraqi Kurdistan. An increasing number of Yezidis gradually took refuge in Western countries (Yazda 2017). The KRG established an office tasked with the liberation of captured Yezidis. A significant number of enslaved women and children were eventually liberated by ransom payments or military operations. The Yezidi religious leadership declared that all survivors, both males and females, remained full members of the community despite their captivity and forced conversion.[8] Around 3,500 Yezidis were liberated five years after the assault (Rudaw 2019). Many of them were ransomed by their families with the finan-

---

8. I obtained a copy of the statement of the document dated February 6, 2015 from the office of the Baba Sheikh in Sheikhan on September 27, 2017.

cial help of Kurdish authorities (Interviewee #22, May 24, 2018; Interviewee #52, June 1, 2018). An old Yezidi woman who lost many members of her family including his sons to IS violence and survived a year of captivity remarked that she was released as a result of an agreement between KRG and the IS that provided electricity to IS-controlled territories in exchange for captives (Interviewee #61, April 30, 2019).

There is no enigma that the IS had genocidal intentions against the Yezidis (Moradi and Anderson 2016). In its own publications, the IS provides an explicit rationale for attacking, killing, and enslaving this "pagan" group. It argues that the very existence of these people is an affront to Allah who will judge Muslims. Hence, Muslims who actively participated in the attacks would be in the good graces of God. Different from the People of the Book, Yezidis were subject to forced conversion and enslavement even if they did not fight Muslims. This is because, the IS argued, Muslim clergy categorized Yezidis either as apostates who deviated from Islam or polytheists (*Dabiq* 2014). The IS's reading of the Koran omitted key verses about peace and coexistence, cited other verses out of context, and ignored both historical and contemporary debates about their interpretations (Jacoby 2019). At the same time, as discussed above, IS portrayal of Yezidis is consistent with how Muslim religious and political authorities portrayed the group for many centuries. What made the IS exceptional in contemporary times is that its actions were directly informed by a literal reading of religious sources. It practiced what it preached. Consequently, IS brutality toward the Yezidis could be described as a reflection of its dehumanizing ideology based on well-established historical and theological justifications. Yet we cannot simply assume that the locals who committed the atrocities involving mass shootings and enslavement were subscribing to this ideological template. An in-depth analysis of their motives in light of competing arguments is necessary.

The Perpetrators

It is well documented that tens of thousands of foreign fighters joined the IS from many different parts of the world. Some of these fighters were involved in Yezidi violence, especially in the enslavement of Yezidi women and children. Female survivors of IS captivity talked and wrote extensively about how they were sold among foreign fighters. For most, if not all, of these fighters, Yezidis were complete strangers belonging to an obscure faith demonized by IS leaders. They had no prior knowledge or reasons to question IS ideologues' description of the group as devil worshippers whose adherents deserved to be converted, enslaved, or killed. For them, Yezidi captives were defenseless people they could exploit at will. When questioned about their involvement in the Yezidi atrocities, these foreign fighters expressed indifference, offered moral equivalences, or aimed to justify their actions explicitly (Duffy 2021, 35–42).

A consistent theme in survivor testimonies is the indignation generated by witnessing widespread participation of their Sunni neighbors in the atrocities. A Kurdish judge investigating IS crimes noted that his commission identified around 3,500 local people, primarily from Mosul, Tal Afar, Ba'aj, and Anbar, who were directly involved in the genocidal violence against the Yezidis (Interviewee #19, May 23, 2018). This striking pattern requires a systematic engagement with the question of how ordinary people turn against their neighbors and engage in unspeakable acts of violence. It can be argued that local Sunnis, primarily Arabs and Turkomans, had no option but to follow IS orders given its highly authoritarian and coercive character. This argument would overlook the fact that the active and willing collaboration of locals was essential to the caliphate's rise in northwestern Iraq in the summer of 2014. The IS managed to capture Mosul and its environments thanks to help from various autonomous armed groups that did not necessarily share its ideological commitments (Abdulrazaq and Stansfield 2016; Gerges 2016). The IS initiated direct assistance to Sunni Arab farmers and enabled the return of Sunni Arab tribes, who had been deported after 2003 (Mohammed 2018). Even after the IS managed to establish state-like institutions and governance over vast territories, Sunni Muslims had some agency to negotiate, evade, and contest its rule (Revkin and Ahram 2020; Aarseth 2021). So a proverbial "cog in the wheel" argument is not helpful in making sense of how local people became executioners and enslavers of their Yezidi neighbors.

Iraqi members of the IS, especially the ones from Nineveh, have had a long history of commercial, tribal, and societal interactions with Yezidis. For them, Yezidis were individuals with familiar names and faces who inhabited the same human geography across generations. These mundane relations could have played a countervailing force against IS ideological dehumanization of Yezidis. Accordingly, some Yezidi interviewees mentioned how their Sunni Muslim neighbors assured them about their safety before and during IS attacks. These neighbors let Yezidis know of the IS plans in advance so that they could flee. They also provided vehicles, treatment, and food and water to the trapped Yezidis, hid them in their houses and gardens, or facilitated the flight of enslaved Yezidi women and children. In some cases, they even risked their own lives by helping captive Yezidis escape to the KRG. A teenager whose father, brother, and six uncles were murdered, told that he and twenty-five other

Yezidis were able to escape in 2016 thanks to the help of shepherds from a local Arab tribe who were then killed by the IS (Interviewee #15, May 22, 2018).

Many other local Sunni Muslims acted viciously. The active participation of many locals in the attacks was a primary reason why Yezidis experienced heavy losses. A middle-aged woman from Siba Sheikh Khidir, the site of one of the worst massacres, said, "My father knew some of them [Sunni Arabs from neighboring villages]. They used to visit our house, sat and had tea with us. When the IS emerged, they joined them and attacked us." She and her family were briefly detained by the IS before they were released thanks to the intervention of a prominent local Arab sheikh (Interviewee #51, May 31, 2018). The sense of betrayal was particularly acute among Yezidis who realized that the IS would not be able to take their women without the collaboration of their Arab kirivs, godfathers of Yezidi boys. Many survivor testimonies contained bitterness about their kirivs who became willing executioners of the IS campaign of terror. In several cases, Yezidis who had managed to escape to Mount Sinjar returned to their villages after being given false assurances by their kirivs that they would be safe under IS rule (Interviewee #14, May 22, 2018; Interviewee #15, May 22, 2018). Given this tragic experience, in some survivor testimonies, the word *kiriv* is used to describe all Sunni Muslims who prey on their Yezidi neighbors. Other survivors used the term *malmîrati* (literally meaning, "may God ruin their house") to describe their erstwhile neighbors. This term emphatically captures their sense of betrayal.[9] An elderly woman who was briefly taken captive by the IS described Sunni Arabs of Mosul as malmîrati who had harassed and intimidated Yezidi women attending school in the city even before its fall to the IS (Interviewee #64, May 2, 2019). Another elderly woman who fled to Mount Sinjar referred to locals who suddenly appeared as IS fighters as malmîrati (Interviewee #81, May 13, 2019).

The intimate nature of violence highly complicates intercommunal reconciliation in the long run. Even if the IS was completely expelled from the Sinjar area by early 2017, local perpetrators continued to live in the area. As a result, many Yezidi survivors did not feel safe to return to Sinjar (Interviewee #57, June 5, 2018). Many Yezidis were also upset that several Sunni Arab sheikhs who had participated in the attacks switched sides, lived freely in Erbil, and declared their support for Kurdish independence referendum in 2017 (Interviewee #4, September 28, 2017). Some Yezidis engaged in revenge attacks

---

9. This curse (*ocağı sönsün* in Turkish) is also used by the older generation of Sunni Kurds to describe local people who expropriated the property of non-Muslims (Armenians and Assyrians) and kidnapped their women during World War I. In a conversation, an old Kurdish man drew a parallel between this historical practice and what the IS did to Yezidis. I thank Serdar Yıldırım for this insight.

against Sunni Arab villagers they held responsible for the 2014 attacks (Amnesty International 2018).

Hatred

Does the religious hatred argument help us understand the puzzle of the intimate violence characterizing the anti-Yezidi violence? In chapter 1, I define religious hatred as a historically formed schema fostering intense animosity toward a group because of its perceived beliefs and innate characteristics. Roger Petersen (2002, 62) argues that hatred could be a strong motive if the target group has frequently attacked with similar justification over an extended period. As discussed above, Muslim religious and political authorities have historically depicted Yezidis as a stigmatized group and justified their execution and enslavement on theological grounds. Most importantly, there is compelling evidence that such depictions played a direct role in instigating and motivating the attacks among the local people.

Many Yezidi interviewees argued that they were targeted because of their religious beliefs and practices, a recurrent pattern according to their collective memory. Hence, they labeled IS attacks as the seventy-third or the seventy-fourth firman. In the words of a Yezidi male survivor, "The IS told people near us [Sunni Muslims], 'Kill Yezidis, take away their properties, capture their girls, the door of heaven will be opened for you; you will go to heaven.' They believed that and attacked us. . . . The Sinjar attack was not a political issue; it was a religious issue" (Dinç 2017, 133–34, 220). In the words of a male Yezidi refugee living in Nebraska, "My son had a Muslim godfather [kiriv]. Not all Muslims are bad. But when ISIS came, they supported ISIS against us. It is in the ontology of Islam . . . [to] kill the infidels" (Interviewee #7, October 25, 2017). Similarly, a Yezidi woman who works as a social worker in the United Kingdom argued that locals perceived Yezidis as devil worshippers and the rise of the IS became an opportunity for them to act on their preexisting beliefs (Interviewee #11, April 20, 2018). From their perspective, local Sunnis were just waiting for the right opportunity to attack them. A Yezidi man who used to work as a translator for the US Army reasoned, "When ISIS came to Shingal, they thought that the caliphate came. They took the opportunity. They were not so powerful as to attack Yezidis previously" (Interviewee #47, May 30, 2018). Yezidis also reported that their kidnappers accused them of being "infidels" deserving to suffer and justified their enslavement with direct references to God (Domle 2015, 65, 87). A Yezidi man displaced from northern Sinjar observed, "There is nothing in Sinjar. The soil is not fertile. They could not have obtained much material gain by attacking us. We were not People of the Book (*Ahl al-Kitāb*) in their eyes. They did not care about our peaceful and friendly nature" (Interviewee #18, May 22, 2018).

These visceral testimonies are powerful but call for a critical interpretation. After all, Yezidis may have their own reasons to attribute religious motives to the perpetrators while downplaying other reasons such as Sunni Arab resentment with Yezidis' alliance with Kurdish forces. Moreover, people do not act as ethnic blocs in times of conflict, as Lee Ann Fujii (2008, 570) argues. They are embedded in local relations and power structures that shape their involvement in violence against each other. Many Sunni Muslims interacted with Yezidis daily. These interactions fostered relations that could have tamed the effects of religious stigmatization. In fact, there is variation in terms of local Sunni participation in Yezidi atrocities. Whereas many locals took part in the atrocities, some others took a stance against the IS.

Some of this variation reflects how tribal affiliations historically shaped intercommunal interactions and Sunni Arab political positions. A section of the Shammar tribe inhabited the border town of Rabia and its environs, located to the northwest of Mount Sinjar. Fleeing Wahhabi raids, the tribe moved to Sinjar from Najd in the Arabian Peninsula at the beginning of the nineteenth century. Shammar had a history of conflict with Yezidi tribes over land issues (Williamson 1974, 29–33, 182). At the same time, Shammar has been supportive of the post-2003 order. Ghazi Mashal Ajil al-Yawer, a head of the tribe, was interim president of Iraq from 2004 to 2005. According to a prominent member of the tribe, Shammar also fought against Salafi jihadist groups (Interviewee #39, May 28, 2018). Consequently, Shammar of Rabia generally did not join the attacks against Yezidis and cooperated with the Kurdish forces (Derzsi-Horváth 2017; Khalek 2017). In contrast, members of Shammar who resided in the plains south of Mount Sinjar actively took part in the attacks (Lajnat al-Buhuth wa al-dirasat 2016, 95–96). Overall, there is a clear pattern that Sunni Arabs who inhabited the villages and towns to the south and west of Mount Sinjar were active participants in the killing and enslavement of Yezidis. Out of thirty-six mass graves identified by a Yezidi NGO, twenty-nine of them were in the south (Yazda 2018). The worst atrocities took place in Siba Sheikh Khidir, Til Ezer, Girzerik, and Kocho, settlements to the south of Mount Sinjar, and Hadran, located on the western edge of the mountain (see figures 2.3, 2.5a, and 2.5b). After the defeat of the IS, Sunni communities in southern Sinjar whose members participated in the atrocities denied their involvement, offered no apology, and joined the paramilitary forces sponsored by the Shiite-dominated Iraqi government (Interviewee #38, May 5, 2019). In

FIGURES 2.5A AND 2.5B. Kocho in February 2014 (top) and in October 2021 (bottom). (Credit: Esri, © OpenStreetMap contributors, HERE, Garmin, METI/NASA, USGS)

contrast, Yezidis residing in northern Sinjar had a higher likelihood of survival as the road to PYD-controlled territory across the border in Syria remained opened (Interviewee #78, May 11, 2019).

To develop a more nuanced understanding of the patterns of local participation in the atrocities, it is important to consider political developments since the early 1990s. According to a local Yezidi researcher, the younger generations of Sunni Muslims tended to be more dismissive of customs of interreligious coexistence and developed more hostile attitudes toward Yezidis (Interviewee #38, May 28, 2018). This generational transformation could be explained as a long-term outcome of the so-called Faith Campaign initiated by Saddam in 1993. The Saddam regime instrumentalized Islam to bolster its public support in a time of deep economic crisis and international sanctions (Baram 2011; Helfont 2018). The campaign relaxed some of the restrictions over public expressions of Islam and enabled more conspicuous preaching by Salafi networks especially in western Mosul, Tal Afar, and Ba'aj (Mohammed 2018). The regime also promoted the notion of the Dajjal, a false and deceiving messiah in Islamic eschatology (al-Shakar 2019). This notion resonated with widespread views of Yezidis as devil worshippers. Salafist tendencies also gained acceptance among Ba'th officers who would play important roles in the rise of the IS and its initial military successes two decades later (*Asharq Al-Awsat* 2015).

A significant number of IS leaders had been involved in local Salafi networks that emerged during the Faith Campaign. A local Sunni Arab observed that individuals from Tal Afar occupied leadership positions in the IS and were directly involved in the assault against Kocho (Interviewee #39, May 28, 2018). A prominent IS leader was Abd al-Rahman Mustafa al-Shakhilar al-Qaduli (aka Abu Ali al-Anbari), the second-in-command of the IS who was thought to be killed in an airstrike in March 2017. He established himself as a teacher and imam in Tal Afar in the mid-1990s (Whiteside 2017; Hassan 2018). After the invasion, al-Anbari formed a local armed organization that was later merged with al-Qaeda. He expressed a virulent hatred of Yezidis. He considered them as infidels and opposed Sunni Muslim participation in the post-2003 Iraqi parliament on the grounds that it provided representation to Yezidis (a single quota seat allocated to the group) (Weiss and Hassan 2016). Similarly, Muhammad Sa'id Abdal Rahman al-Mawla (aka Abu Ibrahim al-Hashimi al-Qurashi), who became the IS leader after the death of Abu Bakr al-Baghdadi in October 2019, was from Tal Afar district. His father was a mosque preacher from the early 1980s until his death in 2001. Al-Qurashi studied Islamic studies at the University of Mosul and graduated in 2000. After the invasion, he gave sermons in the same mosque where his father used to preach. He was detained by the US forces in 2008. In 2014, he became a fierce advocate of the enslavement of Yezidi women and justified his stance on Islamic grounds. Although some Iraqi members of the IS opposed this practice on practical grounds (i.e., fearing that their own women and families may be targeted), al-Baghdadi eventually sided with al-Qurashi and sanctioned the mass enslavement of Yezidi women (Kilani 2021).

Tal Afar emerged as a bastion of resistance to the US occupation after 2003 (Patriquin 2007). In addition to Salafi networks, a legacy of the Faith Campaign, the town was home to a retirement community for low-ranking Ba'th military officers, mostly Sunni Turkoman, many of whom would join the insurgency. As Turkomans were divided along overlapping sectarian (Sunni vs. Shiite) and tribal lines, the city experienced periods of intense indiscriminate violence (Fitzsimmons 2013, 91–94; Yıldız 2017). As many Sunni Turkomans joined the IS by 2013, Shiite and Sunni Turkomans opposing the IS fled from the city. After the fall of Sinjar, the IS brought a large group of Yezidi women and children to the city that served as a distribution center of abductees. IS supporters from Tal Afar heavily participated in this large-scale human trafficking operation. For instance, an underage Yezidi girl was taken by a twenty-one-year-old IS fighter from Tal Afar (Rudaw 2020b). Another Yezidi refugee in Nebraska identified a man from Tal Afar as one of the IS militants in charge of the slave market in Mosul. The man posed as a civilian fleeing Tal Afar in 2017, as IS rule was crumbling (Dunker 2017).

Given these developments since the 1990s, local customs conducive to interreligious coexistence that could have limited the influence of Yezidi stigmas were already extremely fragile. With the outbreak of sectarian civil war in post-2003 Iraq, they became ineffective. Historically, Yezidis did not seek to convert others. At the same time, they also reacted strongly against Yezidis converting to Islam or eloping with non-Yezidis. Such reactions reflected the Yezidi fear that their demographic existence would be further diminished if they could not police their boundaries. They also aroused the ire of local Muslims and paved the way for extremist violence. As mentioned above, the 2007 suicide attacks in two Yezidi settlements happened after the killing of a Yezidi girl by her relatives on the grounds that she had a relationship with a Muslim man.

A similar dynamic took place in Kocho, the Yezidi village that was under IS siege for twelve days, from August 3 to 15, 2015. Kocho was situated among Sunni Arab settlements and had ongoing commercial and social relations with them. At the same time, Sunni Arabs did not hide their abhorrence of Yezidis and refused to eat food cooked by Yezidis on the grounds that it was not halal (Kamal 2017, 34–35). In August 2014, the local IS commander, who was from a neighboring settlement, asked the village head to convert to Islam and gave him three days to decide. He was accompanied by Dakhil, a former Yezidi singer whose elder brother had been killed by Yezidis after converting to Islam during the time of Saddam. The family had then migrated to Anbar province and became Islamized. Dakhil, now a member of the IS, sought his own version of revenge and demanded all Yezidis to convert to Islam (Interviewee

#31, May 26, 2018). Dakhil was with IS militants who raided the village, executed the men, and enslaved women and children on August 15. He was later caught and sentenced to death by a KRG court in May 2019 (Kurdistan 24 2019).

Whereas norms regulating interreligious relations have "ancient" origins, their contemporary relevance and influence wax and wane over time (S. Kaufman 2001, 12). They may lie dormant for extended periods before being easily activated by preachers and political activists in the absence of countervailing customs and religious voices calling for toleration and coexistence. In this case, the rise of Salafi jihadism in northwestern Iraq since the 1990s was a catalyst that activated anti-Yezidi stigmatization among large segments of the local Sunni Arab and Turkomans. When the IS initiated its campaign of extermination against Yezidis in the summer of 2014, it capitalized on well-entrenched religious stigmatization about Yezidis. Anti-Yezidi stigmas made mass execution, kidnapping, and conversion of the Yezidis justifiable in an environment of sectarian violence. Consequently, without considering the role played by religious hatred, an accurate and full understanding of the full repertoire of IS violence against Yezidis will be lacking.

Resentment

An argument based purely on religious hatred does not explain the timing of the attacks. I consider the role of resentment to present a more dynamic understanding of the atrocities. Resentment is a collective state of mind that emerges when a group perceives another group it despises to make *undeserved* gains in political status. It generates collective anger toward that group and a desire to level it down. It should be emphasized that resentment does not necessarily reflect the actual nature of intergroup power dynamics. A previously dominant group experiencing a status loss and losing a privileged access to power would take out its anger on a group who remains weak but is no longer content with its marginalized position and makes political demands. In this sense, resentment is a perfect scapegoating mechanism.

I suggest that an explanation combining resentment with religious hatred provides a compelling account of how political change aggravated intercommunal tensions and led to anti-Yezidi atrocities in post-2003 Iraq. During the Saddam era, when many Sunni Muslims in northwestern Iraq had stronger access to political power and enjoyed relatively privileged positions, there were no large episodes of anti-Yezidi violence. Using Susan Fiske et al.'s (2002) typology, Yezidis were a distant and despised group (low warmth) with low status (lacking competence) in the eyes of their Sunni Muslim neighbors. They were the objects of contempt and disgust but not envy. As an underdeveloped and insulated community, they were perceived to practice "archaic" and "uncivilized" rituals. Furthermore, the Saddam regime had a strong monopoly over means of coercion and did not tolerate any bottom-up acts of violence. The regime punished Yezidis who were affiliated with the Kurdish nationalist movement and pursued a campaign of demographic engineering involving Arabization of Yezidis and their forceful displacement. But there were no indiscriminate massacres targeting the community during this period. To echo Walter Benjamin, the state's positive law had no appetite for the potentially unpredictable and uncontrollable natural law in the hands of a populace.

The fall of the Ba'th rule changed the nature of intercommunal relations. As Sunni Arabs lost political power and social status, Sunni Kurds and Shiite Arabs became the main beneficiaries of the new order and made major gains. In northwestern Iraq, the 2003 invasion paved the way for the rise of Kurdish nationalism and provided some limited opportunities for Yezidis willing to join the Kurdish bandwagon. As discussed above, Yezidis became a crucial demographic bloc to the Kurdish claims over disputed territories in Nineveh province, one of the most contested areas in the entire country. A leading Yezidi politician pointed out that given the highly contested nature of elections in Nineveh, purging Yezidis out of Sinjar in 2014 tilted the demographic balance in favor of Sunni Arabs (Interviewee #20, May 23, 2018). As a Yezidi researcher put it, this political dynamic generated resentment among Sunni Arabs and Turkomans who lost their access to power and increasingly perceived the Yezidis as the lackey of the Kurds (Interviewee #38, May 28, 2018). Consequently, the IS had a strategic goal that resonated with local Sunni Arab and Turkoman Muslims—ethnic cleansing of Yezidis to undermine Kurdish claims over Nineveh.

In the context of Arab-Kurdish struggle over the disputed territories, Yezidis had no option but to side with the Kurds. Salafi jihadism presented an existential threat to Yezidis; secular Kurdish nationalism embraced Yezidis as the "original Kurds." As Yezidis sought security under Kurdish protection, they became direct targets of Sunni Arabs and Turkomans furious with Kurdish nationalist aspirations. In the words of a Yezidi male survivor, "The main reason why [Sunni] Arabs did not like us was Muslim Kurds. For instance, they did not let Arabs come to our village and take care of their business. An Arab could not visit his Yezidi friend freely. . . . We did not want the Peshmerga to behave in that manner. They made [Arabs] our enemies" (Dinç 2017, 82, 211). As observed by a Yezidi man who worked as a translator for the US Army, "After 2003, the KDP was more powerful in Sinjar. . . . They gave salaries to some families. After 2003, we [Yezidis] stopped working for Arabs; we came to work for Kurds" (Interviewee #47, May 30, 2018). A Yezidi female survivor said, "When Kurds entered Sinjar, Arabs started hating us" (Interviewee #55, June 2, 2018). Hence, local Sunni Arabs deeply resented the newly established Kurdish power in Sinjar and perceived Yezidis as beneficiaries of Kurdish patronage and protection.

Overall, we need to underlie the role of resentment to understand the outbreak of anti-Yezidi violence in northern Iraq after 2003. At the same time, it should be noted the resentment argument by itself has two limitations. First, it could not explain Kurdish participation in the anti-Yezidi atrocities. The Kurds of Iraq were the main beneficiaries of the post-2003 order. Although an overwhelming majority of local perpetrators were Sunni Arabs and Turkomans, some Yezidi survivors mentioned how Kurds also participated in the attacks (Dinç 2017, 113, 134, 146, 226; Interviewee #54, June 2, 2018). As with many other ethnicities from a diverse set of countries, Kurds from both Iraq and Turkey joined the IS in non-negligible numbers (Meleagrou-Hitchens and Alaaldin 2016; al-Tamimi 2017; Tezcür and Besaw 2020). A Yezidi couple displaced from Sinjar talked about the story of a Yezidi girl who was "purchased" and kept in captivity by a Kurdish man for several years in Halabja, a conservative town that was the site of chemical attacks by Saddam forces in 1988 (Interviewee #83, May 13, 2019). To explain this pattern, we need to refer back to the hatred argument.

Next, the resentment argument by itself falls short of explaining the full repertoire of IS violence including the abduction of children and sexual enslavement of women. Shiite Arabs and Sunni Kurds were the main groups who benefited from the postinvasion political system. Yet Yezidis, who made only minor gains, became the principal target of the Sunni Arab and Turkoman fury. This discrepancy can be explained by power asymmetries only to a certain extent. Unlike Shiite Arabs and Sunni Kurds, Yezidis were very weak and remained at the complete mercy of the IS and its local supporters. Yet power asymmetries are less helpful when it comes to explaining the full repertoire of IS violence. Although IS fighters executed large numbers of Sunni Kurds and Shiite Arabs and Turkomans, especially captured members of the security forces, and forcefully displaced many communities, including Christians of Mosul and Nineveh plains, Yezidis were the only group subject to systematic kidnapping and sexual violence that were justified exclusively on religious grounds. Consistent with a core insight of feminist scholarship, sexual violence derived from entitlement that comes with the possession of power (Rose 2021). In this specific case, sexual violence reflected power asymmetries coded into religious identities. Consequently, the combination of religious stigmatization and political resentment fueled genocidal anti-Yezidi violence.

Greed

What about the role of greed in the motives of the perpetrators? As discussed before, Sinjar remained one of the least underdeveloped regions of Iraq with very high levels of poverty, illiteracy, and food vulnerability rates (WFP 2016). Many poor Sunni Arabs from the area joined Salafi jihadist groups offering pecuniary incentives after 2003 (Interviewee #56, June 4, 2018). Meanwhile, the invasion brought greater material opportunities for the Yezidis. Some Yezidi men found work in the construction sector or informal economy of the Kurdistan region (Savelsberg, Hajo, and Dulz 2010). Others served in the Iraqi army or worked for the US army to get steady incomes despite the lethal threats they faced (Robson 2018). An increased flow of income enabled Yezidi families to build better homes and purchase durable goods and cars (Spät 2018). These limited improvements were not significant enough to make Yezidis, however, a source of envy. For sure, the attackers robbed Yezidis and looted their houses. For instance, when residents of Kocho were gathered in the school building, they were asked to surrender their cash and valuable items. Their vehicles were also confiscated. Nonetheless, given the general poverty of Yezidis, the scope of theft remained limited. Rather than being a major reason motivating the attacks in the first instance, the desire to seize Yezidi possessions is likely to be an opportunistic outcome that arose when the community was at the complete mercy of the IS. In fact, murders did not always involve robbery. A young Yezidi female lawyer from northern Sinjar survived the attacks but lost three of her uncles to IS violence. She said, "They [my uncles] were beheaded. I have photos and videos. We could only find their bodies. They had their ID cards on them. My elder uncle had five million dinars [around $4,300]. The money was still in his pockets" (Interview #85, May 14, 2019).

Yezidi properties were not the main source of IS greed. IS fighters and collaborators treated the bodies of their captives as commodities to be used, exploited, and traded. Women were repeatedly raped and forced to do all sorts of household chores and agricultural work. Small children were given Muslim names and indoctrinated and trained as fighters in military camps. Some of them lost their lives while engaging in suicidal operations on behalf of the IS. A smaller number of Yezidi men, who were forced to convert, became forced labor as shepherds and manual workers. As mentioned earlier, many captives were released only after hefty ransom payments. A Yezidi activist explained in detail that the ransoming of captured Yezidis became a significant source for local Arabs (Interviewee #21, May 23, 2018). An old Yezidi woman saved her sister from captivity after paying $20,000 (Interviewee #59, April 29,

2019). A Yezidi man paid $7,500 to have his sister released from slavery. Upon the payment of this amount, his sister was given a document indicating her status as a former slave who converted to Islam (Interviewee #52, June 1, 2018). Another Yezidi working for a local NGO observed that some local Arabs helped Yezidis but still took away their money (Interviewee #46, May 30, 2018).

From a prosaic but disturbing perspective, unrestrained access to the bodies of Yezidi women was an important incentive for local men to join the IS campaign. An Arab sheikh from the Shammar tribe, a US and Kurdish ally, reasoned that local Sunnis desired Yezidi women, especially the ones from Kocho, who had a reputation of being "beautiful" and used religion as a pretext. In his view, they would have still taken away women had people of Kocho converted to Islam en masse (Interviewee #39, May 28, 2018). The implication is that whoever gained control of the bodies of these women would have an elevated social status given the patriarchal norms. The widespread smear that Yezidis were "sexually promiscuous" (i.e., engaging in sexual activities during religious rituals and murids offering their wives to sheikhs) fostered popular portrayals of Yezidis as "immoral people." An implication of this smear is the "availability" of Yezidi women for sexual gratification of their kidnappers. Hence, religious justifications and stigmatization were indispensable factors enabling local perpetrators to engage in sexual violence against Yezidi women. Yezidi women, hitherto unreachable to Sunni Muslim men given rigid communal boundaries, became not only accessible but also a major prize for the attackers. In some cases, local men already set their eyes on Yezidi women. According to a story narrated by two Yezidi women from Til Ezer, a Sunni Arab man entered the house of a Yezidi family during the assault. The man was the kiriv of a Yezidi boy. He held the hand of the boy's mother and told her that since she had washed and returned the robe he had worn during the circumcision, she was in his heart. He was waiting for this day to return. He then took the woman away (Interviewee #62, April 30, 2019).

Sexual exploitation of Yezidi women was a motivating force of IS fighters only because this practice was explicitly condoned by their leadership on religious grounds. There is a long history of how rape has been instrumentalized as a weapon of war while being justified in reference to religious texts. In the Christian tradition, Deuteronomy 21:10–14 legitimizes rape during warfare that aimed to defile gendered hierarchy and destroy the reproductive potential of a defeated community (Reeder 2017). Without a similar justification based on Islamic tradition, IS sexual violence against Yezidis would have been haphazard and limited. In this regard, Elisabeth Wood's (2018) distinction between rape as an organizational policy and practice is informative to distinguish IS treatment of Yezidi and non-Yezidi women. The IS pursued rape as an organizational policy, "purposefully adopted in pursuit of" its objectives in a systematic manner (516). At the same time, the group targeted Yezidis much more frequently than any other with this repertoire of violence (Gutiérrez-Sanín and Wood 2017). Moreover, Yezidi victims of IS sexual violence were not just young women. A high-ranking Kurdish health official stated that his team treated victims of rape who were as young as eight and as old as sixty (Interviewee #37, May 28, 2018). In comparison, rape as practice, as different from organizational policy, captures IS sexual violence toward non-Yezidis. The IS tolerated rape of non-Yezidi women by its fighters and supporters. Meanwhile, it neither officially condoned nor provided explicit religious justifications of sexual violence against non-Yezidis. Consequently, the pursuit of sexual gratification was a factor in understanding the motives of perpetrators who relied on religious templates to single out Yezidi women as more exploitable than any other religious group.

Fear and Guilt

An observable implication of the fear argument is that Sunni Arabs and Turkomans preemptively targeted Yezidis because they feared an attack by Yezidis. An observable implication of the guilt argument is that they aimed to absolve their responsibility for serving the Ba'th regime by scapegoating Yezidis. There is no compelling evidence for either of these arguments.

The post-2003 period saw a precipitous decline in public security that contributed to the polarization of intercommunal relations. That was especially true in Sinjar, a region hotly contested between Sunni Kurds and Arabs. In the words of a Sunni Kurd from the area, "After 2003, everyone [Arabs, Kurds, Yezidis] was suspicious of each other [in Sinjar], not sure about others' intentions" (Interviewee #56, June 4, 2018). Political and military control gradually passed from Sunni Arabs to Sunni Kurds, especially after the August 2007 bombings. The KDP emerged as the dominant political and military force in the Sinjar center. Meanwhile, the widespread Sunni Arab participation in insurgencies was met with massive retaliatory violence by the occupying US forces, the Iraqi army, and Shiite armed groups. Sectarian policies pursued by the Nouri al-Maliki government that criminalized entire Sunni Arab communities and brutally repressed mass protests in these communities throughout 2013 fueled popular support for the IS (Gerges 2016). In a speech delivered in 2013, then–prime minister al-Maliki portrayed the counterinsurgency campaign in Anbar, a Sunni Arab–dominated province just south of Nineveh, as the continuation of an ancient war between "the followers of Hussein [Prophet Muhammad's grandson and the third Shiite imam] and the followers of Yazid [the second Umayyad caliph whose army killed Hussein]" (Hassan 2014). In this environment of sectarian insecurity, local Sunni Arabs lived in fear.

Yet Yezidis did not present a threat to Sunni Arabs or Turkomans given their small demographic size, weak economic status, political fragmentation, and underrepresentation. A deeply rooted sense of powerlessness was a constant theme in the narratives of Yezidis from all walks of life. Unlike Christians of Iraq, they lacked any meaningful international visibility and linkages before 2014. They lacked the organizational capacity to respond to sectarian attacks in kind. Yezidi militias, which engaged in revenge killings against local Sunni Arabs, emerged in the wake of the IS genocidal campaign. Yezidis served in the Peshmerga and Iraqi army but had no autonomy to pursue their own agendas. Although they achieved political positions in Sinjar including the district governorship, the real power belonged to the KDP. According to a leading member of the Yezidi community who served as an Iraqi minister, Yezidis were underdogs with no real political leverage in Iraq (Interviewee #42, May 29, 2018). Accordingly, there is also no strong evidence that the IS and its local supporters targeted Yezidis because they perceived the group as a security concern. There was no depiction of Yezidis as a military threat in IS publications. On the contrary, as mentioned earlier, Islamists who criticized IS atrocities argued that Yezidis should have been spared because they did not take arms against Sunni Muslims.

An opposite argument is that the very weakness of the Yezidis made them an ideal target for the IS. A Yezidi male survivor in his sixties suggested that the IS treated Christians "more leniently" because of their Western connections that could result in a military intervention (Interviewee #33, May 26, 2018). In contrast, Yezidis lacked any external patrons who would be motivated to intervene on their behalf. This argument is not compelling either. The IS treatment of Yezidis did not become less vicious after the US military intervention on behalf of the community. The IS neither softened its vicious treatment of the group nor used Yezidi captives as a bargaining chip to get concessions from the United States and other Western powers. Driven by a religious ideology, harming of Yezidis continued unabated.

Regarding the guilt argument, local communities affiliated with a fallen regime may participate in mass atrocities against a minority to vindicate themselves in the eyes of the new rulers. For instance, in Eastern Europe at the time of Nazi invasion in 1941, local communities that had collaborated with the Soviet authorities tried to realign themselves with the Nazi power by accusing Jews of being communists and preying on them. Such a dynamic was not observable in this case. Sunni Arabs and Turkomans in Nineveh were the main beneficiaries of the Saddam regime in terms of access to political power and economic benefits. However, the new political order in Iraq following the US invasion in 2003 did not necessarily identify Yezidis as a minority supportive of the ancien régime. While the security of Yezidis deteriorated after 2003, the attacks came from Sunni extremists and not from Shiite groups that emerged as the hegemonic group in the post-Saddam era. Furthermore, anti-Yezidi violence was condoned by neither Shiite nor Kurdish authorities. So there is no evidence that local Sunni Arabs and Turkomans attacked Yezidis to align themselves with the new order.

There is some historical evidence indicating that the Ba'th regime co-opted certain Yezidi groups (Interviewee #95, October 12, 2019). It established Yezidi battalions and recruited Yezidi informers in Sinjar in the 1980s (Degerald 2018, 261–63). Besides, many Yezidi interviewees expressed that they had felt safer under the secular dictatorship of Saddam. Given these patterns, some Sunni Kurds suggested that Yezidis believed in false promises of former Ba'th members, now affiliated with the IS, who were their acquaintances. In the words of a Sunni Kurd from Sinjar town, "Saddam forced Yezidis to come down the mountain and reside in collective towns. He gave them salaries and food in exchange for their support. Yezidis then got lazy; they started doing nothing. During the IS's attack, some people in Kocho thought that it was Saddam's men; that is why they did not leave" (Interviewee #56, June 4, 2018). A Kurdish social scientist made a similar assessment. He argued that some Yezidis had high positions in the Ba'th party. They welcomed the IS since they mistakenly associated it with the revival of the Ba'th (Interviewee #6, October 24, 2017). Although it is true that some former Ba'th officers joined the ranks of the IS, this reasoning reflects a "blaming the victim" mentality and aims to minimize Kurdish responsibility in abandoning Yezidis to the mercy of Salafi jihadists. Yezidis had been on the very periphery of the Ba'th regime and there is no evidence that they provided any kind of support to the insurgents in the post-2003 period. On the contrary, they suffered tremendously because of insurgent violence and were constant targets of Salafi jihadist groups well before 2014. It would be incredulous to expect them to have any illusions about the nature of the IS. At most, out of desperation, they hoped that the IS would not harm them as long as they did not resist its rule. Consequently, we can eliminate the guilt argument as a relevant factor for the attackers' motive.

Table 2.1 lists the five mechanisms discussed above and reports a summary of empirical findings for each of them based on hoop tests previously discussed. Process tracing based on triangulation of a variety of original sources including in-depth interviews with survivors, bystanders, and informed observers suggest that hatred and resentment and, to a lesser extent, greed were central to the motives of the local perpetrators participating in the anti-Yezidi atrocities.

Table 2.1 Explaining popular participation in mass violence against Yezidis

MECHANISMS	FINDINGS
Hatred	Stigmatization of Yezidis as "devil worshippers" activated by Salafi preachers in recent decades
Resentment	Anger with Yezidis perceived to serve Kurdish territorial ambitions
Greed	Rape and enslavement of Yezidi women justified on religious grounds
Threat	No evidence
Guilt	No evidence

Why Yezidis?

Modern Iraq has a long history of political violence. In some cases, the targets were non-Muslim religious minorities such as the Assyrians during the Simele massacre in 1933 (Zubaida 2000) and the anti-Jewish pogroms in Baghdad in 1941 (Cohen 1966). These episodes of violence were coordinated by state forces and involved active local participation. The pretext for violence was the perceived links of the targeted group with a hostile external power—Great Britain in the case of the Assyrians and Israel in the case of the Jews. Under the Ba'th rule inaugurated in 1968, the Iraqi state employed violence to crush all forms of dissent, especially among Shiite Arabs and Sunni Kurds. The counterinsurgency tactics increasingly entailed indiscriminate violence that targeted entire communities. The Anfal campaign in the late 1980s was the most brutal of all; it involved systematic use of chemical weapons and resulted in the deaths of tens of thousands of Kurds (Hilterman 2007). The Saddam regime repressed mass uprisings in the southern and northern parts of Iraq following the failed invasion of Kuwait in 1991 with extreme forms of violence.

Given this bloody history, it may appear surprising that both the monarchical and republican regimes from the establishment of the Iraqi state in 1921 to the 2003 invasion did not stand out as periods of violence in the collective Yezidi memory. When Yezidis talk about firmans they suffered in the past, they regularly refer to military expeditions during the Ottoman times. As explained by a Yezidi activist with Kurdish sympathies who wrote a book about the history of his community, there were no firmans from 1918 to 2007 (Interviewee #29, May 28, 2018). Hence, modern Iraq was a period of relative respite for the Yezidis. While they remained on the margins of sociopolitical and economic order, they also avoided extreme forms of violence experienced by other communities. Paradoxically, their demographic weakness, limited political ambitions, and lack of external linkages were a blessing under an authoritarian government that tolerated no dissent while keeping Islamic radical movements under check. While the regime instrumentalized Islamic symbols to boost its legitimacy (e.g., Anfal is a Koranic verse), religious justifications were peripheral to its patterns of violence.

With the US invasion in 2003, Sunni and Shiite radical movements gained ascendancy. In this political context, Yezidis qua Yezidis became particularly vulnerable to sectarian violence. As a liminal minority lacking the status of People of the Book and associated with religious stigmas, the very nature of their faith was an anathema especially for Sunni radicalism. The signs of existential danger facing the community were already palpable well before the IS onslaught in 2014. It is not a coincidence that the worst terror attack during this period, coordinated suicide bombings in 2007, targeted Yezidi settlements south of Sinjar.

Since there were no higher education institutions and lack of employment options for people with advanced degrees in Sinjar, many Yezidis seeking better opportunities needed to visit or live in Mosul for many decades. Yet for ordinary Yezidis from Sinjar, visiting and living in Mosul became very perilous after 2003. Yezidi women studying and working in the city ran the risk of being abducted and raped (Interviewee #85, May 14, 2019). Many Yezidis were killed simply because of their religious faith. A university-educated Yezidi woman described how her brother who was a lecturer in the University of Mosul survived his ordeal: "He was kidnapped by a group of extremists. They let him go only after he convinced them that he was a Christian. He was purposefully carrying only his university ID since Iraqi national identity cards have a box about religious affiliation" (Interviewee #25, May 24, 2018). Another young Yezidi woman from northern Sinjar was studying law in the University of Mosul in 2013 (Interviewee #84, May 14, 2019):

> It was during the beginning of the academic year. In the university cafeteria, a man with a long beard approached me and asked me if I am a Yezidi. When I said yes, he gave me an envelope. It has a note describing all Yezidis as "infidels" [*kafirs*] and threatening us with death unless we leave the city. . . . Ten days later, they posted a similar note on the web. It wrote, "Yezidi has no place here [Mosul]. Unless they leave, they will be killed." Consequently, most Yezidi students left.

She and some other students stayed hoping to conclude their university education. Several months later, students from the law faculty of the University of Mosul organized a picnic in Lalish. On the morning of their departure, they learned that all four drivers who were supposed to take them to Lalish were shot and killed. Three of them were Yezidis. After this incident, all Yezidi students left Mosul and transferred their registration to universities located in the KRG. Just being a Yezidi was a sufficient reason for a person to be the victim of violence in the hands of Sunni radicals in northern Iraq.

The IS left a trail of tears and blood in the lands it occupied. The international campaign to defeat the IS resulted in fierce urban fighting reducing cities such as Raqqa and Mosul to rubble (Amnesty International 2019). Hundreds of thousands of people including Christians, Yezidis, Kurds, Shiites, and Sunnis were permanently displaced from their homes. The IS destroyed Shiite religious sites and summarily executed Shiite members of the Iraqi security forces it captured. Nonetheless, there was something particularly vicious about the IS's treatment of Yezidis when compared to its treatment of other non–Sunni Muslim groups. No other ethnic or religious group was as disproportionately affected by the IS waves of violence as the Yezidis. The Christians in Mosul were initially given three options: conversion to Islam, payment of a poll tax (*jizya*), or leave the city. A month later, all Christians were forced to leave. Although their properties were plundered, no large-scale massacre of Christians took place (Barber 2016, 465–68). Yezidis of Sinjar also expected to be given an option of departure, but they were not given such a choice (Interviewee #7, October 24, 2017; Interviewee #9, December 3, 2017; Khalek 2017). Overall, the scope of killing and enslavement of Christians remained limited and less systematic. Although there were several other liminal minorities in the region, they were much smaller than Yezidis. Like Yezidis, Shabaks, a group with distinctive Shiite beliefs that originated in the early sixteenth century (Vinogradov 1974; Leezenberg 2018), and Kākā'i (also called Ahl-e Haqq), a group that originated from a Sufi order in the early fourteenth century (Leezenberg 1997), lack the status of People of the Book. The scale of IS violence targeting these groups remained more limited and less documented because of their smaller size and geographical dispersion.

Most disturbingly, there is overwhelming evidence that Yezidi women were the only group who were subject to systematic rape and abuse. In Mosul hospitals, captive Yezidi women who were subject to horrendous forms of sexual violence were conspicuous as they were the only women who were unveiled (Aarseth 2021, 106). The IS issued religiously justified regulations to its members detailing how to treat captive Yezidi women who were gathered in central areas in Mosul and Tal Afar before being distributed among IS fighters and supporters across Iraq and Syria (HRW 2015; OHCHR 2016). An international human rights lawyer investigating sexual violence in armed conflicts observed that there were no similar locations and practices for Shiite or Christian women (Interview #10, March 15, 2018). This information was corroborated by the Kurdish official in charge of the KRG office established in October 2014 and tasked with liberating individuals captured by the IS. According to the statistics his office compiled, there were a total of 6,417 Yezidis (3,548 females and 2,869 males) who were taken away by the IS. By May 2018, 3,288 of them were liberated. In comparison, his office identified fourteen cases of Christian captives who were liberated (Interview #48, May 31, 2018). There were also reports that several hundreds of Shiite Turkoman women and children were enslaved by the IS (IILHR et al. 2015, 15). Yet the scope of IS sexual violence against the Shiites remained much more limited, and social stigma associated with rape among the Shiite Turkomans resulted in greater levels of silence among liberated women of the community (Altaş 2020). There is also no evidence that IS leadership officially organized, condoned, or encouraged the rape and enslavement of Shiite or Christian women.

In summary, Yezidis became targets of extreme violence because their very identity was a source of stigma in the eyes of Islamic radicals who tapped into the widespread grievances of the Sunni community under the US occupation and the Shiite-dominated Iraqi government. With the rise of the IS and its territorial conquests in 2014, there were no inhibitions preventing the implementation of an eliminationist strategy aiming to destroy the very existence of Yezidism as a separate religious religion in a Muslim political order. In the annals of violence in modern Iraq, Yezidis were the only group who were targeted with a genocidal campaign because of their religious faith.

The Quest for Recognition

A paradoxical and unintended consequence of the IS genocidal campaign was the unprecedented international attention the community has attracted. By and large, Yezidis remained an obscure and "exotic" community until 2014. For the first time in their history, the community benefited from direct military assistance when the United States conducted airstrikes against IS forces besieging Mount Sinjar in August 2014. Several Yezidi survivors, most notably Nadia Murad, the Nobel Peace Laureate in 2018, have become prominent figures, representing the community on many international platforms. Meanwhile, diaspora Yezidis in several Western countries formed associations and engaged in lobbying activities and public campaigns to mobilize attention to the continuing plight of their people. Informed by transitional justice frames of criminal accountability and discourses of political liberalism and feminism, Yezidi activists and their allies have demanded the recognition of IS violence against Yezidis as genocide and the formation of an international tribunal that would punish the perpetrators. Although Iraq tried, convicted, and executed hundreds of people on the grounds that they were members of the IS, these trials did not specifically address crimes committed against Yezidis and lacked due process (HRW 2017a). More recently, the United Nations has sponsored a special team to conduct investigations into crimes committed by the IS. Among other tasks, this team trains Iraqi judges and prosecutors, compiles evidence by interviewing survivors and victims and studying IS documents, and supports the excavation of mass grave sites (UNITAD 2020). Besides, a law enacted by the Iraqi parliament in March 2021 provides financial assistance to Yezidi female survivors and excludes the perpetrators of anti-Yezidi atrocities from any future amnesty.

In a survey conducted among displaced Yezidis in Iraqi Kurdistan in 2016, a vast majority expressed preference for the International Criminal Court (ICC) as the forum to seek justice. Since most of the respondents had a very vague idea of what the ICC does, this preference reflected a deep distrust in domestic courts (Akhavan et al. 2020). Even though the ICC can gain jurisdiction over the crimes against Yezidis via a United Nations Security Council referral, that remains a very distant possibility. Instead, some Western courts have started to try the perpetrators relying on the notion of universal jurisdiction. Most notably, the trial of an IS member accused of participating in genocide against Yezidis started in Germany in April 2020 (Kather and Schwarz 2020). In November 2021, he was found guilty of genocide against the Yezidis and sentenced to life in prison (BBC News 2021).

Yezidi attempts to have the international community recognize the atrocities as genocide achieved some success. Several entities including the Office of the United Nations High Commissioner for Human Rights, the European Parliament, and the German parliament recognized IS violence against Yezidis as genocide. Besides, the Iraqi Kurdish leadership made the Yezidi genocide an integral aspect of its pursuit of independence from Iraq. The Ba'th regime's Anfal campaign involving chemical weapons attacks, massacres, sexual violence, and mass deportation against Kurdish people in the late 1980s has been a central discursive aspect of Kurdish pursuit of independence (Baser and Toivanen 2017). From the Kurdish perspective, the extermination campaign pursued against the Yezidis was the second time in recent history that Kurdish people in Iraq were subject to genocide. Only with an independent Kurdistan, religious minorities would be safe from extremist violence. Mir Tahsin Said Beg, the Yezidi leader who died in 2019, urged displaced Yezidis to vote in favor of the Kurdish independence in the referendum that took place in September 2017 (Rudaw 2017). Other prominent Yezidis, however, remained ambivalent about Kurdish ambitions and demanded an autonomous province for religious minorities in Nineveh under international protection (Interviewee #32, May 26, 2018; Interviewee #95, October 12, 2019).

These developments are monumental given the centuries-long history of Yezidis as a liminal minority. In the wake of IS violence, Yezidis have been elevated from an obscure community with "esoteric" and "ancient" beliefs into a persecuted minority par excellence deserving freedom of religion and protection. Tragically, these symbolic gains have come at the cost of the destruction of the traditional homeland of Yezidis, the Sinjar area, and the global dispersion of Yezidis. In the absence of any permanent political resolution, most Yezidis continue to live in camps under desperate conditions or seek refuge in Western countries (Ayhan 2021, 148–55).

Yezidi efforts to obtain recognition of their religion as a "legitimate" form of belief from Islamic authorities continue to face obstacles. Prominent Islamic clerics and institutions have explicitly condemned IS violence against Yezidis (e.g., Wilson Center 2014; Diyanet 2017). At the same time, highly stigmatized views of Yezidi beliefs, rituals, and symbols continue to be present in mainstream Muslim outlets. For instance, the Qatar Ministry of Awqaf and Islamic Affairs describes Yezidism as a "deviant sect" and claims that Yezidis have "a night which [Yezidis] call '*The Black Night*' where they turn off lights and regard prohibited things and alcoholic drinks as permissible" (Islamweb.net 2012). The website advises Muslims to shun Yezidis until they repent. Prominent Shiite leaders also express similar views. In response to a query, the office of Ayatollah Ali Khamenei, the supreme leader of the Islamic Republic of Iran, implied that Yezidis are infidels and not People of the Book.[10]

Prevailing stereotypical views of Yezidis continue to endanger interreligious coexistence and make their existence in Muslim-majority lands precarious. In Turkey, where Yezidis used to live in significant numbers before their exodus in the late twentieth century, anti-Yezidi stigmatization continues to be prevalent. Yezidis who had a sizable population in Batman, Mardin, Siirt, Şırnak, and Urfa were subject to discrimination not only at the hands of the state but also local Sunni Kurds. This dual pattern of discrimination was intensified especially with the outbreak of the Kurdish insurgency in the 1980s. In recent years, Yezidis returning from Europe were met with intimidation and threats by local villagers who joined the state's paramilitary forces who took over their land (Yağız et al. 2014, 105–17; Interviewee #95, October 12, 2019). Popular

---

10. This was in response to a written question submitted online to www.khameni.ir (received on October 27, 2017). The office of Ayatollah Makarem Shirazi, a high-ranking Iranian Shiite cleric, defined Yezidism as an ancient pre-Islamic Kurdish religion and suggested that they should be avoided in general (response received from www.makarem.ir on October 29, 2017). In contrast, the office of Ayatollah Bayat Zanjani, a prominent reformist cleric, indicated that we should treat others (including Yezidis) humanely as suggested by Islamic ethics (response received from www.bayat.info on November 6, 2017).

stigmatization of Yezidis has persisted even after the genocidal attacks in 2014. A German Yezidi scholar, who was born in Turkey, noted that he received letters from his native town praising IS violence on the grounds that Yezidis are "nonbelievers" (Interviewee #8, May 15, 2019).

A particular object of despise continues to be Peacock Angel associated with the devil in local Muslim imagination. In July 2019, a newly elected mayor of a district in Turkey with a mixed population of Kurds, Arabs, Christians, and Yezidis changed the municipal logo and removed the image of Peacock Angel. The original logo had an image of a mosque minaret, church tower, and Peacock Angel symbolizing coexistence. The new logo kept the minaret and church tower but replaced Peacock Angel with a dome. In the face of protests, the mayor replaced the dome with a cone symbolizing a Yezidi temple but did not restore the image of Peacock Angel (Günaydın 2019). In March 2020, a historical Yezidi cemetery in a neighboring district was attacked and tombstones including Peacock Angel symbols were destroyed (*Ajansa Nûçeyan a Firatê* 2020).

Almost all Yezidis of the Afrin province of Syria were displaced after the Turkish invasion in early 2018 (Rudaw 2020a). Militant groups backed by Turkey destroyed and looted Yezidi cemeteries and temples. Societal tensions also exist in Iraqi Kurdistan despite the protection offered by Kurdish authorities to Yezidis and hospitality shown by Kurdish people in Duhok and Zakho to displaced Yezidis (Interviewee #18, May 22, 2018). One of the most prominent Yezidis in Iraq remarked that many local people still perceive Yezidis as devil worshippers (Interviewee #42, May 29, 2018). Survivors who stayed in camps in the KRG lamented that they have no social relations with their Sunni neighbors who refuse to eat food cooked by Yezidis on the grounds that it is not halal. According to a Yezidi female NGO worker, another persistent common stereotype was that Yezidis are filthy and do not wash themselves (Interviewee #41, May 28, 2018).

Refik Halit Karay, a prominent Turkish intellectual, published a novel called *Yezidin Kızı* (The daughter of Yezid) in 1939 (Karay 1939). The novel is about a rich Yezidi woman returning to Sinjar from Argentina where she was born. Her father, a prominent Yezidi leader, had escaped Ottoman persecution and established himself a successful career in Argentina. The woman hoped to establish a new homeland for Yezidis in eastern Turkey. Many decades later, Yezidis continue to have an insecure inexistence in Iraq and seek security in the diaspora. In a twist of irony, Karay's fictional diasporic longing would be central to the collective psyche of Yezidis in the twenty-first century.

Chapter 3

From Massacres to Denied Victimhood
Alevis of Turkey

In November 1996, a traffic accident in Susurluk, a town in northwestern Turkey, exposed an intricate and corrupt network involving politicians, security forces, and mafioso types. The accident, which happened at the height of a brutal counterinsurgency campaign against the PKK, a militant Kurdish nationalist organization, led to a series of protests by the nascent civil society demanding greater accountability and transparency. An ingenious tactic adopted by protesters was to invite citizens to flash their home lights for a minute at nine o'clock every night. The coalition government led by Prime Minister Necmettin Erbakan was reluctant to support the protests despite Erbakan's credentials as an Islamist outsider. That was a political misjudgment, as the military establishment, which aimed to cover up the scandal, would lead an effort to topple this government in February 1997.

The minister of justice, Şevket Kazan, a close aide of Erbakan, dismissed the protesters as playing "snuffing out candles" (*mum söndü oynuyorlar*) (*Milliyet* 1997). This anti-Alevi smear has a long lineage going back to the Ottoman-Safavid geopolitical rivalry in eastern Anatolia in the early sixteenth century. The Alevis of Anatolia, some of whom expressed their loyalty to the Safavid shah, became internal enemies and targets of indiscriminate persecution by the Ottomans. To avoid persecution, some of these communities held their co-gendered religious rituals (*cem*) nocturnally in secret. This secrecy fomented a whirlwind of rumors that they were engaging in incestuous sexual orgies.

FROM MASSACRES TO DENIED VICTIMHOOD

The smear was also used to demonize other marginalized faith groups such as Mazdakism in Islamic lands and Cathars and Bogomils in Christian lands (D. Kaplan 2014).

As the minister of justice's shameful comment revealed, the historical smear persisted well into the late twentieth century. When a coalition government tried to establish a unit that would serve the Alevi communities in 1963, it faced widespread reaction from the rightist opposition and press invoking the smear of snuffing out candles. The government was ultimately forced to recall its legislative proposal (*Cumhuriyet* 2008). But why did the minister of justice use an anti-Alevi smear to refer to a civil society initiative demanding transparent governance? Claiming the mantle of the historically dominant Sunni view, he was implying that protesters were Alevis who are disloyal to the state. From his perspective, individuals who dared to express dissent and confront illicit practices by state authorities lacked sexual morality, like a "heterodox sect" that defied the Ottoman rule.

In this chapter, I argue that the persistent religious stigmatization played a decisive role in the anti-Alevi massacres that took place in Turkey in the late twentieth century. Empirically, I focus on two violent episodes in neighboring central Anatolian towns in the late twentieth century, Maraş in 1978 and Sivas in 1993. Turkey has a long history of mass violence committed by the state, most infamously in Dersim in 1938 (Goner 2017). Various armed groups also engaged in terror attacks killing a large number of civilians. At the same time, the killings in these two central Anatolian cities were the bloodiest acts of communal violence involving ordinary people as the main perpetrators. In both episodes, thousands of local people, mostly males, took part in acts of intimate violence killing scores of people, predominantly Alevis. Despite the fact that the specific dynamics leading to the massacres were significantly different, in both cases religious stigmatization fomented bottom-up violence.

There is a general hesitancy to accuse ordinary Sunni Muslims of participating in a massacre targeting Alevis both in scholarly accounts and public discussions. On the one hand, the Turkish left accuses the state of complicity and incompetency. On the other hand, the Turkish right favors the conspiratorial "provocation thesis," which suggests that internal and external enemies of the nation incited the passions of people and triggered "undesired outcomes." Although these two rival perspectives entail very different political implications, they both fail to shed light on the question of why and how religious mobilization had strong appeal and was central to mass violence in both cases. In the empirical analyses utilizing a rich variety of original sources including court documents and survivor testimonies, I highlight the agency of ordinary people who participated in the atrocities. As in the previous chapter,

I evaluate various mechanisms motivating them to violence using hoop tests. In both massacres, historically constructed and popularly available templates of Alevi stigmatization played a central role in fueling the rage of locals who were resentful of their loss of political status.

Historical Formations of Alevi Liminality

Alevis have historically been called Kızılbaş, a term used to describe the supporters of Ismail I, the Safavid shah (r. 1501–24), who don long red headgears.[1] With the late nineteenth century, Alevi, which had no negative connotations and signified one's faithfulness to Ali ibn Abi Talib, the son-in-law of Prophet Muhammad, became the predominant term and adopted at both the official and popular levels. Alevis include Turkish- and Kurdish (mostly Zazakî)–speaking groups who have historically been dispersed throughout Anatolia.[2] The Nusayris/Alawites, who are concentrated in northeastern Syria and the southeastern Mediterranean coast of Turkey, have a distinctive historical evolution that sets them apart from Alevis (Winter 2016). Nonetheless, Ottoman fatwas in the early sixteenth century did not discriminate between Alawites and Alevis and demonized both groups. The renowned Islamic scholar Ibn Taymiyyah described Alawites as heretics and polytheists (Talhamy 2010).

A defining element of Alevism has been what it does not practice and believe in as much as what it does (Ertan 2017, 167). In varying degrees, Alevi beliefs and practices have differed from orthodox Sunni teachings. Historically speaking, the Alevis have not shared Islamic beliefs in heaven and hell, fasted during Ramadan, had pilgrimage to Mecca, and prayed in mosques. Unlike Sunnis, Alevis have believed in the transmigration of souls (metempsychosis) to humans, plants, insects, or inanimate objects after death. They have also had co-gendered religious rituals and consumed alcohol, practices sanctioned by orthodox Islam. A predominant view treats Alevism as a "syncretistic folk Islam" whose origins lie in the pre-Islamic beliefs among the Turkic groups who migrated from Central Asia to Anatolia in the medieval ages. This view, which reconstructs Alevism as a heterodox form of Islam, has been internalized by some contemporary Alevi communities. At the same time, it overlooks how labeling of Alevism as a syncretic religion implies its subordination and

---

1. Kızılbaş has often been used pejoratively by Sunni Muslims but adopted by some Alevi communities. I use the term interchangeably with Alevis when writing about Ottoman times.
2. It is now common to use the term *Alevi-Bektaşi* even if Alevism and Bektaşism have distinct historical origins and interactions with the state (Gezik 2012, 220). The Ottomans managed to co-opt an important branch of Bektaşism, which had more urban characteristics and was prevalent in the Balkans.

inferiority to Hanafi-Sunni orthodoxy represented by the Ottoman and Turkish states since the early sixteenth century (for critical discussions, see Sevli 2019, 125–32; Karakaya-Stump 2020, 13–14).

The origins of Alevism could be traced back to the religiously diverse environment of the thirteenth century Anatolia and neighboring regions; the emergence of Alevism as a distinctive religious identity took place in the sixteenth century (Karakaya-Stump 2020, 4–5). The early sixteenth century saw a vast eastern expansion of Ottoman rule. The defeat of the Mamluks delivered Arab lands including Syria, Palestine, Egypt, and Hijaz to the Ottoman sultan who became the protector of the two holiest Islamic cities, Mecca and Medina. The rivalry with the Safavids, which emerged as the ruling dynasty in Iran, turned out to be more protracted (Amanat 2017, 50–59). Although the Ottomans defeated the Safavids in a major battle in 1514, the struggle over Kurdish lands, Iraq, and eastern Anatolia lasted for several centuries. The Ottoman-Safavid imperial rivalry was the critical juncture generating a historically path-dependent process that would last until the late nineteenth and early twentieth centuries. During this period, the alliance between the sultanate and Sunni religious scholars, ulema, was cemented (Kuru 2019). The Ottomans persecuted Alevi communities that were perceived to be loyal to the Safavid dynasty. The experience of Ottoman persecution facilitated the formation of a common and distinctive collective identity among groups in Anatolia whose religious beliefs and rituals diverged from Hanafi-Sunni orthodoxy favored by the Ottoman state. In this sense, the crystallization of the Sunni identity of the Ottoman rule was a decisive factor that brought dissident communities with diverse characteristics under the rubric of an encompassing Alevi identity.

The intense military and ideological rivalry with the Hapsburg Empire in the west and the Safavids in the east had a profound influence on the formation of an imperial mindset among the Ottoman elite (Şahin 2015). The rivalry was a major factor triggering the rise of Ottoman Sunnism, a process characterized by the replacement of religious ambiguity and pluralism with orthodoxy and expectations of popular conformity with this orthodoxy (Terzioglu 2012/2013; Krstić 2019; for a more qualified assessment, see Şahin 2015, 208–10). It also entailed a close and unprecedented cooperation between imperial religious and political authorities. The Safavids, with their claims of descendance from the family of Prophet Muhammad, did not only present a military but also an ideological threat to the Ottoman dynastical rule (Şahin 2015, 197). The rise of Safavid influence led to deification of both Ali and Shah Ismail among Kızılbaş communities in Anatolia in the sixteenth century (Ocak 1996, 267, 279–80). In response, the Ottomans declared themselves as the representative of "true Islam" against the Safavid "heresy" and expanded mosque construction and emphasized the importance of communal Friday prayers. The Ottoman religious authorities issued fatwas and declared Kızılbaş communities as heretical by employing a variety of pejoratives such as *zındık, kafir, mülhid,* and *rafizi* (Karakaya-Stump 2020, 275–81). These terms became part of a linguistic repertoire used to stigmatize Alevis for centuries. In contrast to Christians and Jews who were recognized under the millet system, the Kızılbaş, who were offered no such legitimacy and protection, could be enslaved and killed and had their property expropriated.

When dealing with Kızılbaş communities, the Ottomans faced the challenge of legibility, which entailed collecting and processing information about the loyalty of the population (Scott 1998). Facing Kızılbaş communities that lacked a centralized and hierarchical religious order and hid their identities to avoid persecution, the Ottomans improvised. According to an Ottoman document dating from 1581, the Kızılbaş cursed and reviled the first three caliphs and did not name their children after them, associated Sunnis with Yezid, whose soldiers killed Hussein, the grandson of Prophet Muhammad, in Kerbala in 680, held night meetings where they engaged in sexually immoral relations, and did not pray or fast (Imber 1979, 261). Their rituals (*cem ayinleri*) were portrayed as illicit and secretive gatherings where men and women engaged in sexual debauchery including incest (Karolewski 2008, 442–43). The stigmatized association of Kızılbaş with sexual immorality and incest became a rhetorical tool to label them as the enemies of both the religion and state in official documents (Baltacıoğlu-Brammer 2019, 58). These top-down practices encouraged a culture of denouncements at the popular level where pious Sunni Muslims were expected to identify and testify against their Kızılbaş neighbors in heresy trials (Zarinebaf-Shahr 1997; Karakaya-Stump 2020, 288). Stigmatization of Alevis persisted and transmitted across generations at the popular level long after the Ottoman-Safavid rivalry (M. Greene 2020, 82). A noted Western scholar, Frederick William Hasluck (1878–1920), observed how Sunnis continued to perceive Alevi congregations as occasions for promiscuous practices including orgies in the early twentieth century (Hasluck 1921, 338).

Kızılbaş rituals and doctrines became also more institutionalized and stabilized under Safavid influence (Yıldırım 2019). The process of ideological polarization made both imperial powers less tolerant of Sufism with its emphasis on spirituality and inward orientation that had used to make sectarian differences porous and bridgeable. With the gradual waning of Safavid influence in Anatolia, however, Kızılbaş was transformed from a revolutionary and proselytizing movement into a quietist and insulated community (Karakaya-Stump 2020, chap. 6). From the second half of the seventeenth century to the second half of the nineteenth century, the Ottoman concern with the Alevi communities significantly declined as the Safavids no longer posed a major security threat. Alevis, who practiced endogamy and minimized their interactions with the state, managed to preserve their distinct identity and increase their presence in different parts of rural Anatolia. In the absence of an external patron, localized entities called *ocaks* became central to the sociological and religious life of the Alevis throughout the centuries. The entities, which were "semi-formal and informal social networks and a set of morally sanctioned and quasi-hierarchically structured relationships," were led by *dedes* who were organized along charismatic family lines and treated as authority figures (Karakaya-Stump 2020, 14).

The advent of Christian missionaries and their activities among the non–Sunni Muslim subjects of the empire reinitiated Ottoman interest in the Alevis, which reached its peak during the reign of Sultan Abdülhamid II (r. 1876–1909). The sultan was fearful of an Alevi-Armenian alliance in the contested eastern Anatolia with its ethnoreligious diversity (Kieser 2001, 98, 103). For the Ottoman state, the historically marginalized and excluded "eastern Alevis" became a political problem with the increasing foreign involvement in the region. This pattern would have an enduring legacy and shape the relations between the Turkish state and eastern Alevis throughout the twentieth century (Kieser 2013).

Protestant missionaries aimed to take advantage of the historical distance between the Alevis and the Ottoman state. However, their conversion efforts did not have much success. To limit missionary influence among the Alevis and ensure their loyalty to the state, the Ottoman sultan pursued a policy of assimilation and aimed to recast Alevis as Muslims. This policy entailed conscription, mosque construction in Alevi villages, and sending of Sunni ulema to those villages (Dressler 2013, 45, 69–70; Çakmak 2019, 317–26). While ambiguity and hostility toward Kızılbaş religious beliefs persisted, the term *Alevi* with its more positive connotations and affinities with Sunni Islam gradually replaced pejoratives used to describe the community at the official level (Çakmak 2019, 46, 163). From a broader perspective, the Alevis became a target of Ottoman mission civilisatrice that aimed to establish control over peripheral groups via tax collection, conscription, censuses, and education and incorporate them into the Ottoman rule legitimized by Hanafi-Sunni Islam (Somel 2000; Makdisi 2002). These "correction of belief" (*tashih-i akaid*) policies did target Alevis, Yezidis, Nusayris/Alawites, and Druzes with varying degrees of intensity and commitment (Gölbaşı 2009; Alkan 2012, 31–33; Winter 2016, 221–24; Çakmak 2019). At the same time, Abdülhamid II formed semiautonomous cavalry units led by tribal leaders (*Hamidiye Alayları*) to ensure the loyalty of Sunni Kurds (Klein 2011). The Alevi communities, whose loyalties were suspected, were excluded from these units (Çakmak 2019, 427–28).

Sultan Abdülhamid II lost his throne in 1909. Both the Young Turks that ruled the empire until 1918 and the nascent Turkish Republic that emerged in 1923 continued the policy of assimilation toward the Alevis that replaced the charges of heresy. Although the rise of Turkish secularism made religious belief less pertinent to sociopolitical relations, belonging to the Turkish nation still depended on nominal religious identity. Alevis could be accepted as part of the Turkish nation only if they could be reclassified as Muslims (Dressler 2013, 101). This strategy is reflected in the oft-repeated contemporary assertion claiming that Turkey is a country where 99 percent of the population is Muslim (*yüzde 99'u Müslüman olan bir ülke*). Since Alevis are conventionally estimated to make around 10–15 percent of the population (Aktürk 2012, 129), this hegemonic discourse entails their de facto assimilation into Islam. (See figure 3.1 for an image of a contemporary place of Alevi worship in Istanbul, *cemevi*). The institutionalization of a certain form of Sunni Islam has made the education system inherently discriminatory against Alevis who were also marginalized in the provision of religious services provided by the state (Cesari 2021, 81–82, 92–93). The Turkish state, despite significant changes in the ideological orientation of ruling governments across decades, continues to portray Alevism as part of Islam. The regime's heavy favoritism toward the majority religion makes it very difficult for Alevis to seek recognition as an autonomous religious group (Akan 2022). For instance, in 1966, the chair of the powerful state institution in charge of regulating religious affairs (Diyanet İşleri Başkanlığı) characterized Alevism as a "political view" and argued that the Sunni-Alevi divide was no longer salient. Similar to how Baha'is in Iran and Ahmadis in Pakistan were recast as "political groups" rather than faith groups, he denied Alevism being a separate belief system and indicated that it was an old political problem (Azak 2010, 140). To counter this hegemonic Sunni discourse, Alevi intellectuals as well as secular intelligentsia claimed that Alevis who had been subject to persecution under the Ottomans were deeply committed to the republican regime.

In contemporary Turkey, the very nature of Alevism, whether it is a religion, culture, philosophy, or way of life, is subject to competing views within and outside the community (Lord 2022). Some Alevi groups treat Alevism as a religion with its own distinctive beliefs and rituals (see figure 3.2). Others treat Alevism as a cultural heritage formed by memories of victimhood at the hands of Sunni rulers and the majority (Ertan 2017). Yet some other Alevi groups that are known for their "moderate" orientations seek representation for Alevis within the existing system. They pursue official recognition of their

FIGURE 3.1. Gazi Cemevi in Istanbul, July 2008 (Credit: Author)

FIGURE 3.2. An Alevi ritual in Antalya, June 2014 (Editorial credit: Yusuf Aslan / Shutterstock.com)

worship places, *cemevleri*, and exemption of Alevi children from compulsory courses on Sunni Islam in the public education system. Yet powerful Sunni groups and Diyanet refuse to recognize Alevism as an "official sect" of Islam deserving separate services. Consequently, historical liminality of Alevis continues to hamper the community's ability to be treated with dignity and respect even in an age of politics of recognition (Taylor 1994).

Communists and Unbelievers: A Comparative Analysis of Alevi Massacres

The emergence of Alevi political activism in modern Turkey can be traced to the relatively pluralistic atmosphere of the 1960s and 1970s. The urbanization of Alevis in the second half of the twentieth century brought the gradual dissolution of the traditional and insulative Alevi dede structure. This sociological transformation facilitated the ability of leftist parties and movements to find a popular base among the Alevi youth (Aktürk 2012, 155–60; Ertan 2015). The two decades spanning the military interventions of 1960 and 1980 were the golden years of the Turkish left. Leftist organizations including unions, associations, media outlets, and armed groups became the most dynamic political forces and achieved significant popular mobilization during the 1970s (Kürkçü 2007). For the first and only time in Turkish electoral politics, a center-left party won pluralities in two consecutive elections (1973 and 1977) (Aydın and Taşkın 2015).

The "fight against communism," an umbrella term to denounce all forms of leftist politics, became a unifying mantra of all colors of the political right during this period (Meşe 2016). During the Cold War, the charge of communism entailed loyalty to the Soviet Union with its purported sinister designs over Turkey. The significant presence of the Alevis in leftist politics also triggered historically formed latent Sunni stigmas about the community. The Alevis were not just rebellious as they used to be during the Ottoman times when they were agents of Iran. They also presented an assault against public order and "national values" with their alleged immorality (Ertan 2012, 215–22). For the right, Alevism became synonymous with unbelief and communism. As early as 1950, an Islamist magazine characterized the opposition to compulsory religious courses in the public education system as an Alevi and communist position (*Sebîlürreşad* 1950). The mobilization of Sunni prejudices against the Alevis became a core strategy of the nationalist right by the late 1970s. This strategy would culminate in a series of anti-Alevi massacres in several central Anatolian cities from 1978 to 1980.

The 1980 coup brought the demise of class-based leftist politics and paved the way for the rise of identity politics transforming the patterns of political participation among the Alevis. Unlike the 1960s and 1970s when Alevi identity was subsumed under class politics, organizations and intellectuals claiming to represent Alevis as a distinct group proliferated. Meanwhile, the anti-Alevi stance of the right was softened and partially replaced by attempts to reframe Alevism within an encompassing Islamic framework. Meanwhile, the secular forces in the state bureaucracy including the military and civil society portrayed the Alevis as a bulwark against the rise of both Kurdish and Islamist movements. The growing public assertiveness of Alevis would ultimately result in a violent outburst in Sivas, a central Anatolian city that had also experienced sectarian violence in 1978.

Table 3.1 summarizes the characteristics of two major massacres targeting the Alevis of Turkey in the late twentieth century. These two cases exhibit major differences in terms of prevailing political context, cleavages, pretext for and repertoires of violence, and initiators of the attacks. The Maraş massacre took place in an environment of left-right polarization and nationalized political violence. There was a partial overlap between sectarian and ethnic cleavages, as many Alevis who became the targets of violence were ethnic Kurdish. The initial events that sparked the violence were organized by a secretive group within the state bureaucracy and far-right nationalist party. The violence lasted for several days and involved mob attacks against Alevi homes

Table 3.1 Anti-Alevi massacres in Turkey in the late-twentieth century

CHARACTERISTICS	MARAŞ, DECEMBER 1978	SIVAS, JULY 1993
Political context	Cold war polarization, peak years of leftist mobilization, a center-left party leading a coalition government	Post–cold war identity politics; Islamist party on the rise, a center-left party as a coalition partner
Cleavages	Partially overlapping sectarian and ethnic divisions (Alevi/Kurdish vs. Sunni/Turkish)	Ethnic dimension not salient
Pretext	Bombing of a movie theater attended by right-wing activists	A state-sponsored festival involving a prominent atheist literary figure
Initiators	Elements within the state bureaucracy and far-right nationalist party	Spontaneous/unidentified
Perpetrators	~15,000; overwhelmingly locals	~10,000; overwhelmingly locals
Repertoires of violence	Mob attacks against Alevi homes and businesses that lasted for several days and involving murder, rape, and looting	Primarily arson—mob burning of a hotel where festival participants took refuge
Fatalities	114 according to official figures (at least 83 of them were Alevis and leftists)	37 (33 festival participants, 2 hotel employees, and 2 attackers)

and businesses. The Sivas massacre happened under a very different political environment characterized by the rise of Kurdish violent and nonviolent mobilization and Islamist party politics. Although Sivas had a sizable Alevi Kurdish population in its eastern districts, the ethnic dimension was not a salient factor during the violence. The role of the initiators was much more limited as the mob violence evolved spontaneously. The nature and length of the violence were also very different, as the mob put a siege on and, several hours later, torched a hotel where participants in an Alevi festival took refuge. At the same time, there were two notable parallels between these two massacres. First, a center-left party was part of a coalition government in both cases. This stoked the resentment of the local population who felt politically marginalized. Second, historical templates of religious stigmatization of Alevis were central to the mobilization of the crowds in both cases.

Maraş 1978
A Decade of Polarization and Road to the Coup

Turkey in the late 1970s was rattled by political assassinations. The 1971 military intervention, following six years of a single-party government, inaugurated a period of unstable coalition governments. Eleven different coalition governments, longest of which lasted for twenty-seven months, followed each other in quick succession until the military captured power in September 1980. Under the leadership of Bülent Ecevit, CHP (Cumhuriyet Halk Partisi) adopted a populist center-left position and won pluralities in both the 1973 and 1977 elections (Bilâ 2008; Taşkın 2022). Leftist unions and associations as well as armed groups gained significant grounds during the second half of the decade. They recruited heavily among the Alevis who also overwhelmingly voted for the CHP. Leftist activists were critical of the belief system and hierarchical order of Alevism but embraced its folk poetry and musical traditions in their contentious politics (Neyzi 2002). A number of dissident Alevi *aşıks*, singer-poets, joined the socialist movement and addressed socioeconomic inequalities and political problems in their poetry and music (Avcı 2022).

Meanwhile, the dominant party on the right, the AP (Adalet Partisi), faced significant challenges from far-right parties, the Islamist MSP (Milli Selamet Partisi) and the Turkish nationalist MHP (Milliyetçi Hareket Partisi). The MSP received 12 percent of the vote in the 1973 elections and 9 percent in 1977; the MHP increased its vote share from 3 to 6 percent during the same period.

Both parties drew disproportionate support from voters in central Anatolian provinces such as Maraş, Malatya, Sivas, and Erzincan characterized by sectarian (Sunni-Alevi) and ethnic (Turkish-Kurdish) cleavages and uneven economic development (Gezik 2012, 61, 214).

The MHP pursued a strategy of tension involving extraparliamentary methods to maximize its political influence. It aimed to exploit sectarian and ethnic tensions to foment a civil war atmosphere that would bring the collapse of parliamentary order and facilitate its capture of political power. What it lacked in terms of electoral strength, it more than compensated in terms of access to state bureaucracy and street power. That strategy found a fertile environment in the so-called central Anatolian triangle, the area between Çorum, Erzurum, and Antep, where the increasing socioeconomic and political visibility of Alevis generated resentment among the historically dominant Sunni Turks (Laçiner 1978). Positions in the state and municipal bureaucracy in these cities were highly contested among rival parties (Gürel 2004, 130). The coming of a coalition led by the CHP, which replaced a tripartite AP-MSP-MHP coalition, in January 1978 tilted the balance of power in favor of the left. That fueled the rage of right-wing groups who perceived that Alevis would be the main beneficiaries of the new government and increase their presence in the state bureaucracy (e.g., *Fedai* 1979). Similar to the experience of the Weimar Republic, a fragmented and polarized civil society and party system would contribute to the demise of democratic governance in Turkey by the end of the decade (Berman 1997; Bermeo 2003).

In this increasingly polarized environment, sectarian differences gained intense political saliency. Secretive units affiliated with the MHP and embedded in the state bureaucracy organized bomb attacks in 1978. A bomb mailed to the mayor of Malatya, a religiously and ethnically diverse city, resulted in his death and led to riots that resulted in the killings of eight people in April 1978. In September 1978, sectarian attacks in Sivas, another central Anatolian city, resulted in the deaths of nine people. In May and July 1980, two waves of riots targeting Alevi businesses and homes took place in Çorum. False rumors that a mosque in an Alevi neighborhood was bombed inflamed tensions and dozens of people lost their lives (Dede 2017, 21–22; *New York Times* 1980). The bloodiest riots took place in Maraş in December 1978.

Neighbors Killing Neighbors

On the evening of December 19, 1978, a bomb exploded in a theater showing a movie popular with right-wing groups. There were no serious injuries. Following the attack, a group damaged the CHP provincial center, the post office, and several stores belonging to Alevis and leftist activists. A day later, a coffee shop attended by Alevis and leftists was bombed. On the day of winter solstice, two teachers who were active members of the leading leftist teachers' association were gunned down by unidentified individuals on a narrow street. One of them died immediately, while the other died at the hospital. The following day, a large crowd gathered in front of the hospital to organize the funerals of the two slain teachers. The funeral crowd started to march from the hospital to the main mosque of the city. However, an opposing group confronted the crowd with a rain of stones in front of the mosque. That resulted in a panic and dispersal of the funeral procession. From that moment on, the city fell under mob rule for two days.

The spark of the riot, the bombing of the theater, was organized by agents within the MHP and state bureaucracy aimed to generate chaos that would pave the way for a military takeover. In fact, the CHP-led government was forced to declare martial rule that put large parts of the country under direct military control in the aftermath of the massacre. The military leadership eventually conducted a brutal takeover in September 1980 that would completely transform Turkish politics. The coup would vindicate the MHP's strategy of undermining parliamentary politics. The junta espoused a new ideology, the Turkish-Islamic synthesis (*Türk-İslam sentezi*), that identified religious and ethnic identity as central blocs of loyalty to the state (B. Kaplan 2002; Bora 2017, 401–4).

In Maraş, the attackers faced stiff resistance in Yörük Selim, the only predominantly Alevi neighborhood in the city. Meanwhile, Alevis living in other parts of the city became easy prey for the attackers who also destroyed Alevi and leftist-owned stores and businesses in the city center. Similar to how crosses were painted on the doors of Catholic families during the Saint Bartholomew's Day massacre in 1572 (Carmichael 2009, 31) and the word *Islam* was written in chalk on the doors of Muslim households during the Adana massacres of 1909 (Der Matossian 2022, 146), the Sunni and Turkish stores and businesses and houses were marked by a crescent and star symbol in blue to keep them protected. In contrast, the Alevi houses were marked by red crosses (Salman 2015, 203, 226, 234). The perpetrators used sticks and knives and had access to guns. This pattern fits the "forward panic" model of mass violence where a stronger party overwhelms a weaker party following a period of tension and fear in a conflict setting. In this model, the weaker party does not necessarily present a physical threat to the stronger party whose frustrations and anger translate into a rush of violence in the absence of any inhibiting factor (Collins 2009). The only potentially inhibiting factor in this case was the presence of military units stationed in the city. Yet the military perceived the violence as a "mutual conflict" caused by an external conspiracy and preferred not to "take sides" (Tunç 2015, 355–58). Although the military forces stationed in the city provided partial protection to the Alevis trapped in Yörük Selim, the Alevis living in mixed and Sunni-dominated neighborhoods became easy targets for the mob. As reflected in the testimonies of many survivors, any protection offered by the army was half-hearted and incomplete. Some officers and conscripts were openly hostile to Alevis (Salman 2015, 204, 210–11, 219, 224, 227, 229, 232, 235).

An indictment prepared by the military in April 1979, during the emergency rule, provides valuable insights about the demographic characteristics and affiliations of the individuals who participated in the atrocities in different roles and capacities (T. C. Adana—K. Maraş—G. Antep ve Urfa İlleri Sıkıyönetim Komutanlığı Askeri Savcılığı Adana 1979; hereafter Indictment 1979). It lists the names of 1,114 suspects and asks for criminal penalties for 763. Hereinafter, my analysis is about these 763 suspects with a focus on 581 who were arrested. An overwhelming majority of the suspects (677) were charged with either "causing an armed riot" or "participating in an armed riot." The other charges include homicide, theft, looting, carrying illicit arms, libel, participating in an illegal march (primarily for leftist suspects), and so forth. Some individuals had multiple charges. Other judicial documents including the court decision that is more than a thousand pages remain inaccessible. The military authorities refuse to make these documents public on the grounds that they contain "secret information" and "information about private lives" despite repeated requests by activists and lawyers (Yıldız 2019).

The indictment offers a detailed narration of the violent events that took place in different parts of the city and surrounding areas. One of the most notable aspects of the massacre is its intimate and local nature. Ninety-five percent of the suspects (718 out of 760) were registered in Maraş and 98 percent of them (745 out of 761) were residents of the province during the massacre.[3] While a plurality of them had their families registered in a village (56 percent), a strong majority of them (81 percent) lived in Maraş. A majority of individuals with rural roots (66 percent) became an urban dweller by the time of the massacre, indicating how urbanization transformed socio-economic dynamics in a single generation. Residents of some of the former Armenian villages around the city also actively took part in the assaults and killings (Tunç 2015, 402–9).

---

3. Registry information of three suspects and residence information of two suspects were unrecorded. In Turkey, registry provinces indicate the regional background of one's family. It is not untypical for an individual to be born and live in Istanbul but has her registry in an Anatolian town where her (grand)parents are originally from.

CHAPTER 3

Table 3.2 Profiles of suspects in the Maraş massacre

	LEFTISTS (N = 69)	RIGHTISTS (N = 690)
Arrested*** (arrested = 1)	M: 0.25; Std: 0.43	M: 0.81; Std: 0.39
Male*** (male = 1, female = 0)	M: 0.80; Std: 0.48	M: 0.94; Std: 0.24
Age***	M: 27.4; Std: 10.4	M: 31.2; Std: 10.6 (n = 689)
Married*** (married = 1, single = 0)	M: 0.45; Std: 0.5 (n = 47)	M: 0.77; Std: 0.42 (n = 484)
Education*** (1 to 5, ranging from illiterate to university education)	M: 3.3; Std: 1.28 (n = 49)	M: 1.9; Std: 0.8 (n = 438)
Family registered in Maraş*** (registered in Maraş = 1, otherwise = 0)	M: 0.77; Std: 0.42 (n = 69)	M: 0.96; Std: 0.19 (n = 687)

Source: T. C. Adana—K. Maraş—G. Antep ve Urfa İlleri Sıkıyönetim Komutanlığı Askeri Savcılığı Adana [Indictment] (1979).
Note: M, mean; Std, standard deviation. Two-tailed tests. ***$p < 0.01$.

Table 3.2 provides a comparative overview of the demographic characteristics of leftist (i.e., Alevi) and rightist (i.e., Sunni) suspects. Although many of the leftists were Alevis, there was a significant number of Sunnis supportive of the leftist movements and parties. Almost all rightist suspects were Sunnis (primarily ethnic Turks). There were only sixty-nine leftist suspects and only fifteen of them (25 percent) were arrested. In contrast, 561 out of 690 (81 percent) rightist suspects were arrested. Moreover, most leftist suspects were charged with participating in an "illegal march"—that is, funeral procession of the two slain teachers. Only twenty-three of them (33 percent) were charged with causing or participating in armed conflict. In contrast, 650 out of 692 (94 percent) rightist suspects were subject to these charges. This asymmetry as reflected in judicial documents produced by the military, which had no sympathy for the left, starkly reveals the one-sided nature of the violence.

According to the 1975 census, the province of Maraş had a population of around 640,000 and the city itself had a population of 136,000. In the province, around 65 percent of females were illiterate, and 3 percent of women received education beyond primary school. There were only 186 women with university education in the entire province. Thirty-three percent of males in the province of Maraş were illiterate. The ratio of men with education beyond primary school was 9 percent. There were 1,139 men with university education out of a male population of 262,884 (4.3 out of 1,000). Given this demography, table 3.2 demonstrates significant differences between the leftist and rightist suspects. Rightist suspects were older and less educated. They were also overwhelmingly male (44 women and 646 men). More than

90 percent of them were either illiterate or did not attend beyond primary school. In comparison, more than 50 percent of the leftists had at least a high school education, some of whom came to Maraş either to study or to teach. This stark difference hints that increasing educational attainments of Alevis, a historically stigmatized group, was a factor aggravating Sunni resentment. The latter felt that its superior social status was now under threat.

The massacre could not be described as a "youth rage." The average age of both rightist suspects and the ones who were arrested was around thirty-one. In fact, many rightists, unlike leftists, were also married with children.[4] They included workers, shopkeepers of various sorts, farmers, self-employed artisans, and traders. A significantly fewer number of them were civil servants, teachers, students, and white-collar workers. Only a miniscule number (7 out of 558 about whom we have information) were recorded as being unemployed. Overall, these patterns suggest that the massacre had a popular appeal and mobilized ordinary men and, to a much limited extent, women against their neighbors.

A majority of the rightists were residents of Maraş city. In many cases, they were from the same neighborhoods where Alevi households were attacked. Although some local Sunnis tried to protect their Alevi neighbors with varying degrees of success, many others were actively involved in the atrocities. They identified the Alevi households, partook in the physical assaults, and joined the looting. To give some specific examples, thirteen Alevis including a ten-month-old baby boy and a ten-year-old girl were killed in the Serintepe neighborhood. The victims were members of poor families who recently moved to the city from rural areas. The indictment lists forty-five defendants from the same neighborhood. Fifteen Alevis from six different households were killed in the Yusuflar neighborhood. The indictment lists eighty-one defendants from the same neighborhood. Fourteen Alevis from four different households lost their lives in the Yenimahalle and Sakarya neighborhoods. A hundred suspects were residents of these two adjacent neighborhoods. Nine residents of the Namık Kemal neighborhood were murdered. Ninety-four of the suspects were from the same neighborhood.

In summary, the entire Alevi community of Maraş became the target of mass violence. The wide repertoire of violence involved murder, rape, forced conversions, and looting. The carnage resulted in the deaths of at least 114 people, including small children, women, and the elderly. According to the

---

4. While the information about whether suspects have children (and how many) is less complete, only 8 percent of the married rightist suspects did not have children. The mean number of children for this group (n = 353) was 3.8.

indictment, three of these fatalities were caused by factors only indirectly related to the violent incidents. Two old people died because of heart attacks caused by the upheaval. A three-years-old Alevi boy died when he and his mother were hit by a military vehicle that came to evacuate them. The rest of the fatalities were due to direct attacks. There were instances of sexual assault and rape, which were mentioned only implicitly or indirectly in survivor testimonies (e.g., Salman 2015, 209, 220, 223). The rioters also destroyed 552 houses and 289 shops (Tunç 2015, 331). Eighty-three of the killed were Alevis or leftist Sunnis; twenty-one of them were rightists; seven remained unidentified; political affiliation of three of the dead were unrevealed. After more than forty years, the burial places of the bodies of more than thirty people killed in the massacre were still unknown (Erdem 2019). The judicial process that took place under martial law resulted in thirty-seven capital punishments that were later reduced to prison sentences. Ultimately, all suspects were released. The massacre resulted in the exodus of Alevis from Maraş. An estimated fifteen thousand of them left the city in less than a year (Howe 1980).

The Motives of the Perpetrators

Barbara Slavin and Rosanne Klass (1978) covered the massacre in an article published in the *New York Times* and titled "Another 'Holy War' Erupts in Turkey" that claimed that "the violence was rooted in ancient religious enmity" between Sunnis and Alevis, who were described as "members of a Shiite Moslem sect." In contrast, scholarly studies of the Maraş massacre tends to emphasize the political, organizational, and socioeconomic dynamics at the expense of religious differences. Seyla Benhabib (1979) is critical of the journalistic and popular depictions of the violence as "a holy war" stemming from "ancient hatreds." She suggests political provocateurs capitalized on Sunni resentment with the growing visibility of Alevis due to uneven capitalist development in the region. Similarly, Burak Gürel (2004, 125; my emphasis) argues that the massacre "must not be understood as an Alevi/Sunni conflict" even if he concedes that "the religious (or sectarian) dimension was an effective factor in the *mobilization of the masses*." He argues that religious differences became more salient as a result of political polarization and socioeconomic transformations of the 1970s. Finally, a long commentary that appeared in the leftist magazine *Birikim* (1979) shortly after the massacre focuses on Sunni Turkish resentment with the perceived Alevi and Kurdish gains due to the deeper penetration of capitalist modes of production into the countryside. In a sense, all these interpretations are informed by Friedrich Engels's *The Peasant*

War in Germany ([1850] 1926) that assigns analytical weight to class differences, at the expense of religious differences, as the main dynamic shaping violent political struggles.

I concur with these perspectives that suggest how popular resentment about the increasing public visibility of Alevis instigated mass violence. At the same time, these perspectives leave the question of how provocateurs managed to mobilize thousands of ordinary people into a mob attacking and killing their neighbors and committing the worst atrocity in modern Turkey unanswered. Many victims were poor rural migrants who could not be personal objects of envy. They also lacked the capacity to present a physical threat to the majority-Sunni Turkish population. Here, I provide a novel interpretation and argue that provocateurs succeeded only because they utilized framings that neatly aligned with the preexisting sectarian animosity among the local population.

Before presenting the empirical evidence, an analogy with the post-Reconstruction lynchings that resulted in the deaths of more than 4,400 of Black people in the United States, mostly in the southern states, would be instructive. Socioeconomic resentment among poor whites (Tolnay and Beck 1995, 25) and the desire to suppress Black political representation (Dray 2003, 122–27) directly informed the motives of people who actively participated in these lynchings. Yet lynchings that typically involved the active participation of large crowds across many localities in the South were thinkable and actable only because of the deep ingrained racist norms and expectations. As it does not make sense to study lynchings without taking the entrenched legacy of color line into account, an analysis of the Maraş massacre without discussing the role of religious stigmatization in shaping the motives of the perpetrators is utterly incomplete.

The fact that attackers employed religious discourses to incite violence was extensively documented in victim and witness testimonies (Salman 2015, 182–238). A number of local clerics claimed that one could become a haji—that is, a Muslim who went to pilgrimage in Mecca—by killing an Alevi (Indictment 1979, 142). In many episodes of mass violence, unfounded and rapidly circulating rumors accusing an out-group engaging in acts of aggression play a key role in mobilizing collective rage (Tambiah 1997, 281–87; Fujii 2021, 74; Der Matossian 2022, 92–95). That was also the dynamic in Maraş. The initiators of the massacre spread rumors that Alevis were raping Sunni women in the neighborhoods they were in majority (Indictment 1979, 138, 143; *Gazete Vatan* 2012). Given deeply rooted prejudices about Alevis being sexually promiscuous, such rumors were particularly effective in inflaming religious passions. The rumors also alleged that Alevis, who lacked holy books of their own, were burning copies of the Koran (Tunç 2015, 316–18). The slogans used by the attackers were explicitly sectarian and expressed hatred of the Alevis.

The most common slogans included "Müslüman Türkiye" (Muslim Turkey), "Din elden gidiyor, vurun bu Kızılbaşları" (We are losing our religion, attack Kızılbaş), "Allahını seven, Peygamberini seven yürüsün" (Whoever loves his God and Prophet, march!), "Komünistler/Kızılbaşlar Ulu Cami'yi yakıyor" (Communists/Kızılbaşlar are burning down the Grand Mosque), "Komunist Alevileri öldürün" (Kill the communist Alevis), "Alevileri yaşatmayın" (Do not let Alevis live), "Allah için vurun" (For God's sake, attack them), "Bunları öldüren cennetlik olur" (Whoever kills them goes to heaven), "Bunlara yaşamak haramdır" (It is forbidden for them to live), and "Maraş Alevilere mezar olacak" (Maraş will be the graveyard of Alevis) (Gürel 2004, 125; Salman 2015, 184, 187, 204, 213, 226; Tunç 2015, 378–79).

The perpetrators implemented impromptu religious tests to decide whom to kill and whom to spare. On many occasions, captured Alevis were quizzed about the five requirements of Islam and forced to recite the Shahada (*Kelime-i Şehadet*). Some Alevis who "passed" these tests were let go (Salman 2015, 185, 216). The ones who could not recite were killed (Gürel 2004, 120). The captives were also forced to "convert to Islam" on the spot (Indictment 1979, 125–26, 128, 148, 156, 166, 168). Captured men were checked whether they had circumcision, similar to practices used by the mob targeting Christians in Istanbul during the September 1955 riots (Indictment 1979, 163; Salman 2015, 223; Tunç 2015, 335). Some of the killed Alevis were falsely claimed not to be circumcised (Tunç 2015, 347). The circumcision test served to check the conspiratorial "Armenian connection," fed by widespread rumors that Armenians were fomenting unrest among the population (Gürel 2004, 123). Forced conversions and circumcision checks also demonstrate that local Sunnis did not necessarily perceive Alevis as "genuine Muslims" despite the official discourse and practices that treated the latter as part of Islam.

Given the destruction of the city's sizable Armenian population six decades ago, the popular belief that Alevis and leftists were Armenians in disguise was ominous. Similar to Sivas, Maraş was home to a significant Armenian population before the genocidal Ottoman campaign during World War I. The Armenian presence in Maraş came to a violent end with the Turkish nationalist takeover of the city in 1920. In an interview with an Islamist publication a week after the massacre, a Sunni resident of Maraş who participated in the attacks suggested that violence had nothing to do with the "Alevi-Sunni conflict." He then suggested that when the Armenians took advantage of the weakness of the state and rebelled against the "Muslim nation," Muslims eventually beat them. "Had the Muslims had the intention of cleansing the Armenians, they would not have embraced them for centuries." According to his reasoning, what happened to the Alevis who made up a small minority of the population but dared to support "communists" is similar to what happened to the Armenians (*Tevhid* 1979). Such conspiratorial views associating the Alevis with the Armenians continued to be circulated many decades after the massacre. In a "documentary" shown on the state channel TRT in December 2008, Ökkeş Şendiller, an MHP politician who was one of the primary instigators of the massacre, made references to "seven uncircumcised bodies" and an Armenian leftist militant to argue that "external forces" were behind the "incident." He also slandered Hrant Dink, a prominent Turkish-Armenian intellectual and journalist assassinated by clandestine state forces in January 2007, and falsely claimed that he was also involved in the plot (*Milliyet* 2008; Bianet 2011).

There is some empirical support for the greed mechanism but no support for either the fear or guilt mechanisms. Some Alevis, who migrated to the city of Maraş from nearby villages and towns, had upward social mobility in the last decades, accumulated various economic assets, and established commercial presence (Salman 2015, 196, 202, 209–10). The massacre involved widespread looting of Alevi homes and businesses. In this sense, greed played a role in instigating mass participation in the atrocities. At the same time, many of the victims came from poor families with limited incomes. There is also no conclusive evidence that the perpetrators made significant material gains in the aftermath of the massacre. That contrasts with the killings of the Armenians that resulted in massive looting, dispossession, and property transfers in many parts of Anatolia in the 1910s and 1920s (Kerr 1973; Aktar and Kırmızı 2013; Biner 2020; Kurt 2018, 2021).

The fear mechanism is not convincing at all. Although the military and right-wing politicians and publications framed the events as a "mutual conflict" rather than one-sided violence (e.g., *İslâmî Hareket* 1979; *Tevhid* 1979), Alevis and leftists were incapable of staging a unilateral attack against Sunnis. Most importantly, there was a significant power asymmetry in favor of the latter who made an absolute majority of the population. This asymmetry was reflected in the casualty rate. An overwhelming majority of the victims were Alevis and Sunnis known for their leftist sympathies. Many of the survivors left the town permanently soon after. A secretive far-right cell was responsible for the initial provocative act, the bombing of the movie theater. The Alevis and leftists showed some resistance that resulted in pitched battles in the Yörük Selim neighborhood. However, these were defensive acts against the attackers and did not translate into indiscriminate violence. If not for the military forces, the defenses of Yörük Selim would collapse, and its entire population would be wiped out.

Finally, the guilt mechanism does not capture the motives of the perpetrators. Although there was a center-left party (CHP-led coalition government), its hold over power was shaky. Local Sunni population who supported the right-wing parties remained hostile to this government and did not seek to stay in its good graces. The CHP government was in no position to establish a new political order and shift the loyalties of the local population. In fact, the massacre paved way for the imposition of emergency rule that greatly increased the influence of the military. The government ultimately fell in November 1979 and a junta regime captured power in September 1980.

In summary, the available evidence supports an explanation combining religious hatred with political resentment. As a liminal minority, Alevis were perceived as "disloyal subjects" since the Ottoman rivalry with the Safavids in the early sixteenth century. They remained as "the intimate others" whose religious beliefs and practices were at odds with that of the Sunni majority in various parts of Anatolia. Religious stigmatization by itself did not lead to the outburst of bottom-up violence in the late 1970s, however. As long as sociopolitical hierarchy was intact, Alevis remained a marginalized but tolerated community. In this sense, hatred informed by religious stigmatization was a necessary but not a sufficient mechanism in popular participation in the Maraş massacre. Local Sunni populations became increasingly resentful of Alevis, who made some modest gains thanks to socioeconomic development, in the second half of the twentieth century. The formation of a coalition government led by the center-left CHP that was perceived to favor Alevis during a time of intense political polarization was the main factor aggravating Sunni resentment. The combination of hatred and resentment was the spark that ignited the anti-Alevi violence in Maraş. The massacre achieved its goal and resulted in an Alevi exodus. With Alevis either gone or subdued, Maraş has transformed into the bastion of the Turkish right since then.

Sivas 1993
Identity Politics on the Rise

The mob violence in Sivas in 1993 happened in a completely different political atmosphere. The 1980 military coup brought an end to leftist mobilization while facilitating the rise of neoliberal economics (Erensü and Madra 2022). The politics of distribution led by organized labor was replaced by the politics of recognition pursued by identity-based groups. The Turkish-Islamic synthesis, the ideological blueprint of the new political order, entailed the construction of mosques in Alevi villages and compulsory religious courses in public education (van Bruinessen 2000, 121–22). Meanwhile, Islamist and Kurdish movements became formidable political forces by the early 1990s. Some parts of the state bureaucracy perceived the Alevis as allies in their struggle with these contentious movements throughout the 1990s. Against Islamic revivalism, they were supposed to defend the secular order; against Kurdish revivalism, they were expected to embrace their Turkish roots (Poyraz 2005; Öktem 2008; Sevli 2019). This instrumentalization of the Alevi identity became an additional source of antagonism in the eyes of some Sunni Muslims (Ocak 1999, 148). In this context, Alevi intellectuals and groups became more assertive and demanding, seeking greater public and official recognition of the Alevis as a distinct religious group (Erman and Göker 2000).

The "Alevi memorandum" published in the *Cumhuriyet* newspaper in May 1990 was a milestone symbolizing the participation of Alevis qua Alevis in the public sphere (Ertan 2017, 95, 99). The "Alevi revival" in the post-1980 period involved the formation of various influential and active organizations vying to represent Alevis in sociopolitical affairs in both Turkey and Europe. They ranged from groups that reconfigure Alevism as a Turkish interpretation of Islam to others that formulate Alevism as a separate cultural and belief system (Ertan 2017, 176–201; Sevli 2019, 234–37). The formation of a coalition government where the center-left SHP (Sosyal Demokrat Halkçı Parti), a successor to the CHP, became junior partner in November 1991 provided access to state positions for Alevis for the first time since the late 1970s. Most notably, an Alevi SHP member became the minister of justice.

Selling Snails in a Muslim Neighborhood

Sivas, a historically important Anatolian city, turned into a provincial backwater with a stagnant economy by the late twentieth century. It had one of the highest numbers of migration rates in the country and its share of the country's population declined from 2.6 percent in 1950 to 1.4 percent in 1990. The Alevis had a particularly high migration rate due to their socioeconomic marginalization (Yiğenoğlu 1994, 96–97). The city also experienced a process of cultural ruralization as city dwellers migrated to western cities while villagers moved to the city center. These demographic changes contributed to the marginalization of the left as a political force in the city after the 1970s.

Sivas was not immune to sectarian violence that engulfed Maraş. In September 1978, false rumors about a mosque being bombed in the predominantly Alevi neighborhood of Ali Baba rapidly spread in the city. A crowd formed after the Friday prayers and attacked the neighborhood while shouting slogans such as "Sivas kafirlere mezar olacak" (Sivas will be the graveyard of unbelievers), "Kanımız aksa da zafer İslam'ın" (Victory belongs to Islam even if our blood spills), and "Müslüman Türkiye" (Muslim Turkey). Before public order was restored, nine people lost their lives. Several weeks after the violence, a pamphlet signed by Müslüman gençlik (Muslim youth) and addressing Alevis warned them not to follow communism as they used to follow the Safavid shah in the past. The perception of the Alevis as a fifth column continued to run deep and tap into readily available historical stigmas.

Following the 1980 coup that decimated the left and sped up migration from the province, Alevi sociopolitical activism in Sivas was subdued. Alongside Maraş, Sivas was one of the four provincial cities where the Islamist RP (Refah Partisi), the successor to the MSP, won the mayor's position in 1989. This local victory signified the rise of the nativist elements who were culturally conversative, xenophobic, and reactionary at the expense of religious and ethnic minorities who left the province in disproportionate numbers (Coşkun 1995, 303–33). Consequently, by the 1980s, the Islamist and Turkish nationalist forces established a clear demographic and ideological hegemony in the city.

The Alevi revival and the formation of a coalition government including the SHP provided Alevis some access to political power in the early 1990s. The coalition government appointed a new governor, who used to serve as an adviser to the SHP leader, to Sivas in February 1992. The Pir Sultan Abdal Cultural Association (Pir Sultan Abdal Kültür Derneği, PSAKD, established 1988) became a leading public organization redefining Alevism as a distinctive set of beliefs and cultural practices. In July 1993, the PSAKD, in collaboration with the minister of culture, an SHP member, and the provincial governor, invited a group of artists and intellectuals to attend the Pir Sultan Abdal Festival to be organized in the city of Sivas for the first time. Pir Sultan Abdal was a folk poet from Sivas who was executed by the Ottomans for supporting the Safavids in the mid-sixteenth century. He is an iconic figure whose legendary historical persona and work have deeply influenced contemporary Alevi tradition and popular culture. For the festival, a statue of a folk poet symbolizing Pir Sultan Abdal and his dog was erected in a central square of Sivas. According to the Alevi oral tradition, Pir Sultan Abdal's dogs (called *haram yemez*, sinless) had higher integrity than the corrupt Ottoman governor and judges of Sivas (Koerbin 2011).

Among the invitees to the festival was Aziz Nesin, a prominent Turkish author. Nesin was also one of the few public figures who openly declared his unbelief. He also became the target of a widespread smear campaign when he started to publish a translation of Salman Rushdie's *The Satanic Verses* in a Turkish newspaper a month earlier (BBC News Türkçe 1993). The book, a work of magical realism including narratives about Muhammad and the early years of Islam, was first published in the United Kingdom in 1988. It led to a series of protests among Muslim communities. Tensions escalated when Ruhollah Khomeini, the ruler of the Islamic Republic of Iran, issued a death fatwa against Rushdie in February 1989. Rushdie went into hiding. The Turkish government of the time banned the publication of *The Satanic Verses*. Despite Nesin's attempts, a Turkish translation of the book in its entirety remains unavailable as of 2023.

The participation of Nesin, an outspoken unbeliever, in a festival named after a historical Alevi figure known for his defiance of the Sunni authorities became the catalyst for religious mobilization. On June 30, a day before the start of the festival, a pamphlet signed by Müslümanlar (Muslims) was distributed in the streets of Sivas. It started with a quote from the Koran (Ahzab 6): "The Prophet is more worthy of the believers than themselves, and his wives are [in the position of] their mothers." It then accused Rushdie and Nesin of insulting the prophet and his wives. It bitterly complained that while Rushdie was hiding for his life in a non-Muslim country, Nesin, described as a servant of global imperialism, and his entourage was being hosted by the governor of Sivas. The pamphlet concluded with another Koranic reference (Nisa 76): "Those who believe fight in the cause of Allah, and those who disbelieve fight in the cause of Taghut [worshipping a false god]. So fight against the allies of Satan. Indeed, the plot of Satan has ever been weak."

Nesin spoke on the first day of the festival. He expressed his respect for all beliefs as an unbeliever, talked about the legacy of Pir Sultan Abdal, argued that Alevis have been more tolerant because they never hold power, and offered a critique of all religions including Islam for being outdated. His speech did not include any references to *The Satanic Verses* at all (Aşut 1994, 303–10). On the second day of the festival, one of the local newspapers printed a headline that read, "Müslüman Mahallesi'nde Salyangoz Satılıyor" (They sell snails in a Muslim neighborhood). A picture of Nesin while talking at the festival was beneath the title. This popular idiom indicated that Nesin shamelessly insulted sacred values of Muslim people in their homeland. Another local newspaper characterized the festival as the propaganda of unbelief and warned the festival participants that they live in country that is "99 percent Muslim" (Coşkun 1995, 382).

On the same day, a crowd (between five hundred and one thousand people according to official reports) formed following the Friday prayers in Meydan and Pasha mosques (for a map of the locations, see figure 3.3). It would grow much larger and more aggressive throughout the day (Coşkun 1995, 366–73). To borrow Walter Benjamin's terminology, as in Maraş, local people claiming

134   CHAPTER 3

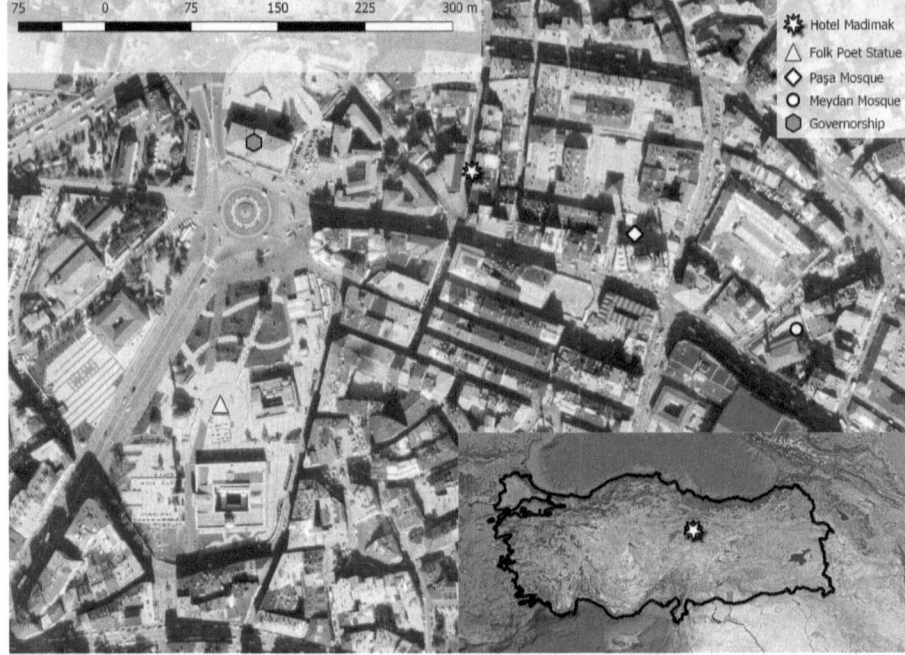

FIGURE 3.3. Main locations of the Sivas massacre (Credit: Joshua Lambert)

the mantle of natural law took control over the city as the state forces that were supposed to uphold the positive law became paralyzed. The crowd marched to the governorship, surrounded by a police barrier, and shouted slogans against the governor and Nesin. As their numbers increased to several thousands, the crowd marched to the Cultural Center, just across the street where the festival was held, and had a brief skirmish with festival attendees. Afterward, the crowd moved back to the governorship and continued to protest the governor. Later, they returned to the Cultural Center and attacked and damaged the folk poet statue, located near the center. Meanwhile, some of the festival guests including Nesin took refuge in the Madımak Hotel. When the crowd started to concentrate in front of the hotel around 4:00 p.m., it was around ten thousand strong.

The besieged guests frantically contacted government figures including the SHP leader who served as deputy prime minister. Yet the security forces failed to take decisive action to disperse the crowd. The RP mayor made a speech to appease the crowd. While expressing sympathy for their "cause," he asked people to go back to their homes. Yet the crowd continued to grow. Both the prime minister and minister of interior asked the governor to "protect" the crowd, the guests trapped in the hotel, and the security forces from one another. They requested that the security forces were not supposed to engage in coercive measures *unless necessary* (Aşut 1994, 334). According to a parliamentary report issued after the massacre, public authorities perceived the violent event as a "sectarian conflict" and feared that the exercise of force against the crowd would result in more widespread attacks against the Alevis in the city (Aşut 1994, 355; DDK 2014, 1360).

As the siege around the hotel continued, the authorities decided to take down the folk poet statue in an attempt to appease the protesters. This concession to the crowd backfired. A number of protesters took charge of the dismantled statue, dragged it in front of the hotel, and put it on fire along with several cars and furniture on the lower floors of the hotel. Meanwhile, the crowd stoned the hotel and prevented fire engines from reaching the hotel. By 8:00 p.m., flames blazed up and engulfed the hotel, as the crowd was shouting "Muslim Turkey."[5] Smoke and fire eventually killed thirty-three festival guests, including seventeen women, and two hotel employees. The victims included prominent artists, poets, and writers as well as youngsters and children (one of them being as young as twelve) who participated in PSAKD cultural activities (Çavdar 2020, 99). Two protesters were shot and killed by the police. Fifty-two guests, including Nesin, narrowly survived the carnage (Aşut 1994, 335–38). Around 9:00 p.m., the security forces managed to disperse the crowd.

Motives of the Perpetrators

Many commentators and politicians engaged in conspiratorial reasoning and sought to shift responsibility for the massacre to external forces with sinister goals aiming to exploit sectarian differences and foster instability in the country (Çaylı 2018). Yet there is no evidence that the violence was initiated and led by an organized force. Years of investigation and judicial processes did not reveal any organizational conspiracy behind the massacre (DDK 2014, 1345). Moreover, almost all people who were arrested and put on trial were locals. Most of them did not have any active roles in political parties and associations. Only a few of them were active members of the RP. Out of 130 people who were put on trial, 34 received life sentences, 47 were imprisoned for several years, and 39 were acquitted. Others remained on the run, died, or eventually benefited from statute of limitations (DDK 2014, 1326).

As in Maraş in 1978, the demographic characteristics of the perpetrators unequivocally show that they were local people. What is extraordinary about

---

5. These scenes were recorded and available at https://youtu.be/qWocQ0HCgF8 (accessed March 26, 2023).

them is how ordinary they were. The initial indictment listed 160 suspects, 94 of whom were arrested (TBB 2004, 171–89, 204–22). Most of them were part of the phalanx surrounding the hotel. Some of them directly participated in the burning of the hotel. One hundred and fifty-three of these suspects had their birth registries in Sivas; only seven of them were from other Anatolian provinces. Out of these 153 people, 84 of them were registered in a village of Sivas and 69 of them registered in the city of Sivas or other urban centers of the province. This pattern suggests that rural migrants to the city were heavily involved in mass violence, as in Maraş. Almost all the suspects (154) were residents of the city at the time. Thirty-nine of 43 neighborhoods of the city had at least one resident among the suspects. The youngest suspect was a seventeen-year-old high school student; the eldest was fifty-nine years old. They were civil servants, workers, and local shopkeepers. Only a few of them were listed as unemployed in police records. Unlike the Maraş massacre, all the suspects were men. Forty-six of them were married and thirty-nine were single (marital information of seventy-seven of them not reported). Out of 117 whose education was reported, nine of them had university education, five of them associate degrees, forty-three were high school graduates, twenty-one middle school graduates, and thirty-four primary school graduates. Overall, these demographics suggest that the mob included cross-cutting segments of the local population.

The accused maintained their innocence throughout and after the trial. Their claims of innocence resonated with the broader public in Sivas and beyond. The number one suspect, a member of the municipal assembly who instigated the crowd, remained a fugitive for many years. At the time of his death in 2011, he was living undetected in a house 650 yards (600 meters) from the old Madımak Hotel (*Hürriyet* 2011). Another individual, who was fifty-nine years old at the time of the massacre and received a life sentence, was released with a presidential pardon in December 2019. A number of public figures organized a campaign to secure his release on health grounds. The same local newspaper that accused Nesin of insulting the sacred values of people twenty-seven years ago welcomed his release with a headline that reads, "Welcome, Grandpa Ahmet" (Hoşgeldin Ahmet Dede) (T24 2020). The defense attorneys ended up taking influential political positions after the AKP (Adalet ve Kalkınma Partisi), the successor party to the RP, came to power in November 2002.

As in Maraş, explicitly Islamist slogans were frequent during the Sivas massacre. According to various reports, the crowd shouted, "Müslüman Türkiye" (Muslim Turkey), "Kanımız aksa da zafer İslam'ın (Victory belongs to Islam even if our blood spills), "İslamiyet'i ezdirmeyeceğiz" (We will not let Islam to be trampled), "İslam'a uzanan eller kırılsın" (The hands threatening Islam will be broken down), "Dinsiz vali istemiyoruz" (We do not want an irreligious governor), "Vali istifa" (Down with governor), "Şerefsiz Vali İstifa" (Down with dishonorable governor), "Şeytan Aziz" (Devil Aziz [Nesin]), and "Sivas Aziz'e Mezar Olacak" (Sivas will be the graveyard of Aziz) (Aşut 1994, 342–43). The veracity of other slogans (e.g., "We established the republic here," "We will overthrow it here," "Down with secularism," "Long live sharia," "Sharia will arrive," "Oppression will end," etc.) remains contested due to the politicization of the judicial process in the polarized atmosphere of the 1990s.

The secularist forces portrayed the massacre as the latest reincarnation of a series of reactionary uprisings exploiting religious sentiments of ordinary people against the secular (*laik*) republican state (Sarıhan 2002, 282–87). After the AKP rose to power in 2002, it aimed to replace this framing of the massacre as a reactionary uprising. It reverted to the "provocation thesis" portraying both Alevis and Sunnis as victims of repressive state policies and blamed the state authorities of the time for not respecting the sacred values of people (DDK 2014, 1392–1401). Despite their dramatically opposing political agendas, both narratives implicitly agreed that religious motives were central to the collective act of violence. Whereas the secularist narrative projected a larger political meaning to the massacre—that is, Islamists aiming to overthrow the regime—the AKP narrative suggested that the crowd whose passions were inflamed came under the influence of provocateurs to defend threatened sacred religious values (1338, 1355). Nonetheless, both narratives were careful not to present the massacre as an event triggered by sectarian animosities.[6]

Hoop tests suggest that greed, fear, or guilt mechanisms did not play any role in the Sivas massacre. Although there was widespread material damage due to rioting, different from Maraş, there was no looting. By the early 1990s, Alevis already occupied a marginal position in the city's economy. Many of the individuals who were part of the crowd were property owners and economically stable. Besides, empirical evidence supports neither fear nor guilt mechanisms. As mentioned above, political power and influence of Alevis was highly diminished in the post-1980 Sivas. Local Alevis did not pose any threat to Sunni domination of local politics. Even less so than in Maraş in 1978, they lacked any capacity for self-defense. Many participants in the festival were Alevis who came from other provinces. In both the 1991 and 1995 elections, the Islamist RP received a large plurality of the votes in the province, 38 percent

---

6. The Kurdish nationalist movement offered a distinct framing and argued the regime aimed to foment sectarian conflict to weaken the Kurdish movement (*Serxwebûn* 1993, 4–5).

and 39 percent, respectively. These ratios were well above its national performances. It also won the municipal elections in 1989 and 1994. Similarly, the guilt hypothesis does not shed light on mass participation in the atrocity. The SHP supported by many Alevis was a junior partner in the government but had no control over the police or military. Its electoral support spiked in the 1989 local elections and were in decline throughout the early 1990s. At a broader level, there was no regime change that would make Alevis scapegoats of the ancien régime.

As in the Maraş massacre, a satisfactory explanation combines hatred based on religious stigmas with resentment. The nature of Sunni resentment in the 1990s was different than that of in the 1970s. In the more recent period, the Alevi groups sought greater public and official recognition of their cultural and religious identities. The Pir Sultan Abdal Festival, which was backed by the SHP, was part of this demand for recognition in a historical heartland of Alevism. This unprecedented post-1980 Alevi visibility in the center of the city under state patronage was the main source of resentment among the local population. That was a direct challenge to the newly consolidated identity of Sivas as a conservative Sunni Muslim city.

Equally important is how the popular fury against the Alevis stemmed from historically constructed religious stigmas. The organization of an Alevi festival in the city center brought three issues to the forefront. First, the erection of a folk poet statue in the city center was a direct challenge to the post-1980 image of Sivas as a "Muslim city." The statue invoked the rebellious and disloyal heritage of Alevis. Sunni Turks of Sivas found the statue, symbolizing Pir Sultan Abdal and his dog, highly offensive (T. C. Devlet Bakanlığı 2010b, 22; DDK 2014, 1346–47). An Ottoman pasha had Abdal, an Alevi folk poet, executed for treason while a republican governor had his statue erected. Next, the participation of Nesin, the most outspoken unbeliever in Turkey, in the festival invoked the stereotypical popular views of Alevis as indigenous unbelievers amid a Muslim society. Third, the very nature of the festival was deemed offensive to Sunni sensibilities. An allegation was that the festival participants had a "noisy" Alevi folkloric dance during the collective Muslim prayer on Friday (T. C. Devlet Bakanlığı 2010b, 67). Moreover, the festival violated the norm of gender segregation as it involved a large number of women who took part in artistic exhibitions and folk plays. These co-gendered activities resonated with the long-lasting smear misrepresenting Alevi rituals as orgies. An intimidating pamphlet distributed a day before the festival accused Nesin of insulting the family of Prophet Muhammad and questioning the integrity of his wives. The implication is that Nesin and mixed-gender festival guests staying in a hotel together had no such sexual morals themselves. In the words of one of the

Table 3.3 Explaining popular participation in mass violence against Alevis

MECHANISMS	MARAŞ 1978	SIVAS 1993
Hatred	Stigmatization of Alevis as unbelievers loyal to an external power	Stigmatization of Alevis as unbelievers lacking morals
Resentment	Political activism and visibility of Alevis	Public visibility of Alevis in a state-sponsored festival
Greed	Looting of Alevi properties and leveling Alevi commercial presence in the city	No evidence
Fear	No evidence	No evidence
Guilt	No evidence	No evidence

perpetrators, the hotel fire that consumed many of them was the fire of hell.[7] Consequently, popular participation during the Sivas massacre capitalized on the historically evolving but persistent stigmatization of Alevis as rebellious and sexually immoral unbelievers. As long as the Alevis knew their place, they were tolerable. Yet the very act of Alevis seeking public recognition triggered a bloody backlash.

In summary, this available empirical evidence and hoop tests suggest that hatred and resentment were central to the motives of people who committed the atrocity in Sivas. In contrast, the other three mechanisms—greed, fear, and guilt—have no strong empirical backing. Table 3.3 summarizes the findings in both the Maraş and Sivas massacres.

Alevi Massacres in a Comparative Perspective

Mass violence was a formative force in the emergence and consolidation of the Turkish nation-state. The two decades preceding the establishment of the republican regime in 1923 was characterized by the "brutalization of political life" in an environment of deep insecurity. As the Ottoman Empire faced existential challenges, violence, ranging from assassinations to massacres, became the preferred method of addressing political conflicts (Gawrych 1986). In particular, eastern Anatolia with its multiethnic population became a zone of both state-led and communal massacres in the final decades of the empire (Levene 1998). Historians disagree regarding the question of whether the Armenian genocide was a culmination of the previous episodes of violence. Some scholars suggest that there was a linear and escalating continuum of mass killings

---

7. 1:35 at https://youtu.be/qWocQ0HCgF8.

starting with the late nineteenth century (Morris and Ze'evi 2019). Others emphasize the contingent nature of the genocidal violence that became thinkable and feasible only due to the outbreak of World War I (Turkyilmaz 2011; Suny 2015). In any case, the destruction of the Armenian population from 1915 to 1923 was the original sin that paved the way for the foundation of modern Turkey. The denial of mass violence committed against the Armenians continues to be the hegemonic position in contemporary Turkey (Göçek 2015). With the expulsion and massacres of Assyrians during the same period and the population exchange with Greece in 1924, Anatolia mostly "purified" of its almost two millennium-long Christian history would be the territorial basis of the new nation-state. The share of the Christians in Anatolia declined from 20 percent in 1912 to 2 percent in 1924 (Suny 2015, 209).

Violence against Armenians in the late nineteenth and early twentieth centuries has been unprecedented in its scope and scale. It is also different from anti-Alevi violence of the late twentieth century in several notable ways. First, the state was the organizer, instigator, and enabler of anti-Armenian violence. Most dramatically, the removal of the Armenian population from the Anatolian hinterland in 1915 was a strategic goal of the revolutionary Young Turk regime that precipitated the involvement of a wide range of local actors who had their own motivations to prey on the Armenians. As in other genocidal campaigns (Mann 2005), the mobilization of state capacity was crucial for the successful execution of mass deportations, conversions, and killings. In comparison, the state was a bystander during the Alevi massacres in Maraş and Sivas. When the Turkish state mobilized its considerable power, it brought an end to mob rule that prevailed in these two cities. That does not absolve the state of its complicity in these crimes especially given the lack of justice and accountability in the aftermath of these massacres. Nonetheless, there is a crucial difference between a state that pursues mass murder as a matter of policy and a state that fails to prevent atrocities due to incompetency and fragmentation.

Next, violence against Armenians could not be understood as the expression of centuries-long communal animosities. Most scholars downplay the role of religion as a motivating factor of perpetrators of violence especially at the elite level (Melson 1982; Levene 1998; Suny 2015; Der Matossian 2022). The Young Turk regime, which seized power in a coup in 1913, was led by a group of young officers whose primary goal was to save the territorial integrity of the empire via top-down modernization. Especially after the disastrous Balkan Wars of 1912–13, Turkish nationalism emerged as the ideological blueprint guiding the regime (Hanioğlu 2008, 166, 188). This ideological blueprint pursued ethnoreligious homogenization via nonviolent and violent means and treated societal diversity as a source of anxiety and threat (Dündar 2008;

Öktem 2022). Since its inception in the early twentieth century, Turkish nationalism has tended to treat non–Turkish Muslim populations as assimilable while excluding non-Muslim populations with their more cosmopolitan outlook and foreign linkages. This modernist nationalist vision seeking an ethnically homogenous homeland, not a religious ideology, was the driving force of the Armenian genocide.

Benny Morris and Dror Ze'evi (2019, 492) offer an opposing interpretation and identify "the ideology of Muslim supremacy" both at the elite and popular levels as a key factor in driving the massacres of not only Armenians but other Christian populations from 1894 to 1924. They write, "To judge from the available documentation, among most of the actual perpetrators of the mass murder and mass expulsion of Christians throughout the thirty-year period, the overriding motivation was religious" (494). From their perspective, the ruling Ottoman and Turkish regimes as well as the Muslim populace perceived Christians of Anatolia as subservient people whose demands for equality supported by powerful Christian states were "an affront to Allah's will and the natural order" (492–93). Jihadist mobilization was a desperate attempt to keep this order intact even at the cost of annihilating Christian presence in the Turkish territory. Their argument builds on Vahakn Dadrian's (1993, 186) claim that the "calculated appeal to religious fanaticism, intended to inflame the passions against the targeted and subordinate Christian minority group, cannot be overestimated as a major factor behind mass murder in the history of the Turko-Armenian conflict." Mark Levene (2020) takes a strong stance against this argument that religion was a central motive in the Armenian genocide. He draws attention to the broader geopolitical context characterized by the gradual disintegration of the empire in the face of internal and external threats as well as the atrocities against Muslim civilians by Christian states or groups and the flow of Muslim refugees from the Caucasus and Balkans as a result of Ottoman territorial losses.

Given this scholarly debate, two analytical clarifications are important. First, elite motives need to be separated from popular motives with some precision. Religious themes were peripheral to the justification for Armenian deportations and killings at the official level. The Ottoman rulers depicted the Armenians as a fifth column whose disloyalty presented an existential threat to the territorial integrity of the state. The preservation of the empire's territorial integrity (the homeland for the nascent secular nation-state) were the primary concerns of the Ottoman (Turkish) elites. In comparison, there is more evidence that local Muslim portrayals of Alevis as *kafirs* facilitated and justified popular violence (Aktar and Kırmızı 2013, 307; Balakian 2009, 144–46). Hence, the argument of Morris and Ze'evi about religious motives may be more relevant when aiming to make sense of the motives of the perpetrators at the popular level. Then the question becomes *how relevant* is religious hatred when evaluated in tandem with greed, resentment, and fear? Muslim animosity toward Armenians was driven by nonreligious motives including greed—that is, conflict over scarce land; envy of prosperous Armenian traders, industrialists, and craftspeople; resentment—that is, perceived gains made by the Armenians during the Tanzimat era that was inaugurated in the 1830s; and fear—that is, anxiety caused by growing Armenian political activism and their linkages with foreign powers. In a sense, popular attacks against Armenians could be a classic case of equifinality—a set of diverse motives harboring the potential for great violence. Given these dynamics, an analytical approach fleshing out the roles of emotions with more precision would be a major contribution to the literature on the Armenian massacres.

Second and most pertinent for the purposes of this book, there is no evidence that the stigmatization of and violence against Armenians (other Christian groups) represents an unbroken historical *continuity*. The Ottoman persecution of the Armenians is a *modern* phenomenon that presents a clear deviation from the millet system, which provided a relative safety to recognized non-Muslim groups of the empire. There was no major Ottoman campaign directly targeting the Armenians until 1894. During this period, the flux of large numbers of Muslim refugees displaced from the Balkans, the Caucasus, and Crimea contributed to the deterioration of intercommunal relations (Midlarsky 2005, 58). This historical pattern is very different from the one experienced by Alevis and Yezidis under Ottoman rule. Given their religious liminality, they were never incorporated into the millet system and targets of periodic military expeditions. As discussed in this and previous chapters, exclusion of and violence against both Alevis and Yezidis were justified utilizing religious stigmas since the sixteenth century.

It is also insightful to draw comparisons between the Kurdish conflict in modern Turkey and the experience of the Alevis. The projection of the state authority in Kurdish lands in the 1920s and 1930s was a brutal process. In particular, the state campaign to pacify Dersim, home to Zazakî-speaking Alevi tribal communities, in 1937–1938 involved massive displacement, mass executions, and poisonous gas attacks resulting in the deaths of at least ten thousand deaths. The campaign was based on a legal framework pursuing resettlement of ethnic minorities on the grounds of national security. It was also justified as a "civilizing mission" targeting a backward area populated by "savage" people who defied state authority for generations. Although there is no scholarly consensus about whether the campaign was genocidal—that is, carrying an intent to destroy the Alevi Kurdish people of Dersim in whole or in part (for opposing interpretations, see van Bruinessen 1994 and Turkyilmaz 2016), there is no doubt that state violence was indiscriminate and excessive. Furthermore, the ethnoreligious identity of Dersim, neither Turkish nor Sunni, was a major factor making violence more permissible and justified. Nonetheless, the official ideology that sanctioned mass violence in Dersim was secular Turkish nationalism that gained racial undertones and marginalized the public presence of religion in the 1930s (Kieser 2011).

The PKK insurgency, which erupted in 1984, has been the most serious internal security threat facing the Turkish state during its centennial existence. By the early 1990s, the PKK, which mobilized considerable popular support, was contesting the state authority not only in mountainous border areas but also in the slums of expanding Kurdish cities (Tezcür 2016). The counterinsurgency campaign of the Turkish state involved evacuations of thousands of villages, mass arrests, systematic torture, and extrajudicial executions. The state ultimately managed to roll back the insurgent gains by the late 1990s, but the PKK with its bases in Iraqi Kurdistan and northern Syria remained intact after four decades. The clashes between the Turkish state and the PKK insurgency occasionally resulted in the deaths of a significant number of security forces that fueled nationalist sentiments and calls for revenge over the years. Yet this emotionally charged atmosphere did not result in the outbreak of large-scale communal riots targeting the Kurds. Although numerous lynchings of and assaults against the Kurds in ethnically mixed localities happened (Bora 2008), the scope and lethality of communal violence remained much more limited compared to the Alevi massacres analyzed in this chapter.

One obvious factor restraining ethnic communal violence was that the civilian and military authorities had no interest in delegating their power to the populace. As Walter Benjamin would expect, the state preferred to face the "Kurdish threat" with lethal violence sanctioned by the positive law instead of vigilante violence over which it would have limited control. As long as the state was capable of leading the fight against the PKK, there was no need for ordinary people to "take justice into their hands." But this still begs the question of why the state has been more willing and capable of stopping anti-Kurdish violence in its tracks while proving complicit or incompetent during Alevi massacres. In response, I suggest the fact that an overwhelming majority of the Kurds were Sunni Muslims, whether nominal or practicing, played a decisive role not only in shaping threat perceptions of the elites but also the motives of the Turkish population.

After the emergence of the PKK, a common trope in the state propaganda was the claim that the insurgency was founded by "Armenians." This propaganda aimed not only to intimidate the Kurdish population by ominously reminding them of the tragic experience of their former neighbors but also aimed to neutralize the PKK influence among Sunni Kurds. Paralleling this trend was the tendency to associate Alevi villages with the PKK (Can and Bora 2000). In the 2010s, the AKP leader, Recep Tayyip Erdoğan, called PKK militants Zoroastrians and atheists who could not represent pious Kurds. In 2013, a university student was given a prison sentence of six years and three months. The court reasoned the student was a member of the PKK since he changed his religious affiliation to Zoroastrianism in his national ID card in 2010 (*Evrensel* 2018). Overall, from the military junta in the 1980s to the AKP government in the 2010s, the notion of Turkish-Kurdish brotherhood based on a shared religious identity was central to official discourses. From the state's perspective, the PKK has been a "religious aberration" threatening the unity of Sunni Turks and Kurds. Although the state authorities discriminate against the Kurds and remain suspicious of their loyalties, the fact that most Kurds are Sunni Muslims alleviate the state's threat perception and is central to its attempts to contain ethnic unrest (Türkmen 2020).

These attempts also resonated at the popular level. In a notorious episode, PKK militants killed thirty-eight civilians in two Sunni Muslim villages in October 1993. Consistent with the state discourse, the parliamentary commission established to investigate a series of violent events concluded that the massacres of "Muslim Turks" were committed by "Armenian-PKK collaborators." According to the commission, the Armenians aimed to take revenge for the resistance they had encountered in the area in 1918 (TBMM 1993, 88). In the aftermath of these attacks, a large mob aimed to storm the predominantly Kurdish neighborhood in the eastern city of Erzurum. The local authorities invited a prominent religious figure to speak to the angry crowd. His speech was crucial in reducing the tension and preventing a full assault. In comparison, local Sunni leaders did not play any restraining role during the anti-Alevi fury in Maraş or Sivas. Common religious bonds between the ethnic Turks and Kurds were the primary reason for the successful intervention by a local religious leader in Erzurum. Consequently, even though Islam has not been a panacea to the Kurdish conflict in Turkey, it has played a significant role in restraining violence at the communal level.

This discussion offers two core insights. First, compared to mass killings of Armenians in the late Ottoman Empire that were organized, led, or sanctioned by state actors, the initiative in the Alevi massacres was in the hands of local Sunnis who openly defied the state authority. Religious animosities based on centuries-old stigmas were central to why and how they participated in communal violence. Hence, violence against Alevis presents a more *continuous* historical pattern than violence against Armenians. Next, despite the Turkish state's heavy-handed repression of the Kurdish dissent characterized by systematic rights violations, there were no episodes of communal violence comparable to what happened in Maraş in 1978 and Sivas in 1993. A primary reason for this contrast is the state's instrumentalization of Sunni Islam to drive a wedge between the PKK and the Kurdish people as well as the moderating influence of shared religious identity in reducing Turkish perceptions of Kurds as a threatening other. Consequently, religious stigmatization featured much more prominently in Alevi massacres than episodes of violence involving the Kurds.

Denied Victimhood and Waiting Room of Remembrance

Responding to a criticism that France sacrificed a lot to keep Algeria under its control, Charles de Gaulle quipped, "Nothing dries quicker than blood" (Rieff 2016, 122). What he meant was that the French people would forget their deaths and move on. In an age of decolonization, his words were prescient. In Turkey, however, the struggle over the remembrance of the Maraş and Sivas massacres endures. As in the American South, there is an ongoing struggle over the "ownership of the past," which entails a "stubborn determination to control its telling and retelling" (Fujii 2021, 107). The Alevi demands for victimhood recognition have met with opposition and deflection from the broader society and the ruling AKP government in the last two decades. The AKP discourse identifies "both sides" as victims of conspiracies aiming to undermine public order and poison sectarian relations. This superficially balanced position generates a false moral equivalency and aims to deny Alevis the status of victimhood. It also characterizes any attempt to commemorate the massacres beyond the official channels as subversive. Consequently, the Alevi politics of remembrance, which is informed by a collective memory of victimhood (Yildiz and Verkuyten 2011; Çavdar 2020), continues to occupy a liminal public space. It is tolerated only when it unremembers that victims were targeted because of their Alevi identities. To borrow from Judith Butler (2009, 23), Alevi lives are characterized by high levels of *precarity*, a politically induced condition that makes them exposed to greater violence. Their lives remain *ungrievable*.

In the Maraş case, the prevailing attitude among rightist politicians and the military was to reframe the event as a bloody conflict between two sides. This has a remarkable similarity with how an Ottoman commission framed the massacre of the Armenians of Adana in 1909 (Der Matossian 2022, 190). Süleyman Demirel, the AP leader who would be president during the Sivas massacre, accused the CHP government of being lenient with the leftists who were supposedly behind the violence (*New York Times* 1978). A high-ranking general who arrived in the city as the massacre was unfolding wrote in his report that extremist elements from both sides were responsible for the violence. He described these sides as "Alevis" and the "people" (Tunç 2015, 372–75). The military leadership also described "Alevis" as an "internal threat" in a report prepared in June 1980. Alongside a crude map showing sectarian distribution in eastern Turkey, Alevis were depicted as a group who supported Kurdish secessionist movements and were provoked by external forces (Benli 2013). Similarly, the Turkish National Intelligence Organization, in a report written a week after the massacre, described the events as a "Turkish-Kurdish conflict" (*Gazete Vatan* 2012).

In this framing, no side could have a rightful claim to victimhood because it was as guilty as the other side. The Alevis were responsible for their own deaths because they deliberately provoked the Sunnis and insulted their "sacred values."[8] This "provocation paradigm" continues to inform how rightist politicians aim to discredit any public activity and demonstration challenging their political and social hegemony. Hence, the commemorations of the event remain contested after more than four decades. A group of AKP parliamentarians representing the province of Maraş held a press conference in 2018, on the fortieth anniversary of the massacre. Similar to how the Tulsa massacre of 1921 that destroyed the Black community in the city was called a "riot" for many decades, they relabeled the massacre as "incidents." For them, the victims of the "incidents" were "our innocent people who were Alevis, Sunnis, Kurds, and Turks." The parliamentarians also labeled an Alevi organization calling for a public commemoration of the massacre in the city as "provocateurs" stoking tensions (*Gazete Manifesto* 2018). As in Sivas, the remaining Alevis in the city were subdued. The first and only *cemevi* in the city was opened in August 2022.

The controversy about the women's march in Istanbul on International Women's Day on March 8, 2019 offers a striking example of the continuing relevance of the provocation paradigm. The governor did not issue a permit for the activists to use the iconic İstiklal Street for their evening march despite the fact that such permits were duly issued in previous years. The police established barricades and used tear gas and plastic bullets to keep attendees off İstiklal. The activists protested the police intervention with whistles and slo-

---

8. This framing of massacre as a mutual conflict is also prevalent in the indictment prepared against leaders of the 1980 military intervention in 2012. Although the indictment holds the junta responsible for fomenting unrest and provoking both sides against each other, it conveniently overlooks the fact that most acts of mass violence targeted leftist groups and sidesteps the agency of ordinary individuals who participated in these acts of violence. For a summary of the indictment, see https://www.failibelli.org/dava/12-eylul-davasi (accessed March 26, 2023).

gans, as calls for the evening prayer were broadcasted from the nearby mosques. The pro-government press then falsely claimed that women protested the call for prayers and accused them of insulting the sacred values of people. A few days later, the minister of interior repeated this accusation and said, "Unfortunately, this ugly event happened. These events make me anxious. Do you know how the Kahramanmaraş incident [sic] erupted? I read how the Kahramanmaraş and Çorum incidents erupted" (*Cumhuriyet* 2019). According to his interpretation, bloody events are likely to happen when a group of provocateurs openly defies symbols and practices dear to the public. When religious passions are awakened, they could be hardly contained. Consequently, public order requires that "marginal elements" know their places. If they do cross the red lines, they would be responsible for the violence they would suffer. The minister of interior's invocation of the Maraş massacre of 1978 demonstrates how its constructed memory continues to intimidate and suppress peaceful dissent more than forty years later. Rather than being an aberration, such references by AKP leaders to pious and loyal citizens, a sort of "moral majority," who could react with justified anger to "provocative actions" of impious minorities have been increasingly frequent in the post-2013 period (Tokdoğan 2018). If these citizens could no longer contain their rage in the face of such "provocations," defying the expectations of Walter Benjamin, then the state would temporarily suspend its monopoly over violence and let vigilante justice take its course (Bora 2008, 35–36).

The ways in which the Sivas massacre is remembered exhibits some striking parallels to the construction of public memory about the Maraş massacre (see figure 3.4). Most visibly, the "provocation paradigm" continues to be central to influential discourses about the violent episode. In a parliamentary session held four days after the massacre, Muhsin Yazıcıoğlu, the leader of a far-right party and a leading figure of the MHP youth organizations in the late 1970s, characterized the festival as "a festival of unbelief." According to him, the violence took place because of Nesin's provocation and had nothing to do with Alevi-Sunni differences (TBB 2004, 135–41).

A similar stance was also prevalent in the AKP's so-called "Alevi openings" (2007–11) that aimed to recast Alevism within a Turkish-Islamic framework (Lord 2017). These openings failed to respond to any major Alevi demands including the legal recognition of Alevi places of worship (*cemevleri*), the end of compulsory mosque building in Alevi villages, the removal of mandatory religious courses from curricula, the elimination or reformation of Diyanet, and the conversion of Madımak into a remembrance museum (Karakaya-Stump 2018). Instead, the overriding political goal was to promote social unity by having Alevis define themselves as Muslims (Çavdar 2020, 83). The only concrete

FIGURE 3.4. A commemoration on the twenty-fourth anniversary of the Sivas massacre in Ankara, July 2017 (Editorial credit: Gencyilmaz Baris/ Shutterstock.com)

change that happened as a result of the AKP's Alevi openings is the expropriation of the building of the old Madımak Hotel and the closure of the kebab restaurant that occupied the lower floors for years. Instead of transforming the building into a museum as requested by Alevi organizations, however, the government opened up a Science and Cultural Center in 2011. On the first floor of this center, a "memory corner" with two large panels on the wall listing the names of the *thirty-seven* (not thirty-three or thirty-five) individuals killed on July 2, 1993 was constructed. The first name on the list was an individual who was part of the crowd who besieged and burned the hotel. He and another attacker received the same posthumous treatment as the people who died in the burning hotel. That way, when people visit the building, they were expected to pay their respects to "all victims." The then–Sivas governor who oversaw the opening of the "memorial" defended this practice as "a human-oriented approach not differentiating among the dead" (Yalçınkaya 2011). Not surprisingly, this was a major affront to the victims' families.[9] As their demands to have the Madımak Hotel transformed into a museum was denied, some of them transformed rooms in their homes into private museums dedicated to their loved ones (Çavdar 2020, 169–75, 191–204).

---

9. After an Alevi association submitted a petition to the Ministry of Interior, the names of the two attackers were finally removed from the panel in May 2022 (*Cumhuriyet* 2022).

AKP policies were in line with the demands expressed by "the people of Sivas" during a meeting that took place during the Alevi openings (T. C. Devlet Bakanlığı 2010b, 106). Discussions during this meeting give the impression that the Sunni people of Sivas are also the victims as their reputation is tarnished as a result of a conspiracy. Leading public personalities from Sivas, except for a few representing Alevi organizations, vehemently opposed the idea of a museum on the grounds that it would provoke sectarian tensions in the city. The mayor argued that such a museum would make the life of the Alevis more difficult in the city (T. C. Devlet Bakanlığı 2010b, 92). His not-so-implicit threat is that the people of Sivas would not tolerate a memorial dedicated to Alevi victimhood, as they did not tolerate a statue dedicated to the memory of Pir Sultan in 1993. The Alevis of Sivas would be safer only if they consented to their public subordinated status. As Alevis' request for public recognition remained a deep source of anxiety for the people of Sivas, such recognition was kept in the waiting room of history. Several businessmen of Sivas, concerned with the negative socioeconomic impacts of the massacre, exhibited a slightly more pragmatic attitude. One of them argued that a memorial similar to the one erected in Solingen, Germany where a neo-Nazi arson attack killed five women and girls from a Turkish migrant family in May 1993 could be erected in Sivas when Turkey becomes as rich as Germany. Until then, the "conditions were not ripe" for such memorials (T. C. Devlet Bakanlığı 2010b, 27).

Another massacre in Başbağlar, a village in a neighboring province, that took place three days after the burning of the hotel plays an instrumental role in the denial of Alevi victimhood. A group of masked men raided a Sunni Turkish village, killed twenty-eight men, and burned down houses and the mosque. Five additional people died in one of the burning houses. Although the massacre is typically attributed to the PKK, the judicial process has been inconclusive (BBC News Türkçe 2020). Regardless, there is no indication that an Alevi organization committed the massacre. Nonetheless, Başbağlar became an effective rhetorical device to establish false moral equivalence and recast the memory of Sivas. It implies that since "both sides" spilled blood, nobody could claim an exclusive right to victimhood (HBVAKV 2011; Yalçınkaya 2011). In fact, references to Başbağlar were common in the Sivas meeting of the AKP's Alevi openings (T. C. Devlet Bakanlığı 2010b). The village has a monument dedicated to the memory of victims and visited by prominent officials and politicians each year on the anniversary of the massacre (Anadolu Ajansı 2019).

This denial of Alevi victimhood is closely associated with the notion that the Sivas massacre was an unresolved conspiracy in which the people of Sivas played no role. According to this hegemonic narrative, individuals who were put on trial and received prison sentences were the victims of another conspiracy by the deep state that falsely portrayed the massacre as a reactionary uprising against the secular republican order. In fact, the final report of the AKP's Alevi openings claimed that the hotel was burned by "persons unknown" (T. C. Devlet Bakanlığı 2010a, 179). This is an eerie reminder of a typical coroner's verdict, "death at the hands of persons unknown," following the lynching of Black people in the American South in the late nineteenth century. Since the lynchings were the expressions of the will of the community, nobody could be held criminally responsible (Dray 2003, ix). Along similar lines, the reaction to the Alevi festival reflected the will of the people who could not be blamed for any wrongdoing. Overall, this reframing of the Sivas massacre is a powerful example of how the AKP government puts Sunni Muslim Turks on the right side of history even when dealing with past wrongs against non-Sunni minorities (Bakiner 2022). This self-righteous framing leaves no room for national reckoning with the massacres.

As a counterpoint, it can be argued that intercommunal reconciliation may benefit from mutual forgetting that would act as an antidote against acts of vengeance. In fact, the notion of *oublience*, erasing acts of intergroup violence from the collective memory, is often perceived as being central to political stability and the avoidance of further violence (Rieff 2016; Clarke 2019). From this perspective, it is perhaps unsurprising that it took 444 years for the first memorial to the victims of the Saint Bartholomew massacre (1572) to be erected in Paris. Even then, it lacked any information about how and by whom the violence was committed. Similarly, a museum and memorial dedicated to the victims of lynchings in the post-antebellum United States opened up in Montgomery, Alabama in 2018, more than a half century after the dismantling of segregation. The problem with the argument that forgetting serves coexistence is that a hegemonic group typically decides what is remembered and unremembered in public. As long as relations of domination persist, as in the case of Turkey, oppressed groups do not forget but are hampered from expressing their collective memory of atrocities in public settings. For them, oublience is an act of self-denial. Hence, forgetting is often feasible and justifiable on democratic grounds only *after* intercommunal reconciliation that calls for a reckoning with the past is achieved.

Contemporary Alevism: Between Liminality and Recognition

The last major anti-Alevi massacre took place in Istanbul in March 1995. Unlike the Maraş and Sivas massacres, this was state-directed violence. A drive-by shooting of four coffeehouses in a predominantly Alevi Kurdish neighborhood killed two people (Marcus 1996; van Bruinessen 1996; Yonucu 2021). Police opened fire on rioters and demonstrators protesting the attack and police brutality. Twenty-two people lost their lives over several days. A number of police officers were put on trial but ultimately received either no or light sentences. In 2005, the European Court of Human Rights found Turkey in violation of Articles 2 and 13 of the convention and ordered compensation payment to the victims' families.

During the earlier AKP years that started in 2002, political space became relatively accommodative of Alevi identity due to the reforms associated with the European Union membership process. The AKP's policy of co-optation reached its zenith with the Alevi openings that lasted from 2007 to 2011. Even though the AKP remained unwilling to recognize the Alevis as a distinct religious group and did not address the main demands of Alevi organizations, public debate and visibility arguably contributed to the diminishing of liminality associated with Alevis at the societal level. For instance, according to a survey conducted in 2014, only 6 percent of the respondents described "Alevi Muslims" as the least liked or most distant group (KONDA 2014b).[10] Alevi activists including families of the victims continued to attend the commemoration at the scene of the Sivas massacre every year and contested official attempts to shape the public memory (Çavdar 2020).

Nonetheless, the othering of Alevis remains prevalent at the official level and suggests the vulnerability of Alevis to sectarian framings in political struggles. The AKP government and municipalities continue to refuse granting legal recognition of cemevleri as places of religious worship (Bianet 2022). After the outbreak of the Syrian civil war where a predominantly Sunni opposition confronted an Alawite-dominated regime, the AKP government repurposed historical templates associating Alevism with disloyalty (Karakaya-Stump 2018). As of 2017, there was not a single Alevi provincial or district governor (T24 2017). Starting with the 2011 parliamentary elections, AKP leaders played the sectarian card to limit the appeal of the main opposition party, the CHP, led by an Alevi Kurdish politician from Dersim, among the Sunni voters (Tezcür 2012, 123). The AKP's sectarianization of politics peaked with the Gezi protests, nonviolent popular protests against then prime minister Erdoğan's top-down and intrusive governance, in the spring and summer of 2013. The fact that many Alevis actively protested a government that pursued discriminatory and exclusionary policies became a

---

10. As a caveat, it should be noted that the respondents were given the self-identity option of "Alevi Muslims" rather than "Alevis" in the survey.

pretext for the AKP government to frame the protests as an Alevi uprising. A notorious police report, based on a sample of 5,513 detainees, claimed that around 3.6 million people participated in the protests and 78 percent of the demonstrators had "Alevi origins." The report left unanswered how sectarian affiliations of the individuals were identified. After all, there are no official statistics about sectarian differences and Alevis are coded as Muslims in official documents (Bianet 2013). The police inference was that almost the entire Alevi population protested since only 5 percent of the respondents self-identified as Alevis in a recent survey (KONDA 2019). It also conveniently overlooked the fact that a large number of the Turkish population was critical of police brutality, which led to the outbreak of the mass protests in the first instance (KONDA 2014a, 18, 20). Consequently, old habits die hard among the security forces. Only if Alevis behave, social peace and public order would be maintained.

CHAPTER 4

Liminality in the Broader Muslim World
Baha'is and Ahmadis

In this chapter, I offer historical narratives of the experience of Baha'is in Iran and Ahmadis in Pakistan and Indonesia. Both faiths emerged as messianic movements led by charismatic leaders who challenged well-established Islamic orthodoxies (i.e., the finality of prophecy) in the second half of the nineteenth century. From the very beginning, they attracted fierce opposition from Muslim clerics and preachers who denounced their teachings as heretical and followers as apostates. As in the case of Yezidis and Alevis, the primary reason why Baha'is and Ahmadis have been persecuted is the fact that their very existence has been an abomination for the representatives of religious orthodoxy. Accordingly, clerics, who often disagree on a wide variety of topics, have been at the forefront of public campaigns of hatred targeting Baha'is and Ahmadis whom they have found beyond the pale of acceptance. They have produced and disseminated stigmas across generations making it very difficult for both communities to find allies and be part of larger coalitions seeking societal and political change. Both Baha'is and Ahmadis have been subject to a variety of chimerical allegations and epithets with political connotations. A common charge is that they are fifth columns serving foreign interests. All these layers of stigmatizations reflect the persistence of their liminality that originated from theological incompatibilities. These allegations and epithets became popular because they tap into and reinforce already existing negative perceptions of these communities.

A crucial difference between Alevis and Yezidis, on the one hand, and Baha'is and Ahmadis, on the other hand, is that the latter have been subject to greater levels of state persecution in contemporary times. As religious differences are explicitly coded into the positive law, Baha'is in the Islamic Republic of Iran and Ahmadis in Pakistan (and to a lesser extent in Indonesia) are deprived of basic citizen rights and experience further marginalization. As the state authorities in Iran and Pakistan push these liminal minorities to the very margins of public life, the severity of bottom-up violence remains more limited.[1]

Compared to Yezidis and Alevis, both Baha'is and Ahmadis came into existence more recently, in the nineteenth century. That both faiths present a fundamental challenge to the core beliefs of Islamic theology lies at the heart of widespread and persistent clerical opposition to Baha'is and Ahmadis. Both groups have been targets of intense stigmatization led by Muslim clerics who perceive the very existence of Baha'ism and Ahmadiyya as an affront to Islam. The Baha'i faith, which emerged from a messianic movement within Shiite Islam, crystallized into a separate religion by the 1860s. Ahmadiyya originated as a messianic movement in colonial India in the 1890s. It has not ventured beyond the orbit of Islam as Ahmadis continue to consider themselves as Muslim. At the same time, it offers a unique interpretation about the finality of Muhammad's prophecy. Hence, both faiths present an irreducible incompatibility with Islamic teachings that Muhammad is the last monotheistic prophet.

Anti-Baha'i and anti-Ahmadiyya discourses have evolved considerably over the decades as religious and moralistic arguments are supplemented and often superseded with a variety of conspiracy theories claiming that they are tools of foreign powers pursuing sinister goals. Yet both groups were targets of discriminatory state practices and laws and episodes of mass violence not because they collectively served the interests of foreign powers, achieved disproportionate political power, or gained economic wealth. The fact that both Baha'is and Ahmadis typically eschew political activism and lack powerful external patrons did not make a dent in the widespread appeal of conspiracy theories. Rather than presenting any demographic, political, or military threat to the dominant groups, their very weakness in these regards has made them convenient targets of scapegoating. Consequently, Baha'is in Iran and Ahmadis in contemporary Pakistan and Indonesia have been among the most per-

---

1. This is obviously not to say that Baha'is in Iran and Ahmadis in Pakistan and Indonesia were free from violence in the hands of nonstate actors. Most notoriously, a terror attack staged by the Pakistani Taliban against two Ahmadi mosques in Lahore in May 2010 resulted in the deaths of more than a hundred members of the community (HRW 2010). In Indonesia, Ahmadis were victims of occasional mob violence in recent years. In Iran, individuals physically attacking Baha'is often enjoy impunity.

secuted religious minorities in the world.² For many Muslim religious authorities, the founders of both faiths have been heretics whose preaching and actions deserve punishment in this world and otherworld.

As liminal minorities, the very existence of Baha'is and Ahmadis presents a deep theological uneasiness for the dominant religion that underlies their stigmatization across generations. The origins of stigmatization are found in historically constructed and crystallized religious differences—that is, incompatible theological beliefs—rather than their presumed political activities or ill-earned material and status gains. In a twist of irony, Baha'is are guilty of believing in a new religion that claims to supersede the revelationary message of Islam; Ahmadis are guilty of believing in a new prophet while simultaneously claiming to be Muslims. In orthodox Muslim discourses, they are not entitled to the recognition offered to the adherents of religions such as Christianity and Judaism who are considered People of the Book. I suggest that this lack of recognition continues to be a predominant factor reinforcing the precariousness of these groups and severely constraining rights and opportunities available to their adherents in countries they originated from. Baha'is lack any sort of legal recognition in Iran and Egypt; Ahmadis in Pakistan are defined in ways that fundamentally are at odds with the self-description of the community (Saeed 2021b). Paradoxically, policies that codify religious differences into the positive law and state practices appeasing popular sentiments and discriminating against these groups make it less urgent for people to take the law into their own hands. To recall Walter Benjamin's typology discussed in chapter 1, as long as religious differences are coded into positive law, popular claims justified on natural law—that is, religious revelation—are kept at bay by state authorities who have a vested interest in not allowing groups and individuals to claim the mantle of natural law and engage in violent acts of "vigilante justice."

The historical experience of Baha'is and Ahmadis also vindicates my application of Jacques Derrida's paradox of iterability to the workings of religious violence. As elaborated in chapter 1, Derrida criticizes Walter Benjamin's distinction between the violence of foundation and preservation. Religious violence in monotheistic religions seeks to derive its legitimacy from the moment of revelation that supersedes any existing laws. Hence, it has a founding

---

2. Both communities spread beyond their homelands. According to World Religion Database in 2020, the largest number of Baha'is lives in India (around 2.1 million) followed by the United States, Kenya, and Vietnam. The Baha'i population in Iran is estimated to be around 250,000 (available at https://www.thearda.com/world-religion/np-sort?var=ADH_705 [accessed March 27, 2023]). In comparison, Ahmadis make sizable minorities in a number of sub-Saharan African countries, especially in Cameroon, Ghana, Liberia, and Tanzania (Pew Research Center 2012b, 128).

character instituting a new legal order. Yet it always remains vulnerable to new religions offering a rival revelation and claiming immunity from the preexisting law on exactly the same grounds. When facing a new claim of revelation, an existing religion reverts to the violence of preservation to nip the challenger in the bud and persecutes its followers. Hence, as the paradox of iterability suggests, Benjamin's distinction between founding and preserving violence is unsustainable as they collapse into each other. That both the Baha'i and Ahmadi faiths make claims of revelations rivaling that of orthodox Islamic beliefs and are potential candidates for founding violence put them at the receiving end of the violence of preservation.

A Denied Faith: Baha'is

The roots of the Baha'is faith lie in Shiite millennialism of the mid-nineteenth century characterized by increasing European influence, growing assertiveness of the Shiite ulema, and weakened rule of the Qajar dynasty (Keddie 2003, 45–48). In 1844, a young merchant from Shiraz, Ali Mohammed Shirazi (b. 1819), claimed himself to be the gate (the *bāb*) of the twelfth imam, who has been in occultation since the ninth century according to the Shiite belief. Several years later, he claimed to be the occulted imam himself and called for the abrogation of Islamic laws (MacEoin 2011). Shirazi's claims presented a direct challenge to the Shiite ulema not only in terms of doctrine but also in terms of social status and material resources (A. Amanat 2008). His followers engaged in several episodes of armed resistance against the Qajars. Shirazi was executed in Tabriz in 1850. Following an unsuccessful assassination attempt on the Qajar shah, the community of Bāb was subject to an intensified wave of persecution. It is estimated that between two thousand and three thousand followers of Shirazi were killed from 1848 to 1852 (MacEoin 1983, 236). Victims in 1852 included Qurrat al-Ayn Tarrat, a preacher and follower of Bāb who gained a posthumous reputation as the first woman who was unveiled in public (Mottahedeh 1998).

The faith found a new direction and spirit under the leadership of Mirza Hussein-Ali Nuri (Baha'u'llah) (1817–92) who was exiled to the Ottoman Empire in 1865. Several years later, he was sent to Acre, a backwater port city located northwest of Jerusalem. During his time there, he reconfigured the Baha'i faith as a distinctive religion. In *Ketab-a aqdas* (1873), Baha'u'llah developed a new code of laws accompanying his new revelation and superseding both Koran and *Bayan* of Bāb (MacEoin 1983). Baha'u'llah espoused a pacifist stance and ideas supportive of modern education, constitutionalism, representative government, and political liberalism (Cole 1992). Over several decades, an overwhelming majority of followers of Bāb became members of the Baha'i faith that also expanded into Western countries. In the face of vehement opposition from the clerics and the Qajar political elite, the new faith struggled to expand its appeal in Iran but still gained new members, some of whom converted from Judaism and Zoroastrianism. By the 1910s, Baha'is in Iran were estimated to be between one hundred thousand and two hundred thousand (P. Smith 1984, 297). They were vulnerable to the charges of apostasy (*murtad*) and subject to various forms of discrimination and violence that often aimed to take over Baha'i properties and women. During periods of political infighting, epidemics, and famine, scapegoating of Baha'is was especially common (Sadeghian 2016). In one of the bloodiest episodes, a pogrom instigated by a local cleric in the city of Yazd killed more than one hundred Baha'is (Fischer 1980, 185).

During the late Qajar rule, similar to Ottoman treatment of Yezidis, Baha'is were categorized as a "deviant sect" (*firqa-ya dalla*) that threatened the collective unity of Shiite Muslims being squeezed between British and Russian imperialism (A. Amanat 2008). Perhaps most insidiously in the eyes of Shiite clerics, and different from both Alevis and Yezidis, Baha'is engaged in proselytization among Muslims. Shiite clerics declared them to be ritually unclean and a threat to the purity of believers (Kazemzadeh 2000). Similar to epithets targeting other liminal minorities, Baha'is were accused of engaging in immoral sexual practices, including exchanging spouses and committing adultery, during their religious rituals. Such accusations persisted well into the twentieth century (Tavakoli-Targhi 2008, 203; M. Amanat 2012, 270). The term *Babi*, which was used interchangeably with Baha'i, became an epithet to describe deviance from traditional Islamic values, modernism, and foreignness (Mottahedeh 1998). In this sense, Baha'is were intimate strangers causing uneasiness and anxiety given their dense international linkages and openness to modern practices including modern education, unveiling, and mixing of genders in public meetings.[3] Baha'is continued to have their center in Acre/Haifa that fell under British control in the post–World War I period (see figure 4.1).

With the advent of the 1930s and 1940s, anti-Baha'i stereotypes started to find a receptive audience among the Iranian secular intelligentsia. These

---

3. The claim that the Baha'i faith is not a religion because it does not have a "book" was also prevalent during the late Ottoman Empire and early Turkish Republic. Abdullah Cevdet, a leading secular intellectual and political activist, was put on trial for penning an article praising the Baha'i faith in 1922. His detractors argued that the Baha'i faith is a "political movement" like socialism and freemasonry. Cevdet had been given a two-year prison sentence before his case was dismissed with the abolition of the law penalizing attacks against sacred matters (Alkan 2005).

FIGURE 4.1. The Baha'i Gardens in Haifa, Israel, July 2019 (Credit: Author)

stereotypes depicted Baha'is as a source of division undermining the unity of the Iranian nation, tools in the service of sinister foreign powers, and being disproportionately represented in the higher echelons of economic and political power. As Shiite Islam, at least its nominal expressions, has become central to the configuration of Iranian nationhood, Baha'is, despite their history as an indigenous religion of Iran, have emerged as the "internal other" (Chehabi 2008). During these years, a conspiracy theory based on a forged document claiming that the Baha'i faith was created at the behest of Russians to destroy the national unity of Iran gained ground. *The Confessions of Dolgoruki*, allegedly written by the Russian ambassador to Iran from 1845 to 1854, is a spy fiction with some eerie resemblance to *The Protocols of the Elders of Zion*. This forgery aimed to portray Baha'is as a threat not only to Shiite Islam but also Iran's national identity. It "successfully promoted the notion of an exclusionary nation which achieved its 'unity' through singling out a minority it considered 'unabsorbable' by depicting it as a cultural and political fifth column" (Yazdani 2011, 42). Parallel to historical developments in early modern Europe where popular hatred toward religious minorities paved the way for the rise of an exclusivist nation-building process (Marx 2003), *The Confessions* made the Baha'is a popular scapegoat helping religious and secular political groups bridge their differences. It also supplemented the conventional stigmatizations of Baha'is with the charges that they are an alien community implanted into the midst of the nation by imperialists. After the foundation of Israel in 1948, it has become commonplace to associate the Baha'i faith with Zionism, as Baha'is are headquartered in Haifa (Tavakoli-Targhi 2008, 220–24). With this development, Baha'i liminality gained a new dimension that would have insidious implications for the future of the community in Iran.[4]

A major anti-Baha'i episode took place in May and June 1955, during Ramadan. In the aftermath of the US- and British-supported coup that overthrew the nationalist prime minister Mohammad Mosaddegh and restored Mohammad Reza to the throne in 1953 (A. Amanat 2017, 548–58), the Shiite clerical establishment had some leverage over the young and insecure shah. When the clerics orchestrated an anti-Baha'i riot, the shah remained complicit to mute their opposition to the oil deal with Western companies and Iran's entry into the pro-Western Baghdad Pact (Akhavi 1980, 77). With the blessing of the palace, a cleric aimed to mobilize "fierce hatred on the part of *Shi'i* true believers" (Akhavi 1980, 76) by denouncing the Baha'i community on national radio. That was followed by the destruction of the dome of the main Baha'i temple in Tehran with the involvement of high-level Pahlavi officials. These events triggered widespread acts of vandalism, looting, and violence targeting Baha'is in different parts of the country. There were also calls for the boycott of Pepsi-Cola since its distributor company was owned by a Baha'i businessman (Fischer 1980, 274; Tavakoli-Targhi 2008, 221–22). Although the regime let the clergy release pent-up rage against the Baha'i community, it did not concede to clerical demands of declaring the Baha'i faith illegal and purging Baha'is from the state bureaucracy (Akhavi 1980, 79–81). As the shah started to consolidate his power by the late 1950s, he had diminishing incentives to accommodate the clerics.

The fallout between the regime and the clerical establishment would result in major disturbances in the early 1960s. Ayatollah Ruhollah Khomeini emerged as the leading figure of religious opposition to the regime's authoritarian secularism and westernization. The conspiracy theory that the Baha'i faith was an imperial machination representing an ontological threat to Iranian

---

4. This conspiracy theory has been circulated in the broader Muslim world. For instance, a book published by Turkey's Presidency of Religious Affairs in the 1990s, the main state body propagating Sunni Islam, included a lengthy excerpt from *The Confessions*. The author of the book, a theology professor who also occupied high-level administrator positions in higher education, calls Baha'u'llah a "Russian spy" and describes the Baha'i faith as a "sinister movement" (*fesad cereyan*). He also claims that it is one of the latest conspiracies against Islam, which include Zionism, crusaders, and imperialists (Fığlalı 1994).

identity became central to Khomeini's religious nationalism. For Khomeini, the Baha'is were not a religious faith but a seditious political movement. This classification, which denies the very existence of Baha'i beliefs, would have ominous implications for the Baha'is once Khomeini replaced the shah in 1979. Khomeini declared his opposition to a bill in 1962 that aimed to eliminate "the profession of Islam as a condition for the electors and the candidates" and use "the term [oath by] 'the Heavenly-Book' instead of the Koran" on grounds that the bill would deliver "Iran to the Baha'is, the presumed agents of Zionism and Imperialism who were implicitly enfranchised by the bill alongside women" (Arjomand 1988, 85). In his lectures in Najaf in 1970 that would be the basis of his political theory of Islamic rule, he alluded to Baha'is when criticizing people opposing the implementation of the Islamic law. He argued that such people are worse "than the person who believes and proclaims that Islam has been superseded or abrogated by another supposed revelation" (Khomeini 1981, 42). In response to President Ronald Reagan's criticism of the executions of Baha'i women in Shiraz in 1983, Khomeini repeated his earlier claim that the Baha'i faith is a political party, the implication being that they are persecuted not because of their faith but political opposition to the regime (Zabihi-Moghaddam 2016).

During the last two decades of the Pahlavi rule, there was widespread perception that Baha'is were given preferred access to the regime and disproportionately represented in the echelons of powers. There were several Baha'is who became notorious for pursuing ostentatious lives and engaging in corruption. For instance, Abdolkarim Ayadi, a Baha'i, was the shah's personal physician who wielded significant influence for a quarter century (Milani 2008, 1058–61). There were many other members of the faith who achieved prominence thanks to their business acumen, artistic creativity, and educational attainments (267–71, 678–85, 599–606). However, Baha'is were not a privileged minority. The community was the subject of various discriminatory practices in terms of employment and taxation (Martin 1984). The shah's intelligence agency, SAVAK, had a close surveillance over the community and often collaborated with a religious network (the Anjuman-i-Tablighat-i Islami, also known as the Hojjatieh, established in the 1940s) known for its fierce antagonism toward the Baha'is (Tavakoli-Targhi 2008, 205). For the growing opposition to the shah's megalomaniac and repressive rule, Baha'is, as a liminal minority, were the perfect scapegoat. That the community pursued political quietism and remained loyal to the regime only fueled popular resentments.

The coming of an Islamist regime to power in Iran presented an existential threat to the Baha'is in Iran. At the eve of the revolution, Baha'is were a tiny minority and numbered around 300,000–350,000 (P. Smith 1984, 297).

Although the community kept a low profile during those turbulent years, their quietism did not reduce the intensity of animosity it faced. The Baha'i cosmopolitanism was an anathema to the xenophobic religious nationalism of the new political order (Cole 2005). The early revolutionary years were characterized by waves of anti-Baha'i persecutions involving executions and imprisonments of both Baha'i leaders and ordinary believers (Abrahamian 2008, 181), lootings of Baha'i properties, dismissal of Baha'is from their jobs, restrictions on their education, and other forms of discrimination making them social outcasts. The Hojjatieh became a very influential group and often led anti-Baha'i activities. Reminiscent of *The Confessions* from the 1940s, the regime figures including diplomats accused Baha'is of being part of a Zionist and imperialist conspiracy (Martin 1984, 57, 72). Although the intensity of violence declined with the second half of the 1980s, Baha'is continued to be the most persecuted religious minority in the Islamic Republic (Sanasarian 2000, 50–53). In the 1990s, a number of Baha'is were put on trial and given death penalty on grounds that they committed apostasy (Cole 2005, 146–50). Even the dead Baha'is were not left alone. In 1992, the authorities demolished the main Baha'i cemetery in the Tehran area and exhumed Baha'i graves so that they could build a "cultural center" (M. Amanat 2012). In 2010, seven leaders of the Baha'i faith were arrested, charged with espionage on behalf of the United States and Israel and acting against Iran's national security, and sentenced to twenty years (later reduced to ten years) (Zabihi-Moghaddam 2016, 138). Until 2005, more than 215 Baha'is were killed or forcefully disappeared (Afshari 2008, 246). More than 60 percent of these killings and enforced disappearances took place from June 1981 to the end of 1984 (248). Similarly, the lack of recognition from Muslim religious authorities and population and geopolitical tensions with Israel deepen the precarity of Egypt's tiny Baha'i community (Johnston 2007; Mahmood 2015).

For some observers, the scope of rights violations targeting Baha'is in postrevolutionary Iran reached genocidal dimensions. From this perspective, only international pressures stopped the Iranian government from continuing its campaign that aimed to annihilate more than a century-old Baha'i presence in the country (Momen 2005). Reza Afshari (2008) offers a more nuanced assessment and suggests that the anti-Baha'i attacks did take place in the absence of a preconceived and systematic plan at the top. Instead, he argues that the egregious violations of Baha'i rights reflect a "highly prejudicial attitude shared by the clergy" (239) and an "indictment of both the state and a significant part of the Iranian society and its illiberal culture" (240). A large segment of the society exhibited "quiet indifference bordering on passive acquiescence" in the face of the persecution of the Baha'is in Iran (273). Only in the 2010s, a few leading secular and religious figures started to exhibit greater tolerance and recognition of the Baha'i faith (Sanyal 2019).

This historical overview suggests that the Baha'i faith is perceived with great animosity and suspicion by Muslim authorities in Iran. As a post-Abrahamic religion, it presents a direct theological threat to the notion of the final prophecy of Muhammad. This theological incompatibility has gradually been supplemented by new stigmas further demonizing the Baha'i community. The view that Baha'is were seditious people with immoral values and in cahoots with the imperial powers against the Iranian nation disseminated widely among Iranian society. There is perhaps no clearer indicator of the Baha'i liminality than the popular hoax that a sinister Russian official was behind the foundation of the faith.

The modest gains made by the community in the later decades of the Pahlavi rule became a source of popular resentment and contributed to the demonization of the Baha'is once the shah was overthrown. Yet the Baha'is never became a privileged minority and were also a convenient scapegoat for the royalist regime, as the clergy-initiated riots in 1955 demonstrated. The collapse of the Pahlavi regime left the community completely vulnerable and at the mercy of hostile forces. As the Islamic Republic persecuted the community utilizing both religious and political arguments, the scope of bottom-up violence against Baha'is remained limited in recent years. Returning to Walter Benjamin's dichotomy, the codification of religious differences into the positive law made it redundant for people to claim the mantle of the natural law and engage in their own "vigilante justice" against a despised minority. The state remained in charge and contained or provoked popular anti-Baha'i passions depending on the political context. The situation of the Ahmadiyya in Pakistan exhibits some resemblances to this unsettling pattern with the difference being that the process of exclusion was more gradual and contested in Pakistan.

Unrecognized Muslims: Ahmadis

Like the Baha'i faith, Ahmadiyya emerged in the second half of the century, at a time when the Muslim world increasingly fell under European influence. Founded by Mirza Ghulam Ahmad (1835–1908), a charismatic Muslim scholar based in British India, Ahmadiyya was at odds with orthodox Islam from its early years. Ghulam Ahmad argued that Jesus survived the crucifixion and died because of natural causes in Kashmir. He also declared himself as the promised messiah who would provide guidance to Muslims who strayed from the path. Even more ambitiously, drawing on medieval messianic Sufi traditions making a distinction between legislative and nonlegislative prophets, Ghulam Ahmad argued that prophecy had a continuous nature and declared himself as a prophet without law-bearing characteristics (Friedmann 2003). Although Ghulam Ahmad's claim to prophethood was shrouded in ambiguity and is interpreted in different manners by his followers, who continued to describe themselves as part of the Islamic *ummah*, Muslim clerics generally condemned him as a heretical figure. According to mainstream Islamic tradition, Muhammad is the twenty-fifth and final prophet. In the Koran, he is referred to as the "seal of prophets." From the clerics' perspective, Ghulam Ahmad's claim to prophecy was a direct assault on one of the core aspects of Muslim faith. He was a "false prophet" guilty of apostasy (Budiwanti 2009). The fact that the Ahmadis had a pro-British stance, rejected the notion of violent jihad, and supported the United Kingdom during the World War I contributed to hostility toward the community among the Muslims in India who embraced the pro-Ottoman khilafat movement. As with the Baha'is, that stance would fuel conspiracy theories accusing the Ahmadis of being pawns of imperialist powers in the subsequent decades (Adil Khan 2015, 7–8, 138). In the first two decades of the twentieth century, a number of Ahmadis were stoned to death in Afghanistan on grounds that they held heretical beliefs and opposed the practice of jihad (131–33).

With the partition of 1947, the Ahmadi community moved to Pakistan and established its headquarters in a town close to Lahore. The Majlis-e Ahrar-e Islam (Ahrar), established by former members of the khilafat movement who opposed the partition, became the main conduit through which anti-Ahmadiyya propaganda was disseminated in Pakistan. Being the most vocal anti-Ahmadi voice helped Ahrar, previously discredited for its opposition to the creation of Pakistan, revitalize itself and emerge as a significant pressure group (Qasmi 2015, 60). As early as 1949, Ahrar demanded that Ahmadis officially be declared as non-Muslims and purged from the state bureaucracy. They accused Ahmadis of conspiring with India (Amjad Khan 2003, 223). Zafarullah Khan (1893–1985), a prominent member of the community who served as the first foreign minister of Pakistan until 1954, became the magnet of Ahrar agitation that portrayed Ahmadis as a sinister force aiming to take over the Pakistani state (Nasr 1994, 132–33; Zaman 2002, 113; Adil Khan 2015, 150). Abul A'la Maududi, the influential founder of the Jamaat-e Islami, joined the chorus by authoring an influential anti-Ahmadi publication (Nasr 1994, 136). Anti-Ahmadi agitation ultimately resulted in widespread disturbances, primarily in Lahore, in 1953. Several hundreds of people, mostly Ahmadis, were killed (Qasmi 2015, 112). Similar to developments during the anti-Alevi massacres in Maraş and Sivas in Turkey, the state managed to restore public order only after the imposition of martial rule in Lahore. The situation elevated the military, which would remain the most powerful political actor in the country for decades to come.

A court of inquiry (the so-called Munir Kyani Commission) established to investigate the disturbances adopted a secular and relatively liberal position. It argued that the state should not pursue a rigid interpretation of the scripture as demanded by the clergy and discriminate against its own citizens on the basis of religion (Qasmi 2015, 19). That was a "moment of accommodation" when the state elites resisted clerical demands to decide who can and cannot be classified as a Muslim (Saeed 2007). This liberal ethos did not last very long. Islamization in Pakistan could be understood as a process with both top-down and bottom-up dynamics. Political elites increasingly used Islamic discourses and symbols to weave a national identity among people with vast ethnic and regional differences (Qasmi 2015, 20). This instrumentalization of Islam proved to be effective as it appealed to popular values and emotions and had substantial mobilization power (Nasr 1994, 139, 182; Saeed 2016, 150, 163). The reconstitution of the Pakistani nation brought the exclusion of the Ahmadi community. Reminiscent of processes in early modern England and France (Marx 2003), the scapegoating of a "heretical religious group" became central to nation building in Pakistan (Saeed 2016, 6).

The period from 1974 to 1993 saw the institutionalization of the exclusion of Ahmadis from the Muslim polity as religious differences were explicitly codified into the positive law. The 1973 constitution that was enacted under relatively democratic circumstances established Islam as the state religion. It also institutionalized a Council of Islamic Ideology to ensure that all laws in the country were compatible with Islam (Forte 1994). Following large-scale riots pitting Sunni Muslims against Ahmadis and popular calls to boycott the community in 1974, the democratically elected Pakistani National Assembly formed a special committee to decide on the status of the community. The assembly was dominated by Prime Minister Zulfikar Ali Bhutto's Pakistan People's Party, which controlled more than 60 percent of the seats (Saeed 2016, 113). The proceedings exhibited the exclusionary logic of majoritarian democracy and legitimized multiple forms of anti-Ahmadiyya discourse including the allegations that the community was created by British imperialism and their religious beliefs are heretical. Acting on the committee's decision, the Pakistani National Assembly unanimously approved a constitutional amendment that declared Ahmadis as non-Muslims (123). The amendment unequivocally noted that the belief in the finality of prophecy of Muhammad is a prerequisite for being defined as Muslim (Article 260) and assigned parliamentary seats to the Ahmadiyya as a non-Muslim group (Article 106).[5] Consequently, a democratically elected body seized the prerogative to classify who is a Muslim and not a Muslim. That a fringe group of Islamist activists and politicians managed to set the national agenda without any significant opposition could be taken as a strong indicator of the popularity of anti-Ahmadiyya positions in the country.

Islamization entailing discriminatory practices against the Ahmadiyya gained a new impetus under the military dictatorship of Muhammad Zia-ul-Haq who came to power in 1977. Most notoriously, in 1984, the regime enacted Ordinance XX, which "prohibited Ahmadis from declaring their faith publicly, propagating their faith, building mosques, or making the call for Muslim prayers" (Amjad Khan 2003, 227). After the 1984 ordinance, the Ahmadiyya leadership fled to London, a move that made the slur that the Ahmadis were pawns of imperialist powers a self-fulfilling prophecy. A 1986 law raised the penalty for blasphemy from fine to imprisonment or death.[6] With the gradual "religio-politicization of the judiciary" that eroded the autonomy of the courts, the exclusion of the Ahmadis from full citizenship rights in Pakistan gained an irreversible character (Saeed 2016, 40). A supreme court decision in 1993 held Ordinance XX valid on the grounds that religious expressions and symbols are exclusive properties that could not be imitated without harming the community that owns them. In fact, the decision drew an analogy with the Coca-Cola Company and argued that as this company does not permit others to sell its product, Muslims have a right to prohibit others from using their symbols to protect the integrity of their faith. The court asked Ahmadis to come up with new names and descriptions to avoid offending Muslim sensibilities (Ahmed 2010; Qadir 2015). With these developments, "the moment of accommodation" of 1954 ultimately gave way to "the moment of criminalization," which severely augmented the precarity of Ahmadis in Pakistan (Saeed 2007).

The Ahmadi liminality was the ultimate reason for the anxiety and threat perception the faith group generated among Sunni clergy and the masses (see

---

5. Abdus Salam, a prominent physicist and a member of the Ahmadiyya, left the country in protest of this decision. In 1979, he would be the first Pakistani to receive the Nobel Prize. The assembly's decision was preceded by a unanimous resolution at an international meeting of the Muslim World League, a Saudi-funded organization with pan-Islamist ambitions, that Ahmadis were non-Muslims. Saudi Arabia also enacted a regulation disqualifying Ahmadis from hajj (Budiwanti 2009; Qadir 2015).

6. In early Islamic history, apostasy was associated with treason and rebellion that deserved the severest punishment. Blasphemy, which is inherently ambivalent, could be committed by non-Muslims but overlaps with apostasy when the responsible party is a Muslim. The criminalization of blasphemy serves as a surrogate in the absence of a law punishing apostasy (Forte 1994).

FIGURE 4.2. An anti-Ahmadi protest in Lahore, Pakistan, September 2018 (Editorial credit: A. M. Syed / Shutterstock.com).

figure 4.2). On the one hand, Ahmadis have plenty of similarities in terms of religious beliefs and practices with Sunni Muslims, the dominant group in Pakistan (Qasmi 2015, 223–25). On the other hand, the basic tenet of the Ahmadi faith—that is, prophecy of Ghulam Ahmad—presents a theological incompatibility fostering accusations of heresy. This paradoxical status of being an "intimate stranger" lies as the basis of the exclusion of the Ahmadiyya from Pakistani nationhood and the intensity of persecution they have faced. As in Iran, the state authorities embraced popular hostilities against a liminal minority and incorporated them into their political agendas. Although this configuration, to a certain extent, set a barrier to the outbreak of bottom-up mass violence, it also deepened Ahmadi marginalization.

The trajectory of the "Ahmadi question" in Indonesia exhibits some remarkable similarities to that in Pakistan even if the scope of their exclusion was more limited. The Ahmadiyya arrived in the Indonesian archipelago in the 1920s. As in British India, the Dutch colonial authorities recognized the Ahmadiyya as a formal religious organization. However, Muhammadiyah (established 1912) and Nahdlatul Ulama (established 1926), highly influential Muslim organizations, took explicit positions against the community from the beginning. Both organizations were established to defend Muslim interest against Dutch colonialism and Chinese influence (Hefner 2000). They also characterized followers of the Ahmadiyya as apostates (Budiwanti 2009; Hicks

2014). In comparison, they exhibited more tolerance toward Christians and Hindus than Ahmadis (Menchik 2016, 67–68). As in Pakistan, Ahmadis were also accused of being tools of British imperialism (75–7). With the foundation of Indonesia as a sovereign state in 1945, the Ahmadis found themselves on the margins of the politico-legal order. The ruling national ideology, Pancasila, made belief in God a prerequisite for full citizenship rights. Islam, Catholicism, Protestantism, Hinduism, Buddhism, and Confucianism enjoy official recognition in contemporary Indonesia. Although this ideology allowed for religious pluralism, it also excluded belief systems, such as the Ahmadiyya, deemed to be "heretical" (71, 78–79).[7]

Similar to the status of Yezidis under the Saddam regime in Iraq, the authoritarian Suharto regime (1967–98) kept a close tab on popular mobilization and limited the scope and frequency of bottom-up violence against the community. At the same time, as in Pakistan, the Ahmadiyya was subject to a series of discriminatory practices. The regime enacted a blasphemy law in 1965 to criminalize beliefs and practices that deviated from religious orthodoxies (Menchik 2015, 69). In 1975, it established the Indonesia Ulema Council (Majelis Ulama Indonesia, MUI) propagating an officially sanctioned view on Islamic orthodoxy and including representatives from many organizations including Muhammadiyah and Nahdlatul Ulama. MUI issued a fatwa declaring Ahmadis as apostates in 1980.

The collapse of the Suharto regime and subsequent democratization of Indonesian politics brought new challenges for Ahmadis. Islamic organizations gained more autonomy and pursued exclusionary practices against the community more conspicuously and vigorously. Despite their differences and rivalries, both modernist and traditional religious leaders shared an anti-Ahmadiyya sentiment (Hicks 2014). MUI issued a new fatwa in 2005 accusing the Ahmadiyya of heresy and apostasy. Even though some liberal Muslim intellectuals and groups were critical of the fatwa, it also provided a fresh impetus to the stigmatization of the Ahmadis at the popular levels (Budiwanti 2009). There were several violent attacks targeting members of the Ahmadiyya that were justified on the grounds of the MUI fatwa (Burhani 2020). Besides, the Indonesian Constitutional Court refused a petition to revoke the 1965 blasphemy law, a decision supported by major Islamic organizations as well as representatives of many religious minorities (Menchik 2016, 85–88). Meanwhile, decentralization accompanying democratization generated electoral

---

7. In Indonesian identity cards, the religious affiliation of each citizen is recorded. These cards are required when dealing with the state bureaucracy and obtaining official documents such as birth, marriage, and death certificates. The nonrecognition of Ahmadiyya prevents members of the community from getting identity cards (HRW 2017b).

incentives for local politicians to adopt anti-Ahmadiyya stances to receive support from powerful brokers in some areas (Soedirgo 2018). As in Pakistan, liminal status of Ahmadis—neither accepted as Muslims nor recognized as a distinct legitimate faith—has aggravated their precarity, fostered popular animosity against the group, and subjected them to "double exclusion" (Burhani 2014, 145).

In contemporary Indonesia and Pakistan, popular perceptions of the Ahmadis are highly negative. In Indonesia, only 12 percent of the respondents answered "yes" when asked if they consider Ahmadis as Muslims. This number declines to 7 percent in Pakistan. In comparison, a plurality (40 percent) of the respondents considers Ahmadis as Muslim in Bangladesh (Pew Research Center 2012b, 93, 133). This relative accommodation of Ahmadis in Bangladesh calls for future research. In Pakistan, four-fifths of the respondents said that blasphemy laws, which often target members of the Ahmadi faith, are necessary to protect Islam, and only a tiny 6 percent argued that such laws unfairly target religious minorities.[8] Ahmadis represent the threat of internal strife in a country where Islam is central to the formation of fragile national identity (Fuchs and Fuchs 2020). Even the very name of the community remains contested as they are pejoratively called Qadianis by the Muslim clerics on the grounds that Ghulam Ahmad is not a prophet of Islam (Ahmed 2010, 313n51). In Indonesia, Sunni Muslims tend to view Ahmadis, a "deviant subgroup," more pejoratively than Christians, a rival out-group. The former presents a direct affront to Sunni Muslim self-identifications (Putra, Holtz, and Rufaedah 2018).

In summary, popular hostilities against both Baha'is and Ahmadis have their origins in theological differences with Islamic orthodoxy even if they have subsequently been embedded in nationalist discourses. The exclusion and persecution of these groups exhibit a remarkable element of continuity and rely primarily on religious stigmatization informed by theological visions. This argument differs from Saeed (2016, 217) who interprets the treatment of Ahmadis in Pakistan as a form of exclusion and criminalization of "religious 'minorities' and 'deviants' in a way that is unprecedented in Islamic history." Although it is very much true that the modern nation-state-building process involved new and intensified forces of violence, liminal minorities had already a very precarious existence before the advent of nationalism as a popular force. Religious stigmatization of these groups gradually encompassed other forms

---

8. This information comes from the same survey conducted by Pew in 2011 and 2012 (available at https://www.pewforum.org/2012/08/09/the-worlds-muslims-unity-and-diversity-5-religious-identity [accessed March 29, 2023]).

of accusations involving resentment toward their perceived political influence, socioeconomic prominence, foreign connections, and cosmopolitanism. They gradually came to symbolize the anxieties and uncertainties of national identity in an era of globalization (Appadurai 2006; Sidel 2006). Their demographic, political, and socioeconomic weakness, rather than their strength, make them ideal targets of scapegoating. Their persistent liminal status hinders their recognition as legitimate religious faiths and lies at the core of their contemporary troubles.

CHAPTER 5

Religious Liminality and Societal Discrimination in a Global Perspective

(WITH JOSHUA LAMBERT)

Alevis in Turkey, Yezidis in Iraq, Baha'is in Iran, and Ahmadis in Pakistan are paradigmatic cases of liminal religious minorities. Their religious faith and practices are constantly questioned and stigmatized by dominant majorities. They have also been subject to intense official and societal discrimination. Although liminal minorities have a concentration in Muslim-majority countries in the Middle East and Asia, they also exist in other regions including South America and Europe. Do liminal minorities in other parts of the world such as Jehovah's Witnesses have a similar experience? How does the notion of liminality advance our understanding of religious discrimination across the globe? How do patterns of discrimination against liminal minorities resemble or differ from discrimination targeting non-liminal groups?

This chapter addresses these questions and offers a plausibility probe about the relevance of the term *religious liminality* to a broader number of cases including non-Muslim-majority societies. We first offer a methodological note about the challenge of making causal inferences about the relationship between religion, on the one hand, and discrimination and violence, on the other, in large-N quantitative studies. Consistent with middle-range theorizing, we advocate a mixed-method approach combining quantitative analyses with in-depth case studies. We identify eleven different religious groups in fifty-one countries as liminal minorities by utilizing information from the Religion and State Project Minorities Module, Round 3—that is, a total of fifty-one minority-state dyads observed over multiple years. The units of analyses in our statistical models are group-years—for example, Baha'is in Iran in 1995 and Jews in Turkey in 2000. We then present statistical models analyzing the patterns of societal discrimination and violence against both liminal and nonliminal religious minorities.

We reach several important findings on the basis of cross-regional analyses. First and expectedly, societal discrimination against all types of religious minorities is more likely to take place in states that heavily regulate religion while lacking robust civil liberties and protections for religious minorities. Next, our statistical models demonstrate that liminal religious minorities are more likely to experience societal discrimination including violent attacks than nonliminal religious groups in non-Muslim-majority countries controlling for a range of demographic, sociopolitical, and economic factors. This finding provides robust empirical evidence that the historical experience of liminality is not unique to countries with Islamic heritage. It is associated with stigmatization, discrimination, and denied equal citizenship beyond the Muslim world. Furthermore, religious minorities, whether liminal or not, are more likely to face discrimination in Muslim-majority countries than anywhere else. At the same time, societal discrimination against nonliminal religious groups such as Jews, various Christian denominations, Hindus, Buddhists, as well as Muslim minorities (e.g., Sunnis in Iran and Iraq and Shiites in Pakistan and Saudi Arabia) in Muslim-majority countries is even more pronounced than discrimination faced by liminal groups who often make tiny minorities. Several dynamics, especially collective threat perceptions aggravated by uneven effects of globalization and geopolitical tensions, generate a hostile environment to religious pluralism in Muslim-majority countries. Overall, the analyses show the conceptual breadth of the term *liminality* and its relevance to the lived experience of religious minorities in different parts of the world.

Conceptualizing and Measuring the Role of Religion in Civil Wars in Large-*N* Studies

There is now accumulating evidence that civil wars with a religious dimension are more difficult to resolve. At the same time, the reasons why such civil wars prove more intractable continue to be debated widely (Svensson 2020). The quantitative literature studying how religious faith informs the patterns of discrimination and violence follows two conventional approaches. The identity-based approach identifies conflicts involving parties with different religious markers as having a religious dimension. The historical examples include Catholics versus Protestants in Northern Ireland, Muslims versus Buddhists in Myanmar, and Shiite Hazaras versus Sunni Pashtuns (Fox 2004; Bormann, Cederman, and Vogt 2017). This approach, which provides parsimonious conceptualization, has two potential limitations. First, it is vulnerable to conceptual overstretching and likely to label a conflict religious even when religion may be peripheral or irrelevant to mobilization and contested issues. As Friedrich Engels ([1850] 1926) argued in the nineteenth century, the underlying reasons for the conflict could be about socioeconomic and political factors even if opposing sides belong to different religious identity groups. Next, the identity-based approach is likely to overlook cases where belligerents belong to the same religious/sectarian identity group but espouse dramatically opposing positions about the role of religion in public affairs. In fact, many violent conflicts in contemporary Muslim countries have such characteristics. The examples include the Salafi jihadist insurgency in Saudi Arabia, the terror campaign of the Pakistani Taliban, as well as the genocidal campaign organized by the Sunni Islamist Sudanese regime that targeted darker skin Sunni Muslim inhabitants of the Darfur region in the early 2000s (Prunier 2011).

The alternative is the issue-based approach aiming to mitigate both problems by giving primacy to stated and expressed positions of these parties (Svensson 2007; Svensson and Nilsson 2018; Toft 2021). Monica Toft (2021, 1612) describes religion as central to civil war if "the rebels fight over whether the state or a rebel-dominated region will be ruled according to a specific religious tradition." She also finds that "religious civil wars" have become more frequent and bloodier in the last several decades (1614, 1618). This approach identifies the conflicts where a party makes religious claims, such as establishing God's rule, defeating infidels, and liberation of sacred spaces and symbols, as having religious incompatibility. A prominent example of such a conflict is the question of control over Jerusalem's Holy Esplanade, which is sacred to both Islam and Judaism. In such contexts, the inherent incompatibility of exclusive control by either side exacerbates the intensity of a conflict (Hassner 2009). In a nutshell, the issue-based approach deems an armed conflict religious if one of the belligerents is motivated, partially or fully, by religious motives including the defense of doctrinal truth from infidels and heretics, eschatological beliefs about the end of the world, and messianic beliefs assigning a divine mission to a self-chosen community.

There are two questions facing the issue-based approach. The first question concerns measurement. Could we validly infer the motives of belligerents from their declared goals and platform? The second question concerns the level of analysis. Assuming elites employ religious symbols and discourse for strategic purposes, what makes such appeals more effective in mobilizing popular support and participation in violent campaigns? The first question implies a methodological limitation. Large-N studies, which rely on publicly available information for coding purposes, do not always have the tools to flesh out the motives of belligerents, which are often multilayered and obfuscated by rhetoric targeting multiple audiences. As discussed in chapter 1, religious faith could be peripheral to the motives of belligerents who primarily pursue material interests, social status, or political power under the cover of purportedly religious goals (Klocek and Hassner 2020). Political elites often have vested interest in manipulating (*instrumentalize*) religious values and sentiments to pursue their own parochial interests (Maoz and Henderson 2020, 59). Using religious symbols and rhetoric may help elites neutralize their opponents, mobilize greater public support, and divert attention from their own shortcomings (Isaacs 2016; Maoz and Henderson 2020, 77–83). Monica Toft (2007, 103–4) argues that political elites engage in an outbidding process to enhance their religious credibility in the eyes of people and mobilize popular support to counter an immediate threat. Such outbidding is more likely to happen when religious rhetoric has a transitional appeal attracting foreign funds and fighters and capitalizes on preexisting religious cleavages in a society. She also suggests that the notion of jihad, which calls for collective defense of Muslim lands from the attacks of unbelievers, has historically been central to Muslim discourses and makes Islam play a greater role in civil wars than any other belief system.

The second question concerns a core conceptual distinction between the motives of elites and ordinary people. Studies employing the issue-based approach tend to *assume* that the elite employment of religious symbols and rhetoric directly appeals to the hearts and minds of people and induces them to participate in collective action. For instance, Toft (2021, 1626) argues that "religion is a motivator for rebellion among Arab Muslims" as civil wars involving belligerents pursuing Islamist goals are preponderant in Arab countries. Along similar lines, Matthias Basedau, Birte Pfeiffer, and Johannes Vüllers (2016) conceptualize civil wars where at least one side makes religious claims as "theological armed conflicts." They suggest that making such claims motivates the targeted audience to fight and "ensures the widespread mobilization of believers" (10).

As argued throughout this book, we cannot simply assume that religious symbols and rhetoric are intrinsically effective means of popular mobilization. There are plenty of historical examples of when religious calls to arms failed spectacularly. By the turn of the millennium, Osama bin Laden's call for jihad against the United States and authoritarian Middle East regimes failed to galvanize significant popular support. Al-Qaeda's pivot toward spectacular terrorist attacks conducted by a small group of cadres could be interpreted as a consequence of this failure. During World War I, the German leadership saw a real asset in the fusion of the caliphate with the Ottoman sultanate. It hoped that the sultan's calls for jihad would find a receptive audience among Indian, North African, and Caucasian Muslims, subject to British, French, and Russian rule, respectively. Yet the three miserable Ottoman military campaigns between December 1914 and April 1915 revealed the limits of such calls (Rogan 2015, 127–28). Nonetheless, the Entente powers continued to be occupied with the threat of insurrection among their large Muslim populations inspired by the call of jihad until the end of the war (189):

> Much of the Allied war effort in the Middle East was driven by what proved to be an unwarranted fear of jihad. While colonial Muslims remained largely unresponsive to the Ottoman sultan-caliph's appeal, the European imperial powers continued to assume that any major Turkish success or Allied setback might provoke the dreaded Islamic uprising in their colonies in India and North Africa. Ironically, this left the *Allies more responsive to the caliph's call than his Muslim target audience*. (404; my emphasis)

The assumption that religious rhetoric intrinsically *mobilizes* people into violent action could not be taken for granted even in cases conventionally treated as "religious violence" par excellence. The IS genocidal campaign against Yezidis in 2014 had a pronounced religious dimension as Sunni Muslims who attacked Yezidis belonged to different religious identities. The IS did not only make religious claims central to its war-making agenda (i.e., the restoration of the Muslim caliphate) but also offered explicit religious justifications for killing and enslaving Yezidis en masse. Nonetheless, these factors by themselves are not sufficient to conclude that religion was central to the motives of the perpetrators of violence. The IS may have had geopolitical reasons to cleanse Sinjar from the Yezidis and used religious discourse as a cover-up. Furthermore, while the IS managed to mobilize a large number of foreign fighters from different parts of the world (Tezcür and Besaw 2020), the effects of Salafi jihadist ideology, as opposed to socioeconomic factors, political grievances, social networks, and organizational resources on IS recruitment remain highly debated (Souleimanov 2020). Besides, the reasons why the IS targeted Yezidis could differ significantly from the reasons why local Sunni Muslims actively took part in the atrocities. The "master" cleavage of a war rarely reflects the local and parochial dynamics driving violence on the ground

(Kalyvas 2003). As demonstrated in chapter 2, religiously inspired motives need to be fleshed out clearly and separated from nonreligious motives in understanding why Yezidis became the targets of a genocidal campaign.

Consequently, we need to be cautious when interpreting the results of cross-national studies that show that the presence of actors making religious claims has a significant relationship with various violent outcomes including civil wars and massacres. In some situations, declared goals and platforms may be a reliable proxy for underlying religious motives; in other situations, they are employed strategically to cover other motives. It is possible to flesh out causal mechanisms through which religious belief may shape motives to engage in discrimination and violence only with more granular data. An explanation presenting religious values and norms as a *cause* of political action could be persuasive when it is evaluated in tandem with other plausible and nonreligious motives including resentment, fear, and greed. Only then can we confidently describe episodes of violence as "religious."

As such, one of the most fruitful ways to study the role of religion in discrimination and armed conflicts is to pursue a mixed-method approach combining in-depth case studies with quantitative methods. Whereas the former enables us to flesh out the causal role of religious beliefs in shaping motivations to fight, the latter identifies the broader general patterns shaping discrimination and violence involving religion. In this spirit, this chapter presents statistical models to provide a comprehensive view of the experience of liminal and nonliminal minorities across the globe.

Identifying Liminal Minorities across the Globe

We identify liminal groups on the basis of the Religion and State Project Minorities Module, Round 3 (RASM3) data set, which provides comprehensive information about 771 religious minorities in 183 countries for a quarter century, from 1990 to 2014 (Fox, Finke, and Mataic 2018). In chapter 1, liminal minorities are defined as groups whose core religious beliefs and practices remain ambivalent, ill-defined, and stigmatized in the eyes of elite and ordinary members of a dominant group. Relatedly, liminal minorities lack official and theological recognition from a dominant religious group. They are also subject to widespread stigmatization informed by religious beliefs. This conceptual framework guides our coding, which is independent from the scope of societal discrimination faced by that group. For instance, according to RASM3, Jewish communities, which are coded nonliminal, are targets of societal discrimination across the globe. In comparison, RASM3 includes several liminal minorities as not facing discrimination. These groups include Baha'is in a variety of Muslim-majority countries such as Malaysia, Mali, and Oman and Druzes in Jordan, Lebanon, and Syria.

Our coding is contextual, temporal, and social. First, it focuses on the relationship between a dominant and a minority religion in a particular country. Stigmatization reflects predominant cleavages and power asymmetries that are prevalent in a society in a particular time (Pescosolido and Martin 2015). A group that is defined as liminal in one country may not be liminal in another country. For instance, Baha'is are coded as a liminal religious minority in Muslim-majority countries but not in other countries. Next, liminality is a dynamic categorization. Mormons throughout the nineteenth and early twentieth centuries could be described as a liminal group in Christian-majority countries. After Mormon leadership started to end the practice of polygamy by the 1890s, however, Mormons gradually achieved greater mainstream status (Saeed 2021b, 272). Hence, we do not code Mormons in the United States as a liminal minority in contemporary times. Third, we are primarily interested in how leaders and members of a dominant religion perceive a religious minority rather than the scope of constitutional and judicial rights granted to this minority. These dimensions, theological views and social values, on the one hand, and official practices, on the other hand, are often closely correlated but are distinct. For instance, Druzes in Lebanon tend to have significant political and legal representation. We code them as a liminal minority given the lack of Islamic recognition of the Druze faith and general Muslim ambivalence about the community.

None of the Abrahamic religious groups, including Catholics, Protestants, Orthodox Christians, Sunnis, Shiites, and Jews, are coded as liminal. Despite their history of mutual antagonism and rivalry, Abrahamic religions grant theological recognition to each other in contemporary times. In contrast, religious groups that emerge in more recent times such as Jehovah's Witnesses and Baha'is lack such recognition. The very nature of these faiths remains subject to fierce controversies. Dominant religions refuse to grant these groups the status of a legitimate separate faith on the grounds that they exhibit cultist, blasphemous, and deviant tendencies. Given these coding decisions, table 5.1 provides a summary of religious groups identified as liminal in RASM3.

Figure 5.1 shows the global distribution of eleven liminal religious minorities present in thirty-eight different countries. Although there is a concentration in the Middle East, many other countries in other parts of the world have liminal minorities. In Europe, Austria, France, and Latvia host communities of Jehovah's Witnesses, which emerged in the United States in the late nine-

LIMINALITY AND DISCRIMINATION IN A GLOBAL PERSPECTIVE

Table 5.1 Liminal minorities and countries

MINORITY	NUMBER OF COUNTRIES
Baha'i[a] (Afghanistan, Brunei, Chad, Djibouti, Egypt, Gambia, Iran, Jordan, Kuwait, Kyrgyzstan, Malaysia, Mali, Oman, Pakistan, Qatar, Sierra Leone, Tunisia, United Arab Emirates, Zanzibar-Tanzania)	19
Jehovah's Witnesses (Austria, Chile, Costa Rica, Ecuador, El Salvador, France, Georgia, Jamaica, Latvia, Mexico)	10
Ahmadi Muslims (Bangladesh, Gambia, Indonesia, Pakistan)	4
Druze (Israel, Jordan, Lebanon, Syria)	4
Sikhs[a] (Afghanistan, Kuwait, Oman, Pakistan)	4
Rastafarians (Barbados, Jamaica, Malawi)	3
Yezidis (Armenia, Iraq, Kurdistan region of Iraq)	3
Alevi (Turkey)	1
Faid al-Djaria Sufi Muslims (Chad)	1
Falun Gong (China)	1
Scientologists (Germany)	1
Total	51

Source: RASM3.

[a]Baha'is and Sikhs are coded as liminal only in Muslim-majority countries.

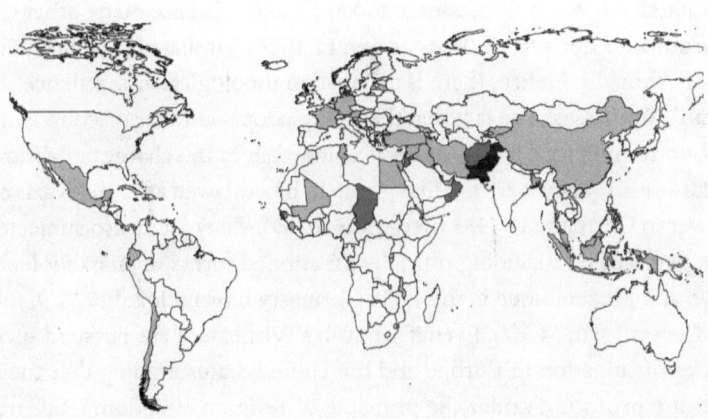

FIGURE 5.1. Liminal minorities across the globe

teenth century. Germany has a presence of Scientologists. In Central and South America, Chile, Costa Rica, Ecuador, El Salvador, Jamaica, and Mexico have minority populations of Jehovah's Witnesses. Pakistan is the only country that is home to three liminal groups: Ahmadis, Baha'is, and Sikhs. These three groups are subject to widespread societal and official discrimination that occasionally translate into acts of violence. There are seven countries with two liminal minorities: Afghanistan (Baha'is and Sikhs), Chad (Baha'is and a Sufi group called Al Faid al-Djaria), Gambia (Baha'is and Ahmadis), Jamaica (Jehovah's Witnesses and Rastafarians), Jordan (Baha'is and Druzes), Kuwait (Baha'is and Sikhs), and Oman (Baha'is and Sikhs).

We briefly explain why we code these eleven minorities as liminal. Yezidis of Iraq and Alevis of Turkey are the two liminal minorities that are analyzed in depth in the previous chapters. The sizable Alevi and Yezidi communities in several European countries, most notably in Germany, are not included in RASM3. Chapter 4 offered a historical discussion of the liminality of both Baha'is and Ahmadis. Baha'is are coded as liminal in Muslim-majority countries given the perceived challenge of the Baha'i faith to one of the core principles of Islamic teachings: Muhammad as the seal of prophets. In RASM3, Baha'is form minorities in eighteen such countries, ranging from Tunisia in North Africa to Brunei in Southeast Asia. As mentioned above, Baha'is in non-Muslim-majority countries are coded as non-liminal. A similar logic applies to Ahmadiyya, which emerged as a separate faith in the late nineteenth century. RASM3 lists Ahmadis as a religious minority in four Muslim-majority countries. All these occurrences are coded as liminal.

Although Jehovah's Witnesses self-identify as Christians, many other Christian groups do not accept them as one of them, similar to Muslim perceptions of Ahmadis. Hence, there is a Christian theological ambivalence about Jehovah's Witnesses. The fact that the group adopts a stance of conscientious objection to military service makes it vulnerable to the charges of disloyalty and extremism. They were the first group to be outlawed after the Nazis came to power in Germany in 1933 (Bergen 2016, 35). They were also subjected to severe persecution including officially sanctioned forms of mass violence in Malawi and Mozambique in the 1970s (Amnesty International 1976, 9; Jubber 1977; Carver 1990, 64–67). Even if Jehovah's Witnesses have pursued successful cases of litigation in Europe and the United States arguing that their activities are protected under the principle of religious freedom (Richardson 2015), they continue to face exclusion and discrimination in many parts of the world. In some countries including Egypt and Russia, the group is officially banned (USCIRF 2020; Majumdar 2021). RASM3 lists Jehovah's Witnesses as a religious minority in ten Christian-majority countries ranging from Chile in South America to Georgia in the Caucuses. All these occurrences are coded as liminal.

The Druze faith emerged as an offshoot of Ismaili Shiism in the early eleventh century (Halm 2004, 178–80). Reincarnation, belief in the rebirth of a particular soul in a new body, is central to the faith (Halabi 2014). Like Yezidis,

LIMINALITY AND DISCRIMINATION IN A GLOBAL PERSPECTIVE

Druzes do not welcome conversion into their faith and practice endogamy. Although there is an established historical tradition of Druzes practicing dissimulation and hiding their true beliefs to avoid persecution in the hands of Muslim rulers and majorities (Nisan 2010), the community does not follow the basic practices of Islam including fasting during the month of Ramadan and praying in mosques. Compared to other liminal minorities in the Muslim world including Ahmadis, Baha'is, and Yezidis, the community enjoys higher levels of official recognition in contemporary times. In RASM3, Druzes are coded as present in four countries: Israel, Jordan, Lebanon, and Syria. The largest number of Druzes live in Syria. They have played historically salient political roles and continue to have judicial autonomy regarding personal matters such as family law (Diab n.d.). In Lebanon, the Druze faith is one of the eighteen officially recognized sects. In contrast, Druzes in Jordan lack official recognition and their own courts and are listed as Muslims. Nonetheless, Druzes occupy an ambivalent position from the perspective of Sunni theology and majority in all these countries.

In Israel, the state aims to dissociate Druzes from Arab identity and Palestinian nationalism (Firro 2001). The community is recognized as a religious group separate from Islam and has its own religious courts and council. Druzes serve in the Israeli army and have access to a separate curriculum and school system. Many Druzes, who make around 2 percent of the Israeli population, also vote for Jewish parties (Nisan 2010). In a sense, they are a "privileged minority" compared to other Arab-speaking citizens of Israel (I. Kaufman 2004). At the same time, they remain subject to various forms of discrimination including land confiscations and restrictions (Yiftachel and Segal 1998). Furthermore, the Basic Law of 2018, which enshrined Israel as the Jewish national state and revoked the status of Arabic as an official language, fostered widespread grievances among the country's Druze minority. The available evidence suggests that there is still widespread ambivalence and ignorance about core Druze beliefs and practices among Jewish citizens of Israel (Miles 2020). In summary, Druzes in all of these four countries are coded as liminal minority given the widespread ambiguity characterizing their classification, ranging from a monotheistic religion to a branch of Shiite Islam, from a separate ethnic group to a deviant sect.

Sikhism, which was founded by Guru Nanak as a monotheistic religion in the Indian subcontinent in the late fifteenth century, is coded as a liminal faith in Muslim-majority countries. That is because Sikhism, similar to the Baha'i faith, presents a major challenge to the Islamic claim of being the final monotheistic religion. According to RASM3, there are four such countries where Sikhs are recorded as a religious minority: Afghanistan, Kuwait, Oman, and Pakistan. There is only limited information about Faid al-Djaria in Chad. It was banned by the government in Chad in 2001 on the grounds that some of their core activities including the mingling of opposite genders in religious rituals are deemed to be un-Islamic (United States Department of State 2002). Given this fundamental disagreement about the nature of religious beliefs and practices of this group, we code it as a liminal minority.

Rastafarians, a movement that emerged in Jamaica among descendants of African slaves in the 1930s, make minorities in Barbados and Jamaica (Price 2003). Although there has been increasing acceptance of Rastafarians as a religious faith in both countries, they continue to face widespread stigmatization and discrimination. They are often stereotyped as "marijuana dealers" (United States Department of State 2019). Hence, their claims to be a religious faith remain contested. Scientology is a movement that emerged in the 1950s in the United States. RASM3 records Scientology only in Germany where it lacks the status of an official religion and is under surveillance by intelligence agencies. It remains subject to intense controversy given its opposition to the practice of psychiatry. It is also accused of controlling all aspects of its members' lives and exploiting them financially (DW 2007). Falun Gong is a spiritual movement that emerged in China in the early 1990s. It is labeled as a heretical cult and a national security threat by the Chinese government by the end of the 1990s. Many adherents of the movement migrated to North America. Its remaining sympathizers in China are subject to persecution (Ownby 2008). They are subject to detention, put in labor camps, and confined to mental hospitals (Saeed 2021b, 267). Given the widespread ambiguity regarding the classification of Falun Gong as a religion, it is coded as a liminal group in China.

The RASM3 data set lists seventy-nine animist groups in various parts of the world, primarily in South America and Africa. According to animism, nonhuman entities such plants could affect human affairs in positive and nefarious ways. It tends to lack a single creed or doctrinal basis and could be compatible with both polytheistic and monotheistic faiths (Park 2020). In RASM3, animists tend to be amalgamations of various faith groups that may or may not form a coherent entity. For these reasons, we do not code animists as liminal. On the basis of this coding procedure, figure 5.2 reveals that liminal minorities make around 7 percent of all minority-year observations in the RASM3 data set. There is a higher concentration of liminal minorities in Muslim-majority countries. Almost two-thirds of liminal minority-year observations are recorded in Muslim-majority countries. There is considerable variation across Muslim-majority countries regarding the scope of religious discrimination. Some of the countries, especially ones around the Persian Gulf such as Saudi Arabia, engage in very high levels of discrimination; other countries, especially ones located in

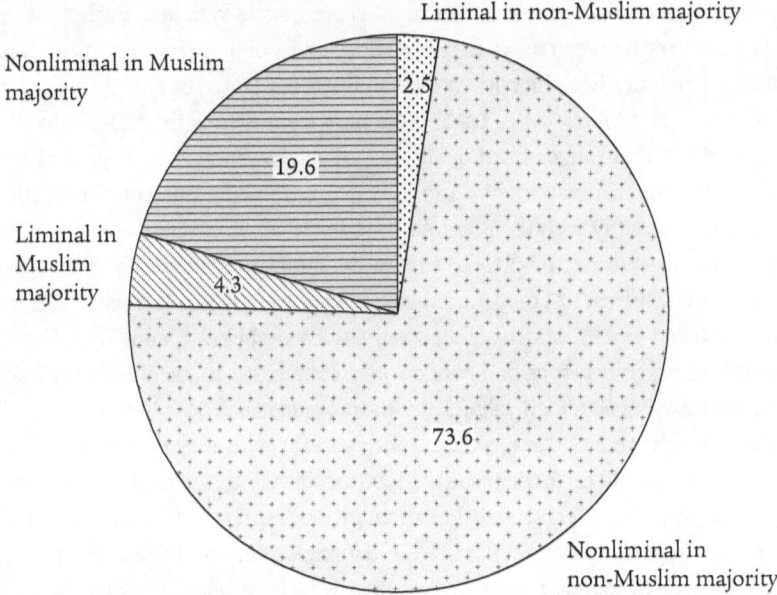

FIGURE 5.2. Liminal and nonliminal minorities in Muslim and non-Muslim countries

sub-Saharan Africa, exhibit greater tolerance (Fox 2016, 125–26, 153). Accordingly, some liminal minorities, such as Baha'is in Egypt and Kuwait, face high levels of governmental discrimination, while other liminal minorities, such as in Gambia and Mali, face very low levels of such discrimination.

Societal Discrimination and Violence against Religious Minorities

Our main premise is that the conceptual distinction between liminal and nonliminal religious groups advance our understanding of discrimination and violence targeting such groups. In our statistical models, the units of analyses in the models are group-years—that is, a religious minority in a particular country in a particular year. For instance, Baha'is in Iran in 1995, a liminal minority, as well as Jews in France in 2000, a nonliminal minority, are separate observations in these models.

Our dependent variable is the Societal Discrimination against Minorities Index of RASM3. This index is most relevant given our interest in how nonstate actors engage in acts of persecution against religious groups. It is composed of twenty-seven indicators that measure different forms of discrimination ranging from symbolic to economic harassment to large-scale violence. Each of these indicators vary between 0 (no discrimination) and 2 or 3 (high levels of discrimination). The index has a high level of reliability as measured by Cronbach's alpha (Fox, Finke, and Mataic 2018, 12–15). We have transformed this index into a binary variable that ranges from 0, absence of discrimination, to 1, presence of any kind of discrimination. We use a binary variable because our theoretical concern is primarily with the presence or absence of discrimination and not the degree to which it occurs. Moreover, the distribution of the index is very left-skewed, meaning that 72 percent of all observations (n = 19,275) receive either a value of 0 or 1 and 90 percent of all observations are below a value of 8. Consequently, using an overspecified continuous dependent variable in our statistical analyses provides no added value. Even more concerning, a few influential outliers at the right end of the spectrum (observations with very high levels of discrimination) would drive the results.[1] More specifically, this variable ranges up to a possible value of 47, and a total of three groups represent all values above 30; Copts in Egypt, Christians in Pakistan, and a single-year observation of Muslims in Myanmar. Ultimately, these cases would drive statistical results when theoretical underpinnings are not related to the scale of violence.

Our main independent variable is a binary variable indicating whether a religious minority is liminal or not. As summarized above, we identify eleven different religious minorities in fifty-one countries as liminal in this data set. We are primarily interested in understanding how liminality is associated with the experiences of societal discrimination across the globe. We also include a series of variables in our models about (a) state-religion relations, (b) religion and demographics, (c) political regime, (d) armed conflict, and (e) economy. A summary of all these variables with descriptive statistics is provided in table AO.2 in the online appendix (https://hdl.handle.net/1813/113348).

Societal and state discrimination on the basis of religion is a major factor contributing to violent religious persecution (Grim and Finke 2011). State discrimination against religious groups is also associated with greater discontent among such groups (Basedau et al. 2017). Moreover, members of religious groups that are favored by the state are more likely to engage in more lethal

---

1. Another option is to adopt a dependent variable using seven variables measuring only forms of discrimination that reach levels of physical violence. We run additional models where the dependent variable is a binary variable taking the value of 0 when there are no acts of violence and the value of 1 in the presence of such acts. The results do not show any significant relationship between liminality and societal violence at $p > 0.10$ level. Given the theoretical framework developed in this book, these results are not surprising. Societal violence against liminal minorities is expected only under specific circumstances when a majority becomes politically resentful. We do not have the ability to test this argument directly given data limitations, as we do not have a variable that could accurately capture the notion of political resentment cross-nationally.

terrorist attacks (Henne, Saiya, and Hand 2020). We use four different variables measuring distinct aspects of the state and religion relationship. Two of these variables come from the Comparative Constitutions Project (CCP) (Elkins, Ginsburg, and Melton 2014). The first variable (*No Separation*) indicates whether the constitution has an explicit decree of separation of church and state. The second variable (*No Freedom of Religion*) indicates whether the constitution provides for freedom of religion. Both variables range between 1 (separation and constitutional provisions for freedom of religion) and 2 (lack of separation and no constitutional provisions). They are also not significantly correlated ($c = 0.09$), justifying their inclusion in the models simultaneously. We expect that settings lacking a constitutional separation between the state and religion and provisions for freedom of religion cultivate greater intolerance toward minority religions among the populace.

We also utilize two additional variables measuring other aspects of the state-religion relations. They come from the Religion and State (RAS) 3 data set, which covers 183 states or statelets for a quarter of a century, between 1990 and 2014 (Fox 2020). The first variable is whether the state has an official religion (*State Religion*). In 2000, 75 out of 188 countries had state religions. A plurality of these countries (n = 29, around 39 percent) had Muslim majorities and twenty-two (30 percent) of them had Catholic majorities. Overall, countries with a concentration of adherents from a single religion are more likely to have state religions than countries with higher levels of religious diversity (Barro and McCleary 2005). Another variable concerning the state-religion relations is the existence of blasphemy laws in favor of a majority religion. Blasphemy laws that ostensibly aim to protect majority religion from defamation are often associated with silencing of dissent and increased levels of terrorist violence. Such laws are conducive to the rise of a culture of impunity where harassment of and violence against religious minorities are tolerated if not condoned (Saiya 2017). They also exhibit strong regional clustering. Apart from Israel and Iraq (post 2003), all other Middle Eastern countries have blasphemy laws favorable to the majority religion. Obviously, a law in the books does not tell anything about its enforceability. Although some of the laws remain dormant and rarely applied, attempts to enforce blasphemy laws vigorously in other countries result in gross human rights violations.[2] In any case, we expect

---

2. An infamous case includes the death sentence given to Asia Bibi, a Christian woman, for committing blasphemy in Pakistan in 2010, a decision later overturned by the supreme court. She eventually took refuge in Canada. Article 216 of the penal code of 2004 of Turkey, ostensibly a secular country, is often used to prosecute individuals expressing opinions critical of religion. Among other things, it criminalizes actions and expressions that openly "degrade" religious beliefs of a segment of the population. Although prosecutors could marshal this article to penalize hate speech targeting

to observe greater societal discrimination against religious minorities in countries with blasphemy laws. Similar to CCP variables, these two RAS variables are slow moving in the sense that it is very unlikely for a state to have an official religion, blasphemy laws, and lack of protections for a religious minority in one year but not in the subsequent year.

We use four variables regarding religion and demographics. *Population* simply indicates the size of a country's population (logged). *Minority Size*, developed by Davis Brown and Patrick James (2018) and used in RASM3, is the ratio of a religious minority to the total population in a country in a given year. According to group threat theory, the relative size of a minority is a central factor shaping its perceptions by a majority. Since larger minorities have a greater political mobilization capacity and compete for scarce resources, they are more likely to be viewed in negative light and face discrimination by members of a majority (Blalock 1957; Quillian 1995). We also control for the percent share of Muslims (*Muslims*) and Christians (*Christians*) in a country. These two variables are five-year rolling averages. The level of societal discrimination experienced by liminal minorities may be conditional on the ratio of Muslim population in a country. That is because Islam's self-image as the last prophetic religion is likely to cultivate a general attitude of antipathy, if not outright hostility, toward any religion that emerged in more recent times. To test this possibility, we include an interaction term between the variables of *Liminal* and *Muslims* in our models.

Figure 5.3 shows the levels of societal discrimination against both nonliminal and liminal groups in countries differentiated according to the relative size of their Muslim population. Liminal minorities in non-Muslim countries are more likely to face discrimination than nonliminal religious minorities. Discrimination against both minority types increases significantly in Muslim-majority countries. Jewish minorities face discrimination very widely. The average societal discrimination score for Jews is 0.8 in Muslim-majority countries and 0.69 in non-Muslim-majority countries. To put it differently, eight out of every ten Jewish communities in Muslim-majority countries and seven out of every ten Jewish communities in non-Muslim-majority countries experience discrimination in a given year. It should also be noted that societal discrimination against Jews tends to be higher than government discrimination across the world (Fox and Topor 2021, 12). The contrasting experience of Baha'is as a nonliminal minority in non-Muslim countries and as a liminal

---

minorities, they often use it to harass dissident voices challenging majoritarian views and hegemonic positions (Bayır 2013, 234–37, 241–43). In a notorious case, the world-famous pianist Fazıl Say received a suspended prison sentence of ten months in 2013.

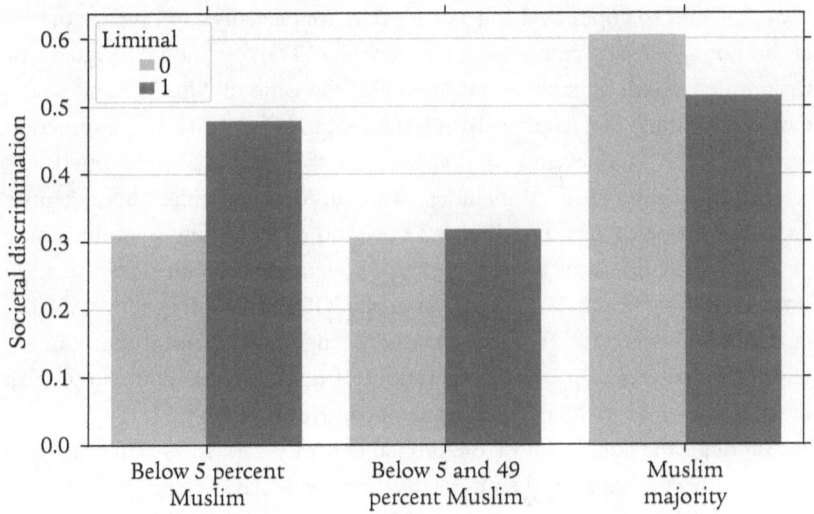

FIGURE 5.3. Societal discrimination, liminal minorities, and Muslim-majority countries

minority in Muslim countries is instructive. The discrimination score for Baha'i communities is 0.07 in the former and 0.56 in the latter. The implication is that whereas Jews are discriminated against in many different parts of the world, Baha'is are subject to widespread discrimination only in Muslim-majority countries where they have a liminal status.

We consider a number of different variables about regime type. Since these variables tend to be highly correlated with each other (see figure AO.1, visualizing correlations among all variables in the online appendix at https://hdl.handle.net/1813/113348), we include two of the theoretically most relevant variables. The first one is the Civil Liberties Index of V-Dem (*Civil Liberties*), which ranges from 0 to 1. Another relevant variable (*Ethnic Exclusion*) measures the ratio of politically relevant ethnic groups excluded from access to political power (Bormann, Cederman, and Vogt 2017). We also include two variables measuring armed conflict obtained from the Uppsala Conflict Data Program (UCDP): whether the country where a religious minority is located experienced a civil war (*Intrastate Conflict*) and interstate war (*Interstate Conflict*) in a given year. Finally, we include two conventional economic variables: *GDP per capita* (logged) and *GDP per capita change*. Intrastate Conflict, Interstate Conflict, GDP per capita, and GDP per capita change are lagged by one year.

Table A.1 included in the appendix presents three mixed-effects models given the variation of covariate structures between group and country-level features. Although certain groups may share common characteristics across national boundaries, we treat them as independent entities with distinct historical and sociopolitical trajectories that are partially captured by the inclusion of a series of country-specific variables. The first model includes our main independent variable about liminality, the ratio of Muslims and Christian populations, the relative size of the religious minority, the interaction term between *Liminal* and *Muslims* as well as four variables about state-religion relations. Model 2 includes two additional variables about regime type: the scope of civil liberties and the ratio of politically relevant ethnic groups excluded from access to executive power. Model 3 includes five additional variables: population, GDP per capita, GDP per capita change, the occurrence of interstate conflict, and the occurrence of intrastate conflict. Given the number of missing observations of these variables, the sample size in the last model is reduced by 15 percent compared to model 1.

Although the coefficient of the liminal minority variable is significant and positive, the coefficient of the interaction term between *Liminal* and *Muslims* is also consistently significant and negative in all three models. To facilitate interpretation, figure 5.4 visualizes how societal discrimination against liminal and nonliminal minorities change as the ratio of Muslim population in a country increases. This figure is based on model 1 since using other models does not reveal different patterns. Although discrimination against nonliminal religious minorities is unlikely in countries with no sizable Muslim population, a liminal minority in such a country has a higher likelihood of discrimination. The likelihood of discrimination against both liminal and nonliminal minorities increases significantly in Muslim-majority countries. Many of these countries embody hegemonic versions of Islam that is nationalized, plays a central role in public education, and informs legal discrimination against other religions, and is associated with restrictions on freedom of speech and gender equality (Cesari 2014, 11–12). Most notably, a nonliminal minority in a country with more than 90 percent Muslim population is twice as likely than a nonliminal minority in a country with no Muslim population to experience societal discrimination. This finding is consistent with research suggesting that religious minorities in the Muslim Middle East prefer a secular dictatorship to a more democratic but majoritarian regime (Mansfield and Snyder 2005/2006; Belge and Karakoç 2015). In fact, the collapse or weakening of authoritarian rule in Egypt, Libya, Syria, and Tunisia unleashed waves of communal hostility and violence targeting non-Muslim minorities in the 2010s (Klocek et al. 2022). Not surprisingly, members of religious minorities in these countries often perceive authoritarian rule as a bulwark against majoritarian discrimination and violence.

We identify several factors to explain the finding that nonliminal minorities in Muslim-majority countries are more likely to face discrimination than liminal minorities. First, Druzes in Jordan, Lebanon, and Lebanon are coded not

LIMINALITY AND DISCRIMINATION IN A GLOBAL PERSPECTIVE

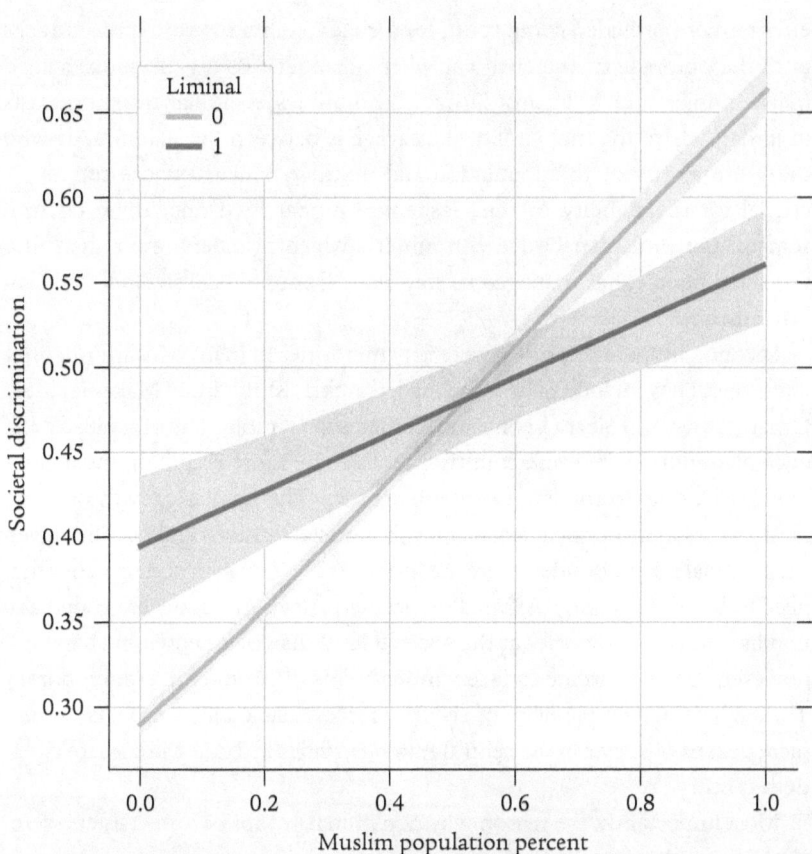

FIGURE 5.4. The effects of religious demographics on societal discrimination against religious minorities

to experience any societal discrimination during the entire period in RASM3. Druzes remain on the periphery of main political cleavages in these three countries. As a well-organized and tight-knit community, Druzes of Lebanon have access to political representation in a highly sectarian system. Organizations representing more powerful and numerous sects such as Shiite Muslims and Maronites have an interest to seek the support of the Druze community. Hence, the intricacies of Lebanese politics are a factor likely to be conducive to its societal acceptance. In Syria, the main sectarian tension involves the Alawite minority that has disproportionate access to political power and the Sunni majority whose members are underrepresented in the echelons of power.[3] This polarized

---

3. Alawites are coded as Shiite Muslims in RASM3.

environment provided some room for Druzes' ability to avoid direct attacks until the outbreak of the civil war when Salafi jihadist organizations staged indiscriminate attacks against Druze communities. A similar situation exists in Jordan where the main political cleavage is between the Palestinians who make a majority of the population and the East Bankers whose support is crucial for the stability of the Hashemite monarchy. Under these circumstances, the Jordanian Druze community, which numbers fewer than fifty thousand people, has managed to stay aloof from political struggles and social tensions.

Second, liminal minorities make tiny minorities in many Muslim-majority countries. They include Baha'is in Chad, Gambia, Kyrgyzstan, Malaysia, Mali, Oman, Qatar, and Sierra Leone and Ahmadis in Gambia. The organized presence of minorities in these countries tends to be more recent, in most cases going back only to the late twentieth century. The further growth of these faith groups in those societies may result in social tensions and hostility given their liminal status. Besides, there are instances of significant coding issues that need to be addressed in RASM3. For instance, Alevis in Turkey are coded as a nondiscriminated minority at the societal level. As documented in chapter 3, however, Alevis continue to face various forms of hostility in contemporary Turkey. The blatant passivity of security forces enabled local crowds to massacre dozens of Alevis in the central Anatolian cities in Turkey in the late twentieth century.

Most importantly, the reason why nonliminal groups become targets of societal discrimination in Muslim-majority countries is a multifaceted phenomenon that differs from the reason why liminal groups are targeted in those countries. A wide variety of nonliminal religious groups are subject to societal discrimination in Muslim-majority countries, including animists, Buddhists, Confucians (in Brunei), various Christian denominations, Jews, Hindus, Muslim minorities—for example, Sunnis in Iraq and Shiites in Iran. At the same time, societal discrimination in Muslim-majority countries is highest against Christian and Jewish minorities (Fox 2020, 80, 122). For instance, Christian communities are likely to suffer during times of geopolitical tensions and interventionist policies pursued by Western states. The US invasion of Iraq in 2003 dramatically increased the scope of discrimination and violence targeting the country's Christian communities. The controversy in 2005 when a Danish newspaper published cartoons of Muhammad, the prophet of Islam, led to attacks against local Christian communities and churches in Nigeria (Reliefweb 2006), Lebanon (Zoepf and Fattah 2006), and Pakistan (Walsh and Aglionby 2006). The perceived connection of local Jewish communities to Israel, which is not recognized by many Muslim-majority states, is likely to trigger collective threat perceptions and generate societal hostility (Fox 2020, 123). Similarly, the high levels of societal discrimination against Hindus in both Bangladesh and Pakistan could be explained by the "India factor." Tensions in bilateral relations as well as riots targeting Muslims in India foster a climate of insecurity for Hindu minorities in these two countries (Rahman 2012; Pattanaik 2013). Consequently, discrimination against nonliminal groups in Muslim-majority countries are likely to be driven by collective threat perceptions aggravated by international conflicts and tend to be distinct from discrimination against liminal groups informed by theological animosity.

Some of the other independent variables exhibit significant coefficients as shown in table A.1 in the appendix. Discrimination against religious minorities, in general, is more likely in countries with a higher ratio of Muslims in all three models. The coefficient of the ratio of Christian population is also significantly and positively associated in models 2 and 3, suggesting that societal discrimination becomes more likely in countries with a higher ratio of Christians. As expected, discrimination against liminal minorities becomes more likely in countries with constitutions that do not provide for freedom of religion. Furthermore, religious minorities in countries with a state religion and blasphemy laws are more likely to suffer from societal discrimination. Whereas discrimination appears more likely to happen in settings with a separation between the state and religion in model 1, that correlation loses its significance in model 3. At the same time and against the expectations of group threat theory, the relative size of a religious minority is not a factor in shaping the patterns of discrimination it is facing. Large minorities are not more likely to experience harassment and violence than tiny religious minorities.

In model 2, observations with higher levels of civil liberties are less likely to have social societal discrimination against religious minorities. The coefficient of the *Ethnic Exclusion* variable remains insignificant. However, it becomes significant and positive in model 3, indicating that higher levels of political exclusion are associated with higher discrimination against religious minorities. Among the five new variables included in model 3, four of them have significant coefficients. Discrimination against religious minorities is more likely in more populous countries. Economic downturns, as measured by low GDP per capita growth, is associated positively with discrimination. However, societal discrimination exhibits a positive association with economic wealth, as measured by GDP per capita. At the same time, the magnitude of this association is very small, and the inclusion of this variable does not have a meaningful impact on our explanatory variables of main theoretical interest. Although interstate wars are not associated significantly with discrimination against religious minorities, such discrimination is more likely to take place during civil wars.

This chapter provides several insights that advance our understanding of the experience of religious minorities across the globe. First, the classification of certain religious groups as liminal provides a valuable conceptual tool to bring greater analytical clarity to make sense of their experiences across the globe. In particular, the finding that liminal minorities are more likely to be subject of discrimination than nonliminal minorities in non-Muslim-majority countries demonstrates the relevance of this conceptualization distinction beyond the specific cases studied in this book. Liminal minorities lack recognition and are often subject to "coercive classification" as states name these groups "in ways that are fundamentally resisted by the group itself" (Saeed 2021b, 262). This factor makes them particularly vulnerable to societal discrimination.

Next, our statistical analyses reveal no significant relationship between the size of a religious minority and the likelihood of it being discriminated against. According to the group threat theory, the larger size of an out-group, the greater threat perception it generates among members of an in-group (e.g., Schlueter and Scheepers 2010; Kopstein and Wittenberg 2018). Baha'is in Iran, Jehovah's Witnesses in European and South American countries, Ahmadis in Indonesia and Pakistan, and Yezidis in Iraq make tiny minorities. Yet they are also subject to regular patterns of societal discrimination that occasionally result in violent riots. As argued throughout this book, popular stigmatization of these groups has deep historical roots and is independent from the question of whether these groups have a capacity for political mobilization or present a major demographic threat to majorities.

Finally, as discussed in previous chapters, societal discrimination does not lead to acts of mass violence as long as the state authority remains intact and aims to maintain public order. In certain historical situations, authoritarian governments could also act as a bulwark against popular violence against stigmatized minorities. The Yezidi experience in Iraq, which is the topic of chapter 2, is particularly instructive. In the eyes of many Yezidis, the highly authoritarian Saddam regime provided protection from potential attacks from their Muslim neighbors. Post-Saddam Iraq generated not only an atmosphere of relative political pluralism but also sectarianism threatening the very survival of Yezidis and other religious minorities. Similarly, Baha'is of Iran had relatively higher levels of safety and opportunities under the Pahlavi monarchy preceding the revolution. Consequently, polities lacking well-established democratic institutions but experiencing waves of popular mobilization present unique risks for liminal minorities.

Conclusion
Transcending Liminality

In conclusion, I address the question of how we can envision interreligious relations beyond liminality and achieve progressive change. What factors lead to emancipation of liminal minorities and promise interreligious relations with greater harmony? I argue that neither democracy nor secularism is sufficient by itself to bring an end to liminality. Democracy inherently involves majority rule that could provide a greater platform to antiliminal positions jeopardizing the rights of stigmatized religious minorities. Although secularism reduces the influence of religious movements over state policies and legislation, it could also foster antiliminal resentment among large segments of society who feel excluded from the political system. Drawing on several key contributions to the vast literature on politics of recognition, I argue that moving beyond liminality entails a self-reflexive transformation in influential religious teachings that grant recognition to stigmatized groups and ideas conducive to genuine interfaith coexistence. Finally, I offer a brief assessment of how taking the role of religious faith in shaping political behavior seriously remains an essential and promising scholarly task in contemporary times.

Embracing Liminality

The cases I analyze in this book make a rather pessimistic reading. In some cases, liminality persists; in other cases, it deepens. Yezidis have attracted unprecedented international awareness and sympathy, but that came only after genocidal attacks that brought their millennial existence in northern Iraq to the brink of destruction. A broader historical perspective, however, presents a more optimistic perspective about the dynamics of change regarding religious coexistence beyond liminality.

The experience of Mormons and Jehovah's Witnesses in the United States demonstrates both the limits and promises of religious pluralism. Both groups, which originated in the United States in the nineteenth century, were subject to the harshest forms of religious persecution for many decades. During periods of pervasive anti-Catholicism and antisemitism (Hofstadter 1966), the government often intervened on behalf of Catholics and Jews, religious minorities who were both larger and had better political connections. In contrast, state authorities often took a hostile position against Mormons and Jehovah's Witnesses and did little to stop persecutions of these religious groups by societal actors. As David T. Smith (2015, 36) argues, these two groups were more likely to be persecuted than Catholics and Jews since there was "a prevailing, powerful discourse in civil society that represents them as something other than a genuine religion." They were often described in pejorative terms as frauds, cults, or seditious political movements masquerading as faith groups (36–38). Employing the conceptual framework developed in this book, both Mormons and Jehovah's Witnesses were liminal minorities whose core beliefs and practices lacked legitimacy in the eyes of the broader American public until the late twentieth century.

In the contemporary United States, popular views of Mormons continue to exhibit traces of liminality even if the general trend is toward greater recognition. Many influential Evangelical Christian leaders continue to regard Mormonism as a "false religion" and "heretical." Nonetheless, Evangelicals and Mormons tend to share common political positions (Gjelten 2018). According to a 2012 survey conducted among Mormons living in the United States, 46 percent of the respondents say that there is "a lot of discrimination against Mormons." Sixty-two percent of them also think that Americans know not too much or nothing about Mormons. Whereas almost all Mormons (97 percent) describe their religion as part of Christianity, according to a 2011 survey, only around half of the non-Mormons think that Mormonism is a Christian religion. At the same time, 63 percent of Mormon respondents in the 2012 survey think that "acceptance of Mormonism is rising" (as opposed to 5 percent who think that it is failing) in the United States. Moreover, 56 percent say that the United States is ready for a Mormon president (Pew Research Center 2012a).

The experience of Mormons in the United States suggests that it is possible to envision progressive change that offers emancipation from the bane of liminality and conducive to durable coexistence. At a fundamental level, countering stigmatization that denies the legitimacy of core beliefs and practices of liminal minorities is indispensable for intercommunal coexistence. That is not to ignore other factors and contingencies contributing to and intensifying the persecution of liminal minorities. As the theoretical framework developed in this book makes it clear, political resentment, popular perception that liminal minorities gain greater access to power while the majority loses status, plays a central role in the outbursts of mass violence targeting liminal minorities. At the same time, these patterns of violence tap into widespread and rarely challenged religious prejudices transmitted across generations. In their study of lynchings of Blacks in the post-Reconstruction South, Tolnay and Beck (1995, 23) observe, "Years of racist propaganda had, in the minds of many whites, lessened blacks to simplistic and often animalistic, stereotypes. These debasing images further depersonalized and dehumanized the victim." As the pervasiveness of racism among the whites in the South enabled the lynchings of Blacks, the pervasiveness of religious stigmas among the Sunni Muslims in Iraq and Turkey enabled the massacres of Yezidis and Alevis, respectively.

The quest for greater religious pluralism involving legitimization of previously liminal beliefs could be conceptualized as a form of politics of recognition that has been central to social justice struggles across the globe since the late twentieth century. As long as a religious group is not considered a legitimate community of believers by a dominant majority, it is unrealistic to expect that popular stigmatization of that group fostering its persecution would be effectively countered. In the absence of such religious legitimacy, members of a dominant religious group would be highly susceptible to conspiratorial narratives claiming that the group engages in all sorts of malicious activities ranging from rituals characterized by sexual promiscuity to spying on behalf of hostile foreigners. As I elucidate throughout this book, such allegations have nothing to do with how members of a liminal minority act and reflect the stereotypical perspective of a dominant religious group. Consequently, overcoming religious misrecognition and unrecognition of these minorities remains at the heart of curbing antiliminal persecutions.

Redressing cultural and symbolic injustices emanating from the denial of dignity of group identities has been at the forefront of progressive politics in the post–Cold War era (Taylor 1994). From a critical perspective, claims of neutrality, impartiality, and meritocracy that supposedly ignore group identities in the allocation of material and symbolic resources cultivate systematic oppression and social domination (Young 1990). These forms of injustice, as different from socioeconomic forms calling for redistribution, are primarily about "social patterns of representation, interpretation, and communication" (Fraser 1995, 71).

Iris Marion Young (1990) identifies five faces of oppression: exploitation, marginalization, powerlessness, cultural imperialism, and violence. All these five faces could be relevant to the experience of liminal minorities. I find cultural imperialism and violence being most pertinent to their experience. Although liminal minorities, especially Yezidis in Iraq, are often subject to deprivation and would directly benefit from redistributive policies, they are stigmatized because of their religious beliefs rather than their poverty. As subjects of cultural imperialism, they are defined and classified by symbols and meanings of a dominant majority whose values directly shape the prevailing norms. In the eyes of a dominant majority, liminal minorities are "both marked out by stereotypes and at the same time rendered invisible" (59). These stereotypes enjoy widespread acceptance and are rarely contested. Moreover, the ways in which members of a liminal minority express themselves remain invisible to a dominant majority. Cultural imperialism in turn enables antiliminal violence. This violence is systematic because it targets members of a liminal minority "simply because they are members of that group" (62). The pursuit of justice on behalf of liminal minorities is then about revaluation of discriminatory values and symbols. The original and primary source of their plight is misrecognition and unrecognition—the ways in which they define their faith receive little to no acceptance by a dominant religious group. In this sense, the injustice suffered by liminal minorities resembles the injustice suffered by gays in many countries. In both cases, the remedy involves a change in exclusivist values harbored by the majority: intolerant religious beliefs in the former, attitudes despising homosexuality in the latter. The most immediate remedy for their experience of injustice entails a transformative change in the perceptions of the dominant group so that their identities are revalued and gain respect.

It can be argued that such a remedy offering a positive recognition to a liminal minority is neither feasible nor desirable. Certain practices of liminal minorities are unacceptable not because they appear abhorrent to members of a dominant group but because they directly violate core liberal values including gender equality, participatory decision making, and individual autonomy. The fact that religious minorities are victims of majoritarianism does not eliminate the possibility that these groups stifle individual rights (Gutmann

2003, 186–88). In fact, liminal minorities could exhibit highly internal patriarchal and authoritarian characteristics. From an intersectional perspective (Crenshaw 1991; McCall 2005), oppression faced by women who are members of a liminal minority is qualitatively different from oppression faced by men of the same group. For instance, the Yezidi community has harbored patriarchal practices severely limiting women's public involvement, at least until the genocidal attacks of 2014. The Baha'i community has an authoritarian structure stifling dissent and discouraging autonomous positions (Cole 2005). Given these dynamics, it is a fair question to ask whether recognition granted to liminal minorities would whitewash their patriarchal and authoritarian practices. It is also probable that such recognition may lead to a backlash among majorities and generate additional layers of stigmatization.

In light of this criticism, we can refer to Nancy Fraser's (1995) approach combining transformative forms, as different from affirmative, of redistribution and recognition as the most promising way to deal with demands for racial and gender justice. Transformative redistribution involves structural reforms of relations of production; transformative recognition destabilizes and blurs group differences and divisions instead of reifying them. The latter assigns new meanings to experience of being in between, the defining aspect of liminality, and revalues it as an irreducible aspect of human fulfillment rather than being a stigma that needs to be shed. For Fraser, the combination of these two transformative remedies is likely to replace hierarchical group boundaries with shifting and more fluid interactions, avoid resentment against affirmative policies, and be conducive to broader coalition building.

A transformative dualistic approach, as elaborated by Fraser, could be most conducive to resilient intercommunal coexistence involving liminal minorities. As religious boundaries become more porous and the experience of inbetweenness gains greater social appreciation, the intensity of stigmatization would also diminish. At the same time, Fraser (1995, 90) notes that her dualistic approach has a drawback when it comes to gender justice, as it is "removed from the immediate interests and identities of women, as they are culturally constructed." Similarly, this approach does not necessarily provide a remedy to the most immediate and urgent issue facing liminal minorities whose religious beliefs and practices continue to lack broader acceptance and legitimacy. An affirmative recognition means that they are no longer treated as blasphemers, heretics, apostates, or infidels who have no or restricted rights. Among other things, an affirmative recognition means for Alevis that their temples (*cemevis*) are granted official status as places of worship; for Yezidis and Baha'is that their claims to being a distinct faith group are respected; for Ahmadis that their peculiar way of prophecy are accepted as part of the richness and diversity of Islam. It also means that all these groups could honor their dead with dignity and could alleviate their sufferings. Demands for commemorative spaces and monuments are central to both Alevi and Yezidi platforms in Turkey and Iraq, respectively. The Legacy Monument and Museum, which was inaugurated in Montgomery, Alabama in 2018 and is dedicated to thousands of lynchings in the American South, provides a powerful lodestar for such recognition efforts.

Such recognition does not mean that internal practices of these groups who tend to violate gender equality, democratic decision making, and religious freedom are legitimized. The fact that the Mormons officially abandoned polygamy in the 1890s in a successful attempt to improve their relations with the US government provides a historical example of how recognition could trigger progressive change within a community. Besides, many religious groups enjoying widespread popularity, legitimacy, and power embody many of these practices to different degrees. To avoid double standards, we cannot withhold recognition from liminal minorities on grounds that they are cultlike, primitive, authoritarian, or patriarchal.

Affirmative recognition sought by liminal minorities is more likely to be achieved in democratic societies with secular political systems limiting the interference of the state in religion and vice versa. However, neither democratization nor secularism inevitably entails such recognition. As discussed earlier, the worst massacres targeting Alevis took place during periods of relative political pluralism and democratic elections in modern Turkish political history. As interviews presented in chapter 2 document, many Yezidis felt safer under the Saddam regime than sectarian pluralism and competitive elections of the post-2003 period. The 1974 constitutional amendment excluding Ahmadis from Muslimhood was enacted by one of the most democratic legislative assemblies in the history of Pakistan. Democratization following the collapse of the Suharto regime in 1998 led to the proliferation of anti-Ahmadi agitation and attacks in many different parts of Indonesia. Consequently, democratization empowering popular sentiments may present new threats to a liminal minority in the absence of powerful countervailing platforms and discourses promoting religious acceptance, inclusiveness, and humility.

Secularism reduces the influence of religious clerics and movements espousing antiliminal hatred over state policies and legislation. In authoritarian regimes with relatively secular policies, Iraq under Saddam until the 1990s being a relevant example, liminal minorities may have a breathing space. Such regimes are likely to keep a lid on outbursts of antiliminal popular violence given their goal to maintain a monopoly over means of coercion. In contrast, the persecution of liminal minorities under authoritarian regimes espousing religious nationalism, such as the postrevolutionary Iran and Pakistan under Zia-ul-Haq, often become the official policy. Yet secularism is not a panacea for liminality by itself. Secular regimes that are perceived to privilege a liminal minority at the expense of a religious majority are particularly vulnerable to episodes of antiliminal mass violence. Sunni Muslim resentment with Alevis in Turkey in the 1970s and 1990s reflects this pattern. Moreover, official policies that assign "minority" status to religious groups tend to impose fixed categorizations that diminish pluralism and indeterminacy inherent to lived religious experience and further marginalize dissident voices that do not neatly fit into such categorizations (Hurd 2014).

For these reasons, the ability and willingness of leaders and movements with credibility and appeal among a dominant majority to grant religious legitimacy to a liminal minority is crucial. There are historical examples demonstrating how religiously inspired political activism could be conducive to progressive change. In civil wars like the violent conflict in Northern Ireland, religious leaders could play transformative roles by virtue of their reputation and expertise (Sandal 2017). In Brazil, Chile, and El Salvador, the Church and Catholic organizations were at the forefronts of human rights activism and democratic struggles in the 1970s and 1980s (Mainwaring 1986; Loveman 1998; Tezcür 2015). During Indonesian democratization in the late 1990s, leaders of main Muslim organization took a stance against ethnonationalist violence instigated by the dying regime and committed to political pluralism (Hefner 2000).

Despite these historical examples, explicit recognition of liminal minorities discussed in this book by prominent religious leaders remains few and far between. The widespread condemnation of IS violence against Yezidis by Muslim clerics and movements did not necessarily entail self-reflexiveness that would encourage a theologically more inclusive attitude toward the Yezidi faith. The unrecognition of Alevis as a separate religious community and efforts to assimilate them into Sunni Islam continues to be the official policy in contemporary Turkey. In Iran, although an increasing number of dissident clerics challenge the exclusionary and conspiratorial discourses about Baha'is, clerical recognition of the Baha'i faith as a distinct religion is extremely rare (Sanyal 2019). Doctrinal truths and entrenched theological orthodoxies make such recognition difficult to come. Nonetheless, a hermeneutical positioning on the part of religious leaders espousing an expansive understanding of rights would eventually transform rigid doctrines and orthodoxies. As proposed by scholars such as Abdullahi An-Na'im (2008, 117), such a positioning enshrines religious freedom as a fundamental right and calls for a systematic reconsideration of notions of apostasy, blasphemy, and heresy. It also means that religious leaders develop a critical view of the past and acknowledge that the persecution of liminal minorities violates fundamental precepts of their faith. A normative embracement of liminality cherishing in-betweenness, ambiguity, and uncertainty would facilitate such a self-reflexive positioning. Only then can we have a modicum of hope for these groups and envision a world beyond hatred, vindictiveness, and liminality.

Reflections on Religion and Violence

I would like to conclude my discussion with two reflections about the contemporary study of religion and political violence. First, the study of politics of religion often assumes the presence of fixed and mutually exclusive identity markers with well-defined boundaries. At the most basic level, differences among major religious traditions such as Christianity, Islam, Hinduism, and Judaism are taken as given and immutable. As I argue throughout this book, such a conceptual approach would not be useful when studying liminal minorities whose belief systems and practices often defy established categorizations and remain ambivalent and ill-defined for dominant majorities.

In the face of this challenge, turning to Hannah Pitkin's attempt to bring Ludwig Wittgenstein's philosophy of language to the study of politics is valuable. In his later work, Wittgenstein argues that words have no universal and unambiguous meanings. Instead, conversations gain meaning only in specific contexts where participants share local and incomplete forms of knowledge that are essential for mutual understanding. Language is not a neutral medium for the transmission of thoughts. This core Wittgenstein insight suggests that conceptual plurality and inconsistency are inherent to human communication (Pitkin 1972, 302). It also invites a greater acceptance of plurality and contradictions in human affairs and a skepticism of broad and systematic generalizations (325–26). The implication of this stance is that rival religious claims that may appear incompatible with each other are an inevitable aspect of the political realm. In fact, liminal religious groups tend to generate existential anxieties among dominant religious groups simply because beliefs and practices of the former pose a direct challenge to truth statements of the latter. Normatively as well as methodologically, embracing this incompatibility is indispensable for the study of politics of liminality. In practical terms, it calls for more nuanced and granular conceptualizations and measurements concerning religious demographics. For instance, the conventional labeling of the population of Turkey as "99 percent Muslim" assumes an artificial level of homogeneity that has no basis in societal experience.

My final reflection is on the broader context characterizing the production of scholarly knowledge about religion. In the last three decades, there have been two monumental influences on how we discuss the role of religious beliefs in violence perpetuated by nonstate actors especially in the US academy. The first is Samuel Huntington's (1996) "clash of civilizations" argument that envisioned a new post–Cold War world order where cultural differences informed by opposing religious traditions would shape the major conflicts across the globe. While Huntington made a general culturalist argument about the propensity of religions for violence, his ominous assessment directly punctured the liberal euphoria of the 1990s and identified Islam as the main source of instability and aggression. The second is the terrorist attacks organized by al-Qaeda on September 11, 2001, that paved the way for the US military occupations of two Muslim-majority countries. These invasions not only inspired highly violent insurgencies tapping into popular grievances and espousing Islamic ideologies but also entailed brutal practices associated with counterinsurgency efforts (Khalili 2012). The rise of the self-styled IS in Iraq and Syria with global outreach by 2013 magnified both trends.

Under the shadow of these influences, scholarship has developed a strong tendency toward arguments that highlight the role of *nonreligious* factors in shaping political attitudes and behavior. Mahmood Mamdani's (2004) *Good Muslims, Bad Muslims* epitomizes this tendency with its crisp historical analysis demonstrating how the interplay between foreign interventions and militant nationalisms shape the contours of politics. His analysis emphatically makes the point that political behavior, including violent resistance against neocolonial pursuits, could not be reduced to the expression of religious identities. Culturalist discourses following the Huntingtonian framework that ascribe a timeless character to such identities—for example, ancient fight between Sunnis and Shiites—often obscure how political violence committed under the banner of religion reflects responses to foreign invasion, state repression, and poor governance. Moreover, the scholarship correctly identifies how leaders instrumentalize religious symbols to seek greater power and mobilize popular support. It provides an indispensable correction to what Mamdani calls "culture talk" that fails to recognize the role of political disagreements and division in violent conflicts.

There is also a significant downside to this tendency. The understandable desire to highlight the role played by noncultural factors in political violence often downplays the centrality of religious faith to human experience. Even though the sweeping predictions of the classical modernization theory about the decline of religion are mostly discredited and abandoned, there is still a general hesitancy to take religion seriously as a causal factor in understanding political behavior in our times. Thankfully, the recent methodological advances and growing acceptance of interdisciplinary approaches in the social sciences make the study of how religious beliefs and faith could motivate violent political behavior more feasible than ever. As Ron Hassner (2009) reminds us, spaces perceived as sacred and providing a connection with the divine have a unique potential to generate intense conflict and violence when they become subject of rival claims. While politicians have their own reasons to stoke conflict, their actions are constrained and shaped by popular sentiments assigning special value to religiously sacred spaces. In a very different context, utilizing a wealth of survey data, Eric McDaniel et al. (2022) argue the growing support for illiberal and undemocratic politicians and policies in the United States reflects the influence of Christian nationalism, a religious ideology that assigns a special role to the United States in God's plan and exhibits intense hostility to those perceived to betray this sacred mission. Along similar lines, I am hoping that this book has demonstrated that certain religious groups by the virtue of beliefs and practices attract unprecedented levels of popular animosity. When combined with political resentment, this animosity gains a fierce character and contributes to mass violence. Coming to terms with this propensity for bottom-up violence is an important scholarly responsibility. Moving forward, it would be very promising to develop a broader historical and geographical perspective to study the conditions under which religiously inspired discourses inciting violence finds a receptive audience at the popular levels and the strategies that could be effective in countering such discourses.

Appendix for Chapter 2

Fieldwork among Yezidis

Conducting fieldwork among individuals who were physically harmed, permanently displaced, lost their loved ones, and remained in captivity due to mass atrocities presents unique professional and ethical challenges for researchers. All these challenges are amplified when interacting with Yezidis who were subject to a genocidal campaign involving systematic rape and enslavement in the hands of the self-styled IS. Given the sensitive and complex issues involved in studying a postgenocidal group, working as a team has had some unique advantages.

My main partner in this fieldwork was Tutku Ayhan, who was a doctoral student at the University of Central Florida during that period. She defended her dissertation titled "Trauma, Resilience, and Empowerment: Post-genocide Experiences of Yezidi Women" in the fall of 2021. We traveled to Iraqi Kurdistan three times (September 2017, May–June 2018, and May 2019) and Germany twice (June 2017 and October 2019), either together or individually. Zeynep Kaya, a scholar based in the United Kingdom, and Bayar Dosky, a scholar based in Duhok, Iraq, were our partners in the fieldwork in Iraqi Kurdistan in 2018. Besides our time together in the field (May–June 2018), our individual trips helped us evaluate some distinctive features of conducting fieldwork as a team. Tutku Ayhan has also conducted a series of interviews virtually.

Prevalent journalistic practices focusing on the plight of Yezidis do not follow basic ethical principles such as not disclosing the identity of the interviewees who stayed under IS captivity for extended periods. They also generate false expectations among survivors that talking to the media would lead to tangible improvements in their situation and force them to narrate their traumatic experiences at great emotional pain (Foster and Minwalla 2018). Even more egregious, some politicians, journalists, and activists instrumentalize and market the suffering of these women for personal gains and visibility, a practice that has also been prevalent in many other settings (Kleinman and Kleinman 1996).

Given these dynamics, I have aimed to offer a contextualized and nuanced portrayal of the various ways Yezidis perceive their relations with other communities. Different from many researchers and journalists who almost exclusively focus on Yezidi women survivors, we interviewed a wide range of actors: (a) Yezidis of Sinjar who were living in camps and host communities in Iraqi Kurdistan, (b) Yezidis who migrated to Western countries both before and after the 2014 attacks, (c) Yezidi political and religious leaders, (d) ordinary Yezidis who lived in Duhok, and (e) non-Yezidi activists, professionals, politicians, and policymakers involved in Yezidi affairs. In this book, I rely on 103 semistructured in-depth interviews conducted with 95 individuals or groups of individuals (see table AO.1 in the online appendix at https://hdl.handle.net/1813/113348). I read and speak Kurmancî, a dialect of Kurdish spoken by most Yezidis. However, differences in vernaculars made it essential for me to have translators during our interviews. Most interviews were recorded and transcribed by a native speaker of Kurmancî. In other interviews, we took copious notes.

We recruited our interviewees utilizing various strategies to capture the diversity of lived experiences as much as possible. First, we relied on media sources and existing contacts to identify individuals who are involved in Yezidi affairs. While some of these individuals occupied formal positions, others had informal types of influence and power. For instance, an ordinary Yezidi man negotiated the release of hundreds of Yezidis from captivity (Interviewee #21). We read about his story in an international media outlet and used our local contacts to obtain his telephone numbers. Working with a local colleague was very helpful in terms of not only identifying the interviewees but also arranging interviews with them. We also relied on referrals from interviewees to reach out to other individuals. This snowball technique provided much help, especially in establishing rapport with survivors or activists who distrust outsiders. Although many of our interlocutors were willing to share their story so that "the world knows about it," they were at times hesitant to answer questions about sensitive local political dynamics. Finally, we interviewed individuals in camps. We have spoken to camp directors, representatives of nongovernmental organizations (NGOs), and camp residents. At times, we asked the camp manager which individuals or families we could interview, and they arranged the meeting; at other times, we relied on our own contacts to reach families. At still other times, serendipity provided new avenues for insightful research. In one of the camps, we were interviewing a Yezidi political activist affiliated with one of the main Kurdish parties (Interviewee #29). During our interview, a friend of his showed up and started to tell his own story. He survived eight months of captivity under the IS with his family and children (Interviewee #30).

We paid special attention to power dynamics characterizing Yezidi-Kurdish relations. Most Yezidis speak Kurdish as their native language, and the Kurdish authorities declare Yezidism as the authentic religion of their people. Some Yezidis are well integrated into Kurdish society. At the same time, there is also significant mistrust among the community toward Sunni Muslims, a mistrust fostered by their long history as a persecuted religious minority. The complicated nature of interreligious affairs directly shaped our quotidian interactions. As with other local communities, it is customary to offer food and refreshments to visitors among Yezidis, regardless of their income levels. As many local Muslims do not consider Yezidi prepared food halal, for a visitor to accept and eat and drink Yezidi offerings contributes to building rapport. Our fieldwork in 2018 coincided with Ramadan, the month of Muslim fasting. Since we were not fasting and able to consume food and refreshments offered by our hosts, they talked more freely about the involvement of Sunni Muslims in atrocities, their disappointment with the flight of Kurdish forces on the day of IS attacks, and the various forms of discrimination they were facing as a religious minority. We also realized that they felt more comfortable speaking about these issues when the translator was a Yezidi rather than a Kurdish person. Consequently, being perceived as an outsider facilitated rapport when talking to Yezidis in an environment of insecurity.

From a holistic perspective, working as a team has helped us interpret the interviews in richer ways. We were able to reach out to a more diverse sample given our positionality and different backgrounds. I arranged meetings with power holders with relative ease using my credentials as a senior researcher from an American university. Tutku Ayhan, as a young woman, was able to engage in extended conversations with female survivors. In some settings, only one of us was present; in other settings, both of us. In the latter situations, sharing and discussing our individual interpretations of the content and context of interviews resulted in insights that would be not available otherwise. We were in a better position to make sense of metadata, "the spoken and unspoken expressions about people's interior thoughts and feelings, which they do not always articulate in their stories or responses to interview questions" (Fujii 2010, 232). We were also better positioned to make impromptu decisions with ethical implications (Cronin-Furman and Lake 2018). To give an example, on numerous occasions, our interviewees in camps expressed an expectation of monetary compensation in exchange for talking to us. This expectation inevitably affected how they responded to certain questions. In one case, a family provided an unrealistically upbeat portrayal of their conditions while mentioning that they would appreciate some help. We reasoned that the family's expectation of benefits from international visitors motivated them to invite us to their container as well as the narrative about the conditions in the camp. After having a discussion, we thought that donating to a local NGO is a more sensible way than paying our interviewees directly. We also bought groceries to be distributed among multiple families. Having the ability to reflect on these ethical issues collectively was a precious asset.

Nonetheless, most of our interviewees just want their voices to be heard by the broader humanity without expecting any tangible benefits. In this sense, our experience has been consistent with other researchers (e.g., Wood 2006; Pearlman 2016), who realized that individuals who suffered tremendously and experienced major losses due to violence are often eager to share their stories. Hence, we believe scholars have a responsibility to represent these testimonies on their own terms as much as possible in their academic and nonacademic outlets so that the world knows about them. In fact, many of our interviewees explicitly requested that the world knows more about them and hear their voices (e.g., Interviewee #18). For some survivors who experienced irreversible losses, speaking up could be a cathartic moment. This was exactly my experience talking to a survivor whose testimony was the core source of the prologue of this book (Interviewee #31). I was initially reluctant to interview him because of his age and health condition. He had surgery and appeared very fragile. After exchanging pleasantries, however, he started to tell his story of survival with great concentration and detail. He was from Kocho, the site of one of the worst massacres during the IS occupation of Sinjar in August 2014. Alongside dozens of members of his family, he was taken to a nearby garden to be executed. He survived due to pure luck as bullets scraped his head and he played dead. At the end of his story, he looked refreshed and vindicated. When I asked him about more than a dozen photocopied photos taped to the wall of his container, he started to name his dead relatives. Those photos were the only remnants of them. I was not a witness to his experiences but at least could amplify his voice, which deserves to be heard.

Another ethical dimension of conducting fieldwork among a marginalized community involves the notion of reciprocity defined as "materials gathered in the field should be returned to the community of origin" (Wood 2006, 383). This notion is particularly pertinent in contemporary Iraq as the US invasion of 2003 resulted in the looting of its national archives and treasures. More recently, the decision of a *New York Times* reporter to compile tens of thousands of IS documents and import them to the United States reignited the debate about the responsibility of journalists and researchers in preserving historical archives in ethical and responsible ways (Bet-Shlimon 2018). In our research, we did not take possession of any original documents. We made copies of various documents after receiving permission from the individuals who presented them to us. We also partnered with local people as collaborators and assistants to enhance research capabilities on the ground. Finally, I am committed to the dissemination of our scholarship among Yezidis via gratis copies (and translated) of our publications as well as donating royalties to NGOs working for the welfare of the community.

Appendix for Chapter 5

Statistical Results

Table A.1 Modeling societal discrimination against religious minorities

	I	II	III
Liminal	0.519*** (0.115)	0.409*** (0.116)	0.379** (0.117)
Muslims	1.262*** (0.087)	1.217*** (0.09)	1.432*** (0.112)
Liminal*Muslims	−1.182*** (0.175)	−1.03*** (0.176)	−1.017*** (0.18)
Christians	0.073 (0.076)	0.299*** (0.079)	0.571*** (0.096)
No separation	−0.267*** (0.041)	−0.203* (0.041)	−0.139 (0.044)
No freedom of religion	0.421*** (0.075)	0.42*** (0.075)	0.161*** (0.079)
State religion	0.289*** (0.027)	0.227*** (0.028)	0.308*** (0.03)
Blasphemy	0.45*** (0.047)	0.403*** (0.047)	0.165*** (0.053)
Minority size	−0.002 (0.002)	−0.004* (0.002)	−0.001 (0.002)
Civil liberties		−0.409*** (0.094)	−0.285** (0.119)
Ethnic exclusion		−0.056 (0.102)	0.449*** (0.115)
GDP per capita			0.0*** (0.0)
GDP per capita change			−0.985*** (0.226)
Population			0.001*** (0.0)
Interstate conflict			−0.032 (0.3)
Intrastate conflict			0.251*** (0.058)
Intercept	−1.146*** (0.114)	−1.001*** (0.13)	−1.36*** (0.17)
Observations	14,985	14,305	12,715
Pseudo-R^2	0.07	0.06	0.06
Log likelihood	−9,092.37	−8,833.76	−7,872.61
AIC	18,204.73	17,691.53	15,779.22
BIC	18,280.88	17,782.35	15,905.88

*$p < 0.1$, **$p < 0.05$, ***$p < 0.01$. Numbers in parentheses are standard errors.

References

Aarseth, Mathilde Becker. 2021. *Mosul under ISIS: Eyewitness Accounts of Life in the Caliphate*. London: I. B. Tauris.

Abca, Yurdaer. 2006. "Yezidilik ve Osmanlı yönetiminde Yezidilik." MA thesis, Eskişehir Osmangazi Üniversitesi.

Abdulrazaq, Tallha, and Gareth Stansfield. 2016. "The Enemy Within: ISIS and the Conquest of Mosul." *Middle East Journal* 70 (4): 525–42.

Abrahamian, Ervand. 1999. *Tortured Confessions: Prisons and Public Recantations in Modern Iran*. Berkeley: University of California Press.

Abrahamian, Ervand. 2008. *A History of Modern Iran*. Cambridge: Cambridge University Press.

Açıkyıldız, Birgül. 2010. *The Yezidis: The History of a Community, Culture and Religion*. London: I. B. Tauris.

The Act of Killing. 2012. Directed by Josh Oppenheimer. Denmark: Final Cut for Real.

Afshari, Reza. 2008. "The Discourse and Practice of Human Rights Violations of Iranian Baha'is in the Islamic Republic of Iran." In *The Baha'is of Iran*, edited by Dominic Parviz Brookshaw and Seena B. Fazel, 232–77. Milton Park, UK: Routledge.

Ahmed, Asad A. 2010. "The Paradoxes of Ahmadiyya Identity: Legal Appropriation of Muslim-ness and the Construction of Ahmadiyya Difference." In *Beyond Crisis: Re-evaluating Pakistan*, edited by Naveda Khan, 273–314. Milton Park, UK: Routledge.

Akan, Murat. 2022. "Capturing Secularism in Turkey: The Ease of Comparison." In *The Oxford Handbook of Turkish Politics*, edited by Güneş Murat Tezcür, 117–38. Oxford: Oxford University Press.

Akhavan, Payam, Sareta Ashraph, Barzan Barzani, and David Matyas. 2020. "What Justice for the Yazidi Genocide? Voices from Below." *Human Rights Quarterly* 42 (1): 1–47.

Akhavi, Shahrough. 1980. *Religion and Politics in Contemporary Iran: Clergy-State Relations in the Pahlavi Period*. Albany: State University of New York Press.

Aktar, Ayhan, and Abdulhamit Kırmızı. 2013. *Diyarbekir 1915*. Istanbul: Hrant Dink Vakfı.

Aktürk, Şener. 2012. *Regimes of Ethnicity and Nationhood in Germany, Russia, and Turkey*. Cambridge: Cambridge University Press.

Ali, Majid Hassan. 2019a. "Aspirations for Ethnonationalist Identities among Religious Minorities in Iraq: The Case of Yazidi Identity in the Period of Kurdish and Arab Nationalism, 1963–2003." *Nationalities Papers* 47 (6): 953–67.

Ali, Majid Hassan. 2019b. "Genocidal Campaigns during the Ottoman Era: The Firmān of Mīr-i-Kura against the Yazidi Religious Minority in 1832–1834." *Genocide Studies International* 13 (1): 77–91.

Ali, Majid Hassan. 2021. "Historical and Political Dimensions of Yezidi Identity before and after the *Firman* (Genocide) of August 3, 2014." In *Kurds and Yezidis in the Middle East: Shifting Identities, Borders, and the Experiences of Minority Communities*, edited by Güneş Murat Tezcür, 43–58. London: I. B. Tauris.

al-Jabiri, Khalid Faraj. 1981. "Stability and Social Change in Yezidi Society." PhD diss., University of Oxford.

Alkan, Necati. 2005. "'The Eternal Enemy of Islām': Abdullah Cevdet and the Baha'i Religion." *Bulletin of the School of Oriental and African Studies* 68 (1): 1–20.

Alkan, Necati. 2012. "Fighting for the Nusayrī Soul: State, Protestant Missionaries and the 'Alawīs in the Late Ottoman Empire." *Die Welt des Islams* 52(1): 23–50.

Allison, Christine. 2001. *The Yezidi Oral Tradition in Iraqi Kurdistan*. Milton Park, UK: Routledge.

Allison, Christine. 2008. "'Unbelievable Slowness of Mind': Yezidi Studies, from Nineteenth to Twenty-First Century." *Journal of Kurdish Studies* 6:1–23.

Alsancakli, Sacha. 2017. "What's Old Is New Again: A Study of Sources in the Sarafnama of Saraf Xan Bidlisi (1005–7/1596–99)." *Kurdish Studies* 5(1): 11–31.

al-Tamimi, Aymeen. 2017. "The Islamic State and the Kurds: The Documentary Evidence." *CTC Sentinel* 10 (8): 33–38.

Amanat, Abbas. 2008. "The Historical Roots of the Persecution of Babis and Baha'is in Iran." In *The Baha'is of Iran*, edited by Dominic Parviz Brookshaw and Seena B. Fazel, 170–83. Milton Park, UK: Routledge.

Amanat, Abbas. 2017. *Iran: A Modern History*. New Haven, CT: Yale University Press.

Amanat, Mehrdad. 2012. "Set in Stone: Homeless Corpses and Desecrated Graves in Modern Iran." *International Journal of Middle East Studies* 44 (2): 257–83.

Amnesty International. 1976. *Amnesty International Briefing on Malawi*. London: Amnesty International. Accessed April 28, 2022. https://www.amnesty.org/en/wp-content/uploads/2021/06/afr360011976en.pdf.

Amnesty International. 2018. *Iraq: Violent Yezidi and Shi'a Backlash against Islamic State*. London: Amnesty International. Accessed October 15, 2020. https://www.amnesty.org.uk/iraq-violent-yezidi-and-shia-backlash-against-islamic-state.

Amnesty International. 2019. *Syria: Unprecedented Investigation Reveals US-Led Coalition Killed More than 1,600 Civilians in Raqqa "Death Trap."* London: Amnesty International. Accessed October 15, 2020. https://www.amnesty.org/en/latest/news/2019/04/syria-unprecedented-investigation-reveals-us-led-coalition-killed-more-than-1600-civilians-in-raqqa-death-trap.

Anderson, Benedict. 1991. *Imagined Communities: Reflections on the Origin and Spread of Nationalism*. Rev. ed. London: Verso.

An-Na'im, Abdullahi Ahmed. 2008. *Islam and the Secular State*. Cambridge, MA: Harvard University Press.

Appadurai, Arjun. 2006. *Fear of Small Numbers: An Essay on the Geography of Anger*. Durham, NC: Duke University Press.

Appleby, Scott R. 2000. *The Ambivalence of the Sacred: Religion, Violence, and Reconciliation*. Lanham, MD: Rowman & Littlefield.

Arabacı, Caner. 2004. "Eşref Edip Fergan ve *Sebîlürreşad* Üzerine." In *Modern Türkiye'de Siyasi Düşünce: İslâmcılık*, 6:96–128. Istanbul: İletişim Yayınları.
Arendt, Hannah. 1958. *The Human Condition*. Chicago: University of Chicago Press.
Arjomand, Said Amir. 1988. *The Turban for the Crown: The Islamic Revolution in Iran*. Oxford: Oxford University Press.
Aşut, Attila. 1994. *Sivas kitabı: Bir toplu öldürümün öyküsü: anılar, belgeler, incelemeler*. Ankara: Edebiyatçılar Derneği.
Avcı, Mustafa. 2022. "Political Music in Turkey: The Birth and Diversification of Dissident and Conformist Music (1920–2000)." In *The Oxford Handbook of Turkish Politics*, edited by Güneş Murat Tezcür, 751–70. Oxford: Oxford University Press.
Aydın, Suavi, and Yüksel Taşkın. 2015. *1960'dan Günümüze Türkiye Tarihi*. Istanbul: İletişim Yayınları.
Ayhan, Tutku. 2021. "Trauma, Resilience, and Empowerment: Post-genocide Experiences of Yezidi Women." PhD diss., University of Central Florida.
Ayhan, Tutku, and Güneş Murat Tezcür. 2021. "Overcoming 'Intimate Hatreds': Reflections on Violence against the Yezidis." In *Conceptualizing Mass Violence*, edited by Navras J. Aafreedi and Priya Singh, 167–80. Milton Park, UK: Routledge.
Azak, Umut. 2010. *Islam and Secularism in Turkey: Kemalism, Religion and the Nation State*. London: I. B. Tauris.
Baer, Marc. 2004. "The Double Bind of Race and Religion: The Conversion of the Dönme to Turkish Secular Nationalism." *Comparative Studies in Society and History* 46 (4): 682–708.
Baer, Marc. 2013. "An Enemy Old and New: The Dönme, Anti-Semitism, and Conspiracy Theories in the Ottoman Empire and Turkish Republic." *Jewish Quarterly Review* 103 (4): 523–55.
Bakiner, Onur. 2022. "Truth, Justice, and Commemoration Initiatives in Turkey." In *The Oxford Handbook of Turkish Politics*, edited by Güneş Murat Tezcür, 669–68. Oxford: Oxford University Press.
Balakian, Grigoris. 2009. *Armenian Golgotha: A Memoir of the Armenian Genocide, 1915–1918*. New York: Vintage Books.
Baltacıoğlu-Brammer, Ayse. 2019. "'Those Heretics Gathering Secretly . . .': Qizilbash Rituals and Practices in the Ottoman Empire according to Early Modern Sources." *Journal of the Ottoman and Turkish Studies Association* 6 (1): 39–60.
Baram, Amatzia. 2011. "From Militant Secularism to Islamism: The Iraqi Ba'th Regime 1968–2003." Woodrow Wilson International Center for Scholars Occasional Paper.
Barber, Matthew. 2016. "They That Remain: Syrian and Iraqi Christian Communities amid the Syria Conflict and the Rise of the Islamic State." In *Christianity and Freedom: Contemporary Perspectives*, edited by Allen D. Hertzke and Timothy Samuel Shah, 2:453–88. Cambridge: Cambridge University Press.
Barkey, Karen. 2005. "Islam and Toleration: Studying the Ottoman Imperial Model." *International Journal of Politics, Culture, and Society* 19 (1–2): 5–19.
Barkey, Karen. 2008. *Empire of Difference: The Ottomans in Comparative Perspective*. Cambridge: Cambridge University Press.

REFERENCES

Barro, Robert J., and Rachel M. McCleary. 2005. "Which Countries Have State Religion?" *Quarterly Journal of Economics* 120 (4): 1331–70.

Basedau, Matthias, Jonathan Fox, Jan H. Pierskalla, Georg Strüver, and Johannes Vüllers. 2017. "Does Discrimination Breed Grievances—and Do Grievances Breed Violence? New Evidence from an Analysis of Religious Minorities in Developing Countries." *Conflict Management and Peace Science* 34 (3): 217–39.

Basedau, Matthias, Birte Pfeiffer, and Johannes Vüllers. 2016. "Bad Religion? Religion, Collective Action, and the Onset of Armed Conflict in Developing Countries." *Journal of Conflict Resolution* 60 (2): 226–55.

Baser, Bahar, and Mari Toivanen. 2017. "The Politics of Genocide Recognition: Kurdish Nation-Building and Commemoration in the Post-Saddam Era." *Journal of Genocide Research* 19 (3): 404–26.

Batatu, Hanna. 1978. *The Old Social Classes and the Revolutionary Movements of Iraq*. Princeton, NJ: Princeton University Press.

Bauman, Chad M. 2020. *Anti-Christian Violence in India*. Ithaca, NY: Cornell University Press.

Bayır, Derya. 2013. *Minorities and Nationalism in Turkish Law*. Farnham, UK: Ashgate.

Belge, Ceren, and Ekrem Karakoç. 2015. "Minorities in the Middle East: Ethnicity, Religion, and Support for Authoritarianism." *Political Research Quarterly* 68 (2): 280–92.

Bellah, Robert. 2011. *Religion in Human Evolution: From the Paleolithic to the Axial Age*. Cambridge, MA: Harvard University Press.

Benhabib, Seyla. 1979. "The Next Iran or the Next Brazil? Right-Wing Groups behind Political Violence in Turkey." *MERIP Reports* 77:16–17.

Benjamin, Walter. 2003. *Walter Benjamin: Selected Writings, 1: 1913–1926*. Edited by Marcus Bullock and Michael W. Jennings. Cambridge, MA: Harvard University Press.

Bennett, Andrew, and Jeffrey T. Checkel, eds. 2015. *Process Tracing: From Metaphor to Analytic Tool*. Cambridge: Cambridge University Press.

Ben-Nun Bloom, Pazit, Gizem Arikan, and Allon Vishkin. 2021. "Religion and Democratic Commitment: A Unifying Motivational Framework." *Political Psychology* 42:75–108.

Bergen, Doris L. 2016. *War & Genocide: A Concise History of the Holocaust*. 3rd ed. Lanham, MD: Rowman & Littlefield.

Berkey, Jonathan. 2003. *The Formation of Islam: Religion and Society in the Near East, 600–1800*. Cambridge: Cambridge University Press.

Berlinerblau, Jacques. 2001. "Toward a Sociology of Heresy, Orthodoxy, and *Doxa*." *History of Religions* 40 (4): 327–51.

Berman, Sheri. 1997. "Civil Society and the Collapse of the Weimar Republic." *World Politics* 49 (3): 401–29.

Berman, Sheri. 2020. *Democracy and Dictatorship in Europe: From the Ancien Régime to the Present Day*. Oxford: Oxford University Press.

Bermeo, Nancy. 2003. *Ordinary People in Extraordinary Times: The Citizenry and the Breakdown of Democracy*. Princeton, NJ: Princeton University Press.

Bet-Shlimon, Arbella. 2018. "Preservation or Plunder? The ISIS Files and a History of Heritage Removal in Iraq." *Middle East Research and Information Project*.

Accessed May 8, 2022. https://merip.org/2018/05/preservation-or-plunder-the-isis-files-and-a-history-of-heritage-removal-in-iraq/.
Bet-Shlimon, Arbella. 2019. *City of Black Gold: Oil, Ethnicity, and the Making of Modern Kirkuk*. Redwood City, CA: Stanford University Press.
Bilâ, Hikmet. 2008. *CHP, 1919–2009*. Istanbul: Doğan Kitap.
Biner, Zerrin Ozlem. 2020. *States of Dispossession: Violence and Precarious Coexistence in Southeast Turkey*. Philadelphia: University of Pennsylvania Press.
Birikim. 1979. "Türkiye'de . . . Maraş'dan Sonra?" *Birikim* 46 (7): 32–55.
Blalock, H. M. 1957. "Percent Non-White and Discrimination in the South." *American Sociological Review* 22 (6): 677–68.
Bora, Tanıl. 2008. *Türkiye'nin Linç Rejimi*. Istanbul: İletişim Yayınları.
Bora, Tanıl. 2017. *Cereyanlar: Türkiye'de Siyasi İdeolojiler*. Istanbul: İletişim Yayınları.
Bormann, Nils-Christian, Lars-Erik Cederman, and Manuel Vogt. 2017. "Language, Religion, and Ethnic Civil War." *Journal of Conflict Resolution* 61 (4): 744–71.
Bourdieu, Pierre. 1987. "What Makes a Social Class? On the Theoretical and Practical Existence of Groups." *Berkeley Journal of Sociology* 32:1–17.
Bournoutian, George. 1997. "Eastern Armenia from the Seventeenth Century to the Russian Annexation." In *The Armenian People from Ancient Times to Modern Times, Vol. II*, edited by Richard G. Hovannisian, 81–107. New York: Macmillan.
Bowles, Samuel. 2008. "Being Human: Conflict: Altruism's Midwife." *Nature* 456 (7220): 326–27.
Brass, Paul R. 1997. *Theft of an Idol: Text and Context in the Representation of Collective Violence*. Princeton, NJ: Princeton University Press.
Brenner, Michael. 2018. *In Search of Israel: The History of an Idea*. Princeton, NJ: Princeton University Press.
Brooke, Steve. 2017. "From Medicine to Mobilization: Social Service Provision and the Islamist Reputational Advantage." *Perspectives on Politics* 15 (1): 42–61.
Brown, Davis, and Patrick James. 2018. "The Religious Characteristics of States: Classic Themes and New Evidence for International Relations and Comparative Politics." *Journal of Conflict Resolution* 62 (6): 1340–76.
Brubaker, Roger. 2015. "Religious Dimensions of Political Conflict and Violence." *Sociological Theory* 33 (1): 1–19.
Brunsma, David L., Daniel Delgado, and Kerry Ann Rockquemore. 2013. "Liminality in the Multiracial Experience: Towards a Concept of Identity Matrix." *Identities* 20 (5): 481–502.
Budiwanti, Erni. 2009. "Pluralism Collapses: A Study of the Jama'ah Ahmadiyah Indonesia and Its Persecution." Asia Research Institute Working Paper Series 117.
Buffon, Veronica, and Christine Allison. 2016. "The Gendering of Victimhood: Western Media and the Sinjar Genocide." *Kurdish Studies* 4 (2): 176–96.
Bulut, Halil İbrahim. 2017. "Mehmet Şerefettin Yaltkaya ve 'Yezîdîler' başlıklı makalesi (Tahlil, Değerlendirme ve Sadeleştirme)." *e-Makalat Mezhep Araştırmaları Dergisi* 10 (1): 1–50.
Burhani, Ahmad Najib. 2014. "Hating the Ahmadiyya: The Place of 'Heretics' in Contemporary Indonesian Muslim Society." *Contemporary Islam* 8 (2): 133–52.

Burhani, Ahmad Najib. 2020. "'It's a Jihad': Justifying Violence towards the Ahmadiyya in Indonesia." *TRaNS: Trans-Regional and -National Studies of Southeast Asia* 9 (1): 99–112.

Bushman, Brad J., Robert D. Ridge, Enny Das, Colin W. Key, and Gregory L. Busath. 2007. "When God Sanctions Killing: Effect of Scriptural Violence on Aggression." *Psychological Science* 18 (3): 204–7.

Butler, Judith. 2009. *Frames of War: When Is Life Grievable?* New York: Verso.

Çakar, Mehmet Sait. 2007. *Yezidîlik: tarihi metinler—Kürtçe ve Arapça nüshaları*. Istanbul: Vadi Yayınları.

Çakmak, Yalçın. 2019. *Sultanın Kızılbaşları: II. Abdülhamid dönemi Alevi algısı ve siyaseti*. Istanbul: İletişim Yayınları.

Can, Kemal, and Bora Tanıl. 2000. "MHP'nin güç kaynağı olarak Kürt meselesi." *Birikim* 134–35 (Haziran/Temmuz). Accessed May 28, 2022. https://birikim dergisi.com/dergiler/birikim/1/sayi-134-135-haziran-temmuz-2000/2327/mhp-nin-guc-kaynagi-olarak-kurt-meselesi/3296.

Carmichael, Cathie. 2009. *Genocide before the Holocaust*. New Haven, CT: Yale University Press.

Carver, Richard. 1990. *Where Silence Rules: The Suppression of Dissent in Malawi*. New York: Human Rights Watch.

Cavanaugh, William T. 2009. *The Myth of Religious Violence: Secular Ideology and the Roots of Modern Conflict*. New York: Oxford University Press.

Çavdar, Ozan. 2020. *Sivas Katliamı: Yas ve Bellek*. Istanbul: İletişim Yayınları.

Çaylı, Eray. 2018. "Conspiracy Theory as Spatial Practice: The Case of the Sivas Arson Attack, Turkey." *Environment and Planning D: Society and Space* 36 (2): 255–72.

Çelik, Adnan, and Namik Kemal Dinç. 2015. *Yüz yıllık ah!: Toplumsal hafızanın izinde 1915 Diyarbekir*. Istanbul: İsmail Beşikci Vakfı.

Cesari, Jocelyne. 2014. *The Awakening of Muslim Democracy: Religion, Modernity, and the State*. Cambridge: Cambridge University Press.

Cesari, Jocelyne. 2021. *We God's People: Christianity, Islam and Hinduism in the World of Nations*. Cambridge: Cambridge University Press.

Cetorelli, Valeria, and Sareta Ashraph. 2019. *A Demographic Documentation of ISIS's Attack on the Yazidi Village of Kocho*. London: LSE Middle East Centre.

Cetorelli, Valeria, Isaac Sasson, Nazar Shabila, and Gilbert Burnham. 2017. "Mortality and Kidnapping Estimates for the Yazidi Population in the Area of Mount Sinjar, Iraq, in August 2014: A Retrospective Household Survey." *PLoS Medicine* 14 (5): 1–15.

Chandra, Kanchan. 2006. "What Is Ethnic Identity and Does It Matter?" *Annual Review of Political Science* 9:397–424.

Charnysh, Volha, and Evgeny Finkel. 2017. "The Death Camp Eldorado: Political and Economic Effects of Mass Violence." *American Political Science Review* 111 (4): 801–18.

Chehabi, Houchang E. 2008. "Anatomy of Prejudice: Reflections on Secular Anti-Baha'ism in Iran." In *The Baha'is of Iran*, edited by Dominic Parviz Brookshaw and Seena B. Fazel, 184–99. Milton Park, UK: Routledge.

Choi, Jung-Koo, and Samuel Bowles. 2007. "The Coevolution of Parochial Altruism and War." *Science* 318 (5850): 636–40.

Chu, Petra ten-Doesschate. 2010. *Nineteenth-Century European Art*. 3rd ed. London: Pearson.
Chua, Amy. 2018. *Political Tribes: Group Instincts and the Fate of Nations*. London: Penguin.
CIA. 2021. "The World Factbook: Turkey." Accessed May 21, 2021. https://www.cia.gov/the-world-factbook/countries/turkey/#people-and-society.
Clark, Kenneth. 1959. *Looking at Pictures*. London: John Murray.
Clarke, Joseph. 2019. "Introduction: Religion and Violence in France: 1500 to the Present." *French History* 33 (2): 165–76.
Cohen, Hayyim J. 1966. "The Anti-Jewish 'Farhūd' in Baghdad, 1941." *Middle Eastern Studies* 3 (1): 2–17.
Cole, Juan R. I. 1992. "Iranian Millenarianism and Democratic Thought in the 19th Century." *International Journal of Middle East Studies* 24 (1): 1–26.
Cole, Juan R. I. 2005. "The Baha'i Minority and Nationalism in Contemporary Iran." In *Nationalism and Minority Identities in Islamic Societies*, edited by Maya Shatzmiller, 127–63. Montreal: McGill-Queen's University Press.
Collier, David. 2011. "Understanding Process Tracing." *PS: Political Science & Politics* 44 (4): 823–30.
Collier, Paul, and Anke Hoeffler. 1998. "On Economic Causes of Civil War." *Oxford Economic Papers* 50 (4): 563–73.
Collins, Randall. 2009. *Violence: A Micro-sociological Theory*. Princeton, NJ: Princeton University Press.
Cook, Michael. 2016. *Ancient Religions, Modern Politics: The Islamic Case in Comparative Perspective*. Princeton, NJ: Princeton University Press.
Coşkun, Zeki. 1995. *Aleviler, Sünniler ve . . . Öteki Sivas*. Istanbul: İletişim Yayınları.
Crenshaw, Kimberlé. 1991. "Mapping the Margins: Intersectionality, Identity Politics, and Violence against Women of Color." *Stanford Law Review* 43 (6): 1241–99.
Cronin, Patricia. 2004. *God's Rule: Government and Islam*. New York: Columbia University Press.
Cronin-Furman, Kate, and Milli Lake. 2018. "Ethics Abroad: Fieldwork in Fragile and Violent Contexts." *PS: Political Science & Politics* 51 (3): 1–8.
Crouzet, Denis. 1990. *Les guerriers de Dieu: La violence au temps des troubles de religion (vers 1525–vers 1610)*. 2 vols. Paris: Champ Vallon.
Dadrian, Vahakn N. 1993. "The Secret Young-Turk Ittihadist Conference and the Decision for the World War I Genocide of the Armenians." *Holocaust and Genocide Studies* 7 (2): 173–201.
Davis, Natalie Zemon. 1973. "The Rites of Violence: Religious Riot in Sixteenth-Century France." *Past & Present* 59 (1): 51–91.
Dawkins, Richard. 2016. *The God Delusion*. 10th anniversary ed. London: Transworld.
DDK (T. C. Cumhurbaşkanlığı Devlet Denetleme Kurulu). Araştırma ve inceleme raporu. Raporu konusu: 1-2Temmuz 1993 tarihlerinde Sivas ilinde meydana gelen "Madımak olayının" oluş şekli, amacı, sonucu ve tesirleri itibariyle incelenmesi, 2014.
Dede, Leyla. 2017. "The Role of Memory in Shaping Social Relations: A Case Study about the Remembrance of Çorum Massacre in 1980." MA thesis, Şehir University.

Degerald, Michael K. 2018. "The Legibility of Power and Culture in Ba'thist Iraq from 1968–1991." PhD diss., University of Washington.

Dehqan, Mustafa. 2008. "A Shabak Contemporary Polemic against the Yezidi Religion." *Oriente moderno* 88 (1): 200–204.

Der Matossian, Bedross. 2022. *The Horrors of Adana: Revolution and Violence in the Early Twentieth Century*. Redwood City, CA: Stanford University Press.

Deringil, Selim. 1999. *The Well-Protected Domains: Ideology and the Legitimation of Power in the Ottoman Empire, 1876–1909*. London: I. B. Tauris

Derrida, Jacques. 2002. *Acts of Religion*. Edited by Gil Anidjar. New York: Routledge.

Derzsi-Horváth, Andras. 2017. "Iraq after ISIL: Rabi'a. Global Public Policy Institute Web Essay." Accessed October 15, 2020. https://www.gppi.net/2017/08/04/iraq-after-isil-rabia.

Diefendorf, Barbara. 1985. "Prologue to a Massacre: Popular Unrest in Paris, 1557–1572." *American Historical Review* 90 (5): 1067–91.

Dinç, Namık K. 2017. *Êzîdîlerin 73. Fermanı: Şengal soykırımı*. İstanbul: Zan Vakfı.

Diyanet. 2017. *Exploitation of Religion and Terrorist Organization DAESH*. Ankara: Diyanet İşleri Başkanlığı. Accessed October 15, 2020. https://dosya.diyanet.gov.tr/DIYKDosya/YayinDosya/94342976-b84f-495c-b7 b.c.-d8a32498d6a4.pdf.

Domle, Khidir. 2015. الموت الاسود: مآسي نساء الإيزيدية في قبضة داعش [al-Mawt al-aswad: ma'āsī nisā' al-Īzīdīyah fī qabḍat Dā'ish = The black death]. Duhok, Iraq. https://www.worldcat.org/title/922713944?oclcNum=922713944.

Douglas, Mary. 1966. *Purity and Danger: An Analysis of Concepts of Pollution and Taboo*. Milton Park, UK: Routledge.

Dray, Philip. 2003. *At the Hands of Persons Unknown: The Lynching of Black America*. New York: Random House.

Dressler, Markus. 2013. *Writing Religion: The Making of Turkish Alevi Islam*. Oxford: Oxford University Press.

Duffy, Liam. 2021. "Western Foreign Fighters and the Yazidi Genocide." Accessed March 11, 2022. https://www.counterextremism.com/press/cep-launches-report-highlighting-role-western-foreign-fighters-yazidi-genocide.

Dündar, Fuat. 2008. *Modern Türkiye'nin Şifresi: İttihat ve Terakki'nin Etnisite Mühendisliği (1913–1918)*. Istanbul: İletişim Yayınları.

Elkins, Zachary, Tom Ginsburg, and James Melton. 2014. "Characteristics of National Constitutions, Version 2.0." Comparative Constitutions Project, 29–42. https://comparativeconstitutionsproject.org.

Engels, Friedrich. (1850) 1926. *The Peasant War in Germany*. Accessed June 1, 2022. https://www.marxists.org/archive/marx/works/1850/peasant-war-germany.

Eppel, Michael. 2016. *A People without a State: The Kurds from the Rise of Islam to the Dawn of Nationalism*. Austin: University of Texas Press.

Erdem, Hakan Y. 1996. *Slavery in the Ottoman Empire and Its Demise, 1800–1909*. New York: St. Martin's.

Erdener, Eda. 2017. "The Ways of Coping with Post-war Trauma of Yezidi Refugee Women in Turkey." *Women's Studies International Forum* 65:60–70.

Erensü, Yahya, and Yahya Madra. 2022. "Neoliberal Politics in Turkey." In *The Oxford Handbook of Turkish Politics*, edited by Güneş Murat Tezcür, 159–85. Oxford: Oxford University Press.

Erginbaş, Vefa. 2020. "Reading Ottoman Sunnism through Islamic History: Approaches toward Yazīd b. Muʿāwiya in Ottoman Historical Writing." In *Historicizing Sunni Islam in the Ottoman Empire, c. 1450–c. 1750*, edited by Tijana Krstić and Derin Terzioğlu, 451–78. Leiden: Brill.

Erman, Thaire, and Emrah Göker. 2000. "Alevi Politics in Contemporary Turkey." *Middle Eastern Studies* 36 (4): 99–118.

Ertan, Mehmet. 2012. "Türk sağının Kızılbaş algısı." In *Türk Sağı: Mitler, fetişler, düşman imgeleri*, edited by İnci Özkan Kerestecioğlu and Güven Gürkan Öztan, 203–42. Istanbul: İletişim Yayınları.

Ertan, Mehmet. 2015. "Örtük politikleşmeden kimlik siyasetine: Aleviliğin politikleşmesi ve sosyalist sol." *Birikim* 309–10:43–56.

Ertan, Mehmet. 2017. *Aleviliğin politikleşme süreci: Kimlik siyasetinin kısıtlılıkları ve imkanları*. Istanbul: İletişim Yayınları.

Evliya, Çelebi. 2013. *Günümüz Türkçesiyle Evliya Çelebi Seyahatnamesi*. Edited and transliterated by Seyit Ali Kahraman and Yücel Dağlı. Istanbul: Yapı Kredi Yayınları.

Fassin, Didier. 2013. "On Resentment and Ressentiment: The Politics and Ethics of Moral Emotions." *Current Anthropology* 54 (3): 249–61.

Fehr, Ernst, and Simon Gächter. 2002. "Altruistic Punishment in Humans." *Nature* 415 (6868): 137–40.

Fığlalı, Ethem Ruhi. 1994. *Bâbîlik ve Bahâîlik*. Ankara: Türkiye Diyanet Vakfı Yayınları.

Filonik, Jakub. 2013. "Athenian Impiety Trials: A Reappraisal." *Dike: Rivista di storia del diritto greco ed ellenistico* 16:11–96.

Firro, Kais M. 2001. "Reshaping Druze Particularism in Israel." *Journal of Palestine Studies* 30 (3): 40–53.

Fischer, Michael M. 1980. *Iran: From Religious Dispute to Revolution*. Cambridge, MA: Harvard University Press.

Fiske, Susan T., Amy J. C. Cuddy, Peter Glick, and Jun Xu. 2002. "A Model of (Often Mixed) Stereotype Content: Competence and Warmth Respectively Follow from Perceived Status and Competition." *Journal of Personality and Social Psychology* 82 (6): 878–902.

Fitzsimmons, Michael. 2013. *Governance, Identity, and Counterinsurgency: Evidence from Ramadi and Tal Afar*. Carlisle, PA: Strategic Studies Institute and US Army War College Press.

Flyvbjerg, Bent. 2006. "Five Misunderstandings about Case-Study Research." *Qualitative Inquiry* 12 (2): 219–45.

Forbes, Frederick. 1839. "A Visit to the Sinjar Hills in 1838, with Some Account of the Sect of Yezidis, and of Various Places in the Mesopotamian Desert, between the Rivers Tigris and Khabur." *Journal of the Royal Geographical Society of London* 9:409–30.

Forte, David F. 1994. "Apostasy and Blasphemy in Pakistan." *Connecticut Journal of International Law* 10 (27): 27–68.

Foster, Johanna E., and Sheerizan Minwalla. 2018. "Voices of Yazidi Women: Perceptions of Journalistic Practices in the Reporting on ISIS Sexual Violence." *Women's Studies International Forum* 67:53–64.

Fox, Jonathan. 2004. "The Rise of Religious Nationalism and Conflict: Ethnic Conflict and Revolutionary Wars, 1945–2001." *Journal of Peace Research* 41 (6): 715–31.

Fox, Jonathan. 2016. *The Unfree Exercise of Religion: A World Survey of Discrimination against Religious Minorities*. Cambridge: Cambridge University Press.

Fox, Jonathan. 2020. *Thou Shalt Have No Other Gods before Me: Why Governments Discriminate against Minorities*. Cambridge: Cambridge University Press.

Fox, Jonathan, Roger Finke, and Dane R. Mataic. 2018. "New Data and Measures on Societal Discrimination and Religious Minorities." *Interdisciplinary Journal of Research on Religion* 14:3–36.

Fox, Jonathan, and Lev Topor. 2021. *Why Do People Discriminate against Jews?* Oxford: Oxford University Press.

Fraser, Nancy. 1995. "From Redistribution to Recognition? Dilemmas of Justice in a 'Post-socialist' Age." *New Left Review* 212:68–93.

Fredrickson, George M. 2015. *Racism: A Short History*. Princeton, NJ: Princeton University Press.

Friedmann, Yohanan. 2003. *Prophecy Continuous: Aspects of Ahmadi Religious Thought and Its Medieval Background*. Oxford: Oxford University Press.

Fuccaro, Nelida. 1997. "Ethnicity, State Formation, and Conscription in Postcolonial Iraq: The Case of the Yazidi Kurds of Jabal Sinjar." *International Journal of Middle East Studies* 29 (4): 559–80.

Fuccaro, Nelida. 1999. *The Other Kurds: Yazidis in Colonial Iraq*. London: I. B. Tauris.

Fuchs, Maria-Magdalena, and Simon Wolfgang Fuchs. 2020. "Religious Minorities in Pakistan: Identities, Citizenship and Social Belonging." *South Asia: Journal of South Asian Studies* 43 (1): 52–67.

Fujii, Lee Ann. 2008. "The Power of Local Ties: Popular Participation in the Rwandan Genocide." *Security Studies* 17 (3): 568–97.

Fujii, Lee Ann. 2009. *Killing Neighbors: Webs of Violence in Rwanda*. Ithaca, NY: Cornell University Press.

Fujii, Lee Ann. 2010. "Shades of Truth and Lies: Interpreting Testimonies of War and Violence." *Journal of Peace Research* 47:231–41.

Fujii, Lee Ann. 2021. *Show Time: The Logic and Power of Violent Display*. Ithaca, NY: Cornell University Press.

Gaddis, Michael. 2015. *There Is No Crime for Those Who Have Christ: Religious Violence in the Christian Roman Empire*. Berkeley: University of California Press.

Gawrych, George. 1986. "The Culture and Politics of Violence in Turkish Society, 1903–14." *Middle Eastern Studies* 22 (3): 307–30.

Gerges, Fawaz A. 2016. *ISIS: A History*. Princeton, NJ: Princeton University Press.

Gezik, Erdal. 2012. *Alevi Kürtler: Dinsel, etnik ve politik sorunlar bağlamında*. Istanbul: İletişim Yayınları.

Göçek, Fatma Müge. 2015. *Denial of Violence: Ottoman Past, Turkish Present, and Collective Violence against the Armenians, 1789–2009*. Oxford: Oxford University Press.

Goertz, Gary. 2006. *Social Science Concepts: A User's Guide*. Princeton, NJ: Princeton University Press.

Goffman, Ervin. 1963. *Stigma: Notes on the Management of Spoiled Identity*. Hoboken, NJ: Prentice Hall.

Gökçen, Amed. 2012. *Osmanlı ve İngiliz arşiv belgelerinde Yezidiler*. Istanbul: Bilgi Üniversitesi Yayınları.

Gökçen, Amed. 2015. *Kadim bir nefes: Ezidi ağıtları*. İstanbul: Bilgi Üniversitesi Yayınları.

Gölbaşı, Edip. 2009. "'Heretik' Aşiretler ve II. Abdülhamid Rejimi: Zorunlu Askerlik Meselesi ve İhtida Siyaseti Odağında Yezidiler ve Osmanlı İdaresi." *Tarih ve Toplum* 9:87–156.

Gölbaşı, Edip. 2013. "Turning the 'Heretics' into Loyal Muslim Subjects: Imperial Anxieties, the Politics of Religious Conversion, and the Yezidis in the Hamidian Era." *Muslim World* 103 (1): 3–23.

Gómez, Ángel, Lucia López-Rodríguez, Hammad Sheikh, Jeremy Ginges, Lydia Wilson, Hoshang Waziri, and Scott Atran. 2017. "The Devoted Actor's Will to Fight and the Spiritual Dimension of Human Conflict." *Nature Human Behaviour* 1 (9): 673–79.

Goner, Ozlem. 2017. *Turkish National Identity and Its Outsiders: Memories of State Violence in Dersim*. Milton Park, UK: Taylor & Francis.

Greene, Joshua David. 2013. *Moral Tribes: Emotion, Reason, and the Gap between Us and Them*. London: Penguin.

Greene, Molly. 2020. "Violence and Religion in the Ottoman Empire." In *The Cambridge World History of Violence Vol. III*, edited by Robert Antony, Stuart Caroll, and Caroline Dodds Pennock, 77–95. Cambridge: Cambridge University Press.

Greengrass, Mark. 1999. "Hidden Transcripts: Secret Histories and Personal Testimonies of Religious Violence in the French Wars of Religion." In *The Massacre in History*, edited by Mark Levene and Penny Roberts, 69–88. New York: Berghahn.

Grim, Brian J., and Roger Finke. 2011. *The Price of Freedom Denied: Religious Persecution and Conflict in the Twenty-First Century*. New York: Cambridge University Press.

Gross, Jan Tomasz, and Irena Grudzinska Gross. 2016. *Golden Harvest: Events at the Periphery of the Holocaust*. Oxford: Oxford University Press.

Grossman, Dave. 1995. *On Killing: The Psychological Cost of Learning to Kill in War and Society*. Boston: Little, Brown.

Grzymała-Busse, Anna. 2016. "The Difficulty with Doctrine: How Religion Can Influence Politics." *Government and Opposition* 51 (2): 327–50.

Guest, John S. 1993. *Survival among the Kurds: A History of the Yezidis*. Milton Park, UK: Routledge.

Gülsoy, Ufuk. 2002. "Sıra Dışı Bir Dini Topluluk: Osmanlı Yezidileri (XIX. ve XX. Yüzyıllar)." *Türk Kültürü İncelemeleri Dergisi* 7:129–62.

Gürel, Burak. 2004. "Political Mobilization in Turkey in the 1970s: The Case of the Kahramanmaraş Incidents." PhD diss., Boğaziçi University.

Gutiérrez-Sanín, Francisco, and Elisabeth Jean Wood. 2017. "What Should We Mean by 'Pattern of Political Violence'? Repertoire, Targeting, Frequency, and Technique." *Perspectives on Politics* 15 (1): 20–41.

Gutmann, Amy. 2003. *Identity in Democracy*. Princeton, NJ: Princeton University Press.

REFERENCES

Güven, Dilek. 2006. *Cumhuriyet dönemi azınlık politikaları bağlamında: 6–7 Eylül Olayları*. Istanbul: İletişim Yayınları.

Hackett, Conrad, and David McClendon. 2017. "Christians Remain World's Largest Religious Group, but They Are Declining in Europe." Pew Research Center, April 5. Accessed September 2, 2020. https://www.pewresearch.org/fact-tank/2017/04/05/christians-remain-worlds-largest-religious-group-but-they-are-declining-in-europe/.

Haidt, Jonathan. 2012. *The Righteous Mind: Why Good People Are Divided by Politics and Religion*. New York: Knopf Doubleday.

Halabi, Rabah. 2014. "Invention of a Nation: The Druze in Israel." *Journal of Asian and African Studies* 49 (3): 267–81.

Halm, Heinz. 2004. *Shi'ism*. 2nd ed. New York: Columbia University Press.

Hanioğlu, Şükrü. 2008. *A Brief History of the Late Ottoman Empire*. Princeton, NJ: Princeton University Press.

Hasluck, Frederick William. 1921. "Heterodox Tribes of Asia Minor." *Journal of the Royal Anthropological Institute of Great Britain and Ireland* 51:310–42.

Hassan, Hassan. 2014. "More than ISIS, Iraq's Sunni Insurgency." *Cairo Review*, June 20. Accessed October 6, 2020. https://www.thecairoreview.com/tahrir-forum/more-than-isis-iraqs-sunni-insurgency.

Hassan, Hassan. 2018. "The True Origins of ISIS." *The Atlantic*. Accessed October 15, 2020. https://www.theatlantic.com/ideas/archive/2018/11/isis-origins-anbari-zarqawi/577030.

Hassner, Ron E. 2009. *War on Sacred Grounds*. Ithaca, NY: Cornell University Press.

Hassner, Ron E. 2016. *Religion on the Battlefield*. Ithaca, NY: Cornell University Press.

Hayden, Robert M. 1996. "Imagined Communities and Real Victims: Self-Determination and Ethnic Cleansing in Yugoslavia." *American Ethnologist* 23 (4): 783–801.

Hayes, Peter. 2017. *Why? Explaining the Holocaust*. New York: Norton.

HBVAKV (Hacı Bektaş Veli Anadolu Kültür Vakfı). 2011. *Alevi Çalıştayları Nihai Raporu Üstüne bir Değerlendirme*. Ankara: Hacı Bektaş Veli Anadolu Kültür Vakfı.

Hedström, Peter, and Petri Ylikoski. 2010. "Causal Mechanisms in the Social Sciences." *Annual Review of Sociology* 36:49–67.

Hefner, Robert W. 2000. *Civil Islam: Muslims and Democratization in Indonesia*. Princeton, NJ: Princeton University Press.

Helfont, Samuel. 2018. *Compulsion in Religion: Saddam Hussein, Islam, and the Roots of Insurgencies in Iraq*. Oxford: Oxford University Press.

Henne, Peter S., Nilay Saiya, and Ashlyn W. Hand. 2020. "Weapon of the Strong? Government Support for Religion and Majoritarian Terrorism." *Journal of Conflict Resolution* 64 (10): 1943–67.

Hicks, Jacqueline. 2014. "Heresy and Authority: Understanding the Turn against Ahmadiyah in Indonesia." *South East Asia Research* 22 (3): 321–39.

Hilterman, Joost. 2007. *A Poisonous Affair: America, Iraq, and the Gassing of Halabja*. Cambridge: Cambridge University Press.

Hirschman, Albert O. 1997. *The Passions and the Interests: Political Arguments for Capitalism before Its Triumph*. 20th anniversary ed. Princeton, NJ: Princeton University Press.

Hodgson, Marshall G. S. 1974. *The Venture of Islam: Conscience and History in a World Civilization. Vol. 3. The Gunpowder Empires and Modern Times*. Chicago: University of Chicago Press.

Hofstadter, Richard. 1966. *The Paranoid Style in American Politics and Other Essays*. Cambridge, MA: Harvard University Press.

Holt, Mack P. 1993. "Putting Religion Back into the Wars of Religion." *French Historical Studies* 18 (2): 524–51.

Holt, Mack P. 2012. "Religious Violence in Sixteenth-Century France: Moving beyond Pollution and Purification." *Past & Present* 214 (Suppl. 7): 52–74.

Horowitz, Donald L. 2000. *Ethnic Groups in Conflict*. Updated ed. Berkeley: University of California Press.

Horowitz, Michael C. 2009. "Long Time Going: Religion and the Duration of Crusading." *International Security* 34 (2): 162–93.

Housley, Norman. 2008. *Religious Warfare in Europe 1400–1536*. Oxford: Oxford University Press.

Human Rights Watch (HRW). 2009. *On Vulnerable Ground: Violence against Minority Communities in Nineveh Province's Disputed Territories*. New York: Human Rights Watch. Accessed November 1, 2020. https://www.hrw.org/report/2009/11/10/vulnerable-ground/violence-against-minority-communities-nineveh-provinces-disputed.

Human Rights Watch (HRW). 2010. *Pakistan: Massacre of Minority Ahmadis*. New York: Human Rights Watch. Accessed May 1, 2021. https://www.hrw.org/news/2010/06/01/pakistan-massacre-minority-ahmadis#.

Human Rights Watch. (HRW). 2015. *Slavery: The ISIS Rules*. New York: Human Rights Watch. Accessed November 1, 2020. https://www.hrw.org/news/2015/09/05/slavery-isis-rules.

Human Rights Watch (HRW). 2017a. *Flawed Justice: Accountability for ISIS Crimes in Iraq*. New York: Human Rights Watch. Accessed November 1, 2020. https://www.hrw.org/report/2017/12/05/flawed-justice/accountability-isis-crimes-iraq.

Human Rights Watch (HRW). 2017b. *Indonesia's Ahmadiyah Push Back against Discriminatory Laws*. New York: Human Rights Watch. Accessed May 1, 2021. https://www.hrw.org/news/2017/06/23/indonesias-ahmadiyah-push-back-against-discriminatory-laws.

Huntington, Samuel. 1968. *Political Order in Changing Societies*. New Haven, CT: Yale University Press.

Huntington, Samuel. 1996. *The Clash of Civilizations and the Remaking of the World Order*. New York: Simon & Schuster.

Hurd, Elizabeth Shakman. 2014. "Alevis under Law: The Politics of Religious Freedom in Turkey." *Journal of Law and Religion* 29 (3): 416–35.

Imber, Colin H. 1979. "The Persecution of the Ottoman Shī'ites according to the Mühimme Defterleri, 1565–1585." *Der Islam* 56 (2): 245–73.

Institute for International Law and Human Rights (IILHR), Minority Rights Group International (MRG), Unrepresented Nations & Peoples Organization (UNPO), and No Peace Without Justice (NPWJ). 2015. *Between the Millstones: The State of Iraq's Minorities since the Fall of Mosul*. Brussels: IILHR, MRG,

REFERENCES

UNPO, NPWJ. https://minorityrights.org/wp-content/uploads/2015/08/Between-the-Millstones-English.pdf.

Isaacs, Matthew. 2016. "Sacred Violence or Strategic Faith? Disentangling the Relationship between Religion and Violence in Armed Conflict." *Journal of Peace Research* 53 (2): 211–25.

Jacobs, Alan. 2015. "Process Tracing the Effects of Ideas." In *Process Tracing: From Metaphor to Analytic Tool*, edited by Andrew Bennett, and Jeffrey T. Checkel, 41–73. Cambridge: Cambridge University Press.

Jacoby, Tim. 2019. "Islam and the Islamic State's Magazine, *Dabiq*." *Politics and Religion* 12 (1): 32–54.

Jaffrelot, Christophe, ed. 2007. *Hindu Nationalism: A Reader*. Princeton, NJ: Princeton University Press.

Johnson, Dominic, and Oliver Krüger. 2004. "The Good of Wrath: Supernatural Punishment and the Evolution of Cooperation." *Political Theology* 5 (2): 159–76.

Johnson, Megan K., Wade C. Rowatt, and Jordan P. LaBouff. 2012. "Religiosity and Prejudice Revisited: In-group Favoritism, Out-group Derogation, or both?" *Psychology of Religion and Spirituality* 4 (2): 154–68.

Jubber, Ken. 1977. "The Persecution of Jehovah's Witnesses in Southern Africa." *Social Compass* 24 (1): 121–34.

Juergensmeyer, Mark. 2000. *Terror in the Mind of God: The Global Rise of Religious Violence*. Updated ed. Berkeley: University of California Press.

Juergensmeyer, Mark. 2009. "Religious Violence." In *The Oxford Handbook of the Sociology of Religion*, edited by Peter B. Clarke, 890–908. Oxford: Oxford University Press.

Kalyvas, Stathis N. 2003. "The Ontology of 'Political Violence': Action and Identity in Civil Wars." *Perspectives on Politics* 1 (3): 475–94.

Kamal, Asma Mustafa. 2017. حكايات نساء داعش: سبايا ومحظيات. Cairo: Mu'assasat Batānah.

Kaplan, Benjamin J. 2002. "Fictions of Privacy: House Chapels and the Spatial Accommodation of Religious Dissent in Early Modern Europe." *American Historical Review* 107 (4): 1031–64.

Kaplan, Doğan. 2014. "Alevilere atılan "mum söndü" iftirasının tarihsel kökenleri üzerine." *Hünkar: Alevilik Bektaşilik Akademik Araştırmalar Dergisi* 2:41–53.

Kaplan, Sam. 2002. "Din-u Devlet All over Again? The Politics of Military Secularism and Religious Militarism in Turkey Following the 1980 Coup." *International Journal of Middle Eastern Studies* 34 (1): 113–27.

Karadaghi, Kamran. 1993. "The Two Gulf Wars: The Kurds on the World Stage, 1979–1992." In *A People without a Country*, 214–40. London: Zed Books.

Karakaya-Stump, Ayfer. 2018. "The AKP, Sectarianism, and the Alevis' Struggle for Equal Rights in Turkey." *National Identities* 20 (1): 53–67.

Karakaya-Stump, Ayfer. 2020. *The Kizilbash-Alevis in Ottoman Anatolia: Sufism, Politics and Community*. Edinburgh: University of Edinburgh Press.

Karay, Refik Halit. 1939. *Yezidin kızı*. Istanbul: Semih Lûtfi Kitabevi.

Karolewski, Janina. 2008. "What Is Heterodox about Alevism? The Development of Anti-Alevi Discrimination and Resentment." *Die Welt des Islams* 48 (3): 434–56.

Kather, Alexandra Lily, and Alexander Schwarz. 2020. "First Yazidi Genocide Trial Commences in Germany." *Just Security.* Accessed October 15, 2020. https://www.justsecurity.org/69833/first-yazidi-genocide-trial-commences-in-germany.

Kaufman, Ilana. 2004. "Ethnic Affirmation or Ethnic Manipulation: The Case of the Druze in Israel." *Nationalism and Ethnic Politics* 9 (4): 53–82.

Kaufman, Stuart J. 2001. *Modern Hatreds: The Symbolic Politics of Ethnic War.* Ithaca, NY: Cornell University Press.

Kazemzadeh, Firuz. 2000. "The Baha'is in Iran: Twenty Years of Repression." *Social Research* 67 (2): 537–58.

Keddie, Nikki. 2003. *Modern Iran: Roots and Results of Revolution.* New Haven, CT: Yale University Press.

Kelly, Michael J. 2010. "The Kurdish Regional Constitutional within the Framework of the Iraqi Federal Constitution: A Struggle for Sovereignty, Oil, Ethnic Identity, and the Prospects for a Reverse Supremacy Clause." *Penn State Law Review* 114 (3): 707–808.

Kerborani, Bahadin. 2021. "Paying the Price of Dasht-i Karbala: Historical Perceptions of Yezidis in the Ottoman Era." In *Kurds and Yezidis in the Middle East: Shifting Identities, Borders, and the Experiences of Minority Communities,* edited by Güneş Murat Tezcür, 99–114. London: I. B. Tauris.

Kerr, Stanley Elphinstone. 1973. *The Lions of Marash.* Albany: State University of New York Press.

Khalili, Laleh. 2012. *Time in the Shadows: Confinement in Counterinsurgencies.* Stanford, CA: Stanford University Press.

Khan, Adil Hussain. 2015. *From Sufism to Ahmadiyya: A Muslim Minority Movement in South Asia.* Bloomington: Indiana University Press.

Khan, Amjad Mahmood. 2003. "Persecution of the Ahmadiyya Community in Pakistan: An Analysis under International Law and International Relations." *Harvard Human Rights Journal* 16:217–44.

Khenchelaoui, Zaim, and Jean Burrell. 1999. "The Yezidis, People of the Spoken Word in the Midst of People of the Book." *Diogenes* 47 (187): 20–37.

Khomeini, Ruhollah. 1981. *Islam and Revolution: Writings and Declarations of Imam Khomeini (1941–1980).* Translated and annotated by Hamid Algar. Northridge, CA: Mizan Press.

Kierkegaard, Søren. (1843) 2021. *Fear and Trembling: A New Translation.* New York: Liveright.

Kiernan, Ben. 2007. *Blood and Soil: A World History of Genocide and Extermination from Sparta to Darfur.* New Haven, CT: Yale University Press.

Kieser, Hans-Lukas. 2001. "Muslim Heterodoxy and Protestant Utopia. The Interactions between Alevis and Missionaries in Ottoman Anatolia." *Die Welt des Islams* 41 (1): 89–111.

Kieser, Hans-Lukas. 2011. "Dersim Massacre, 1937–1938, Mass Violence & Résistance." Accessed May 27, 2022. http://bo-k2s.sciences-po.fr/mass-violence-war-massacre-resistance/en/document/dersim-massacre-1937–1938, ISSN 1961–9898.

Kieser, Hans-Lukas. 2013. *Iskalanmış barış: Doğu vilayetleri'nde misyonerlik, etnik kimlik ve devlet 1839–1938.* Revised ed. Istanbul: İletişim Yayınları.

Kılıçdağı, Ohannes. 2014. "Socio-political Reflections and Expectations of the Ottoman Armenians after the 1908 Revolution: Between Hope and Despair." PhD diss., Boğaziçi University.

King, Desmond S., and Rogers M. Smith. 2005. "Racial Orders in American Political Development." *American Political Science Review* 99 (1): 75–92.

Klein, Janet. 2011. *The Margins of Empire: Kurdish Militias in the Ottoman Tribal Zone.* Redwood City, CA: Stanford University Press.

Kleinman, Arthur, and Joan Kleinman. 1996. "The Appeal of Experience; the Dismay of Images: Cultural Appropriations of Suffering in Our Times." *Daedalus* 125:1–23.

Klocek, Jason, Hyun Jeong Ha, and Nathanael Gratias Sumaktoyo. 2022. "Regime Change and Religious Discrimination after the Arab Uprisings." *Journal of Peace Research* 60 (3).

Klocek, Jason, and Ron E. Hassner. 2020. "War and Religion: An Overview." In *Oxford Encyclopedia of Politics and Religion*, edited by Paul A. Djupe, Mark J. Rozell, and Ted G. Jelen. Oxford: Oxford University Press.

Koerbin, Paul. 2011. "Pir Sultan Abdal: Encounters with Persona in Alevi Lyric Song." *Oral Tradition* 26 (1): 191–220.

KONDA. 2014a. "Gezi raporu: Toplumun 'Gezi parkı olayları' algısı Gezi parkındakiler kimlerdi?" KONDA, June 5. Accessed November 1, 2020. https://konda.com.tr/wp-content/uploads/2017/02/KONDA_GeziRaporu2014.pdf.

KONDA. 2014b. "Konda barometresi temalar: Bir arada yaşamak." KONDA, November. Accessed November 1, 2020. https://konda.com.tr/tr/rapor/bir-arada-yasamak.

KONDA. 2019. "Türkiye'de toplumsal cinsiyet raporu: Hayat tarzları 2018 Araştırması." KONDA, November. Accessed November 1, 2020. https://konda.com.tr/wp-content/uploads/2019/11/KONDA_ToplumsalCinsiyetRaporu.pdf.

Kopstein, Jeffrey S., and Jason Wittenberg. 2018. *Intimate Violence: Anti-Jewish Pogroms on the Eve of the Holocaust.* Ithaca, NY: Cornell University Press.

Kouymjian, Dickran. 1997. "Armenia from the Fall of the Cilician Kingdom (1375) to the Forced Emigration under Shah Abbas (1604)." In *The Armenian People from Ancient Times to Modern Times Vol. II*, edited by Richard G. Hovannisian, 1–50. New York: Macmillan.

Kreyenbroek, Philip G. 1995. *Yezidism: Its Background, Observances and Textual Tradition.* New York: Edwin Mellen.

Krstić, Tijana. 2019. "State and Religion, 'Sunnitization' and 'Confessionalism' in Süleyman's Time." In *The Battle of Central Europe: The Siege of Szigetvár and the Death of Süleyman the Magnificent and Nicholas Zrínyi (1566)*, edited by Pál Fodor, 65–91. Leiden: Brill.

Kürkçü, Ertuğrul. 2007. "Türkiye Sosyalist Hareketine Silahlı Mücadelenin Girişi." In *Modern Türkiye'de Siyasi Düşünce: Sol*, 8:494–509. Istanbul: İletişim Yayınları.

Kurt, Ümit. 2018. "Theatres of Violence on the Ottoman Periphery: Exploring the Local Roots of Genocidal Policies in Antep." *Journal of Genocide Research* 20 (3): 351–71.

Kurt, Ümit. 2021. *The Armenians of Aintab: The Economics of Genocide in an Ottoman Province.* Cambridge, MA: Harvard University Press.

Kurtz, Lester R. 2015. *Gods in the Global Village: The World's Religions in Sociological Perspective*. 4th ed. Thousand Oaks, CA: Sage.

Kuru, Ahmet T. 2009. *Secularism and State Policies toward Religion: The United States, France, and Turkey*. Cambridge: Cambridge University Press.

Kuru, Ahmet T. 2019. *Islam, Authoritarianism, and Underdevelopment: A Global and Historical Comparison*. Cambridge: Cambridge University Press.

Kuyucu, Ali Tuna. 2005. "Ethno-religious 'Unmixing' of 'Turkey': 6–7 September Riots as a Case in Turkish Nationalism." *Nations and Nationalism* 11 (3): 361–80.

Kuziemko, Ilyana, Ryan W. Buell, Taly Reich, and Michael I. Norton. 2014. "'Last-Place Aversion': Evidence and Redistributive Implications." *Quarterly Journal of Economics* 129 (1): 105–49.

LaBouff, Jordan, Wade Rowatt, Megan Johnson Shen, and Callie Finkle. 2012. "Differences in Attitudes toward Outgroups in Religious and Nonreligious Contexts in a Multinational Sample: A Situational Context Priming Study." *International Journal for the Psychology of Religion* 22 (1): 1–9.

Laçiner, Ömer. 1978. "Malatya Olayı—Türkiye'de Faşist Hareketin Yapısı ve Gelişimi." *Birikim* 39:12–24.

Lajnat al-Buhuth wa al-dirasat. 2016. كارثة شنگال، 3–آب—2014: مجموعة بحوث ودراسات. [Karithat Shangal: majmuat bhuth wa dirasat] (August 3, 2014). Duhok, Iraq: al-Hay'ah al-'Ulyā li-Markaz Lālish al-Thaqāfī wa-al-Ijtimā'ī.

Lange, Matthew. 2017. *Killing Others: A Natural History of Ethnic Violence*. Ithaca, NY: Cornell University Press.

Langer, Robert, and Udo Simon. 2008. "The Dynamics of Orthodoxy and Heterodoxy: Dealing with Divergence in Muslim Discourses and Islamic Studies." *Die Welt des Islams* 48:273–88.

Lapidus, Ira M. 2002. *A History of Islamic Societies*. 2nd ed. Cambridge: Cambridge University Press.

Layard, Austen Henry. 1850. *Nineveh and Its Remains: With an Account of a Visit to the Chaldean Christians of Kurdistan, and the Yesidis, or Devil Worshippers; and an Inquiry into the Manners and Arts of the Ancient Assyrians*. Vol. 2. London: J. Murray.

Leach, Colin Wayne, and Russell Spear. 2008. "'A Vengefulness of the Impotent': The Pain of In-group Inferiority and Schadenfreude toward Successful Out-groups." *Journal of Personality and Social Psychology* 95 (6): 1383–96.

League of Nations. 1925. Question on the Frontier between Turkey and Iraq. Report submitted to the Council by the Commission instituted by the Council Resolution of September 30th, 1924. Geneva.

Leezenberg, Michiel. 1997. "Between Assimilation and Deportation: The Shabak and the Kakais in Northern Iraq." In *Syncretistic Religious Communities in the Near East*, edited by Kehl-Bodrogi, Otter-Beaujean, and Barbara Kellner-Heikele, 155–74. Leiden: Brill.

Leezenberg, Michiel. 2018. "Transformations in Minority Religious Leadership: The Yezidis, Shabak, and Assyrians in Northern Iraq." *Sociology of Islam* 6 (2): 233–60.

Levene, Mark. 1998. "Creating a Modern 'Zone of Genocide': The Impact of Nation- and State-Formation on Eastern Anatolia, 1878–1923." *Holocaust and Genocide Studies* 12 (3): 393–433.

Levene, Mark. 2020. "Through a Glass Darkly: The Resurrection of Religious Fanaticism as First Cause of Ottoman Catastrophe." *Journal of Genocide Research* 22 (4): 553–60.

Lewis, Bernard. 1953. "Some Observations on the Significance of Heresy in the History of Islam." *Studia Islamica* 1:43–63.

Lewis, Bernard. 1968. *The Emergence of Modern Turkey*. 2nd ed. Oxford: Oxford University Press.

Link, Bruce G., and Jo C. Phelan. 2001. "Conceptualizing Stigma." *Annual Review of Sociology* 27:363–85.

Link, Bruce G., and Jo C. Phelan. 2014. "Stigma Power." *Social Science & Medicine* 103:24–32.

Longrigg, Stephen Hemsley. 1925. *Four Centuries of Modern Iraq*. Oxford: Oxford University Press.

Lord, Ceren. 2017. "Rethinking the Justice and Development Party's 'Alevi Openings.'" *Turkish Studies* 18 (2): 278–96.

Lord, Ceren. 2018. *Religious Politics in Turkey: From the Birth of the Republic to the AKP*. Cambridge: Cambridge University Press.

Lord, Ceren. 2022. "The Transnational Mobilization of the Alevis of Turkey: From Invisibility to the Struggle for Equality." In *The Oxford Handbook of Turkish Politics*, edited by Güneş Murat Tezcür, 455–80. Oxford: Oxford University Press.

Loveman, Mara. 1998. "High-Risk Collective Actions: Defending Human Rights in Chile, Uruguay, and Argentina." *American Journal of Sociology* 104 (2): 477–525.

Loveman, Mara. 2005. "The Modern State and the Primitive Accumulation of Symbolic Power." *American Journal of Sociology* 110 (6). 1651–83.

Luft, Aliza. 2019. "The Contribution of Social Movement Theory of Understanding Genocide." *Contention* 7 (2): 1–30.

MacEoin, Denis. 1983. "From Babism to Baha'ism: Problems of Militancy, Quietism, and Conflation in the Construction of a Religion." *Religion* 13 (3): 219–55.

MacEoin, Denis. 2011. "BĀB, ʿAli Moḥammad Širāzi." *Encyclopaedia Iranica* 3 (3): 278–84. Accessed May 1, 2021. http://www.iranicaonline.org/articles/bab-ali-mohammad-sirazi.

Mahmood, Saba. 2015. *Religious Difference in a Secular Age: A Minority Report*. Princeton, NJ: Princeton University Press.

Mainwaring, Scott. 1986. *The Catholic Church and Politics in Brazil*. Redwood City, CA: Stanford University Press.

Maisel, Sebastian. 2008. "Social Change amidst Terror and Discrimination: Yezidis in the New Iraq." Middle East Institute Policy Brief 18.

Major, Brenda, and Laurie T. O'Brien. 2005. "The Social Psychology of Stigma." *Annual Review of Psychology* 56:393–421.

Majumdar, Samirah. 2021. "41 Countries Ban Religion-Related Groups; Jehovah's Witnesses, Baha'is among the Most Commonly Targeted." Pew Research Center, November 15. Accessed March 25, 2022. https://www.pewresearch.org/fact-tank/2021/11/15/41-countries-ban-religion-related-groups-jehovahs-witnesses-bahais-among-the-most-commonly-targeted/.

Makdisi, Ussama. 2002. "Ottoman Orientalism." *American Historical Review* 107 (3): 768–96.
Malešević, Sinisa. 2017. *The Rise of Organised Brutality*. Cambridge: Cambridge University Press.
Mälksoo, Maria. 2012. "The Challenge of Liminality for International Relations Theory." *Review of International Studies* 38 (2): 481–94.
Mamdani, Mahmood. 2001. *When Victims Become Killers: Colonialism, Nativism, and the Genocide in Rwanda*. Princeton, NJ: Princeton University Press.
Mamdani, Mahmood. 2004. *Good Muslim, Bad Muslim: America, the Cold war, and the Roots of Terror*. New York: Random House.
Mamdani, Mahmood. 2020. *Neither Settler nor Native: The Making and Unmaking of Permanent Minorities*. Cambridge, MA: Harvard University Press.
Mann, Michael. 2005. *The Dark Side of Democracy: Explaining Ethnic Cleansing*. New York: Cambridge University Press.
Mansfield, Edward, and Jack Snyder. 2005/2006. "Prone to Violence: The Paradox of the Democratic Peace." *National Interest* 82:39–45.
Maoz, Zeev, and Errol A. Henderson. 2020. *Scriptures, Shrines, Scapegoats, and World Politics: Religious Sources of Conflict and Cooperation in the Modern Era*. Ann Arbor: University of Michigan Press.
Marcus, Aliza. 1996. "'Should I Shoot You?': An Eyewitness Account of an Alevi Uprising in Gazi." *Middle East Report* 199:24–26.
Martin, Douglas. 1984. "The Persecution of the Baha'is of Iran 1844–1984." *Baha'i Studies* 12 (13): 1–87.
Marx, Anthony W. 2003. *Faith in Nation: Exclusionary Origins of Nationalism*. Oxford: Oxford University Press.
Masoud, Tarek. 2014. *Counting Islam: Religion, Class, and Elections in Egypt*. Cambridge: Cambridge University Press.
McCall, Leslie. 2005. "The Complexity of Intersectionality." *Signs: Journal of Women in Culture and Society* 30 (3): 1771–800.
McDaniel, Eric L., Irfan Nooruddin, and Allyson F. Shortle. 2022. *The Everyday Crusade: Christian Nationalism in American Politics*. Cambridge: Cambridge University Press.
McDoom, Omar Shahabudin. 2012. "The Psychology of Threat in Intergroup Conflict: Emotions, Rationality, and Opportunity in the Rwandan Genocide." *International Security* 37 (2): 119–55.
McDoom, Omar Shahabudin. 2021. *The Path to Genocide in Rwanda: Security, Opportunity, and Authority in an Ethnocratic State*. Cambridge: Cambridge University Press.
McKay, Ryan, Charles Efferson, Harvey Whitehouse, and Ernst Fehr. 2011. "Wrath of God: Religious Primes and Punishment." *Proceedings of the Royal Society B: Biological Sciences* 278 (1713): 1858–63.
Mearsheimer, John. 2018. *The Great Delusion: Liberal Dreams and International Realities*. New Haven, CT: Yale University Press.
Meleagrou-Hitchens, Alexander, and Ranj Alaaldin. 2019. "The Kurds of ISIS." *Foreign Affairs*. Accessed October 15, 2020. https://www.foreignaffairs.com/articles/syria/2016-08-08/kurds-isis.

Melson, Robert. 1982. "A Theoretical Inquiry into the Armenian Massacres of 1894–1986." *Comparative Studies in Society and History* 24 (3): 481–509.

Menchik, Jeremy. 2016. *Islam and Democracy in Indonesia: Tolerance without Liberalism.* Cambridge: Cambridge University Press.

Meral, Ziya. 2018. *How Violence Shapes Religion: Belief and Conflict in the Middle East and Africa.* Cambridge: Cambridge University Press.

Meşe, Ertuğrul. 2016. *Komünizmle Mücadele Dernekleri: Türk sağında antikomünizmin nşası.* Istanbul: İletişim Yayınları.

Midlarsky, Manus I. 2005. *The Killing Trap: Genocide in the Twentieth Century.* Cambridge: Cambridge University Press.

Midlarsky, Manus I. 2020. "Genocide and Religion in Times of War." In *Oxford Encyclopedia of Politics and Religion*, edited by Paul A. Djupe, Mark J. Rozell, and Ted G. Jelen. Oxford: Oxford University Press.

Milani, Abbas. 2008. *Eminent Persians: The Men and Women Who Made Modern Iran, 1941–1979.* Vols. 1–2. Syracuse, NY: Syracuse University Press.

Miles, William. 2021. "Open 'Secrets' and Uncomfortable Truths: Druze, Jews and Israel's New Nationality Law." *Anthropology Now* 12 (3): 56–63.

Moffett, Mark. 2019. *The Human Swarm.* New York: Basic Books.

Moghadam, Assaf. 2009. "Motives for Martyrdom: Al-Qaida, Salafi Jihad, and the Spread of Suicide Attacks." *International Security* 33 (3): 46–78.

Mohammed, Omar. 2018. "'Mosul Will Never Be the Same': An Interview with Omar Mohammed." Middle East Research and Information Project, 287. Accessed November 1, 2020. https://merip.org/2018/10/mosul-will-never-be-the-same/.

Momen, Moojan. 2005. "The Babi and Baha'i Community of Iran: A Case of 'Suspended Genocide'?" *Journal of Genocide Research* 7 (2): 221–41.

Monroe, Kristen Renwick. 2008. "Cracking the Code of Genocide: The Moral Psychology of Rescuers, Bystanders, and Nazis during the Holocaust." *Political Psychology* 29 (5): 699–736.

Moore, Robert I. 2007. *The Formation of a Persecuting Society.* 2nd ed. Malden, MA: Blackwell.

Moradi, Fazil, and Kjell Anderson. 2016. "The Islamic State's Êzîdî Genocide in Iraq: The Sinjār Operations." *Genocide Studies International* 10 (2): 121–38.

Morris, Benny, and Dror Ze'evi. 2019. *The Thirty-Year Genocide: Turkey's Destruction of Its Christian Minorities, 1894–1924.* Cambridge, MA: Harvard University Press.

Mottahedeh, Negar N. 1998. "Mutilated Body of the Modern Nation: Qurrat al-'Ayn Tahirah's Unveiling and the Iranian Massacre of the Bábís." *Comparative Studies of South Asia, Africa and the Middle East* 18 (2): 38–50.

Mueller, John. 2000. "The Banality of 'Ethnic War.'" *International Security* 25 (1): 42–70.

Murad, Jasim Elias. 1993. "The Sacred Poems of the Yazidis: An Anthropological Approach." PhD diss., University of California, Los Angeles.

Nasr, Seyyed Vali Reza. 1994. *The Vanguard of the Islamic Revolution: The Jama'at-i Islami of Pakistan.* Berkeley: University of California Press.

Neyzi, Leyla. 2002. "Embodied Elders: Space and Subjectivity in the Music of Metin-Kemal Kahraman." *Middle Eastern Studies* 38 (1): 89–109.

Nicolaus, Peter, and Serkan Yuce. 2019. "A Look at the Yezidi Journey to Self-Discovery and Ethnic Identity." *Iran and the Caucasus* 23 (1): 87–104.

Nietzsche, Friedrich. 1910. *Human All-Too-Human*. Edinburgh: T. N. Foulis.
Nietzsche, Friedrich. 1977. *A Nietzsche Reader*. Translated by R. J. Hollingdale. London: Penguin.
Nirenberg, David. 2013. *Anti-Judaism: The Western Tradition*. New York: Norton.
Nisan, Mordechai. 2010. "The Druze in Israel: Questions of Identity, Citizenship, and Patriotism." *Middle East Journal* 64 (4): 575–96.
Norenzayan, Ara. 2013. *Big Gods: How Religion Transformed Cooperation and Conflict*. Princeton, NJ: Princeton University Press.
Ocak, Ahmet Yaşar. 1996. *Türk sufîliğine bakışlar*. Istanbul: İletişim Yayınları.
Ocak, Ahmet Yaşar. 1999. *Türkler, Türkiye ve İslam: Yaklaşım, yöntem ve yorum denemeleri*. Istanbul: İletişim Yayınları.
Office of the United Nations High Commissioner for Human Rights (OHCHR). 2016. "'They Came to Destroy': ISIS Crimes against the Yazidis." New York: OHCHR. Accessed October 15, 2020. https://www.ohchr.org/Documents/HRBodies/HRCouncil/CoISyria/A_HRC_32_CRP.2_en.pdf.
Okçu, Davut. 1993. *İslamdan ayrılan cereyanlar: Yezidilik ve Yezidiler*. Istanbul: Birleşik.
Öktem, Kerem. 2008. "Being Muslim at the Margins: Alevis and the AKP." *Middle East Report* 246:5–7.
Öktem, Kerem. 2022. "Ruling Ideologies in Modern Turkey." In *The Oxford Handbook of Turkish Politics*, edited by Güneş Murat Tezcür, 53–74. Oxford: Oxford University Press.
Olson, Robert William. 1973. *The Siege of Mosul: War and Revolution in the Ottoman Empire, 1720–1743*. Ann Arbor: UMI.
Ownby, David. 2008. *Falun Gong and the Future of China*. Oxford: Oxford University Press.
Öz, Yusuf. 2007. "Mardin Yezidileri, inanç, sosyal hayat ve coğrafi dağılım." MA thesis, Marmara University.
Öztürk, Ramazan. 1996. *Sessiz tanık: Fotoğraflarla Türkiye ve dünya, 1974–1995*. Istanbul: Sabah Yayıncılık.
Park, G. Kerlin. 2020. "Animism." *Encyclopedia Britannica*, October 29. Accessed April 30, 2022. https://www.britannica.com/topic/animism.
Parry, Oswald H. 1895. *Six Months in a Syrian Monastery*. London: Horace Cox.
Patriquin, Travis. 2007. "Using Occam's Razor to Connect the Dots: The Ba'ath Party and the Insurgency in Tal Afar." *Military Review* 87 (1): 16–17.
Pattanaik, Smruti S. 2013. "Majoritarian State and the Marginalised Minorities: The Hindus in Bangladesh." *Strategic Analysis* 37 (4): 411–29.
Pearlman, Wendy. 2016. "Narratives of Fear in Syria." *Perspectives on Politics* 14:21–37.
Pescosolido, Bernice A., and Jack K. Martin. 2015. "The Stigma Complex." *Annual Review of Sociology* 41:87–116.
Petersen, Roger D. 2002. *Understanding Ethnic Violence: Fear, Hatred, and Resentment in Twentieth-Century Eastern Europe*. Cambridge: Cambridge University Press.
Pettigrew, Thomas F. 1979. "The Ultimate Attribution Error: Extending Allport's Cognitive Analysis of Prejudice." *Personality and Social Psychology Bulletin* 5 (4): 461–74.
Pew Research Center. 2012a. *Mormons in America—Certain in Their Beliefs, Uncertain of Their Place in Society*. New York: Pew Research Center. Accessed June 4,

2022. https://www.pewresearch.org/religion/2012/01/12/mormons-in-america-executive-summary/.

Pew Research Center. 2012b. *The World's Muslims: Unity and Diversity*. New York: Pew Research Center.

Pew Research Center. 2021. *Religion in India: Tolerance and Segregation*. New York: Pew Research Center. Accessed March 6, 2023. https://www.pewresearch.org/religion/2021/06/29/religion-in-india-tolerance-and-segregation/.

Philpott, Daniel. 2004. "Christianity and Democracy: The Catholic Wave." *Journal of Democracy* 15 (2): 32–46.

Philpott, Daniel. 2007. "Explaining the Political Ambivalence of Religion." *American Political Science Review* 101 (3): 505–25.

Philpott, Daniel. 2019. *Religious Freedom in Islam: The Fate of a Universal Human Right in the Muslim World Today*. Oxford: Oxford University Press.

Pitkin, Hannah. 1972. *Wittgenstein and Justice*. Berkeley: University of California Press.

Pollmann, Judith. 2006. "Countering the Reformation in France and the Netherlands: Clerical Leadership and Catholic Violence 1560–1585." *Past & Present* 190 (1): 83–120.

Posen, Barry R. 1993. "The Security Dilemma and Ethnic Conflict." *Survival* 35 (1): 27–47.

Poyraz, Bedriye. 2005. "The Turkish State and Alevis: Changing Parameters of an Uneasy Relationship." *Middle Eastern Studies* 41 (4): 503–16.

Price, Charles Reavis. 2003. "Social Change and the Development and Co-optation of a Black Antisystemic Identity: The Case of Rastafarians in Jamaica." *Identity: An International Journal of Theory and Research* 3 (1): 9–27.

Prunier, Gerard. 2011. *Darfur: The Ambiguous Genocide*. Ithaca, NY: Cornell University Press.

Putra, Idhamsyah Eka, Peter Holtz, and Any Rufaedah. 2018. "Who Is to Blame, the Victims or the Perpetrators? A Study to Understand a Series of Violence Targeting the Accused Heretic Group Ahmadiyya." *Psychology of Religion and Spirituality* 10 (2): 166–73.

Pyszczynski, Tom, Abdolhossein Abdollahi, Sheldon Solomon, Jeff Greenberg, Florette Cohen, and David Weise. 2006. "Mortality Salience, Martyrdom, and Military Might: The Great Satan versus the Axis of Evil." *Personality and Social Psychology Bulletin* 32 (4): 525–37.

Qadir, Ali. 2015. "When Heterodoxy Becomes Heresy: Using Bourdieu's Concept of Doxa to Describe State-Sanctioned Exclusion in Pakistan." *Sociology of Religion* 76 (2): 155–176.

Qasmi, Ali Usman. 2015. *The Ahmadis and the Politics of Religious Exclusion in Pakistan*. London: Anthem.

Quillian, Lincoln. 1995. "Prejudice as a Response to Perceived Group Threat: Population Composition and Anti-immigrant and Racial Prejudice in Europe." *American Sociological Review* 60 (4): 586–611.

Rahman, Tariq. 2012. "Pakistan's Policies and Practices towards the Religious Minorities." *South Asian History and Culture* 3 (2): 302–15.

Reed, Adolph L. Jr. 2022. *The South*. New York: Verso.

Reeder, Caryn A. 2017. "Deuteronomy 21.10–14 and/as Wartime Rape." *Journal for the Study of the Old Testament* 41 (3): 313–36.

Reşo, Xelîl Cindî. 2014. "Mîrgeha: Şêxan û Şingal û Kilîs." *Kürt Tarihi Dergisi* 15: 34–45.
Revkin, Mara R., and Ariel I. Ahram. 2020. "Perspectives on the Rebel Social Contract: Exit, Voice, and Loyalty in the Islamic State in Iraq and Syria." *World Development* 132:104981.
Richardson, James T. 2015. "Managing Religion and the Judicialization of Religious Freedom." *Journal for the Scientific Study of Religion* 54 (1): 1–19.
Rieff, David. 2016. *In Praise of Forgetting: Historical Memory and Its Ironies*. New Haven, CT: Yale University Press.
Roberts, Penny. 2012. "Peace, Ritual, and Sexual Violence during the Religious Wars." *Past & Present* 214 (Suppl. 7): 75–99.
Rodogno, Davide. 2012. *Against Massacre: Humanitarian Interventions in the Ottoman Empire, 1815–1914*. Princeton, NJ: Princeton University Press.
Rogan, Eugene. 2015. *The Fall of the Ottomans: The Great War in the Middle East*. New York: Basic Books.
Rose, Jacqueline. 2021. *On Violence and on Violence against Women*. New York: Farrar, Straus, and Giroux.
Rumelili, Bahar. 2012. "Liminal Identities and Processes of Domestication and Subversion in International Relations." *Review of International Studies* 38 (2): 495–508.
Sadeghian, Saghar. 2016. "Minorities and Foreigners in a Provincial Iranian City: Bahā'is in the Russian Consulate of Isfahan in 1903." *Journal of Persianate Studies* 9 (1): 107–32.
Saeed, Sadia. 2007. "Pakistani Nationalism and the State Marginalisation of the Ahmadiyya Community in Pakistan." *Studies in Ethnicity and Nationalism* 7 (3): 132–52.
Saeed, Sadia. 2016. *Politics of Desecularization: Law and the Minority Question in Pakistan*. Cambridge: Cambridge University Press.
Saeed, Sadia. 2021a. "Islam, Modernity, and the Question of Religious Heterodoxy: From Early Modern Empires to Modern Nation-States." In *Negotiating Democracy and Religious Pluralism: India, Pakistan, and Turkey*, edited by Karen Barkey, Sudipta Kaviraj, and Vatsal Naresh, 31–58. Oxford: Oxford University Press.
Saeed, Sadia. 2021b. "Religion, Classification Struggles, and the State's Exercise of Symbolic Power." *Theory and Society* 50:255–81.
Şahin, Kaya. 2015. *Empire and Power in the Reign of Süleyman: Narrating the Sixteenth-Century Ottoman World*. Cambridge: Cambridge University Press.
Saiya, Nilay. 2017. "Blasphemy and Terrorism in the Muslim World." *Terrorism and Political Violence* 29 (6): 1087–105.
Salman, Nurhak. 2015. *Tanıkların Anlatımıyla Maraş Katliamı*. Istanbul: Pêrî Yayınları.
Sanasarian, Eliz. 2000. *Religious Minorities in Iran*. Cambridge: Cambridge University Press.
Sandal, Nukhet A. 2017. *Religious Leaders and Conflict Transformation: Northern Ireland and Beyond*. Oxford: Oxford University Press.
Sanyal, Ankita. 2019. "Baha'is in Post-revolution Iran: Perspectives of the Ulema." *Contemporary Review of the Middle East* 6 (1): 58–74.
Sapolsky, Robert M. 2017. *Behave: The Biology of Humans at Our Best and Worst*. London: Penguin.

REFERENCES

Sarıhan, Ali, ed. 2002. *Madımak yangını: Sivas katliamı davası*. Vol. 1. Ankara: Barosu Yayınları.

Savelsberg, Eva, Siamend Hajo, and Irene Dulz. 2010. "Effectively Urbanized: Yezidis in the Collective Towns of Sheikhan and Sinjar." *Études rurales* 186:101–16.

Scheler, Max. (1915) 1994. *Ressentiment*. Milwaukee: Marquette University Press.

Schlueter, Elmar, and Peer Scheepers. 2010. "The Relationship between Outgroup Size and Anti-outgroup Attitudes: A Theoretical Synthesis and Empirical Test of Group Threat and Intergroup Contact Theory." *Social Science Research* 39 (2): 285–95.

Schmidt, Dana Adams. 1964. *Journey among Brave Men*. Boston: Little, Brown.

Schwartz, Regina M. 1997. *The Curse of Cain: The Violent Legacy of Monotheism*. Chicago: University of Chicago Press.

Scott, James C. 1998. *Seeing like a State: How Certain Schemes to Improve the Human Condition Have Failed*. New Haven, CT: Yale University Press.

Scott, James C. 2009. *The Art of Not Being Governed: An Anarchist History of Upland Southeast Asia*. New Haven, CT: Yale University Press.

Selengut, Charles. 2003. *Sacred Fury: Understanding Religious Violence*. Lanham, MD: Rowman & Littlefield.

Semelin, Jacques. 2001. "In Consideration of Massacres." *Journal of Genocide Research* 3 (3): 377–89.

Sethi, Manisha. 2021. "Jainism in Danger? Temple Entry and the Rhetoric of Religion and Reform in post-Colonial India." *Modern Asian Studies* 55 (5): 1718–54.

Serxwebûn. 1993. "TC Özel Savaşının Bitmeyen Katliamları." *Serxwebûn* 139:4–5.

Sevli, Sabir Güler. 2019. *Ötekinin ötekisi—etno-dinsel Bir kimlik olarak Alevi Kürtlüğün inşası*. Istanbul: İletişim Yayınları.

Shariff, Azim F., and Ara Norenzayan. 2007. "God Is Watching You: Priming God Concepts Increases Prosocial Behavior in an Anonymous Economic Game." *Psychological Science* 18 (9): 803–9.

Shaw, Martin. 2003. *War and Genocide: Organized Killing in Modern Society*. New York: Polity.

Sidel, John T. 2006. *Riots, Pogroms, Jihad: Religious Violence in Indonesia*. Ithaca, NY: Cornell University Press.

Sinnerbrink, Robert. 2006. "Deconstructive Justice and the 'Critique of Violence': On Derrida and Benjamin." *Social Semiotics* 16 (3): 485–97.

Smith, David Livingstone. 2011. *Less than Human: Why We Demean, Enslave, and Exterminate Others*. New York: St. Martin's.

Smith, David T. 2015. *Religious Persecution and Political Order in the United States*. Cambridge: Cambridge University Press.

Smith, Peter. 1984. "A Note on Babi and Baha'i Numbers in Iran." *Iranian Studies* 17 (2/3): 295–301.

Snyder, Timothy D. 2015. *Black Earth: The Holocaust as History and Warning*. New York: Seal Books.

Soedirgo, Jessica. 2018. "Informal Networks and Religious Intolerance: How Clientelism Incentivizes the Discrimination of the Ahmadiyah in Indonesia." *Citizenship Studies* 22 (2): 191–207.

Somel, Selçuk Akşin. 2000. "Osmanlı modernleşme döneminde periferik nüfus grupları." *Toplum ve Bilim* 89:178–201.

Souleimanov, Emil Asian. 2020. "Civil War and Religion: Salafi-Jihadist Groups." In *Oxford Encyclopedia of Politics and Religion*, edited by Paul A. Djupe, Mark J. Rozell, and Ted G. Jelen. Oxford: Oxford University Press.

Spät, Eszter. 2018. "Yezidi Identity Politics and Political Ambitions in the Wake of the ISIS Attack." *Journal of Balkan and Near Eastern Studies* 20 (5): 420–38.

Stark, Rodney. 2001. *One True God: Historical Consequences of Monotheism*. Princeton, NJ: Princeton University Press.

Stark, Rodney, and Roger Finke. 2000. *Acts of Faith: Explaining the Human Side of Religion*. Berkeley: University of California Press.

Stepan, Alfred C. 2000. "Religion, Democracy, and the 'Twin Tolerations.'" *Journal of Democracy* 11 (4): 37–57.

Straus, Scott. 2006. *Order of Genocide: Race, Power, and War in Rwanda*. Ithaca, NY: Cornell University Press.

Suny, Ronald Grigor. 2015. *They Can Live in the Desert but Nowhere Else: A History of the Armenian Genocide*. Princeton, NJ: Princeton University Press.

Svensson, Isak. 2007. "Fighting with Faith." *Journal of Conflict Resolution* 51 (6): 930–49.

Svensson, Isak. 2020. "Civil War and Religion: An Overview." In *Oxford Encyclopedia of Politics and Religion*, edited by Paul A. Djupe, Mark J. Rozell, and Ted G. Jelen. Oxford: Oxford University Press.

Svensson, Isak, and Desirée Nilsson. 2018. "Disputes over the Divine: Introducing the Religion and Armed Conflict (RELAC) Data, 1975 to 2015." *Journal of Conflict Resolution* 62 (5): 1127–48.

Swidler, Ann. 1986. "Culture in Action: Symbols and Strategies." *American Sociological Review* 51 (2): 273–86.

Szakolczai, Arpad. 2015. "Liminality and Experience: Structuring Transitory Situations and Transformative Events." In *Breaking Boundaries: Varieties of Liminality*, edited by Agnes Horvath, Bjørn Thomassen, and Harald Wydra, 11–38. New York: Berghahn.

Talebi, Shala. 2011. *Ghosts of Revolution: Rekindled Memories of Imprisonment in Iran*. Redwood City, CA: Stanford University Press.

Talhamy, Yvette. 2010. "The *Fatwas* and the Nusayri/Alawis of Syria." *Middle Eastern Studies* 46 (2): 175–94.

Tambiah, Stanley J. 1997. *Leveling Crowds: Ethnonationalist Conflicts and Collective Violence in South Asia*. Berkeley: University of California Press.

Tarcov, Nathan. 2014. "Machiavelli's Critique of Religion." *Social Research* 81 (4): 193–216.

Taşkın, Yüksel. 2022. "Populism in Turkey: Historical and Contemporary Patterns." In *The Oxford Handbook of Turkish Politics*, edited by Güneş Murat Tezcür, 275–93. Oxford: Oxford University Press.

Tavakoli-Targhi, Mohamad. 2008. "Anti-Baha'ism and Islamism in Iran." In *The Baha'is of Iran*, edited by Dominic Parviz Brookshaw and Seena B. Fazel, 200–231. Milton Park, UK: Routledge.

Taylor, Charles. 1994. "The Politics of Recognition." In *Multiculturalism: Examining the Politics of Recognition*, edited by Amy Gutmann, 25–86. Princeton, NJ: Princeton University Press.

Taylor, Charles. 2007. *A Secular Age*. Cambridge, MA: Harvard University Press.
TBB (Türkiye Barolar Birliği). 2004. *Sivas Davası*. Vol. 1. Istanbul: Türkiye Barolar Birliği Yayınları.
TBMM (The Grand National Assembly of Turkey). 1993. "(10/53, 57, 104, 113, 119, 120, 121, 122, 124, 125, 149 ve 158) Esas Numaralı Meclis Araştırma Komisyonu Raporu." Accessed May 27, 2022. https://www5.tbmm.gov.tr/sirasayi/donem19/yil01/ss871.pdf.
T. C. Adana—K. Maraş—G. Antep ve Urfa İlleri Sıkıyönetim Komutanlığı Askeri Savcılığı Adana [Indictment]. 1979. *İddianame: Kahramanmaraş Toplumsal Olayları*, April 16. Genelkurmay Basımevi.
T. C. Devlet Bakanlığı. 2010a. *Alevi Çalıştayları Nihai Rapor*. Ankara.
T. C. Devlet Bakanlığı. 2010b. "Madımak Değerlendirme Toplantısı." Sivas. Accessed September 15, 2020. http://www.necdetsubasi.com/pdf1?download=23:madimak&start=40.
Teater, Kristina M., and Laura Dudley Jenkins. 2020. "Religious Regulation in India." *Oxford Encyclopedia of Politics and Religion*, edited by Paul A. Djupe, Mark J. Rozell, and Ted G. Jelen. Oxford: Oxford University Press.
Ternon, Yves. 2014. "The Impossible Rescue of the Armenians of Mardin." In *Resisting Genocide: Multiple Forms of Rescue*, edited by Jacques Semelin, Claire Andrieu, and Sarah Gensburger, 383–94. Oxford: Oxford University Press.
Terzioglu, Derin. 2012/2013. "How to Conceptualize Ottoman Sunnitization: A Historiographical Discussion." *Turcica* 44:311–18.
Teymûr, Paşa Ahmed. 2008. *Arap kaynaklarına göre Yezidiler ve Yezidiliğin doğuşu* (çev. Eyüp Tanrıverdi, ed. Ahmet Taşğın). Istanbul: Ataç.
Tezcür, Güneş Murat. 2012. "Trends and Characteristics of the Turkish Party System in Light of the 2011 Elections." *Turkish Studies* 13 (2): 117–34.
Tezcür, Güneş Murat. 2015. "Catholic and Muslim Human Rights Activism in Violent Internal Conflicts." *Politics & Religion* 8 (1): 111–34.
Tezcür, Güneş Murat. 2016. "Ordinary People, Extraordinary Risks: Participation in an Ethnic Rebellion." *American Political Science Review* 110 (2): 247–64.
Tezcür, Güneş Murat, and Clayton Besaw. 2020. "Jihadist Waves: Syria, the Islamic State, and the Changing Nature of Foreign Fighters." *Conflict Management and Peace Science* 37 (2): 215–31.
Thomassen, Bjørn. 2015. "Thinking with Liminality: To the Boundaries of an Anthropological Concept." In *Breaking Boundaries: Varieties of Liminality*, edited by Agnes Horvath, Bjørn Thomassen, and Harald Wydra, 39–58. New York: Berghahn.
Tilly, Charles. 2001. "Mechanisms in Political Processes." *Annual Review of Political Science* 4: 21–41.
Todorov, Tzvetan. 2019. *Goya: Aydınlanmanın gölgesinde (Goya: A la sombra de las Luces)* Istanbul: Othello.
Toft, Monica Duffy. 2003. *The Geography of Ethnic Violence*. Princeton, NJ: Princeton University Press.
Toft, Monica Duffy. 2007. "Getting Religion? The Puzzling Case of Islam and Civil War." *International Security* 31 (4): 97–131.
Toft, Monica Duffy. 2021. "Getting Religion Right in Civil Wars." *Journal of Conflict Resolution* 65 (9): 1607–34.

Toft, Monica Duffy, Daniel Philpott, and Timothy Samuel Shah. 2011. *God's Century: Resurgent Religion and Global Politics*. New York: Norton.

Tokdoğan, Nagehan. 2018. *Yeni Osmanlıcılık: Hınç, nostalji, narsizm*. Istanbul: İletişim Yayınları.

Tolnay, Stewart E., and Elwood M. Beck. 1995. *A Festival of Violence: An Analysis of Southern Lynchings, 1882–1930*. Champaign: University of Illinois Press.

Tripp, Charles. 2007. *A History of Iraq*. Cambridge: Cambridge University Press.

Tunç, Aziz. 2015. *Maraş Kıyımı: tarihsel arka planı ve anatomisi*. Istanbul: Fırat Basım Yayın.

Turan, Ahmet. 1989. "Yezidiliğin aslı, kurucusu ve tarihçesi." *Ondokuz Mayıs Üniversitesi İlahiyat Fakültesi Dergisi* 3 (3): 42–82.

Türkmen, Gülay. 2020. *Under the Banner of Islam: Turks, Kurds, and the Limits of Religious Unity*. Oxford: Oxford University Press.

Turkyilmaz, Yektan. 2011. "Rethinking Genocide: Violence and Victimhood in Eastern Anatolia, 1913–1915." PhD diss., Duke University.

Turkyilmaz, Zeynep. 2016. "Maternal Colonialism and Turkish Women's Burden in Dersim: Educating the 'Mountain Flowers' of Dersim." *Journal of Women's History* 28 (3): 161–86.

Turner, Victor. 1969. *The Ritual Process: Structure and Anti-structure*. Chicago: Aldine.

Tyler, Imogen, and Tom Slater. 2018. "Rethinking the Sociology of Stigma." *Sociological Review Monographs* 66 (4): 721–43.

Üngör, Uğur Ümit. 2012. *The Making of Modern Turkey: Nation and State in Eastern Anatolia, 1913–1950*. Oxford: Oxford University Press.

United Nations Assistance Mission for Iraq (UNAMI). 2009. *District Analysis Summary. Sinjar District and Qahtaniya Sub-district*. Baghdad: UNAMI.

United Nations High Commissioner for Refugees (UNHCR). 2005. *Background Information on the Situation of Non-Muslim Religious Minorities in Iraq*. Geneva: UNHCR. Accessed October 15, 2020. https://www.refworld.org/pdfid/4371cf5b4.pdf.

United Nations Human Settlements Programme in Iraq (UNHABITAT). 2015. *Emerging Land Tenure Issues among Displaced Yazidis from Sinjar, Iraq*. Baghdad: UNHABITAT. Accessed October 15, 2020, https://unhabitat.org/sites/default/files/documents/2019-04/emerging_land_tenure_issues_among_displaced_yazidis_from_sinjar_iraq.pdf.

United Nations Investigative Team to Promote Accountability for Crimes Committed by Da'esh/ISIL (UNITAD). 2020. *Fifth Report of the Special Adviser and Head of the United Nations Investigative Team to Promote Accountability for Crimes Committed by Da'esh/Islamic State in Iraq and the Levant*. Baghdad: UNITAD. Accessed March 10, 2021. https://undocs.org/Home/Mobile?FinalSymbol=S%2F2020%2F1107&Language=E&DeviceType=Desktop.

United States Commission on International Religious Freedom (USCIRF). 2020. *The Global Persecution of Jehovah's Witnesses*. Washington, DC: USCIRF. Accessed March 25, 2022. https://www.uscirf.gov/sites/default/files/2020%20Issue%20Update%20-%20Jehovahs%20Witnesses.pdf.

United States Department of State. 2002. *Report on International Religious Freedom: Chad*. Washington, DC: U.S. Department of State. Accessed April 30, 2022. https://www.justice.gov/file/211611/download.

United States Department of State. 2019. *Report on International Religious Freedom.* Washington, DC: U.S. Department of State. Accessed April 30, 2022. https://www.state.gov/reports/2019-report-on-international-religious-freedom.

United States Institute of Peace (USIP). 2011. *Iraq's Disputed Territories: A View of the Political Horizon and Implications for U.S. Policy.* Washington, DC: USIP. Accessed October 15, 2020. https://www.usip.org/publications/2011/04/iraqs-disputed-territories.

Ure, Michael. 2015. "Resentment/Ressentiment." *Constellations* 22 (4): 599–613.

van Bruinessen, Martin. 1994. "Genocide in Kurdistan? The Suppression of the Dersim Rebellion in Turkey (1937–38) and the Chemical War against the Iraqi Kurds (1988)." In *Conceptual and Historical Dimensions of Genocide*, edited by George J. Andreopoulos, 141–70. Philadelphia: University of Pennsylvania Press.

van Bruinessen, Martin. 1996. "Kurds, Turks and the Alevi Revival in Turkey." *Middle East Report* 200:7–10.

van Bruinessen, Martin. 2000. "Transnational Aspects of the Kurdish Question." European University Institute Working Paper RSC No.2000/22.

Varshney, Ashutosh. 2001. "Ethnic Conflict and Civil Society: India and Beyond." *World Politics* 53 (3): 362–98.

Varshney, Ashutosh. 2003. "Nationalism, Ethnic Conflict, and Rationality." *Perspectives on Politics* 1 (1): 85–99.

Verghese, Ajay. 2020. "Taking Other Religions Seriously: A Comparative Survey of Hindus in India." *Politics and Religion* 13 (3): 604–38.

Vinogradov, Amal. 1974. "Ethnicity, Cultural Discontinuity and Power Brokers in Northern Iraq: The Case of the Shabak." *American Ethnologist* 1 (1): 207–18.

Walzer, Michael. 1968. "Exodus 32 and the Theory of Holy War: The History of a Citation." *Harvard Theological Review* 61 (1): 1–14.

Weiss, Michael H., and Hassan Hassan. 2016. "Everything We Knew about This ISIS Mastermind Was Wrong." *Daily Beast.* Accessed February 1, 2021. https://www.thedailybeast.com/everything-we-knew-about-this-isis-mastermind-was-wrong.

Weitz, Eric D. 2003. *A Century of Genocide: Utopias of Race and Nation.* Princeton, NJ: Princeton University Press.

Whiteside, Craig. 2017. "A Pedigree of Terror: The Myth of the Ba'athist Influence in the Islamic State Movement." *Perspectives on Terrorism* 11 (3): 2–18.

Wilde, Melissa J. 2007. *Vatican II: A Sociological Analysis of Religious Change.* Princeton, NJ: Princeton University Press.

Wilkinson, Steven I. 2004. *Votes and Violence: Electoral Competition and Ethnic Riots in India.* Cambridge: Cambridge University Press.

Williamson, John F. 1974. "A Political History of the Shammar Jarba Tribe of Al-Jazirah: 1800–1958." PhD diss., Indiana University.

Wimmer, Andreas. 2008. "The Making and Unmaking of Ethnic Boundaries: A Multilevel Process Theory." *American Journal of Sociology* 113 (4): 970–1022.

Wimmer, Andreas. 2013. *Waves of War: Nationalism, State Formation, and Ethnic Exclusion in the Modern World.* Cambridge: Cambridge University Press.

Winter, Stefan. 2016. *A History of the 'Alawis: From Medieval Aleppo to the Turkish Republic.* Princeton, NJ: Princeton University Press.

Wolff, Philippe. 1971. "The 1391 Pogrom in Spain. Social Crisis or Not?" *Past & Present* 50:4–18.
Wood, Elisabeth Jean. 2006. "The Ethical Challenges of Field Research in Conflict Zones." *Qualitative Sociology* 29:373–86.
Wood, Elisabeth Jean. 2018. "Rape as a Practice of War: Toward a Typology of Political Violence." *Politics & Society* 46 (4): 513–37.
World Food Programme (WFP). 2016. *Iraq: Socio-economic Atlas*. Rome: WFP.
Yağız, Özlem, D. Yıldız Amca, Uçak Emine Erdoğan, and Necla Saydam. 2014. *Malan barkirin: Evlerini yüklediler zorunlu göç anlatıları*. İstanbul: İthaki Yayınları.
Yalçınkaya, Ayhan. 2011. "Hafıza savaşlarından sahiplenilmiş şehitliğe: Madımak Katliamı örnek olayı." *SBF Dergisi* 66 (3): 333–94.
Yazda. 2017. *An Uncertain Future for Yezidis: A Report Marking Three Years of an Ongoing Genocide*. Accessed October 15, 2020. https://www.yazda.org/reports-and-publications.
Yazda. 2018. *Working against the Clock: Documenting mass graves of Yazidis killed by the Islamic State*. Accessed October 15, 2020. https://www.yazda.org/reports-and-publications.
Yazdani, Mina. 2011. "The Confessions of Dolgoruki: Fiction and Masternarrative in Twentieth-Century Iran." *Iranian Studies* 44 (1): 25–47.
Yiftachel, Oren, and Michaly D. Segal. 1998. "Jews and Druze in Israel: State Control and Ethnic Resistance." *Ethnic and Racial Studies* 21 (3): 476–506.
Yiğenoğlu, Çetin. 1994. *Şeriatçı şiddet ve ölü ozanlar kenti Sivas*. Istanbul: Ekin Yayınları.
Yildiz, Ali Aslan, and Maykel Verkuyten. 2011. "Inclusive Victimhood: Social Identity and the Politicization of Collective Trauma among Turkey's Alevis in Western Europe." *Peace & Conflict* 17 (3): 243–69.
Yıldırım, Rıza. 2019. "The Safavid-Qizilbash Ecumene and the Formation of the Qizilbash-Alevi Community in the Ottoman Empire, c. 1500–c. 1700." *Iranian Studies* 52 (3/4): 449–83.
Yıldız, Tunahan. 2017. "Mezhep çatışmasına bir etnik grup ve yerel bağlam üzerinden bakmak: Irak Türkmenleri ve Telafer örneği." *Türkiye Ortadoğu Çalışmaları Dergisi* 4 (2): 41–73.
Yonucu, Deniz. 2018. "The Absent Present Law: An Ethnographic Study of Legal Violence in Turkey." *Social & Legal Studies* 27 (6): 716–33.
Yonucu, Deniz. 2021. "Counterinsurgency in Istanbul: Provocative Counterorganization, Violent Interpellation and Sectarian Fears." *British Journal of Middle Eastern Studies* 49 (5): 896–914.
Young, Iris Marion. 1990. *Justice and the Politics of Difference*. Princeton, NJ: Princeton University Press.
Zabihi-Moghaddam, Siyamak. 2016. "State-Sponsored Persecution of Baha'is in the Islamic Republic of Iran." *Contemporary Review of the Middle East* 3 (2): 124–46.
Zaman, Muhammad Qasim. 2002. *The Ulama in Contemporary Islam: Custodians of Change*. Princeton, NJ: Princeton University Press.
Zarinebaf-Shahr, Fariba. 1997. "Qızılbash 'Heresy' and Rebellion in Ottoman Anatolia during the Sixteenth Century." *Anatolia moderna. Yeni Anadolu* 7 (1): 1–15.
Zimmer, Heinrich Robert. 1951. *Philosophies of India*. Princeton, NJ: Princeton University Press.

Zubaida, Sami. 2000. "Contested Nations: Iraq and the Assyrians." *Nations and Nationalism* 6 (3): 363–82.

Journalistic and Miscellaneous Online Sources

Ajansa Nûçeyan a Firatê. 2020. "Saziyên Êzidiyan êrişa li dijî goristana Hesen Beg şermezar kirin." *Anf kurdi*, April 5. Accessed October 15, 2020. https://anfkurdi.com/kurdistan/saziyen-Ezidiyan-erisa-li-diji-goristana-hesen-beg-sermezar-kirin-126306.

Altaş, Gülbahar. 2020. "IŞİD mağduru Türkmen kızların kaderi belirsiz: Aşiret ve kültürel yapı normal hayata dönmelerine engel!" *Independent Türkçe*, April 26. Accessed May 31, 2021. https://www.indyturk.com/node/169006/dünya/işid-mağduru-türkmen-kızların-kaderi-belirsiz-aşiret-ve-kültürel-yapı-normal.

Anadolu Ajansı. 2019. "'Başbağlar Katliamı' şehitleri unutulmadı." *AA*, July 5. Accessed June 3, 2021. https://www.aa.com.tr/tr/turkiye/basbaglar-katliami-sehitleri-unutulmadi/1524159.

Arraf, Jane, and Sangar Khaleel. 2021. "3,000 Yazidis Are Still Missing. Their Families Know Where Some of Them Are." *New York Times*, October 21. Accessed May 29, 2022. https://www.nytimes.com/2021/10/03/world/middleeast/yazidis-missing-isis.html.

Asharq Al-Awsat. 2015. "كبار قادة «داعش» اليوم من نتاج «الحملة الإيمانية» التي أطلقها صدام في التسعينات". *Aawsat*. Accessed November 30, 2021. https://aawsat.com/home/article/425556/كبار-قادة-«داعش»-اليوم-من-نتاج-«الحملة-الإيمانية»-التي-أطلقها-صدام-في-التسعينات.

Benli, Mesut Hasan. 2013. "Asker, Alevileri iç tehdit saymış: 'Aleviler devlete sızmaya çalışıyor.'" *Radikal*, July 11. Accessed June 3, 2021. http://www.radikal.com.tr/turkiye/asker-alevileri-ic-tehdit-saymisaleviler-devlete-sizmaya-calisiyor-1141286.

BBC News Türkçe. 1993. "Arşiv Odası: Aziz Nesin, 1993." *BBC News Türkçe*, May 30. Accessed June 3, 2021. https://youtu.be/WtAgLYretEw.

BBC News Türkçe. 2020. "Başbağlar Katliamı: 27 yıl önce Erzincan'ın Kemaliye ilçesine bağlı köyde neler yaşandı?" *BBC News Türkçe*, July 5. Accessed June 3, 2021. https://www.bbc.com/turkce/haberler-turkiye-44722856.

BBC News. 2005. "Iraq Voters Back the New Constitution." *BBC News*, October 25. Accessed October 15, 2020. http://news.bbc.co.uk/2/hi/middle_east/4374822.stm.

BBC News. 2021. "Yazidi Genocide: IS Member Found Guilty in German Landmark Trial." *BBC News*, November 30. Accessed March 4, 2022. https://www.bbc.com/news/world-europe-59474616.

Bianet. 2011. "Court of Appeals: No Defamation of Hrant Dink." *Bianet*, December 2. Accessed November 1, 2020. https://bianet.org/english/print/134473-court-of-appeals-no-defamation-of-hrant-dink.

Bianet. 2013. "Polisten Gezi Direnişi analizi." *Bianet*, November 25. Accessed November 1, 2020. https://bianet.org/bianet/toplum/151567-polisten-gezi-direnisi-analizi.

Bianet. 2022. "İzmit'te cemevlerine yasal statü verilmesi AKP ve MHP'den döndü." *Bianet*, July 7. Accessed October 29, 2022. https://bianet.org/bianet/insan

-haklari/264247-izmit-te-cemevlerine-yasal-statu-verilmesi-akp-ve-mhp-den-dondu.

Cumhuriyet. 2008. "Bir uzun mücadele." Cumhuriyet, December 7. Accessed March 1, 2021. https://www.cumhuriyet.com.tr/haber/bir-uzun-mucadele-26942.

Cumhuriyet. 2019. "Soylu'dan 8 Mart yorumu: Siz Kahramanmaraş olayının nasıl çıktığını biliyor musunuz?" Cumhuriyet, March 14. Accessed June 3, 2021. https://www.cumhuriyet.com.tr/haber/soyludan-8-mart-yorumu-siz-kahramanmaras-olayinin-nasil-ciktigini-biliyor-musunuz-1293799.

Cumhuriyet. 2022. "Madımak Oteli'ni yakmaya gelen iki kişi, dokuz yıl sonra anıttan kaldırıldı." Cumhuriyet, May 11. Accessed October 29, 2022. https://www.cumhuriyet.com.tr/turkiye/madimak-otelini-yakmaya-gelen-iki-kisi-dokuz-yil-sonra-anittan-kaldirildi-1934680.

Dabiq. 2014. "The Revival of Slavery before the Hour." *Dabiq* (October):13–17.

Diab, Razi A. N.d. "Religion and the Law in Syria. Arab Center for International Humanitarian Law and Human Rights Education." *ACIHL*. Accessed April 30, 2022. https://acihl.org/articles.htm?article_id=26.

Dunker, Chris. 2017. "Yazidi Refugee Now Living in Lincoln Recounts Terrifying Story of Her Enslavement." *Lincoln Journal Star*. Accessed March 7, 2023. https://journalstar.com/news/local/yazidi-refugee-now-living-in-lincoln-recounts-terrifying-story-of-her-enslavement/article_c635f4c1-b7a3-5598-b969-4f47588d34a1.html.

DW. 2007. "Germany: Scientologists Complain of State-Sanctioned Discrimination." DW, September 26. Accessed April 30, 2022. https://www.dw.com/en/germany-scientologists-complain-of-state-sanctioned-discrimination/a-2798580.

Emont, Jon. 2017. "Why Are There No New Major Religions?" *The Atlantic*, August 6. Accessed May 21, 2021. https://www.theatlantic.com/international/archive/2017/08/new-religions/533745/.

Erdem, Ali Kemal. 2019. "O günün tanığı HDP Milletvekili Özen: Maraş Katliamı başarılı oldu . . . Independent Türkçe." *Indyturk*. Accessed December 19, 2019. https://www.indyturk.com/node/105611/haber/maraş-katliamının-tanığı-hdp-milletvekili-özen-maraş-katliamı-başarılı-oldu.

Evrensel. 2018. "Nüfus cüzdanına Zerdüşt yazdırınca 'örgüt üyesi' sayıldı." *Evrensel*, March 11. Accessed May 27, 2022. https://www.evrensel.net/haber/347450/nufus-cuzdanina-zerdust-yazdirinca-orgut-uyesi-sayildi.

Fedai. 1979. "Kahramanmaraş olaylarının ardından." *Fedai* 5 (2): 13. Accessed April 14, 2021. https://katalog.idp.org.tr/pdf/1476/2872.

Gazete Manifesto. 2018. "AKP'li Maraş milletvekilleri Maraş Katliamı anmasını hedef gösterdi: Sol gruplar anma bahanesiyle toplumu geriyorlar." *Gazete Manifesto*, December 21. Accessed June 3, 2021. https://gazetemanifesto.com/2018/akpli-maras-milletvekilleri-maras-katliami-anmasini-hedef-gosterdi-sol-gruplar-anma-bahanesiyle-toplumu-geriyorlar-228122.

Gazete Vatan. 2012. "MİT'e göre Maraş olayları Türk-Kürt çatışmasıymış." *Gazete Vatan*, April 29. Accessed June 3, 2021. http://www.gazetevatan.com/mit-e-gore-maras-olaylari-turk-kurt-catismasiymis-446874-gundem.

REFERENCES

Gjelten, Tom. 2018. "Evangelicals and Mormons Are Political Allies, but Theological Rivals." NPR, January 6. Accessed May 13, 2021. https://www.npr.org/2018/01/06/575964167/evangelicals-and-mormons-are-political-allies-but-theological-rivals.

Günaydın, Abdülhakim. 2019. "Ezidilerin dini lideri Şehmus Peşimam: Midyat Belediyesi'nin yeni logosunda Ezidilere ait bir şey yok." *Independent Türkçe*, September 9. Accessed October 15, 2020. https://www.indyturkish.com/node/48521/haber/ezidilerin-dini-lideri-%C5%9Fehmus-pe%C5%9Fimam-midyat-belediyesi%E2%80%99nin-yeni-logosunda.

Haksöz. 2007. "Katliam zincirine yeni bir halka: Yezidiler." *Haksöz* (September): 37. Accessed February 13, 2021. https://katalog.idp.org.tr/yazilar/1012341/katliam-zincirine-yeni-bir-halka-yezidiler.

Howe, Marvine. 1980. "Verdicts Due in '78 Turkish Riots." *New York Times*, July 5. Accessed December 1, 2020. https://www.nytimes.com/1980/08/08/archives/verdicts-due-in-78-turkish-riots.html.

Hürriyet. 2011. "İnsanları yaktığı ilde öldü." *Hurriyet*, July 12. Accessed June 3, 2011. https://www.hurriyet.com.tr/gundem/cumhurbaskani-yardimcisi-oktaydan-sehit-guvenlik-korucusu-cahit-celik-icin-bassagligi-mesaji-41824794.

İslâmî Hareket. 1979. "Kardeşlik mi bıraktınız bre! . . . Maraş hadisesinin içyüzü." *İslâmî Hareket* 1 (12): 1, 3, 9. Accessed April 14, 2021. https://katalog.idp.org.tr/yazilar/29777/kardeslik-mi-biraktiniz-bre.

Islamweb.net. 2012. "Yezidism . . . Emergence, founder and beliefs." Islamweb.net, February 15. Accessed October 15, 2020. https://www.islamweb.net/en/fatwa/56882/.

Johnston, Cynthia. 2007. "Baha'is in Egypt Fight for Recognition as People." Reuters, February 20. Accessed, April 23, 2021. https://www.reuters.com/article/us-egypt-bahai/bahais-in-egypt-fight-for-recognition-as-people-idUSL2757830620070221.

Khalek, Rania. 2017. "Genocide in Iraq: When Local Sunni Became ISIS and Slaughtered Their Neighbors." Alternet. Accessed November 1, 2020. https://www.alternet.org/2017/10/genocide-iraq-when-local-sunni-became-isis-and-slaughtered-their-neighbors/.

Kilani, Feras. 2021. "A Caliph without a Caliphate: The Biography of ISIS's New Leader." Newlinesmag. Accessed, March 11, 2021. https://newlinesmag.com/reportage/a-caliph-without-a-caliphate-the-biography-of-isiss-new-leader.

Kurdistan 24. 2019. "Iraq Sentences Yezidi Man to Death for Joining ISIS, Committing Crimes against Minority Group." Kurdistan 24, March 25. Accessed October 15, 2020. https://www.kurdistan24.net/en/news/2a36d0c0-838f-4fb2-b233-eaf382d79f3d.

Le Monde. 1972. "Search for New Alliances Reported." *Le Monde*, April 7. [Original in French]

Milliyet. 1997. "Aydınlardan 'bir dakika' öfkesi." *Milliyet*, February 2. Accessed March 1, 2021. https://www.milliyet.com.tr/siyaset/aydinlardan-bir-dakika-ofkesi-5387565.

Milliyet. 2008. "Devletin kanalında büyük ayıp." *Milliyet*, December 27. Accessed March 1, 2021. https://www.milliyet.com.tr/gundem/devletin-kanalinda-buyuk-ayip-1033362.

New York Times. 1935. "Rebellious Yezidis Are Subdued in Iraq." *New York Times*, October 26. Accessed December 1, 2020. https://www.nytimes.com/1935/10/26/archives/rebellious-yezidis-are-subdued-in-iraq-punitive-force-ends.html.

New York Times. 1978. "Martial Law Is Set in 13 Cities." *New York Times*, December 26. Accessed December 1, 2020. https://www.nytimes.com/1978/12/26/archives/martial-law-is-set-in-13-turkish-cities-cabinet-acts-after-93-are.html.

New York Times. 1980. "New Rioting Strikes Turkish City." *New York Times*, August 8. Accessed December 1, 2020. https://www.nytimes.com/1980/07/05/archives/new-rioting-strikes-turkish-city.html.

New York Times. 2019. "Erdogan Uses Video of New Zealand Attacks at Election Rallies." *New York Times*, March 17. Accessed May 19, 2021. https://www.nytimes.com/2019/03/17/world/middleeast/erdogan-video-new-zealand-mosque-attack.html.

Öğmüş, Harun. 2014. "İŞİD gerçekten İslami kaygı taşısaydı." *Yüzakı* 115 (September): 14–15. Accessed February 13, 2021. https://katalog.idp.org.tr/yazilar/1410408/isid-gercekten-islami-kaygi-tasisaydi.

Özköse, Adem. 2009. "Yezidilik ve Yezidiler." *Gerçek Hayat* (May 8–14): 24–25. Accessed February 13, 2021. https://katalog.idp.org.tr/yazilar/1713269/yezidilik-ve-yezidiler.

Özköse, Adem. 2014. "Yezidilik ve Yezidiler." *Genç Dergisi* (November): 22–23. Accessed February 13, 2021. https://katalog.idp.org.tr/yazilar/1302010/yezidilik-ve-yezidiler.

Pear, Robert. 1988. "Khomeini Accepts 'Poison' of Ending the War with Iraq; U.N. Sending Mission." *New York Times*, July 21. Accessed May 19, 2021. https://www.nytimes.com/1988/07/21/us/khomeini-accepts-poison-of-ending-the-war-with-iraq-un-sending-mission.html.

Poetry Foundation. 2018. "Bar Codes and Mass Graves: A Reading by Seven Emerging Êzîdî Poets." *Poetry Foundation*. Accessed June 2, 2022. https://www.poetryfoundation.org/harriet/2018/12/bar-codes-and-mass-graves-a-reading-by-seven-emerging-zd-poets.

Prager, Joshua. 2006. "A Chilling Photograph's Hidden History." *Wall Street Journal*, December 2. Accessed March 6, 2023. https://www.wsj.com/articles/SB116499510215538266.

Reliefweb. 2006. "Nigeria: Muhammad Cartoon Protests Spark Attacks on Christians." *Reliefweb*, February 20. Accessed October 25, 2022. https://reliefweb.int/report/nigeria/nigeria-muhammad-cartoon-protests-spark-attacks-christians.

Robson, Seth. 2018. "Special Forces Soldiers Fight to Grant Last Wish of Iraqi Interpreter Killed in Action." *Stars and Stripes*. Accessed March 1, 2021. https://www.stripes.com/news/middle-east/special-forces-soldiers-fight-to-grant-last-wish-of-iraqi-interpreter-killed-in-action-1.546347.

Rudaw. 2015. "Barzanî: Kurdên êzîdî nasnameya netewî ya kurdî parastine." Rudaw, August 3. Accessed March 10, 2022. https://www.rudaw.net/kurmanci/kurdistan/0308201516.

Rudaw. 2017. "Ji Mîre Êzidiyên cîhanê banga referandûmê." Rudaw, September 23. Accessed October 15, 2020. https://www.rudaw.net/kurmanci/kurdistan/230920175.

REFERENCES

Rudaw. 2019. "Di 4 sal û 10 mehan de 3476 Kurdên Êzidî hatine rizgarkirin." Rudaw, June 4. Accessed February 26, 2021. https://www.rudaw.net/kurmanci/kurdistan/040620191.

Rudaw. 2020a. "Çekdarên ser bi Tirkiyê ve mezargehên Êzidiyan şikandin." Rudaw, April 27. Accessed March 1, 2021. https://www.rudaw.net/kurmanci/kurdistan/2704202021.

Rudaw. 2020b. "Leyla ji destê DAIŞê rizgar bû lê ji ber koronayê nikare vegere nav malbata xwe." Rudaw, May 6. Accessed October 15, 2020. https://www.rudaw.net/kurmanci/kurdistan/0605202010.

Sebîlürreşad. 1950. "Aleviler, Kızılbaşlar Komünist midir?" Sebîlürreşad 4 (90): 237. Accessed April 14, 2021. https://katalog.idp.org.tr/pdf/5313/9595.

Sebîlürreşad. 1954. "Yezidî mezhebini Şeyh Adî mi kurmuştur?" Sebîlürreşad 7 (173): 364–65. Accessed February 13, 2021. https://katalog.idp.org.tr/yazilar/94025/yezidi-mezhebinin-seyh-adi-mi-kurmustur.

Sebîlürreşad. 1962. "Yezidî mezheb." Sebîlürreşad 14 (344): 303–4. Accessed February 13, 2021. https://katalog.idp.org.tr/yazilar/96377/yezidi-mehzeb.

Sebîlürreşad. 1965. "Yezidî mezhebi." Sebîlürreşad 15 (360): 147–48. Accessed February 13, 2021. https://katalog.idp.org.tr/yazilar/96671/yezidi-mehebi.

al-Shakar, Hamid. 2019. "الإيمانية لصدام حسين ١٩٩٢م وولادة مرجعية محمد الصدر ودخول الوهابية لسُنة العراق ظاهرة الحملة!" Accessed, November 30, 2021. https://www.youtube.com/watch?v=6cgF-lQqmFY.

Slavin, Barbara, and Rosanne Klass. 1978. "Another 'Holy War' Erupts, in Turkey." New York Times, December 31. Accessed May 19, 2021. https://www.nytimes.com/1978/12/31/archives/the-world-in-summary-pekings-new-helmsmen-chart-a-different-course.html.

T24. 2017. "Aleviler liyakatsız değildir; ne vali ne emniyet müdürü, 957 ilçede kaymakam bile yok." T24, October 15. Accessed June 3, 2022. https://t24.com.tr/haber/aleviler-liyakatsiz-degildir-ne-vali-ne-emniyet-muduru-957-ilcede-kaymakam-bile-yok,464979.

T24. 2020. "Sivas katliamı hükümlüsünün tahliyesini 'Hoşgeldin Ahmet Dede' manşetiyle duyuran gazetenin sahibi AKP'li çıktı." T24, February 3. Accessed June 3, 2021. https://t24.com.tr/haber/sivas-katliami-hukumlusunun-tahliyesini-hosgeldin-ahmet-dede-mansetiyle-duyuran-gazetenin-sahibi-akp-li-cikti,859065.

Tevhid. 1979. "Kahramanmaraş faciasını bizzat yaşayan bir Müslüman anlatıyor: Faciada üç gün." Tevhid (4):13–16. Accessed April 14, 2021. https://katalog.idp.org.tr/yazilar/37290/faciada-uc-gun.

al-Thawrah. 1972. "New Official Holidays Law Passed." Al-Thawrah, September 15. [English translation of Arabic article]

Tohum. 1965. "Yezidî adetleri." Tohum 17:27–28. Accessed February 13, 2021. https://katalog.idp.org.tr/yazilar/35047/yezidi-adetleri.

Walsh, Declan, and John Aglionby. 2006. "Church Ablaze as Cartoon Protests Continue across Globe." The Guardian, February 19. Accessed October 25, 2022. https://www.theguardian.com/world/2006/feb/20/pakistan.muhammadcartoons.

Wilson Center. 2014. "Muslims against ISIS Part 1: Clerics & Scholars." Wilson Center, September 24. Accessed March 1, 2021. https://www.wilsoncenter.org/article/muslims-against-isis-part-1-clerics-scholars.

Yıldız, Canan. 2019. "Bir avukatın Maraş Katliamı'ndaki 'devlet sırlarına' ulaşma mücadelesi." *T24*, December 19. Accessed, March 1, 2021. https://t24.com.tr/haber/bir-avukatin-maras-katliami-ndaki-devlet-sirlarina-ulasma-mucadelesi,852771.

Zoepf, Katherine, and Hassan M. Fattah. 2006. "Beirut Mob Burns Danish Mission Building over Cartoons." *New York Times*, February 6. Accessed October 25, 2022. https://www.nytimes.com/2006/02/06/world/middleeast/beirut-mob-burns-danish-mission-building-over-cartoons.html.

Index

Abdal, Pir, Sultan, 132, 133
abduction. *See* kidnapping of Yezidis
Abdülhamid II, Sultan, 74, 115–16
Abrahamic religions, 10, 22–23, 44–45, 51–52, 55, 176. *See also* Christians/Christian minorities; Jews/Judaism
Adi ibn Musafir, Sheikh, 69–70, 74–75
agents, foreign. *See* fifth column
Ahmad, Mirza Ghulam, 162–63, 165–66
Ahmadis/Ahmadiyya, 27, 32, 153–54, 155, 162–68, 176–78
Ahrar (Majlis-e Ahrar-e Islam), 163–64
AKP (Adalet ve Kalkınma Partisi) and AKP government, 137, 143–44, 145–46, 147–50, 151–52
Alawites, 112, 186–88
Alevi-Bektaşi, 112n
Alevi massacres/anti-Alevi violence: comparative analysis and perspective on, 118–20, 139–45; denied victimhood and remembrance for, 31–32, 122–23, 129, 137, 145–52; in Istanbul, 150–51; in Maraş, 31–32, 111, 119–30, 145–47; motives in, 13–14, 31–32, 62, 126–30, 132, 135–39, 141–42, 149; perpetrators of, 121–26, 133–34, 135–36, 144–45; in Sivas, 31–32, 111, 119–20, 130–39, 147–50
Alevis/Alevism: and assimilation, 26–27, 115–16, 197–98; contemporary liminality of, 150–52, 188; global distribution of, 178; history of liminality and beliefs of, 11–12, 25, 26–27, 55–56, 112–18; recasting of, as Muslims, 115–16, 119, 147–48, 151–52; recognition of, 26–27, 31–32, 113–14, 116–18, 130–31, 138–39, 150–52, 197–98; stigmatization of, 31, 110–14, 118, 119–20, 130, 138–39, 144–45
alienation, 6, 59–60
al-Qaeda, 83, 173–74, 199
altruism, 30, 42–45

ambivalence of liminal belief systems: for major religions, 22–23, 26, 48, 175–76, 178–79, 198; in the theoretical framework, 48, 50–51, 55–56, 59
Anfal campaign, Iraq, 103–4, 107
anger, 9–10, 59–60, 65, 95, 122–23, 146–47. *See also* resentment
animist groups, 180–81
animosity. *See* hatred
An-Na'im, Abdullahi, 197–98
antisemitism, 51–52, 55, 61, 102, 192. *See also* Jews/Judaism
AP (Adalet Partisi), 120–21
apostasy, accusations of: against Ahmadis, 153, 162–63, 166–68; against Baha'is, 153, 156–57, 160–61; in Islamic history, 165n; in the theoretical framework, 35–36; against Yezidis, 73, 87
Armenians/Armenian genocide, 15–18, 38–39, 64, 128–29, 139–42, 143–44, 145–46. *See also* Christians/Christian minorities
assimilation/assimilability: of Alevis, 26–27, 115–16, 197–98; of Armenians, 140–41; in liminality, 51, 54, 55; of non-Turkish Muslims, 140–41; and Turkish nationalism, 17–18; of Yezidis, 74
Assyrians, 15–16, 17–18, 103, 139–40
authorities, religious: in Alevi liminality, 26, 113–14; in Baha'i and Ahmadi liminality, 154–55, 160–61; and Baha'is in Iran, 162; in condemnation of anti-Yezidi violence, 75; in religious liminality, 11–12, 53–54; in Yezidi stigmatization, 71, 74–75

Ba'ath regime. *See* Hussein, Saddam and regime
Baha'is/Baha'ism, 27, 32, 55–56, 153–54, 156–62, 176–78, 184–85, 190
Baha'u'llah (Mirza Hussein-Ali Nuri): *Ketab-a aqdas*, 156–57

245

INDEX

Bangladesh, 168
Başbağlar massacre, 149–50
behavior, political and prosocial, 21, 22, 23, 24, 42–43, 199–200
belief, religious: in discourses on religion and violence, 199–200; freedom of, 20–21, 58–59, 108, 182–83, 189; and mass violence, 6; as motive in religious violence, 42–45, 174–75; in political violence, 20–23; in religious liminality, 10, 11–12, 34–35; supernatural, 30, 34, 42–45, 49–50; in the theoretical framework, 34–35, 38–39, 40–41, 42–45, 49–50, 51–56, 58–59
Benjamin, Walter, 35, 45–46, 48–49, 65–66, 155–56
bin Laden, Osama, 173–74
blasphemy/blasphemy laws, 165, 165n, 167–69, 183–84, 189

captives: Alevi, 128; Yezidi, 1–2, 3–4, 68–69, 79–80, 84, 85–89, 98–100, 105–6. *See also* kidnapping of Yezidis
Catholics/Catholic Church, 39, 40–42, 48, 192, 197. *See also* Abrahamic religions
cemevleri (Alevi places of worship), 116–18, 151–52
children: in the Alevi massacres, 125–26, 135; in the Yezidi genocide, 4, 9, 29, 67–68, 73, 86–87, 94–95, 98–99
CHP (Cumhuriyet Halk Partisi), 120, 121, 122, 130, 131, 145–46, 151–52
Christians/Christian minorities: in Alevi liminality, 115–16; atrocities against, in Iraq, 15–16; in global perspective on liminality and discrimination, 176, 178, 183–84, 188–89; justifications for rape in, 99–100; motives for atrocities against, 18–19; in the roots of Yezidism, 25; in transcending liminality, 192–93, 199–200; views on Judaism of, 48; and the Yezidi genocide, 71, 101, 105–6. *See also* Armenians/Armenian genocide; People of the Book
church-state separation, 182–83, 189
civil wars: in the Alevi massacres, 151–52; in global perspective on liminality and discrimination, 171–75, 185–86, 187–88, 189–90; Iraqi, 94; role of religion in, 19, 171–75; in scale of religious violence, 14; Syrian, 67–68, 84, 151–52; in the Yezidi genocide, 67–68, 84, 94. *See also* wars/warfare
"clash of civilizations" argument, 199–200

classification of liminal minorities: of Ahmadis as Muslims, 164–65; of Alevis as Muslims, 115–16, 119, 147–48, 151–52; of Baha'is as a political movement, 159–60; "coercive" of liminal minorities, 190; in global perspective on liminality and discrimination, 179, 180; in the theoretical framework, 54; in transcending liminality, 194; of Yezidis as "syncretic," 69–70
clerics, Muslim: in the Alevi massacres, 127–28; in Baha'i and Ahmadi liminality, 32, 153, 154, 156–57, 159–60, 162–63, 165–66, 168; in condemnation of anti-Yezidi violence, 75; condemnation of IS violence by, 197–98; in the Yezidi liminality, 74–75. *See also* authorities, religious
codification of religious difference, 12–13, 35, 45–46, 154, 155, 162, 164–65
coexistence, religious: as argument for denied victimhood, 149; subordination of liminal minorities in, 10; in the theoretical framework, 41–42, 62, 65–66; in transcending liminality, 191, 192–93, 195–96; of Yezidis and Muslims, 4, 92–94, 108–9
commemoration of violence, 145–50, 151, 195–96
communism/anti-communism, 64–65, 118, 127–29, 131–32
compatibility/incompatibility, theological, 153, 154, 155, 162, 165–66, 172, 198
conceptualization of religious violence, 35–50
Confessions of Dolgoruki, The (anonymous), 157–59
conformity, 5, 49–50, 52–53, 55–56, 113–14
conspiracy theories: absence of legitimacy in belief in, 193; on Ahmadis as foreign agents, 154–55, 162–64; in the Alevi massacres, 31–32, 111–12, 122–23, 128–29, 135, 145, 149–50; on Baha'is as foreign agents, 154–55, 157–61; conspiratorial provocation thesis, 111–12
conversions, forced: of Alevis, 128; of Armenians, 140; in liminality, 55; of Yezidis, 2–5, 9, 68, 72–73, 75–76, 86–88, 94–95, 98–99, 105
criminalization, 100–101, 165, 165n, 167, 168–69, 183–84, 183–84n
crusading, 41n, 49–50

dehumanization, 53, 87, 88–89, 193
democratic systems/democratization, 60, 167–68, 191, 196

demonization. *See* stigmatization
Derrida, Jacques, 35, 46–47, 155–56
Dersim, Kurdish Turkey, 142–43
development/underdevelopment, socio-economic, 13–14, 82–83, 95–96, 98, 120–21, 126–27
deviance, 26, 32, 69–70, 87, 108, 157, 168–69
diasporas: Baha'i and Ahmadi, 155n; Yezidi, 69–70, 106–7, 109
displacement, 67–68, 79, 82, 95–96, 97, 105, 109, 142–43
dissent, 41–42, 103–4, 146–47, 183–84
Diyanet, 116, 118, 147–48
Dönme converts, 55
Druzes of Lebanon, 176–79, 186–88

economics/economic factors: in the Alevi massacres, 13–14, 119, 126–27, 129, 130; in the Armenian genocide, 16–17; in defining religious violence, 37–38; development/underdevelopment, 13–14, 82–83, 95–96, 98, 120–21, 126–27; in global patterns, 185–86, 189–90; in violence against liminal minorities, 13–14, 18–19; in the Yezidi genocide, 82
endogeneity, 70–71, 114–15, 178–79
Engels, Friedrich, 37–38, 171–72
enslavement of Yezidis: motives for, 90–92, 93–95, 97; sexual, stigmatization in, 31; of women and children, 4, 9, 67–68, 73, 86–89, 93, 94–95, 97, 105–6
envy, 38, 60, 61, 141–42. *See also* greed
equifinality, 141–42
Erdoğan, Recep Tayyip, 39–40, 143–44, 151–52
eschatology, 30, 40–42, 65, 92–93
ethnic cleansing. *See* genocide
European Union, 151
exclusion of religious minorities: of Ahmadis, 162, 164–69; of Alevis, 115–16, 140–41, 142, 151–52; of Baha'is, 157–59, 168–69; in defining religious violence, 39, 48, 50, 52; ending, in transcending liminality, 194, 196, 197–98; in the formation of nationalism, 19; in global perspective, 178, 185–86, 189–90; prevention of, in sustaining pluralism, 65
executions, mass: of Baha'is in Iran, 159–61; intimacy of, 5–8; in Iran, as religious violence, 35–37, 45–46; in the Yezidi genocide, 3–4, 67–68, 83, 84–87, 90

Faid al-Djaria, 179–80
faith, religious. *See* belief, religious

Faith Campaign (Hussein regime), 92–93
Falun Gong, 180
fear: in the Alevi massacres, 115, 122–23, 129, 137–38; in the Armenian genocide, 16–17, 141–42; of jihad, in WWI, 173–74; of Judaism, 48; in the theoretical framework, 52–53, 59, 63; in the Yezidi genocide, 100–101
fifth column, 118, 153, 154–55, 157–61, 162–64
"forward panic" model of mass violence, 122–23

gender: deviation from norms of, in stigmatization, 52–53, 138–39; ending gendered discrimination, in transcending liminality, 194–96; in the massacres of Alevis, 138–39; in the Yezidi genocide, 4, 28, 82–83, 98–100, 124–25
genocide: Armenian, 15–18, 38–39, 64, 128–29, 139–42, 143–44, 145–46; Baha'i, 161–63; motives for, 63–65; nationalism in, 19–21; political context scale of violence in, 14; role of civil war in, 171–72; Rwandan, 21–22, 28–29, 63. *See also* Yezidi genocide
geopolitics: in Alevi liminality, 26, 110–11; in the Alevi massacres, 141; in anti-Christian violence in Turkey, 141; in anti-Yezidi violence in Sinjar, 174–75; in the Armenian genocide, 17; in Baha'i liminality, 160–61; in patterns of liminality and discrimination, 171, 174–75, 188–89
Gezi protests, 151–52
globalization, 9–10, 18–19, 59, 168–69, 171
Goya, Francisco: *The Disasters of War*, 6–7; *The Third of May 1808*, 5
greed, 13, 38, 64, 98–100, 102, 129, 137–38, 141–42. *See also* envy
group threat theory, 61, 184, 189, 190
guilt as motive, 64–65, 100, 101–2, 130, 137–38

Hamidiye Cavalry, 18–19
Hanafi-Sunni orthodoxy, 112–13, 115–16
hatred: in the Alevi massacres, 130, 138–39, 144–45; defined, 53; in discourses on religion and violence, 21–22, 199–200; measuring relevance of, 141–42; stigmatization in, 59, 68; in the Yezidi genocide, 68, 72, 83–84, 90–95

INDEX

heresy/heretics: of Ahmadis, 154–55, 163–66, 167–68; of Alevis, 26–27, 112, 116; of Baha'is, 153, 154–55; in liminality, 11–12; in Mormonism, 192–93; of Yezidis, 69–70, 73, 75–76. *See also* insult, religious

Hindus/Hinduism, 18–19, 56–58, 189

Hojjatieh, 160–61

Holocaust, 63, 64. *See also* genocide; Jews/Judaism

homogenization, religious, 38–39, 54, 140–41, 198

Huguenots, 39, 40–41, 55

Hussein, Saddam and regime: beneficiaries of, 101–2; in modernization of Yezidis, 78–80; violence in Anfal campaign by, 103–4, 107; and the Yezidi genocide, 83–84, 92–94, 95–97; Yezidi resettlement by, 2, 82; in Yezidi security, 58, 79–80, 190, 196–97

Ibn Taymiyyah, 71, 112

ideology: and Ahmadi recognition, 164–65, 166–67; in Alevi liminality, 113–15, 116; in the Alevi massacres, 122, 124, 131–32, 140–41, 142–43; in anti-Armenian violence, 140–41; in defining religious violence, 37–38, 46–47, 48–50; and discrimination, in global perspective, 174–75; genocidal, in debates on religion and political violence, 21; in IS brutality against Yezidis, 87–89; in motives for mass violence, 6–7, 59–60, 63; of Muslim supremacy, in massacres of Christians, 141; secular, in configuration of religious liminality, 58–59; in transcending liminality, 199–200; in Yezidi encounters with modernity, 76, 78–79

impunity for perpetrators: in the Alevi massacres, 125–26, 147–49, 151; in anti-Ahmadi violence, 154n; in the Armenian genocide, 17; blasphemy laws in culture of, 183–84; liminality of victims in, 15, 29; in the Yezidi genocide, 29, 106–7, 108–9

India, 18–19, 32, 56–58, 154, 155n, 162–63, 188–89. *See also* Ahmadis/Ahmadiyya

Indonesia, 27, 28–29, 32, 154–55, 166–68, 196, 197

institutionalization of religion: in Alevi liminality, 114–15, 116; in global perspective on liminality and discrimination, 180, 183–84, 189; in the Kurdish constitution, 80–81; in nonrecognition of Ahmadis, 164–65; in the theoretical framework, 20–21, 35, 58–59

instrumentalization of religion: in civil wars, 172–73; in comparisons of the Alevi massacres and Armenian genocide, 144–45; in debates on religion and political violence, 20; in nonrecognition of Ahmadis in Pakistan, 164; use of religious symbols in, 199; in the Yezidi genocide, 92–93, 103–4

insult, religious, 39–40, 121, 127–28, 131–35, 138–39, 146–47, 148–49. *See also* heresy/heretics

insurgency/counterinsurgency: Kurdish/PKK insurgency, 78–79, 100–101, 108–9, 110, 143–45; US invasions in, 199; and the Yezidi genocide, 78–79, 83, 100–101, 102, 103

International Criminal Court (ICC), 107

interventions, foreign: and the Armenian genocide, 18–19; on behalf of Christian minorities, 101; in discourses on religion and violence, 199; in discrimination and violence against minorities, 188–89; in Yezidi encounters with modernity, 75–76, 77–78; in the Yezidi genocide, 67–68

Iran, 35–37, 79–80, 154, 157–60. *See also* Baha'is/Baha'ism

Iraq: Arabization in, 79, 95–96; atrocities against Christians in, 15–16; massacre of Assyrians in, 15–16, 17–18; political pluralism and sectarianism in, 190; sectarian war in scope of violence in, 14; US invasion of, 31, 80, 81–82, 93, 96–97, 98, 101–2, 103–4, 188–89. *See also* Yezidi genocide; Yezidis/Yezidism

IS (Islamic State): condemnations of violence by, 75, 108, 197–98; impunity of, 29, 108–9; international campaign against, 105, 106–7; investigations into crimes committed by, 106–7; Kurds in, 97; religious motives of, 105, 174–75; status loss of Sunni Arabs in violence by, 62; use of rape by, 99–100, 105–6. *See also* Yezidi genocide

ISI (Islamic State of Iraq), 83

Islamic law, 73, 80–81, 156, 159–60

Israel, 158–59, 160–61, 179, 188–90

Jainism, 56–58

Jehovah's Witnesses, 176–78, 192

Jews/Judaism: antisemitism, 51–52, 55, 61, 192; fear of, 48, 63; in global perspective on liminality and discrimination, 175–76, 184–85, 188–89; liminality of, 51–52; motives for mass violence against, 63, 64–65 jihad/jihadism: calls for, in defining religious civil war, 173–74; against Christians in Turkey, 141; in global perspective on liminality and discrimination, 172–75, 187–88; rejection of, in nonrecognition of Ahmadis, 162–63; religious nationalism in, 21; US invasion of Iraq in rise of, 31; in the Yezidi genocide, 67–68, 83–84, 93, 95, 96–97, 102, 174–75

justification, religious: in defining religious violence, 36–37, 39–40, 41, 45, 49–50, 65; for mass atrocities, 17–18; for sexual violence, 98–100, 105–6; for the Yezidi genocide, 71, 90–95, 97, 105–6. *See also* motives

Kākā'is, 105
KDP (Partiya Demokrat a Kurdistanê), 80–81, 82, 96–97, 100–101
Khan, Zafarullah, 163–64
Khomeini, Ruhollah, Ayatollah, 35–37, 132–33, 159–60
kidnapping of Yezidis: in encounters with political modernity, 75, 76, 83; in the genocide, 4, 9, 67–68, 73, 84–85, 86–87, 94–95, 97, 104
Kierkegaard, Søren: *Fear and Trembling*, 42
kirivs (godfathers of Yezidi boys), 4, 86, 89, 90–91, 99
Kızılbaş (Alevis), 112–16
Kocho, Sinjar, 2–5, 7, 84, 86, 92, 94–95
Kurdistan, Iraqi, 1–5, 25, 80–81, 109. *See also* PKK (Kurdistan Workers' Party)
Kurdistan Regional Government (KRG), 67, 80–81, 86–87, 107
Kurds: in contemporary discrimination against Yezidis, 108–9; in the formation of Yezidi liminality, 72–73; insurgency by, 78–79, 100–101, 108–9, 110, 143–45; rise in power of, in Sunni animosity, 13; in syncretism of beliefs into Yezidism, 25–26; use of genocide in pursuit of independence, 107; in the Yezidi genocide, 72–73, 96–97, 100–101, 103; Yezidis as, 78–79, 80–81; Yezidis under rule of, 80–84

Lalish Temple, Iraqi Kurdistan, 76, 77
Lebanon, Druzes in, 176, 178–79, 186–88
legibility/illegibility of liminal religious minorities, 10–12, 51–52, 70–71, 73–74, 114, 167–68
legitimacy/illegitimacy of belief and practice: in Alevism, 113–14; in global perspective, 176; in liminality, 10, 11–12, 51–52, 55–56, 113–14; in the paradox of iterability, 45, 46–47, 155–56; recognition in, 7–8, 108; in transcending liminality, 192, 193, 195–96, 197; in Yezidism, 74–75, 108. *See also* recognition

liberalism/illiberalism: and Ahmadis in Pakistan, 164; of Bahai's, 156–57, 161–62; in discourses on religion and violence, 20–21, 199–200; in identity politics in Sivas, 130–31; in transcending liminality, 194–95, 199–200

local people. *See* neighbors
looting, 7, 64, 72–73, 98, 105, 125–26, 129. *See also* greed
loyalty/disloyalty: of Alevis, 118, 130, 138, 141–42, 151–52; of Baha'is, 160; in liminality of Jehovah's Witnesses, 178; in religious liminality, 11–13, 17–18; Sunni Islam associated with, 74, 76; of Yezidis, 73, 74
Luther, Martin, 42
lynching: of Black people in the US, 61–62, 127, 149–50, 193, 195–96; of Kurds, 143

Madimak Hotel massacre, Sivas, 1992, 133–35, 147–48
Maliki, Nouri al-, and government, 84, 100–101
Mamdani, Mahmood: *Good Muslims, Bad Muslims*, 199
Mandaeans, 70
Maraş, Turkey, 31–32, 111, 119–30, 145–47
markers, religious, 21–22, 23, 45–46, 54, 171–72, 198
Marxism/Marxist perspectives, 22
Maududi, Abul A'la, 163–64
memorials. *See* commemoration of violence
memory, collective, 26, 72–73, 90–91, 103–4, 145–50, 151
messianism, 32, 41n, 153–54, 162–63
MHP (Milliyetçi Hareket Partisi), 120–21, 122, 133
millennialism, Shiite, 156
millet system, 16, 51–52, 73–74, 75–76, 113–14, 142
Mir Tahsin Said Beg, 107
missionaries, 18–19, 76, 115–16
mobilization to violence: in the Alevi massacres, 111–12, 118, 119–20, 126–28, 132–33, 141; in debates on religion and political violence, 20, 23; in defining religious violence, 38–40, 41; in global

mobilization to violence (*continued*)
perspective on liminality and discrimination, 171–72, 173–75; institutionalization of Islam in, 164; religious justification of violence in, 10, 65; resentment in, 13; in the theoretical framework, 50, 58–59, 65
modernity/modernization: in the Armenian genocide, 140–41; in Baha'ism, 156–57; in mass atrocities, 16–17, 18–19; in state interactions with liminal minorities, 12–13; in the theoretical framework, 35, 46, 57–59, 65; Yezidi encounters with, 74–84
monotheism, 21, 44–45
morality/immorality: in Alevi liminality, 111, 114–15, 118, 138–39; in the Alevi massacres, 31–32, 138–39; in defining religious violence, 40–43, 44, 45–46, 49–50; in denial of Alevi victimhood, 145, 147, 149–50; in denial of Baha'ism, 157, 162; in historical configurations of liminality, 52–53; in religious liminality, 10, 17; sexual, 52–53, 111, 114, 138–39, 157; in the Yezidi genocide, 87–88, 99; in Yezidi liminality, 73
Mormons, 55, 176, 192–93, 196
Mosul, Iraq, 67–68, 78–79, 83, 84, 88, 104–6
motives: in the Alevi massacres, 13–14, 31–32, 62, 126–30, 132, 135–39, 141–42, 149; in the Armenian genocide, 63–65, 141–42; in defining religious civil war, 172, 173–75; for mass killings, 6–7; methods of inferring, 24; of ordinary people in mass atrocities, 30; pleasing God as, 22, 23, 34; religious homogenization as, 38–39; in the theoretical framework, 34, 41, 42, 44–45, 65; in the Yezidi genocide, 13, 62, 68–69, 90–106, 174–75. *See also* justification, religious
Muhammadiyah, 166–67
Murad, Nadia, 106–7

Nahdlatul Ulama, 166–67
nationalism: in the Alevi massacres, 31–32, 38, 132, 142–43; and authoritarianism, in liminality, 197–98; in Baha'i and Ahmadi liminality, 32, 157–60, 164; Christian, in the United States, 199–200; in debates on religion and political violence, 19–21; in defining religious violence, 39; in global perspective on liminality and discrimination, 164; Hindu, 56; in mass atrocities, 17–18; militant, in discourses on religion and violence, 199; in precarity of liminal minorities, 168–69; in the theoretical framework, 38, 58–59; Turkish, 17–18, 38, 132, 140–41, 142–43; in Yezidi encounters with modernity, 76, 78–79; in the Yezidi genocide, 96
nation-state-building, 20–21, 157–59, 164, 168–69
natural law: and the Alevi massacre, 133–34; and liminality in the broader Muslim world, 155, 162; in the theoretical framework, 35, 45–46, 48–49, 62, 65–66; and the Yezidi genocide, 95–96
neighbors: agency of, in mass atrocities, 11, 30, 111, 146n; in the Alevi massacres, 121–26, 133–34, 135–36, 144–45; documentation of involvement in atrocities, 28; as perpetrators in Rwanda, 28–29; religious motives of, 38–39; in the Yezidi genocide, 9, 13, 68, 84, 85, 86–87, 88–90, 91–93
Nesin, Aziz, 132–35, 138–39
Nietzsche, Friedrich, 20, 42
Nineveh province, 78–79, 81–82, 84–87, 96–97
nonbelievers, 43–44, 108–9
nonliminal religious minorities, 18, 170–71, 172, 175–76, 178, 181, 184–85, 186–89

Oppenheimer, Joshua: *The Act of Killing*, 28–29
orthodoxy, Islamic: Baha'i and Ahmadi conflicts with, 153, 155–56, 162–63, 167, 168–69; in religious liminality, 11–12, 13, 26, 27, 71, 112–14; in the theoretical framework, 55–56; transformation of, in transcending liminality, 197–98
Ottoman Empire: Alevi liminality in, 11–12, 31–32, 54, 112–16; anti-Yezidi campaigns by, 71–74; Armenian genocide in, 64, 128–29, 139–40, 141–42; atrocities against religious minorities in, 15–17, 18–19; "corrections of belief" policies of, 74, 115–16; motives for genocide of, 38–39; role of religion in wars of, 173–74; stigmatization of Alevis in, 110–11; violence in response to existential threats to, 139–40; in Yezidi encounters with modernity, 74, 75–77. *See also* Turkey/Turkish nation-state/Turkish Republic
Ottoman-Safavid rivalry and wars, 16, 26, 110–11, 113–14, 130

INDEX 251

Pakistan: blasphemy laws in, 183–84n; discrimination against Hindus in, 188–89; liberal minority groups in, 176–78; nonrecognition of Ahmadis in, 32, 154–55, 162, 163–69, 196; Sikh liminality in, 179–80; stigmatization of Baha'is in, 27

Pakistan People's Party, 164–65

Pancasila, 166–67

paradox of iterability (Derrida), 35, 46–47, 155–56

patriarchal structures, 99, 194–95, 196

Peacock Angel, 69, 71, 74–75, 109

People of the Book, 25–26, 51–52, 71, 87, 90–91, 104, 108, 155. *See also* Christians/Christian minorities; Jews/Judaism

perpetrators: in the Alevi massacres, 121–30, 147–49; impunity for, 15, 17, 64, 147–49, 151, 154n, 183–84; as victims, in denial of Alevi victimhood, 147–49; in the Yezidi genocide, 68, 84, 86–90, 97, 98–100, 102. *See also* motives; neighbors

Peshmerga, 5, 67–68, 84, 86–87, 96–97

Pir Sultan Abdal Festival, 132–33, 138–39, 147–48

PKK (Kurdistan Workers' Party), 2–3, 143–45, 149. *See also* Kurds

plunder. *See* looting

pluralism, religious: in the Alevi massacres, 118; in debates on religion and political violence, 22–23; in global perspective, 171; and nonrecognition of Ahmadis in Indonesia, 166–67; in the theoretical framework, 48, 54, 57–58, 65; in transcending liminality, 192, 193, 196–97, 198

pogroms, 13–14, 61, 103, 156–57

polarization, 58, 63, 100–101, 114–15, 119–21, 126–27, 130, 187–88

political participation: of Alevis, 118, 120–22, 131; of Baha'is, 156–57, 160; denied to Ahmadis in Indonesia, 167–68; in lynching of Black people in the US, 127; of Yezidis, 72, 73–74, 78, 80–82, 83–84, 92–93

political parties, 39–40, 62, 80–82, 118–22, 124. See also under *name of party*

polytheism, 5, 25, 56–57, 87, 112, 180–81

positive law: and the Alevi massacres, 133–34; codification of religious difference into, 12–13, 154, 155, 162, 164–65; in the theoretical framework, 35, 45–46, 48–49, 65–66

power/power dynamics: in the Alevi massacres, 129; in debates on religion and political violence, 22–23; economic, in mass atrocities, 18–19; in global perspective on liminality and discrimination, 176, 186–88; in the theoretical framework, 37–38, 46–47, 52, 60–61; in the Yezidi genocide, 95, 96, 97, 100–101

prophecy/prophets, 154, 155, 162–63, 164–66, 168, 184, 195–96

Protestants/Protestantism, 39, 40–41, 55, 115–16. *See also* Christians/Christian minorities

provocation thesis, 111–12, 137, 146–47

Qurrat, al-Ayn Tarrat, 156

race/racism, 19–20, 51–52, 61–62, 65, 127, 142–43, 193

rape and sexual violence: instrumentalization of, as weapon, 99–100; rumors of, in the Alevi massacres, 127–28; as weapon of war, 98–99; in the Yezidi genocide, 28, 72–73, 97, 98–100, 104, 105–6

Rastafarians, 180

recognition: affirmative, in transcending liminality, 195–96; of Ahmadis and Baha'is, 155, 160–69; of Alevis, 26–27, 31–32, 113–14, 116–18, 130–31, 138–39, 150–52; of Alevi victimhood, 31–32, 122–23, 129, 137, 145–52; of Armenians, 142; in global perspective, 175–76, 179, 188–90; of Jainism, 57–58; politics of, 7–8, 15, 106–9, 150–52; potential of, in peace, 7–8; in religious liminality, 10, 11, 15, 16, 22–23; theological, 7–8, 10, 51–52, 175–76; in transcending liminality, 191, 192–93, 194–96, 197–98; of the Yezidi genocide, 106–8; of Yezidis, 71, 73–74, 75–76, 78–79, 80, 108–9. *See also* legitimacy/illegitimacy of belief and practice

reconciliation, intercommunal, 29, 89–90, 150

repertoires of violence, 13–14, 41, 45, 53, 97, 99–100, 119–20, 125–26

resentment: in the Alevi massacres, 13–14, 62, 119–20, 121, 126–27, 130, 138–39; in the Armenian genocide, 16–17; of Baha'is and Ahmadis, 168–69; in bottom-up violence, 12–14; in discourses on religion and violence, 21–22, 199–200; in the theoretical framework, 36, 38, 59–62, 65; in violence against liminal minorities, 7–8, 10; in the Yezidi genocide, 13, 31, 68, 95–97

resettlement, forced. *See* displacement
resentment, 59–61
revenge, 59–60, 89–90, 94–95, 101, 144, 150
revivalism, religious, 35, 55, 58–59, 130–31
Reza, Mohammad, Shah, 159–60
rights: of citizenship for Baha'is and Ahmadis, 154, 161–62, 165, 167–68; enforcement of blasphemy laws in, 183–84; individual, recognition in, 194–95
riots: in the Alevi massacres, 121–23, 125–26, 137–38, 146, 150–51; anti-Ahmadi, 32, 163–64; anti-Baha'i, 32, 159, 162; anti-Kurd, 143; in mass atrocities against religious minorities, 15–16, 17–18; against religious minorities, in global perspective, 188–89, 190
ritual/ritualism, 40, 50–51, 110–11, 112–13, 114, *117*, 138–39; Alevi, in liminality, 114, *117*; co-gendered, in stigmatization of Alevis, 110–11, 112–13, 138–39; in defining religious violence, 40; and liminal phases, 50–51
Rushdie, Salman: *The Satanic Verses*, 132–33
Rwandan genocide, 28–29, 63

sacred books, 54, 70, 74–75
Safavids, 16, 26, 110–11, 112, 113–15, 130. *See also* Iran
Salafi jihadism: in global perspective on liminality and discrimination, 187–88; religious nationalism in, 21; rise of, in Iraq, 31, 95; in the Yezidi genocide, 67–68, 83–84, 93, 95, 96–97, 102, 174–75. *See also* suicide attacks
Salam, Abdus, 165n
scapegoating: of Alevis, 137–38; of Baha'is and Ahmadis, 154–55, 156–59, 160, 162, 164, 168–69; in defining targets of religious violence, 49–50; of liminal minorities, 30; in the theoretical framework, 62, 65; of Yezidis, 83–84, 95, 100
Scheler, Max, 60–61
Scientologists/Scientology, 176–78, 180
Second Vatican Council (1962–65), 48
sectarianism: and Alevi liminality, 114–15; in the Alevi massacres, 119–21, 126–28, 131–32, 134–35, 137; in denied victimhood of Alevis, 31–32, 145–46, 149; in framings of political struggle, 151–52; in global perspective on liminality and discrimination, 171–72, 186–88, 190; in the politics of Alevi recognition, 151–52; in the

theoretical framework, 40, 41, 54; in Yezidi encounters with modernity, 83–84; in the Yezidi genocide, 84, 94, 95, 100–101, 104; and Yezidi liminality, 73
secularism/secularization: and Ahmadi liminality, 164; and the Alevi massacres, 13–14, 119, 130–31, 136–37, 142–43; in Baha'i liminality, 157–60, 161–62; in global patterns, 186; Kurdish, 78–79, 80, 96–97; and religious liminality, 12–14, 18–19, 20–21, 30, 31–33; in the theoretical framework, 34–35, 37–38, 39, 45–46, 49–50, 57–59, 62, 65–66; in transcending liminality, 191, 196–97; Turkish, 116, 130–31, 142–43; and the Yezidi genocide, 96–97, 102
September 11 terror attacks, 199
sex/sexual intercourse, 17, 26, 40, 52–53, 70–71, 74–75, 99, 110–11, 114, 127–28
sexual violence. *See* rape and sexual violence
Shabaks, 105
Shammar tribe, 91–92
Shiite Muslims and Islam: in anti-Baha'i violence, 32, 159; as beneficiaries of the Ba'thist fall, 96, 97; in defining Yezidism, 108n; in denial of Baha'ism, 157–58, 159; in Iranian nationhood, 157–59; IS violence against, 105–6; in origins of Baha'i faith, 154, 156; rise of radical movements of, 104; and Yezidis, 78–79, 108
Shirazi, Ali Mohammed, 156
SHP (Soysyal Demokrat Halkçi Parti), 131, 132, 137–38
Sikhs/Sikhism, 176–78, 179–80
Sinjar, Iraq: Kurdish power in, 80, 82–83, 96–97; post-2003 power dynamics in, 100–101; strategic importance of, as Syrian-Iraqi border zone, 77–78; Yezidi genocide in, 1–5, 67–68, 73, 84–103
Sivas, Turkey, 31–32, 111, 119–20, 121, 130–39, 147–50
Socrates, trial of, 35–37, 45–46
spaces, sacred, 19, 22–23, 39–40, 172, 199–200
state religions/state-religious relationships: in discrimination and violence against minorities, 189; in exclusion of Ahmadis, 164–65; in societal discrimination, 182–84, 185–86
states/state authorities: complicity of, 32, 35, 48–49, 111–12, 140, 143, 159; in curbing bottom-up violence, 162; incompetence of, in religious violence,

111–12, 140, 143; monopoly on coercion and violence of, 14, 45–46, 65–66, 95–96, 196–97; in persecution of Baha'is and Ahmadis, 154; in recognition of liminal minorities, 15; in the theoretical framework, 48–49, 52, 53–54; in transcending liminality, 192
status loss, 10, 12–13, 60–62, 95, 96
stigmatization: of Ahmadis, 154, 155, 167–69; of Alevis, 112–14, 118, 119–20, 130, 138–39, 144–45; of Armenians, 142; in atrocities, 16, 17, 30, 32–33; in backlash against recognition, 194–95; of Baha'is, 154, 155, 162, 168–69; countering, in transcending liminality, 193; in global perspective, 175–76, 190; in historical patterns of violence, 31; of liminal minorities, 7–8, 10; in outbreaks of violence, 23; of Rastafarians, 180; in religious liminality, 10, 12–14; in the theoretical framework, 34, 38, 52–53, 59, 62; of Yezidis, 13, 68, 70–72, 74–75, 87, 90–91, 92–93, 95, 97, 99, 104, 106, 108–9
suicide attacks, 4, 21, 67–68, 80, 83, 94, 104. *See also* Salafi jihadism
Sunni Islam: in Alevi liminality, 113–14, 115–16, 117–18; in global perspective on liminality and discrimination, 178–79; instrumentalization of, in the PKK insurgency, 144–45; in nonrecognition of Alevism, 197–98; in Ottoman attempts to assimilate Yezidis, 76; subordination of Alevism to, 26–27. *See also* orthodoxy, Islamic
Sunni Kurds, 72–73, 96–97, 100–101, 103, 108–9, 142–45
Sunni Muslims: Alevi subordination to, 26–27; al-Maliki policies in repression of, 100–101; in atrocities against liminal minorities, 16–17, 28, 31–32; as beneficiaries of the Hussein regime, 101–2; condemnation of attacks on Yezidis by, 83n; in global perspective on liminality and discrimination, 171–72, 174–75, 187–88; in nonrecognition of Ahmadis, 164–66, 168; in reframing of Alevi massacres, 147–50; refusal to recognize Alevis by, 116, 118; and religious liminality, 11–12, 26–27, 62, 193; rise of radical movements of, 104; in scapegoating of Yezidis, 83–84. *See also* Alevi massacres/anti-Alevi violence; Yezidi genocide
survivors of violence: agency of, 28; testimonies of, 68–69, 84, 86–89

Syria: Druzes in, 178–79; sectarian tensions in, 186–88; and the Yezidi genocide, 2–3, 4, 67–68, 84, 91–92, 105–6, 109

Tal Afar, Iraq, 92–94
terror, acts of: and blasphemy laws, 183–84; in discourses on religion and violence, 199; resentment in, 61–62
threat perceptions: in Alevi liminality, 113–14; in the Armenian genocide, 140–42; in atrocities against liminal minorities, 17, 18–19; in defining religious violence, 43–44, 48–49; existential, 22–23, 48–49, 63, 96–97, 104, 141–42, 160–61, 198; in global perspective on discrimination and violence, 188–89, 190; in Ottoman modernization of Yezidis, 76; in persecution of Baha'is in Iran, 162; in reframing of Alevi massacres, 145–46; in religious liminality, 11–13, 14, 22–23, 48–49, 198; in the theoretical framework, 34–35, 48–49, 58–59, 63; in the Yezidi genocide, 96–97, 104
tolerance/intolerance: of Ahmadis, 166–67; of Alevis, 114–15, 138–39, 145, 149; of Baha'is, 161–62; in global perspective, 180–81, 182–84; of People of the Book, 25; in religious liminality, 16, 17, 20–21; in transcending liminality, 194; in the Yezidi genocide, 95
transcendence: in defining religious violence, 44, 45, 49; of liminality, 50–51, 58, 191–200
Turkey/Turkish nation-state/Turkish Republic: Alevis as Muslim in, 26–27, 54, 55–56, 115–16, 147–48, 151–52; as instigator of anti-Armenian violence, 140–41; mass violence in emergence and consolidation of, 139–40; in the origins of Alevi liminality, 116–17; in the PKK insurgency, 143–45; prosecution of blasphemy in, 183–84n; religious homogenization in, 26–27, 38–39, 54, 140–41, 198; and Yezidis, 25, 69, 74–75, 108–9. *See also* Alevis/Alevism; Ottoman Empire
Turkish-Islamic synthesis, 122, 130–31, 147–48
Turkomans, 83–85, 86, 94, 101–2, 105–6

United States: Christian nationalism in, 199–200; invasion of Iraq by, 31, 80, 81–82, 93, 96–97, 98, 101–2, 103–4, 188–89; lynching of Black people in, 61–62, 127, 149–50, 193, 195–96 victimhood: in Alevi liminality, 116–17, 118; of Alevis, denied, 31–32, 122–23, 129, 137, 145–52; blaming the victim mentality, 102, 104–5; group, defining, 48–50; mindset of, in resentment, 59–60; Yezidi, 26, 28, 31, 71–72, 102

visibility, public: of Alevis, 31–32, 54, 121, 126–27, 138, 151; of minorities, in oppression, 194; in the theoretical framework, 61–62, 65; of Yezidis, 13, 101

wars/warfare: civil wars, role of religion in, 171–75; degenerate, genocide in, 14; French, heretics and eschatology in, 40–42; in global perspective on liminality and discrimination, 185–86, 189–90; interstate, in discrimination and violence against minorities, 189–90; rape as weapon of, 98–99; World War I, 17, 76–77, 173–74

Yazid ibn Mu'awiya, 71, 78–79

Yezidi genocide: IS in, 1–5, 9, 14, 67–68, 84–103, 174–75; motives in, 13, 62, 68–69, 90–106, 174–75; perpetrators of, 87–90; recognition of, 106–9. *See also* genocide

Yezidis/Yezidism: in encounters with modernity, 74–84; global distribution of, 178; history and beliefs of, 25–26; history of massacres of, 17; impunity for perpetrators of violence against, 29; liminality of, 11–12, 13, 55–56, 69–74; oral tradition of, 70–71; in political modernity, 78–79; religious identity in genocidal violence against, 103–5; stigmatization of, 31, 108

Young Turks and Young Turk regime, 15–16, 116, 140–41

Zionism, 41n, 157–59, 160–61

Zoroastrianism, 69–70, 78–79, 143–44

www.ingramcontent.com/pod-product-compliance
Lightning Source LLC
Chambersburg PA
CBHW031347230426
43670CB00006B/460